BLACK
SEXUAL
POLITICS

BLACK SEXUAL POLITICS

AFRICAN AMERICANS, GENDER, AND THE NEW RACISM

PATRICIA HILL COLLINS

Routledge
New York & London

Published in 2004 by
Routledge
29 West 35th Street
New York, New York 10001
www.routledge-ny.com

Published in Great Britain by
Routledge
11 New Fetter Lane
London EC4P 4EE
www.routledge.co.uk

Routledge is an imprint of the Taylor & Francis Group.
Printed in the United States of America on acid-free paper.

10 9 8 7 6 5 4 3 2 1

Library of Congress Cataloging-in-Publication Data

Collins, Patricia Hill.
     Black sexual politics : African Americans, gender, and the new racism / Patricia
Hill Collins.
          p. cm.
Includes bibliographical references and index.
     ISBN 0-415-93099-5 (cloth : alk. paper)
     1. African Americans—Social conditions—1975- 2. African American men. 3.
African American women. 4. Sex role—United States. 5. African American—Sexual
behavior. 6. African American—Race identity. 7. Racism—United States. 8. United
States—Race relations. 9. Sexism—United States. I. Title.
     E185.86.C58167 2004
     306.7'089'96073—dc22   2003022841

CONTENTS

PART III
Toward a Progressive
Black Sexual Politics

ACKNOWLEDGMENTS

I begin by thanking students from the University of Cincinnati for their support of this project. Special thanks go to the students who enrolled in "Seminar in Black Sexual Politics" and in "Introduction to Black Gender Studies," two new courses in which I explored many of the ideas in this book. The issues in their lives convinced me of the need for this book. Undergraduate students also greatly helped my thinking about contemporary hip-hop culture. Several University of Cincinnati undergraduate student majors and minors in African American Studies assisted me as student researchers on various parts of this project. Adetra "Quay" Martin and Tanya Walker helped me to complete research on films and popular culture. Special thanks also go to Eric Styles, Kyle Riddle, Terri Holland, Erin Ledingham, Keith Melson, Khalila Sanders, and Torrie Wiggins for their insights.

Graduate students in Women's Studies and Sociology also provided important help. Valerie Ruffin made invaluable contributions to this project, both as my research assistant when she was a student at the University of Cincinnati and as a keen editorial eye concerning early drafts of this project. Special thanks also go to Stephen Whittaker for his thorough research in the literature of masculinities and for reading early drafts of some of the chapters. Jennifer Gossett, Sarah Byrne, and Jamie McCauley also shared ideas that improved the final quality of this manuscript. Vallarie Henderson and Tamika Odum assisted me with final manuscript preparation.

My University of Cincinnati colleagues also provided much-needed support for this project. I want to thank Patrice L. Dickerson for assistance with demographic material and

viii ACKNOWLEDGMENTS

William Jackson for his suggestions and critical eye concerning Black film. I also enjoyed co-teaching "Introduction to Black Gender Studies" with Marla Frederick and benefited from the insights of Regina Langley. Both helped me think through ideas concerning race, gender, and religion.

Sharing the ideas in this project with colleagues greatly strengthened this book. I especially appreciate being invited to participate in two exciting conferences on *Progressive Black Masculinities* held in 2001 and 2002 at the Baldy Center at the University of Buffalo Law School. Organized by Professor Athena Matua, these conferences helped me think through issues of Black masculinity. Teresa Miller and John Calmore greatly stimulated my thinking on the prison industry and the treatment of African American men within it. Special thanks to Devon Carbado, Kendall Thomas, Thomas Glave, Mark Anthony Neal, Beverly Guy-Sheftall, Bahati Kuumba, and many other conference participants whose thinking greatly enriched my own. I also want to thank colleagues at other institutions who invited me to present chapters from this manuscript. A partial list includes Rebecca Walter at George Mason University, Tom Greaves at Bucknell University, Jeff Schulz at Arcadia University, Diane Vaughn at Boston College, Gerald Early at Washington University at St. Louis, Tukufu Zuberi at the University of Pennsylvania, and Tariq Modood at the University of Bristol, U.K., where I spent a total of four weeks as a visiting professor in January and June of 2002.

In 2002–2003, I spent a year as a visiting professor at the University of Kentucky, Lexington. The intellectual stimulation that I encountered there enabled me to finish the manuscript. The support that I received from everyone was wonderful. My deep thanks go to Mike Nietzel from the Provost's Office, Joan Callahan and Debra Harley in Women's Studies, and Gerald Smith in African American Studies. University of Kentucky graduate students read parts of this manuscript and gave me helpful comments. In this regard, special thanks go out to Yaphet Bryant for her editorial comments on chapters dealing with Black popular culture and to John Youngblood for his insights concerning the Black Church as well as issues that face gay, lesbian, bisexual, and transgendered Black people. I also want to thank Rachel Clark, my phenomenal graduate research assistant for the year who gave new meaning to the term "stealth feminist."

The University of Kentucky and the University of Cincinnati both helped defray costs associated with this book. The Provost's Office at the

University of Kentucky provided support that helped with the costs of manuscript preparation. At the University of Cincinnati, the support provided by the Taft Fund for costs of travel and manuscript preparation has been invaluable over the years. I also wish to thank Provost Anthony Perzigian for his tireless support of my scholarship during lean financial times. The three deans of the College of Arts and Sciences who held tenure while I completed this project—Joseph Caruso, Chuck Groetsch, and Karen Gould—also provided encouragement and support. Administrative and secretarial support also made my life much easier. I wish to thank Josephine Wynne for her professionalism and her ability to manage the Department of African American Studies during my tenure as chair of the department.

This project would not have come to fruition without the support of the terrific team at Routledge. Ilene Kalish, my tireless editor at Routledge, has been with me through this entire project and her enthusiasm (and energy!) has not waned throughout. I would also like to thank the entire editorial team who worked on the manuscript, with special thanks to Kimberly Guinta, Mark Lerner, and Danielle Savin for their invaluable contributions during the production process. I would also like to thank Tricia Rose, who read and gave helpful suggestions on the final manuscript, as well as the anonymous reviewers provided by Routledge.

I also wish to thank my family for their continued backing. My spouse, Roger and my father, Albert Hill, have been among my strongest and most consistent supporters. I also want to acknowledge the unconditional love offered by my two senior cats who kept me company as I wrote.

Finally, I dedicate this book to Valerie, my beautiful and talented daughter. May the world come to see her and others of her generation as the hope of our future.

NO TURNING BACK

The spring of 1964 held great promise for African Americans. On August 28, 1963, a crowd estimated at between 200,000 and 500,000 Americans of all races had marched on Washington, D.C., petitioning the federal government to make good on its commitment to equal and fair treatment under the law. As the largest mass demonstration at that time ever organized by African Americans, the march made it clear that Black people were not turning back. Despite the bombing of Birmingham's Sixteenth Street Baptist Church that killed four young girls just two weeks after the march, and the assassination of President Kennedy the following November, the tide of history was turning. The passage of momentous civil rights legislation that, for African Americans, was designed to redress the devastating effects of slavery and racial segregation was on the horizon.

That spring, I was a sixteen-year-old high school student in a college preparatory public high school in Philadelphia. Because, along with other Black people, my parents had been denied educational opportunities, they recognized the importance of education for African American empowerment. I was one of the many Black kids who benefited from our parents' personal sacrifices as well as broader civil rights struggles. Schooled in this philosophy, I tried to do everything that I could to be personally excellent. Almost every day I carried home a pile of heavy textbooks and almost every night I worked my way through hours of homework. School was tough, but I believed that it would be worth the effort. Just like the White girls who attended school with me, I was promised a bright future, and I wanted to be prepared.

One day that spring, I took a break from an endless round of studying and went to the movies. As I sat in the theater waiting for the film to begin, I could see two twelve- or thirteen-year-old African American boys seated about three rows ahead of me. Like me, they too had paid their money and were anxious for the film to begin. But unlike me, they just could not sit still. One opened the side door of the theater, beckoned to his friend, and both laughed as they ran back and forth through the theater door. Finally, they closed the door and sat down. All seemed to be well until a White male usher who was barely older than me seemed to appear from nowhere. Barreling down on the two boys, he grabbed each by their shirts, pushed open the side door of the theater, and threw both of them into the alley. From where I was seated, I could see into the alley and I watched in amazement as he threw one boy to the ground and kicked him while shouting, "That'll teach you not to sneak in!"

I was shocked by this brutality. How could I sit still and pretend that nothing had happened? I headed to the back of the movie theater to find the manager. When I arrived, I found that at least six African American adults, some older than my parents, had gotten there before me. Buttonholing the middle-aged White male manager, they began to complain. They too had been watching the boys and vehemently testified that the boys had done nothing wrong, and certainly nothing that merited that level of physical and verbal assault. Ignoring them, the manager turned to his teenaged employee and asked him what had happened. Red-faced and stammering, the usher denied hurting the boys and, if that were not enough, claimed that he had seen the boys sneak into the theater. After hearing his employee's testimony, the manager turned back to the adults. "You must have been mistaken," he flatly stated. He turned his back on all of us and simply walked away.

I was shocked yet again. If these Black adults were disbelieved, clearly I would be too, no matter what my credentials. On that day I learned that, in some situations, gender, age, social class, and education do not matter if you are Black. The usher and the movie theater manager could see only race and their perceptions of race clouded their judgment. I also began to see how differences among African Americans caused by these very same factors could lead to differential treatment. The boys were harmed because they were young, Black, and male—the usher would not have dared to grab in the same fashion the irate middle-aged Black woman complaining about the assault. I saw how, in that situation, being young, Black, and female also meant that my testimony would be routinely ignored, no matter how impressive my elite high school credentials. Each Black person in that theater had a common struggle, but the form it took differed greatly as well as our responses to it. As disheartened as I was by the outcome, I'm glad that I joined the group in the back that complained. Most of the African Americans in the theater sat quietly by, trying to ignore the confrontation in the rear of the theater, diligently munching on their popcorn instead.

That event was one of many that taught me that while good ideas and solid evidence certainly matter (the kind that I was studying in school), power relations that elevate some groups over others can matter even more in determining whose view of truth will prevail. In short, knowledge and power are deeply linked, and achieving social justice requires attending to both.

Over the years, in my work as a scholar I have tried to place my work in service to social justice. For me, this has meant mapping differences in penalty and privilege that accompany race, class, and similar systems of social injustice and trying not to elevate one group's suffering over that of another. In my first book, *Black Feminist Thought*, I aimed to foster Black women's empowerment by identifying and legitimating Black women's intellectual production.[1] I believed then as I do now that people become empowered when they think and speak for themselves (even if, as was the case in the theater, they are ignored or disbelieved). Ideas matter greatly in this struggle for empowerment, and Black women's intellectual production (Black feminist thought) has been essential to the progress and sanity of African American women. Because ideas do matter, they remain targets of criticism, cooptation, and silencing. In *Fighting Words*, I cast a critical eye on Black feminist thought itself and revisited this question of how knowledge and power are interrelated.[2] I wanted to know what standards we might apply to seemingly progressive social theories to see whether they maintained their oppositional purpose. In both works, I argued that it is not enough to imagine empowerment for Black women in isolation from deep-seated changes in the social structure overall. Black women can never become fully empowered in a context of social injustice.

But what about Black men? Little did I know that what I observed in that movie theater in 1964 was an example of a much-larger pattern that is carried out every day in schools, streets, workplaces, and the mass media. Ushers, assistant principals, security guards, and the police subject Black men to varying levels of verbal and physical violence that leave them fearful, angry, and far too often, dangerous to others and to themselves. Black women often take up the slack, enduring low-paying jobs, endless hours of childcare, lonely nights without love, and a sense of powerlessness that things will never change. In the movie theater, we could see how American race relations that conceptualized race in terms of family bound the manager and usher together. They were part of the White family and we were disadvantaged because we did not belong. The manager believed the son within his racial family and disbelieved the Black people who he felt were no kin to him. We could see how America's racial family drama generated benefits for its White sons (in this case, being believed) and fostered physical punishment for its Black ones. Race certainly mattered, but the theater episode was also about masculinity, social class, age, and the power that they conferred. The invisible authority that took tangible form in the manager's and usher's actions also worked to silence us. We were in the metaphorical theater of race together, and we could see then how young Black boys (and girls) were harmed by racial discrimination. We had few illusions that we owned the theater or that we might be allowed to manage it. In 1964, Black people knew that, despite our differences, we shared a common problem.

Much has changed since then. In the post–civil rights era, the power relations that administer the theater of race in America are now far more hidden. Ironically, the protests of Black boys are circulated in mass media within a celebrated global hip-hop culture, yet the substance of that protest continues to be ignored. Middle-class Black people may manage the theaters of academia, city hall, and the military, yet many seem far less willing than the folks in the movie theater to defend the interests of the one out of every three Black youth who live below the poverty level. Ironically, movie theaters themselves have disappeared from Black inner-city areas, leaving Black boys and girls marooned in neighborhoods where basketball seems to provide the best way out. Wondering whether they are "black enough," assimilated upper- and middle-class Black youth growing up in White neighborhoods and attending private schools play video games and socialize in suburban multiplex theater complexes, often paying top dollar to see the latest film that features authentic "ghetto" Black hip-hop artists.

As a result of these changes, it is increasingly difficult to see how relations of race, class, gender, and sexuality that framed my 1964 study break drama are remarkably intact today. Recognizing that racism even exists remains a challenge for most White Americans and, increasingly, for many African Americans as well. They believe that the passage of civil rights legislation eliminated racially discriminatory practices and that any problems that Blacks may experience now are of their own doing. Violations against Black men and women continue to occur, but one-third of African Americans have moved into the middle class and Black people are more visible in positions of authority in schools, companies, hospitals, and government. Many Black people have difficulty seeing their connections to other Black people, let alone rushing to the back of the theater in defense of Black boys whom they do not even know.

In the post–civil rights era, gender has emerged as a prominent feature of what some call a "new" racism. Ironically, many African Americans deny the existence of sexism, or see it as a secondary concern that is best addressed when the more pressing problem of racism has been solved. But if racism and sexism are deeply intertwined, racism can *never* be solved without seeing and challenging sexism. African American men and women both are affected by racism, but in gender-specific ways. Those African American boys were attacked by the usher because they were Black *and* male, not simply because they were Black.

The gender-specific contours of racism are even more pronounced today. This was painfully clear to me one week when I taught my book *Black Feminist Thought* to two very different classes. The first consisted of college undergraduates and was disproportionately filled with young Black women who, because they were single parents, routinely asked whether they could bring their children to class. They were the lucky ones. Unlike their friends relegated to dead-end jobs and a punitive social welfare bureaucracy, they had made it to college. For the other class, I visited a college program in a local prison to talk about the exact same subject matter. This time, the class was disproportionately filled with young Black men who rarely got to see their children. Students in both classes were denied sexual partners. Both were harmed by experiences such as these that alienated Black women and Black men from one another and from themselves. Education, housing, jobs, and health care—African American men and women have gender disparate experiences in all of these areas. What sense does it make to talk about "Black people" as if all Black people are male when gender differences are so pronounced?

Talking about gender does not mean focusing solely on women's issues. Men's experiences are also deeply gendered. Thus, gender ideology not only creates ideas about femininity but it also shapes conceptions of masculinity. Regardless of race, ethnicity, social class, citizenship status, and sexual orientation, all men and women encounter social norms about gender. These norms influence people's sense of themselves as men and women as well as perceptions of masculinity and femininity. For African Americans, the relationship between gender and race is intensified, producing a Black gender ideology that shapes ideas about Black masculinity and Black femininity. This Black gender ideology is not simply a benign set of ideas affecting individual African American women and men. Instead, it is used to justify patterns of opportunity and discrimination that African American women and men encounter in schools, jobs, government agencies, and other American social institutions.

This Black gender ideology also draws upon widespread cultural beliefs concerning the sexual practices of people of African descent. Sexuality is not simply a biological function; rather, it is a system of ideas and social practices that is deeply implicated in shaping American social inequalities. Because ideas about sexuality are so integral to understandings of Black gender ideology as well as broader gender ideology in the United States, neither Black masculinity nor Black femininity can be adequately understood let alone transformed without attending to the politics of sexuality.[3]

Black sexual politics occur at the particular intersection of gender, race, and sexuality that African Americans face. But African Americans are not the only ones who grapple with issues of sexual politics. A wide constellation of social groups, for example, White women, Latino men, gay and lesbian Asian immigrants, wealthy Americans, older indigenous people, and young married Asian mothers, encounter distinctive sexual politics based on their placement in systems of gender, race, and sexuality. Sexual politics can be defined as a set of ideas and social practices shaped by gender, race, and sexuality that frame all men and women's treatment of one another, as well as how individual men and women are perceived and treated by others. Because African Americans have been so profoundly affected by racism, grappling with racism occupies a prominent place within Black sexual politics.

Black sexual politics consists of a set of ideas and social practices shaped by gender, race, and sexuality that frame Black men and women's treatment of one another, as well as how African Americans are perceived and treated by others. Such politics lie at the heart of beliefs about Black masculinity and Black femininity, of gender-specific experiences of African Americans, and of forms that the new racism takes in the post–civil rights era. To confront social inequality, African Americans need an analysis of Black masculinity and Black femininity that questions the links between prevailing Black sexual politics, their connection to Black gender ideology, and struggles for African American empowerment in response to the new racism. Taking into account the new challenges of the post–civil rights era, such an analysis would strive to point the way toward a more progressive Black sexual politics within African American communities. This politics in turn might both catalyze a more effective antiracist politics and contribute to a broader social justice agenda.

Toward these ends, *Black Sexual Politics: African Americans, Gender, and the New Racism* analyses how relations of gender and sexuality within contemporary African American communities reproduce and/or resist new forms of racism. Poverty, unemployment, rape, HIV/AIDS, incarceration, substance abuse, adolescent pregnancy, high rates of Black children in foster care, intraracial violence (especially by young Black males as both victims and perpetrators), and similar issues have a disproportionate impact on African Americans. All of these social problems take gender-specific forms, and none will be solved without serious attention to the politics of gender and sexuality. Black women can never become fully empowered in a context that harms Black men, and Black men can never become fully empowered in a society in which Black women cannot fully flourish as human beings. Racism is a gender-specific phenomenon, and Black antiracist politics that do not make gender central are doomed to fail because someone will always be left behind. If either women or men remain subordinated, then social injustice persists.

The need for a progressive Black sexual politics has always existed, yet the gender-specific social problems of today make this need even more pressing. Not only has developing a progressive Black sexual politics become more needed, contemporary intellectual and/or political trends have created new possibilities for success. Over thirty years of Black feminist advocacy has produced a corpus of work that continues to challenge prevailing gender relations.[4] During this same period, the majority of African American men have been highly resistant to any discussions that they perceived as being critical of them, and some have loudly criticized Black feminism.[5] Recently, however, many African American men have demonstrated an increased willingness to *analyze* Black masculinity. In part, this new receptivity reflects the willingness of many Black men to see that African American women and others who advocate on behalf of Black women are not necessarily *against* Black men. If gender and sexuality have been such important features in explaining African American women's realities, then gender and sexuality are equally important in explaining the realities of African American men. The success of social movements in challenging historical ideas and practices concerning sexuality also creates new intellectual and political space to revisit questions of race and sexuality. Moving from an exclusive focus on Black women to a broader one that encompasses how the politics of gender and sexuality frame the experiences of women and men alike creates new questions for investigation and, perhaps, a new antiracist politics that might follow.[6]

KEY FEATURES OF THE VOLUME

Black Sexual Politics: African Americans, Gender, and the New Racism has several distinguishing features. First, this is a volume of critical social theory.[7] Critical social theory consists of bodies of knowledge and sets of institutional practices that actively grapple with the central questions facing groups of people differently placed in specific political, social, and historical contexts characterized by injustice. For example, because African Americans face social injustices within American society, critical social theory for this group would engage questions of racism and economic inequalities. In the specific political, social, and historical context of the post–civil rights era, rethinking the meaning of gender and sexuality for antiracist political action constitutes a central question facing this group. As a work of critical social theory, *Black Sexual Politics* uses a conceptual framework concerning the intersections of race, gender, and sexuality to raise questions that might help African American women and men and their supporters craft a more progressive Black sexual politics. This book is neither an empirical social science study of current conditions within African American communities nor a manifesto for government officials or community organizations to follow. Because this book does not put forth rules that, when followed, promise to produce the ideal romantic partners, it is not a how-to book on how to fix Black love relationships.[8] *Black Sexual Politics* does not tell readers what to think. Rather, it examines what we might think about.

To some, *Black Sexual Politics* may appear to be heavy on problems and short on solutions. This is because this book is a diagnostic project. It does not aim to be prescriptive but instead is analytical. In fact, being overly prescriptive and giving African American women and men new rules to follow is a large part of the problem itself. Take, for example, the cottage industry of Black self-help books that sprang up in the 1990s, all designed to help African Americans cope with strained love relationships. These books populate local bookstores, crowding out more thoughtful, scholarly treatments, and yet come as close as many African Americans get to serious discussions of gender and sexuality. Long on advice and short on analysis, many of these books can be dangerous, some even going so far as to counsel Black men to handle an unruly Black woman by "soundly slapping her in the mouth."[9] *Black Sexual Politics* rejects this prescriptive approach, arguing instead that becoming empowered means learning how to think for ourselves and making decisions that are in our own best interests.

I think that failing to address questions of gender and sexuality will compromise antiracist African American politics in the post–civil rights era. What good is the empowerment of African American women if it comes at the expense of Black men? Black college women who look around their classrooms and see the shrinking numbers of Black men can either gloat that they have less competition or they can become outraged by this situation and begin strategizing about what to do about it. What good is the empowerment of African American men if it comes on the backs of Black women? Black male ministers whose congregations are usually 70 percent Black female can either enjoy the Sunday dinners, presents, and other benefits that can accrue to men in such situations or they can minister to the daily struggles of Black women who put money in the collection plate by becoming champions for Black women's rights.

What makes a progressive Black sexual politics "critical" is its commitment to social justice, not exclusively for African American men and women, but for all human beings. In this sense, a more progressive Black sexual politics is one specific site of a broader, global struggle for human rights. It is important to stress that although this particular book is about African Americans, this specific project of developing a more progressive Black sexual politics resembles other social justice projects that grapple with similar issues. For example, women and men of African descent in South Africa, Brazil, Nigeria, and Great Britain face similar challenges in obtaining habitable housing, good nutrition, literacy, high-quality jobs, effective health care, and stopping the spread of HIV/AIDS. African Americans' struggles in these areas resemble those of people of African descent globally. Yet because these important social issues also transcend the particular forms they take among Black populations, they also constitute the foundation of social justice projects in a global context. Intersecting oppressions of race, class, gender, ethnicity, and sexuality touch everyone's lives and social justice projects occur across societies and among very different types of people. Because *Black Sexual Politics* examines one local manifestation of a more general, global phenomenon, I invite non–African American readers to consider how the questions raised here might inform their own social justice projects.

Second, this book treats race, class, gender, and sexuality as intersecting versus competing frameworks for developing a progressive Black sexual politics. Deeming race to be more important than gender or class as more valid than sexuality can compromise the social justice core of a progressive Black sexual politics. Take, for example, how models that rank oppressions can harm a Black political agenda regarding cancer. Under models that view race as primary and gender as secondary, higher rates of some cancers among African Americans than Whites would be seen as an important issue for African Americans because Black people as a group are harmed by these racial differentials. But cancers do not affect men and women in the same way. For example, differential incidence and mortality rates for prostate cancer in African American men and breast cancer in African American women constitute gender-specific differences within this racial consensus.[10] Because the vast majority of men will never get breast cancer and it is impossible for African American women to get prostate cancer, these two cancers present a potentially divisive crosscutting issue in setting an African American agenda for challenging cancer. What sense would it make to identify either prostate cancer or breast cancer as the typical Black experience around which to organize antiracist politics? A Black political agenda on cancer that did not take gender into account would effectively ignore the issues of half of the Black population, distort our understanding of the racial effects of cancer on African Americans, and hamper the effectiveness of antiracist politics.

To avoid this type of ranking, *Black Sexual Politics* uses a theoretical framework of intersectionality. Intersectional paradigms view race, class, gender, sexuality, ethnicity, and age, among others, as mutually constructing systems of power. Because these systems permeate all social relations, untangling their effects in any given situation or for any given population remains difficult. I have consistently tried to theorize intersectionality in the overall corpus of my work and *Black Sexual Politics* constitutes yet another piece of this larger theoretical project. In this volume I emphasize intersections of race, gender, and sexuality. Doing so does not mean that I think that class, nation, age, and/or ethnicity are less important for antiracist initiatives. I have done my best to analyze these other systems of oppression, especially social class. However, moving race, gender, and sexuality into the center of analysis should highlight their interaction within African American communities as well as reveal new angles of vision on how these systems interconnect.

Although *Black Sexual Politics* draws upon the intersectional paradigms developed in my earlier work, gender and sexuality are also more visible here because developing an intersectional analysis of Black sexual politics has tangible political ramifications for antiracist scholarship and activism. This project breaks with earlier gender scholarship (including my own) that equates sex with male and female biology and gender with socially constructed ideas of masculinity and femininity. Rather, as presented here, biological sex, the social construction of gender, and sexual orientation constitute distinct yet interconnected phenomena that, in turn, interconnect with race. Because discussions of sexuality always attract definitional difficulties, I do not offer a definition here because I feel that standard dictionary definitions are far more conservative than the meanings suggested here.[11] At the same time, it is important to clarify the three interrelated meanings of sexuality that I use in *Black Sexual Politics*.[12] Sexuality can be viewed as an entity that is manipulated within each distinctive system of race, class, and gender oppression, for example, the importance of rape to patriarchy, child prostitution to contemporary global sex work, or lynching to racial subordination. Sexuality also can be seen as a site of intersectionality, a specific constellation of social practices that demonstrate how oppressions converge. For example, not only did the institutionalized rape of enslaved Black women support racial domination, it potentially produced children who would profit slaveowners, and it reinforced a gender regime. Sexuality also can be analyzed as heterosexism, a freestanding system of oppression similar to racism, sexism, and class oppression, which shares similar goals and social practices.

Third, I focus on African American communities because I fear that the rush to abandon the black/white paradigm of race in the United States in favor of other seemingly more universal paradigms potentially distorts the uniqueness of African American struggles and can also support new forms of racism. Some would suggest that in the context of the changing racial/ethnic composition of the United States, studying African Americans is passé. They suggest that rejecting the historical specificity of studying African Americans and replacing the black/white race relations paradigm with more abstract theories of race and racism can fix this seeming provincialism within African American intellectual production. Everyone must be represented for racial theory to have merit. Studying race and racism on this level of abstraction enables racial theory to move away from the kinds of social issues that have long been important to African Americans and that have catalyzed Black freedom struggles. For example, while accurate, eloquent arguments about how "race" is a social construction have virtually no merit in addressing issues such as the denial of voting rights to African American citizens in Florida during the 2000 presidential election or the continued high rates of Black infant mortality in inner-city neighborhoods. This move also redefines Black intellectual production that focuses on social issues that are of concern to Black people as being myopic and reflecting special interests. One important dimension of the new racism is to cover over the harm done to victims and to mute their protest. Telling African Americans to take a number and wait their turn in a long line of special interest groups vying for recognition in an oppression contest rewrites the specificity of American race relations in an especially pernicious way.[13]

I recognize how much African Americans share with many other groups, both in the United States and globally. For example, I think that many of my arguments also apply to Puerto Ricans, indigenous peoples, Chicanos, Vietnamese, Cambodians, Haitian immigrant populations, and poor and working-class White Americans, albeit through the historical specificity of their distinctive group histories. Issues of poverty, poor health, homelessness, poor education, joblessness, and family disruption that face African American women and men also affect these groups, groups throughout the African Diaspora, and formerly colonized peoples in general. Moreover, there is no clear line roping off African Americans from these and other groups—there are Africans Americans who are Black *and* Puerto Rican, who have relatives among indigenous peoples, who are immigrants, and who are biracial and/or live in multiracial families. At the same time, examining the particularities of African American experience in its own right is inherently valuable, especially in analyzing Black sexual politics, the topic under consideration here. In fact, because the specificity of African American issues can be lost in categories such as "people of color," "race relations," "minority groups," or "people of African descent," placing the experiences of African Americans within other paradigms may actually *harm* the project of developing a progressive Black sexual politics that might work in the United States.

African American experience simultaneously reflects the problems faced by other groups of oppressed people; yet, it is also a unique history that must be explained in its own right. *Black Sexual Politics* recognizes that African Americans constitute a distinctive group that, according to the 2000 census, numbered approximately 36.4 million people.[14] Within the race relations framework of the United States, African Americans remain a "minority group." But 36.4 million people constitute a large population. For example, Black Americans outnumber the population of Ghana (20 million), Kenya (32 million), and Senegal (10 million) and most other African nations. There are more African Americans than the population of Belgium (10 million), Switzerland (7 million), Iraq (24 million), and Israel (6 million). In fact, African Americans constitute one of the largest national populations of people of African decent, following Nigeria (134 million), Congo-Kinshasa (56 million), and Brazil.[15] Beyond sheer size, there is the matter of history. Unlike Hispanics and Asian Americans, terms used since 1965 by the federal government to classify new immigrant populations from widely heterogeneous backgrounds, African Americans constitute a distinctive ethnic group or "people" whose history in the United States is prolonged and unique. African Americans now have close to a 400-year history in America, and North American slavery and racial segregation (apartheid) constitute a specific history that has affected no other group in the United States in the same way. The social institutions and belief structures of African Americans reflect African and European influences, and they have evolved continually over time in response to migrations of people of African descent from continental Africa, the Caribbean, and Latin America into the group itself as well as cultural borrowing and sharing with indigenous peoples, Latinos, Asians, and European immigrant groups. Moreover, because African Americans live within the borders of the remaining world superpower and are citizens of the United States, this group is strategically placed to see the workings of contemporary global politics. For example, African Americans have experienced multiple migrations—from the forced migration of the Atlantic slave trade, to the great migration from the rural South to the cities of the North in the early twentieth century, to the current reverse migration back to the South in search of opportunities. African Americans demonstrate the possibilities and limitations of migration as a strategy for addressing poverty and powerlessness. The global spread of hip-hop from the streets of the South Bronx through global mass media reflects the continued significance of African Americans to both American and global culture. African American experiences are indicative of economic processes of global capitalism, the larger political patterns of transnationalism, and the growing importance of global mass media.

For African Americans, claiming the theoretical space to raise issues that concern Black people in ways that deviate from the paradigms advanced by more powerful groups remains difficult. Given the demographic, historical, social, and political significance of African Americans in both American and global contexts, I ask why it remains so unfashionable in the United States for Black people to talk about issues that concern us on our own terms? Why is this choice routinely criticized as reflecting special interests as opposed to being yet another lens that can be used to examine universal issues that join us all? Why can I not use the specificity of African American experience to investigate important, universal themes without running the risk of having this book marginalized as representing Black "special interests"?

A fourth distinguishing feature of *Black Sexual Politics* concerns how heterogeneity *within* African American populations fosters a distinctive political history concerning class, gender, sexuality, age, color, and ethnicity. I am fully aware of how different 36.4 million Black people are from one another and am frequently surprised when others so forcefully argue that not all Black people are alike. Any person who has grown up in the United Stated with even rudimentary access to African American organizations and communities knows that Black Americans come in all shapes, colors, sizes, and political persuasions. Racial segregation, however, has created large numbers of White Americans who lack sustained, personal experience with African Americans. This group routinely must be convinced of Black humanity, a task that requires that they jettison racial stereotypes and learn to see and value Blacks as individuals. For me, evidence for the humanity of Black people lies in the beauty of Black individualism. In all of my work, this has been my starting point, not my destination.

My concern lies less with recognizing differences among Black people than in the recent rush to study differences to the point of virtually ignoring unemployment, infant mortality, HIV/AIDS, domestic violence, racial profiling, and other important social issues that disproportionately affect African Americans as a group. In this volume, I remain focused on the collective struggles for social justice that have long lay at the heart of African American culture and communities. I argue that these struggles must be reframed through a prism of difference, in this case, gender and sexuality, in ways that do not become overly preoccupied with the question of difference itself. Unfortunately, so much attention within American scholarship is lavished on differences among Americans, or on a race relations paradigm that compares African Americans and other groups (often a requirement for publication), or in excising out a segment of African Americans and reinserting them within some other category (sexual minorities, or women's organizations) that it is difficult to find forums to address the very real social issues that confront *all* African Americans as a group, regardless of age, region, gender, sexual orientation, or social class.

Sexual politics is one such issue, yet the various threads needed for analyses of gender and sexuality, for example, marriage and family relations, violence, unemployment, reproductive rights, prison reform, and school performance are scattered in many places. Because some themes primarily affect men, they are not even seen as being part of an overarching Black sexual politics agenda. Addressing the myriad issues discussed here requires hard-hitting dialogues and new behaviors *among* African Americans that take into account differences of class, gender, age, sexuality, nationality, ability, and appearance among African Americans. In this

volume, I emphasize these internal issues. But I also recognize that bringing about social change needs serious conversations and action strategies
between African Americans and all individuals, organizations, and social
groups engaged in a variety of social justice initiatives. Ideally, we need
projects that examine the interactions among Black and Latino sexual politics, or those of Blacks and new immigrant groups, especially how different forms of sexual politics influence one another. Clearly dialogues need
to occur between conservative Black Christian churches that advance one
stance on homosexuality and movements for lesbian, gay, bisexual, and
transgendered (LGBT) rights that advance another. African Americans
will learn much about charting a new course when armed with information
about how Jewish men and women confront similar yet different issues, or
how urbanization shapes the sexual politics of many groups in cities
around the world. Developing a progressive Black sexual politics that fosters social justice requires engaging people who are positioned inside and
outside of African American communities.

    A fifth dimension of *Black Sexual Politics* concerns my choices con-
cerning language. This volume synthesizes the main ideas of fields as
diverse as critical race theory, feminism, sociology, political economy, queer
theory, and cultural studies. These fields can produce multiple languages,
many of which talk past one another. Despite the richness of the ideas
expressed, arcane jargon can impoverish these very same areas of inquiry.
As of this writing, the major works in many academic fields are virtually
unreadable to academics outside those fields, let alone undergraduate students and the educated lay public. Because this book is interdisciplinary, I
have included a glossary of terms used in this volume in order to help readers understand ideas from many fields. The definitions are cast in simple
language, and they are designed to help readers navigate through more difficult sections of the text. I also include a glossary because some academic
conventions do more to turn off readers than turn them on to the ideas
expressed. For example, despite good intentions, the current fashion of
putting quotation marks around the term "race" can be seen as yet another
example of exclusionary language available to the privileged (and morally
superior) few. My students routinely ask me why the term *race* has quotes
around it because they honestly do not know. However well intentioned,
this usage typically signals that the author realizes that "race" is socially
constructed and that the author does not wish to reify "race" by treating it

as real. I reject this position on two grounds. First, why select "race" for quotation marks and not "gender" or "sexuality"? What is it about "race" that makes it more constructed than other systems of power? Second, despite its constructed nature, the effects of "race" remain real for millions of people. As the experiences of the two boys in the movie theater illustrate, one can experience the effects of racism, no matter how it is justified. No matter that by 1964, biological theories of "race" had been largely discredited. The usher who threw them out of the theater simply did not care.

The use of language in *Black Sexual Politics* also reflects the ongoing capitalization problem that has dogged the terms *Negro* and *Black*. Following conventions in the 2000 U.S. census, I capitalize the term *Black* when it serves to name a racial population group with an identifiable history in the United States. For African Americans, the term *Black* is simultaneously a racial identity assigned to people of African descent by the state, a political identity for petitioning that same state, and a self-defined ethnic identity. Because some African Americans use some variant of the terms *Black people, African Americans, Black Americans,* and *people of African descent* as self-definitions, I capitalize all of these terms.[16]

My reliance on Black popular culture and mass media as important sources of evidence for the arguments presented here constitutes a final distinguishing feature of *Black Sexual Politics*. I rely heavily on discourse analysis. As used here, a discourse is a set of ideas and practices that when taken together organize both the way a society defines certain truths about itself and the way it puts together social power. This means that race, gender, and sexuality have ideological dimensions that work to organize social institutions. In the post–civil rights era, Black popular culture and mass media have both grown in importance in creating ideologies of inequality. Black popular culture consists of the ideas and cultural representations created by Black people in everyday life that are widely known and accepted. In contrast, mass media describes the appropriation and repackaging of these ideas for larger audience consumption. Black popular culture as examined here is indicative of larger political and economic forces on the macro level that in turn influence the micro level of everyday behavior among African Americans. Conversely, everyday behavior becomes the cultural stuff that is mined by Black popular culture and a mass media with an insatiable appetite for new material. In the spirit of doing interdisciplinary scholarship, I felt it necessary to incorporate as many examples as possible from Black popular culture and mass media because I see their significance for global youth cultures and African American youth in particular. Given this book's subject matter of Black masculinity and Black femininity in the context of the new racism, and the significance of African American youth within hip-hop culture, including Black popular culture seemed especially important.

This decision to incorporate Black popular culture and mass media also speaks to the question of audience. I have found that the undergraduates I teach, especially African American students, gain much of their sense of the world not solely from books but also from films, music, videos, and the Internet. Despite the significance of a range of forms of Black popular culture to Black sexual politics, this project relies heavily on film, especially popular films that are readily available on video. These films enter into this project in two ways. For one, I have found that Black popular culture generally and videos in particular catalyze critical thinking and lively classroom discussions among students from diverse backgrounds. Film lends itself to rich discussions of gender and sexuality because students can use these films as jumping off points to analyze difficult topics. Despite its value, because the mega-star of today can be forgotten tomorrow, one drawback of relying too heavily on Black popular culture concerns its fleeting nature. Given this caveat, I tried to identify selected well-known examples within Black popular culture that illustrate the theoretical arguments concerning race, class, gender, and sexuality. I encourage those grounded in media studies who agree with me and/or who take issue with my arguments to generate better examples. Hopefully, more complex analyses of gender and sexuality will follow.

In *Black Sexual Politics*, I also use selected films as exemplars of trends in Black popular culture. Films and videos provide social scripts that show people appropriate gender ideology as well as how to behave toward one another. Despite the protests by defenders of the media who claim that sounds and images have little effect on consumers, the billions spent on advertising dollars suggests otherwise. Certainly images and representations do not *determine* behavior, but they do provide an important part of the interpretive context for explaining it. Social scripts suggest how to behave. Despite the power of mass media, I remind readers that being given a script of how to behave as a Black man or woman in no ways means that one must follow it. For African Americans, rejecting what is expected is often the first step in resistance.

OVERALL ORGANIZATION OF THE VOLUME

Each of the three parts of *Black Sexual Politics: African Americans, Gender, and the New Racism* stresses different dimensions of Black sexual politics. The three chapters in Part I, "African Americans and the New Racism," provide a conceptual and historical foundation for understanding contemporary Black sexual politics. The challenges of the new racism require several progressive agendas, not just the one examined here. For example, a more progressive analysis of social class that takes new forms of global capitalism into account might enable African Americans to see the strengths and limitations of affirmative action, reparations, Black entrepreneurship, and other current economic development strategies. Similarly, a more nuanced analysis of how other immigrants from areas of the Caribbean, Latin America, and continental Africa are influencing the contours of African American ethnicity and of Black organizations, cultures, and communities might catalyze a more dynamic antiracist African American politics. Developing a more progressive Black sexual politics concerning issues of gender and sexuality constitutes one important piece of a broader antiracist, social justice project.

Chapter 1, "Why Black Sexual Politics?" builds on this Introduction by examining why African Americans need to develop a political agenda that takes gender and sexuality seriously. Chapter 2, "The Past Is Ever Present: Recognizing the New Racism" examines issues of Black political economy that underpin contemporary African American gender relations. Rejecting a view of history in which one type of racial formation gives way to another, the chapter argues instead that remnants of several past racial formations affect patterns of class and gender within contemporary African American communities. Chapter 3, "Prisons for Our Bodies, Closets for Our Minds: Racism, Heterosexism, and Black Sexuality" uses the prison and the closet as complementary and competing metaphors for understanding oppressions of race and sexuality in order to examine how racism and heterosexism draw strength from one another. Of race, class, gender, and sexuality as systems of oppression, for many people, heterosexism remains the most difficult to understand and, in many cases, to even see as being a system of oppression. The approach taken here conceptualizes heterosexism as a system of power that suppresses heterosexual and homosexual African American men and women in ways that foster Black subordination.

The three chapters in Part II, "Rethinking Black Gender Ideology" examine how the interconnections of race, class, gender, and sexuality take ideological forms, especially within contemporary Black popular culture and/or global mass media, and how this ideology increasingly influences public life. Under the new racism, representations of Black masculinity and Black femininity become important in explaining class relations within African American communities, within U.S. society, and, because these images now travel, within a global context. These ideologies take gender-specific forms and become deployed in defending the treatment of African Americans within contemporary social institutions.

Chapter 4, "Get Your Freak On: Sex, Babies, and Images of Black Femininity," and chapter 5, "Booty Call: Sex, Violence, and Images of Black Masculinity," examine how past-in-present ideas about sexuality and violence influence contemporary Black popular culture that in turn is commodified, displayed, and sold by a powerful mass media. Both chapters examine how class-specific representations of African American women and African American men that now circulate throughout global mass culture help structure the new racism in the United States. Not only are sexuality and violence part of representations of Blackness, these mass media images circulate in a climate where social institutions are increasingly saturated with relations of sexualized violence. Chapter 6, "Very Necessary: Redefining Black Gender Ideology," analyzes how prevailing gender ideology uses a framework of "weak men, strong women" to advance troublesome notions of Black masculinity and Black femininity. Unpacking this ideology should enable African American men and women to see the range of choices that they actually have in becoming the kinds of Black men and women they want to be.

The three chapters in Part III, "Toward a Progressive Black Sexual Politics," examine three important sites where change needs to occur in moving toward a more progressive Black sexual politics. Chapter 7, "Assume the Position: The Changing Contours of Sexual Violence," takes a closer look at the changing contours of violence as an important form of political control that has emerged within the new racism. Lynching and rape as forms of sexual violence historically visited upon African American men and women have been linked within U.S. sexual politics. However, the chapter questions whether these constructs remain adequate for explaining the violence visited upon African Americans in the post–civil rights era.

Rather, institutionalized rape and institutionalized lynching constitute *different* expressions of the *same* type of social control that is especially suited to the new racism. Chapter 8, "No Storybook Romance: How Race and Gender Matter," examines the dissonance between ideologies of love relationships within mass media and the rules that govern such relationships within the context of everyday life. How people treat one another in everyday life, especially within intimate love relationships, is ground zero for a progressive Black sexual politics. Chapter 9, "Why We Can't Wait: Black Sexual Politics and the Challenge of HIV/AIDS," examines how the global spread of HIV/AIDS might serve as a catalyst for developing a more progressive Black sexual politics. How does developing a more progressive Black sexual politics move antiracism forward?

I end *Black Sexual Politics* with a short afterword titled "The Power of a Free Mind." As comforting as it may be to try to turn back the hands of time and retreat into an imagined Black past where men and women knew their place, this simply is not an option. African Americans cannot relive the events of 1964, pining for the civil rights days when, despite their differences, the cluster of vocal Black people in the back of the theater saw social injustice through a common lens and complained en masse. The new racism is far more slippery and grappling with its contradictions requires new tools. What will it take for African Americans to develop a progressive Black sexual politics? How can all people who work for social justice imagine a future that is different? There are no easy answers to these questions, only the conviction that the power of a free mind might forge new paths that we might all follow. When it comes to struggles for social justice, there's no turning back.

PART I

AFRICAN AMERICANS
AND THE NEW RACISM

ONE

WHY BLACK
SEXUAL POLITICS?

2001: The career of Jennifer Lopez skyrockets. A Puerto Rican woman, Lopez's rise to fame came after her feature film appearance as Selena, the first Chicana superstar. News of J-Lo is everywhere; especially her much discussed love relationship and subsequent break-up with hip-hop artist Puff Daddy (aka P Diddy). One special feature of Lopez's routinely makes the news—her seemingly large bottom. From late night American talk shows to South African radio programs to Internet websites, J-Lo's butt is all the rage. Recognizing its value, it is rumored that Lopez insures her buttocks for 1 billion dollars, as one website mischievously described it, 500 million dollars per cheek.

2000: The photo insert for *Survivor*, Destiny's Child third CD, shows the three African American women standing legs akimbo, holding hands, and dressed in animal skin bikinis. Selling over 15 million albums and singles worldwide, *Survivor*'s success reflects a savvy marketing strategy that promoted the song "Independent Woman" as part of the soundtrack for the hit movie *Charlie's Angels* and foreshadowed the success of group member Beyoncé Knowles. *Survivor*'s message of female power also fuels its popularity. Counseling women to be resilient and financially independent,

Destiny's Child proclaim, "I'm a survivor, I'm gonna make it." *Survivor* suggests sexual independence as well. In their highly popular song "Bootylicious," written by Beyoncé, they refer to their butts as "jelly" and ask, "Can you handle it?" The term *bootylicious* proves to be so popular that, along with *hottie* and *roadrage*, it is added to the 2002 edition of *Merriam-Webster's Collegiate Dictionary*.

1925: Born in a poor community in East St. Louis, Missouri, African American entertainer Josephine Baker moves to Paris. She becomes a sensation in the American production of *La Revue Nègre*. Performing bare-breasted in a jungle setting and clad only in a short skirt of banana leaves, Ms. Baker's rump-shaking banana dance becomes an instant hit with Parisian audiences. When asked whether she will return to the United States, Ms. Baker replies, "they would make me sing mammy songs and I cannot feel mammy songs, so I cannot sing them." Instead, in 1937 Ms. Baker becomes a French citizen and garners lifelong accolades as the "Black Venus" of France. Upon her death in 1975, she receives a twenty-one-gun salute, the only such honor given by France to an American-born woman.[1]

1816: After several years of being exhibited in Paris and London as the "Hottentot Venus," Sarah Bartmann, a Khoi woman from what is now South Africa, dies. In the London exhibit, she is displayed caged, rocking back and forth to emphasize her supposedly wild and dangerous nature. She wears a tight-fitting dress whose brown color matches her skin tones. When ordered to do so, she leaves her cage and parades before the audience who seems fascinated with what they see as her most intriguing feature—her buttocks. Some in the audience are not content to merely look. One eyewitness recounts with horror how Bartmann endures poking and prodding, as people try to ascertain for themselves whether her buttocks are real. In the context of popular London shows that display as forms of entertainment talking pigs, animal monsters and human oddities such as the Fattest Man on Earth, midgets, giants, and similar "freaks of nature," these reactions to Bartmann's exhibition are not unusual. Upon Sarah Bartmann's death, George Cuvier, one of the fathers of

modern biology, claims her body in the interests of science. Her
subsequent dissection becomes one of at least seven others completed on the bodies of women of color from 1814 to 1870. Their
goal—to advance the field of classical comparative anatomy.[2]

Contemporary sexual politics in the United States present African
American women and men with a complicated problem. From the display
of Sarah Bartmann as a sexual "freak" of nature in the early nineteenth century to Josephine Baker dancing bare-breasted for Parisian society to the
animal-skin bikinis worn by "bootylicious" Destiny's Child to the fascination with Jennifer Lopez's buttocks, women of African descent have been
associated with an animalistic, "wild" sexuality. Expressed via an ever-
changing yet distinctive constellation of sexual stereotypes in which Sarah
Bartmann's past frames J-Lo's present, this association of sexuality with
Black women helps create ideas about racial difference. Black men have
their own variety of racial difference, also constructed from ideas about violence and dangerous sexuality. African American heavyweight boxer Jack
Johnson certainly sparked controversy when, in 1910, he fought the formerly unbeaten White champion Jim Jeffries. During the fight itself, over
30,000 men stood outside the *New York Times*' offices, waiting to hear the
outcome. Johnson's bloody victory sparked race riots in every Southern
state. Johnson's predilection for White women only fueled the fires of
White reaction. When authorities discovered that Johnson was having an
affair with an eighteen-year-old blonde from Minnesota, they charged him
under the Mann Act with engaging in white slavery. Johnson's ability to
wield violence and his seeming attractiveness to White women made him
threatening to White middle-class men.[3] For both women and men,
Western social thought associates Blackness with an imagined uncivilized,
wild sexuality and uses this association as one lynchpin of racial difference.
Whether depicted as "freaks" of nature or as being the essence of nature
itself, savage, untamed sexuality characterizes Western representations of
women and men of African descent.[4]

For their respective audiences, the distinctive sexualized spectacles performed by Bartmann, Baker, Destiny's Child, and Lopez invoke sexual
meanings that give shape to racism, sexism, class exploitation, and heterosexism. Each spectacle marks the contradictions of Western perceptions of
African bodies and of Black women's agency concerning the use of their

bodies. Together they frame an invented discourse of *Black sexuality*.[5] For French and British audiences, Sarah Bartmann served as a sign of racial difference used to justify the growing belief in the superiority of White civilization and the inferiority of so-called primitive peoples necessary for colonialism. Her treatment helped create modern Black sexual stereotypes of the jezebel, the mammy, and the welfare queen that, in the United States, helped uphold slavery, Jim Crow segregation, and racial ghettoization.[6] Illustrating through stark historical example how common sense understandings of race and gender flow smoothly into those of biology, medicine, and Western science itself, her body marked the intersection of entertainment, science, and commerce. Sarah Bartmann could be enjoyed while alive and, upon her death, studied under the microscope for the burgeoning field of comparative anatomy. As South African writer Yvette Abrahams and filmmaker Zola Maseko's video recording on the life of Bartmann point out, we know little about Bartmann's agency in this arrangement.[7] What Bartmann lost by being displayed as a "freak" is far clearer to us through our modern sensibilities than what she might have gained for herself and her family.

Bartmann may not have been aware of the power of the sexual stereotypes that were created in her image, but women of African descent who followed most certainly were.[8] Black women struggled to exercise agency and self-definition concerning these images and the social practices that they defended. Evidently aware of the sexual stereotypes applied to women of African descent, Josephine Baker played the part of the "primitive," but for her own reasons.[9] Baker entertained the French with her openness about her body, an important example of how an imagined, uncivilized, wild sexuality remained associated with Blackness within Western social thought and continued as a sign of racial difference. But was Baker really sexually liberated, or was her performance a carefully planned illusion that, in the African American trickster tradition, was designed to titillate and manipulate the tastes of her European audiences? Baker's biography suggests a level of sophistication that enabled her to move far beyond her initial depiction as a bare-breasted "primitive." Baker may have initially done banana dances, but from her point of view, she escaped performing the ubiquitous "mammy songs" assigned to Hattie McDaniel, Ethel Waters, and other talented African American women then performing in the United States. In France, Baker ensured that she was well compensated for her performances.

The work of contemporary artists such as Destiny's Child also invokes the contradictions of sexualized spectacle and Black women's agency or self-determination. Transported from the immediacy of live stage performances, Destiny's Child perform in the intimate yet anonymous terrain of CDs, music videos, movies, Internet websites, and other forms of contemporary mass media. Here each consumer of "Independent Woman" or "Bootylicious" can imagine a one-on-one relationship with one, two, or all three members of Destiny's Child, whose images and artistry are purchased, rented, or downloaded under the control of the consumer. Under conditions of racial segregation, mass media provides a way that racial difference can safely enter racially segregated private spaces of living rooms and bedrooms. Destiny's Child may not be like the girls next door, but they can be seen on home theater and heard via headphones within the privacy of individual consciousness. In this new mass media context, Black sexual stereotypes are rendered virtually invisible by their ubiquity; yet, they persist through a disconnected mélange of animal skins, sexually explicit lyrics, breast worship, and focus on the booty. Destiny's Child may entertain and titillate; yet, their self-definitions as "survivors" and "independent women" express female power and celebration of the body and booty. The women in Destiny's Child are also wealthy. Just who is being "controlled" in these new arenas? For what purpose? Their message contains a defiance denied to Bartmann and Baker—"It's my body, it's my booty, and I'll do what I want with it—can you handle it?"

What are we to make of Jennifer Lopez? As a Latina,[10] where does she fit in this story of Western constructions of "wild" Black sexuality, the social construction of racial difference, and Black people's reactions to them? Like Josephine Baker before her, Jennifer Lopez is celebrated and makes a considerable amount of money. Elevating Jennifer Lopez's buttocks to icon status invokes historical meanings of Black female sexuality and takes the politics of race and sexuality to an entirely new plane. In this case, a Latina brushed with the hint of Blackness and not clearly of African descent carries the visible sign of Black sexuality. In order to be marketed, Black sexuality need not be associated solely with bodies that have been racially classified as "Negro," "mulatto," or "Black." Western imaginations have long filled in the color, moving women from Black to White and back again depending on the needs of the situation. In antebellum Charleston, South Carolina, and New Orleans, Louisiana, White men desired quadroons and octoroons as prostitutes because such women looked like White women, but they were actually Black women, with all that that implied about women's sexuality.[11] J–Lo's fluid ethnicity in her films, from the Chicana in *Selena* to the racial/ethnic ambiguity in subsequent roles, illustrates the shifting contours of racial/ethnic classification. When it comes to "hot-blooded" Latinas, one might ask which part of their "blood" carries the spice of sexual looseness?[12] This all seems to be a far cry from the commodification of Sarah Bartmann's buttocks—or is it?

The fact that these examples involve women of actual or imputed African descent is no accident because the racial difference assigned to Black people has often come in gender specific forms. In the nineteenth century, women stood as symbols of race and women from different races became associated with differentially valued expressions of sexuality. During this period marked by the rise of European nationalism, England, France, Spain, Portugal, Germany, the Netherlands, and Italy all jockeyed with varying degrees of success to define themselves as nation-states. Each followed its own distinctive path in constructing its own national identity and that of its colonies. Yet they shared one overriding feature—the treatment of women within each respective nation-state as well as within the colonies were important to national identity.[13] Ideas of pure White womanhood that were created to defend women of the homeland required a corresponding set of ideas about hot-blooded Latinas, exotic Suzy Wongs, wanton jezebels, and stoic native squaws. Civilized nation-states required uncivilized and backward colonies for their national identity to have meaning, and the status of women in both places was central to this entire endeavor. In this context, Black women became icons of hypersexuality.[14]

Men of African descent were also seen as hypersexual beings that have generated similar icons.[15] During the era of live entertainment, and until the onset of the technologies that made mass media possible, men were objectified differently from women. The West African slave trade and Southern auction blocks treated both Black women's and men's bodies as objects for sale, yet women participated in sexual spectacles to a greater degree than did men, because Western ideas about women and femininity itself have long been more tightly wedded to ideas about women's physical beauty and sexual attractiveness. Even today, men are far more likely to stare at and comment upon women's breasts, buttocks, legs, face, and other body parts than are women to subject men's bodies to this type of scrutiny. Like all women, Black women were objects to be seen, enjoyed, purchased, and used, primarily by White men with money. African women's sexuality may have piqued the prurient interest of Western audiences, but African men's sexuality was seen as dangerous and in need of control. Live expressions of Black male sexuality needed to be hidden from White spectators, especially audiences that might contain White women. Until recently, the very tenets of female respectability made it impossible for a female audience to cheer on a live male sex show, especially a White female audience viewing Black men as sexual beings. Assumptions of heterosexuality also inhibit males viewing other males as sexual objects. A situation in which White men view Black male bodies as sexual objects potentially creates a homoerotic space that is incompatible with ideas of straight White masculinity.

Mass media technologies profoundly altered this reliance on face-to-face spectatorship and live entertainment. Television, video, DVD, and the Internet enabled images of Black women and men to enter living rooms, bedrooms, family rooms, and other private domestic spaces. Black male images could now enter private White spaces, one step safely removed because these were no longer live performances and Black men no longer appeared in the flesh. These technological advances enabled the reworking of Black male sexuality that became much more visible, yet was safely contained. Take, for example, the stylized music video performances of hip-hop artists. Camera angles routinely are shot from a lower position than the rapper in question, giving the impression that he is looming over the viewer. In real life, being this close to young African American men who were singing about sex and violence and whose body language included fists, angry gestures, and occasional crotch-grabbing might be anxiety provoking for the typical rap and hip-hop consumer (most are suburban White adolescents). Yet viewing these behaviors safely packaged within a music video protects consumers from any possible contact with Black men who are actually in the videos. Just who are these videos for? What are the imagined race, gender, and sexual orientations of the viewers? Black men have long given performances that placed sexuality center stage—Elvis Presley, Mick Jagger, and rapper Eminem all recognized and profited from this reality—but the sexual implications of viewing Black men in the flesh rarely made it out of African American settings where such performances had a different meaning. It is one thing to visit a Black nightclub to hear singer Millie Jackson's live performance of raunchy blues or gather in a neighbor's living room to listen to Redd Foxx records. It is entirely another to sit in an interracial audience and listen to comedian Eddie Murphy's uncensored boasting concerning Black male sexual prowess; or to count the times within a music video that the camera hones in on rapper Ja Rule's crotch.

Western perceptions of the sexuality of men of African descent also became central to the national identities of European nation-states engaged in colonial projects. England, France, and other colonial powers constructed their national identities by manipulating ideas about men in the home country and in their colonies. The United States followed a similar path, with ideas about race and masculinity intertwined with ideas about American citizenship.[16] Like their female counterparts, men of African descent were also perceived to have excess sexual appetite, yet with a disturbing additional feature, a predilection for violence. In this context, the "White heroes" of Western Europe and the United States became constructed in relation to the "Black beasts" of Africa.[17] Moreover, both were used to signal the hierarchical relationship between colonizers and colonies. Overall, colonialism, slavery, and racial segregation relied upon this discourse of Black sexuality to create tightly bundled ideas about Black femininity and Black masculinity that in turn influenced racial ideologies and racial practices.

As these systems of racial rule recede in the post–civil rights era, what if anything is taking their place? Over one hundred years ago, African American intellectual William E. B. DuBois predicted that the problem of the twentieth century would be the presence of the color line. By that, DuBois meant that the policies of colonialism and racial segregation were designed to create, separate, and rank the various "races" of man. Until legally outlawed in the 1950s and 1960s, the color line policies of Jim Crow racial segregation kept the vast majority of African Americans from quality educations, good jobs, adequate health care, and the best neighborhoods. In contrast, the problem of the twenty-first century seems to be the seeming *absence* of a color line. Formal legal discrimination has been outlawed, yet contemporary social practices produce virtually identical racial hierarchies as those observed by DuBois. By whatever measures used in the United States or on a global scale, people of African descent remain disproportionately clustered at the bottom of the social hierarchy. The effects of these historical exclusions persist today under a new racism.[18]

It is important to note that the new racism of the early twenty-first century has not replaced prior forms of racial rule, but instead incorporates elements of past racial formations. As a result, ideas about race, gender, sexuality, and Black people as well as the social practices that these ideas shape and reflect remain intricately part of the new racism, but in changed ways. The new racism thus reflects a situation of permanence and change. Just as people of African descent were disadvantaged within prior forms of economic organization, a similar outcome exists today. On a global scale, wealth and poverty continue to be racialized. This is permanence. At the same time, racial hierarchy is produced in a context of massive economic, political, and social change that organizes racial hierarchy differently. The processes used to maintain the same outcome are also different. In a similar fashion, ideas about sexuality and gender that were very much a part of prior forms of racial rule remain as important today. They too are differently organized to produce remarkably similar results.

First, new forms of global capitalism frame the new racism. Globalization itself is certainly not new—it was a core characteristic of former patterns of racism. The African slave trade had a global reach and its legacy created the contemporary African Diaspora. The colonial wealth of Europe was based on a global system of racial subordination of people of color. Yet the increasing concentration of capital in the hands of fewer and fewer corporations distinguishes the contemporary global capitalism from its nineteenth-century counterpart. Today, relatively few transnational corporations are driving the world economy and their decisions affect the global distribution of wealth and poverty. These new forms of global organization have polarized world populations. On one end are elites who are wealthy beyond the imagination, and who have the freedom to come and go as they please, wherever and whenever they want. The locals, the people who are stuck in one place, without jobs, and for whom time seems to creep by, populate the other end.[19]

People of African descent are routinely disadvantaged in this global economy in which corporations make the decisions and in which "the company is free to move; but the consequences of the move are bound to stay."[20] Within a global context, Black people and other people of color are those more likely to lose jobs in local labor markets. They are the ones who lack control over oil, mineral wealth, or other natural resources on their land; who lose their land to global agribusiness; and who are denied basic services of electricity and clean water, let alone the luxury goods of the new information age. The benefits of telecommunications and other new technologies have had a far greater impact on Whites than on people of African descent and other people of color. For example, though Europe and North America constitute 20 percent of the world's population, two-thirds of all televisions and radios are owned and controlled in these two regions.[21]

The new racism is also characterized by a changing political structure that disenfranchises people, even if they appear to be included. In the United States, for example, people may vote, but corporations and other propertied entities wield tremendous influence in deciding the outcome of elections because they fund campaigns. All levels of government have been affected by a growing concentration of economic power that has fostered corporate influence over public policy. This same process operates in a transnational context. Global corporations increasingly dominate national, regional, and local governance. This concentrated economic power erodes the authority of national governments and has created unprecedented migrations of people and jobs both within and between nation-states. The ineffectiveness of transnational governance and domestic policies of racial desegregation in reducing Black poverty suggests an important link joining the experiences of people of African descent with postcolonial governance and the experiences of African Americans in the United States with racial desegregation. The outcome is reconfigured social hierarchies of race, class, gender, and sexuality, with people of African descent clumped at the bottom. Patterns of desegregation and subsequent resegregation of African Americans in the United States resemble the decolonization and recolonization that characterizes the global context.[22]

The new racism also relies more heavily on mass media to reproduce and disseminate the ideologies needed to justify racism. There are two themes here—the substance of racial ideologies under the new racism and the forms in which ideologies are created, circulated, and resisted. Ideas about Black sexuality certainly appear in contemporary racial ideologies. But the growing significance of Black popular culture and mass media as sites for creating and resisting racial ideologies is also striking. The films, music, magazines, music videos, and television shows of global entertainment, advertising, and news industries that produce superstars like Jennifer Lopez help manufacture the consent that makes the new racism appear to be natural, normal, and inevitable.[23]

The challenges of the new racism have been especially pronounced for African American women and men, the subjects of this book. The issues associated with the politics of the new racism and with the manipulation of ideologies within them, in the case of African Americans, the discourse on Black sexuality, affect everyone. But the specific form that race and gender politics take for African Americans can serve as an important site for examining these larger issues. Moreover, the African American community contains a crucial subpopulation in these debates. A generation of young African American men and women who were born after the struggles for civil rights, Black power, and African nation-state independence has come of age under this new racism. Referred to as the hip-hop generation, this group has encountered, reproduced, and resisted new forms of racism that continue to rely on ideas about Black sexuality. Expecting a democratic, fair society with equal economic opportunities, instead, this group faced disappearing jobs, crumbling schools, drugs, crime, and the weakening of African American community institutions. The contradictions of the post–civil rights era affect all African Americans, yet they have been especially pronounced for Black youth.[24]

AMERICA—A SEXUALLY REPRESSIVE SOCIETY?

Sexualized Black bodies seem to be everywhere in contemporary mass media, yet within African American communities, a comprehensive understanding of sexual politics remains elusive. In a social context that routinely depicts men and women of African descent as the embodiment of deviant sexuality, African American politics has remained curiously silent on issues of gender and sexuality. As a result, African Americans lack a vibrant, public discussion of the complex issues that the prevailing discourse on Black sexuality has raised for African American men and women. In more candid moments, however, some African American thinkers stress how damaging the absence of a self-defined Black sexual politics can be. As African American cultural critic Cheryl Clarke pointed out over twenty years ago:

> Like all Americans, black Americans live in a sexually repressive culture. And we have made all manner of compromise regarding our sexuality in order to live here. We have expended much energy trying to debunk the racist mythology which says our sexuality is depraved. Unfortunately, many of us have overcompensated and assimilated the

Puritan value that sex is for procreation, occurs only between men
and women, and is only valid within the confines of heterosexual
marriage. . . . Like everyone else in America who is ambivalent in these
respects, black folk have to live with the contradictions of this limited
sexual system by repressing or closeting any other sexual/erotic urges,
feelings, or desires.[25]

Given the saturation of American mass media with sexual themes, and the
visibility of sexualized spectacles that include men and women of African
descent within movies, music videos, and popular music in particular,
Clarke's comments may seem to be odd. How can American culture be
"sexually repressive" when sexuality seems to be everywhere? White
actresses routinely play roles that include graphic sex scenes. Moreover,
Black women are not downtrodden rape victims, but instead, also seem to
be in control of their own sexuality. Director Spike Lee's African
American leading lady Nola Darling seemed to be calling the shots in *She's
Gotta Have It*, Lee's groundbreaking film about Black female sexuality.
Destiny's Child and J-Lo certainly do not seem "repressed." How can
African Americans be sexually "closeted" when Black sexuality itself
serves as an icon for sexual freedom?

For African Americans, these questions are crucial, especially in the
context of the post–civil rights era in which Black popular culture and
mass media are increasingly important for racial rule. Sexual regulation
occurs through repression, both by eliminating sexual alternatives and by
shaping the public debates that do exist. In order to prosper, systems of
oppression must regulate sexuality, and they often do so by manufacturing
ideologies that render some ideas commonsensical while obscuring others.
The expanding scope of mass media makes this process more visible and,
more important, in the United States, does seem to have produced a "sexually repressive culture."

The treatment of human sexuality in American society reflects a curious
combination of censorship and excessive visibility (e.g., hypervisibility), of
embarrassed silences and talk-show babble. On the one hand, since colonial
times, selected groups within U.S. society have striven to suppress a wide
range of sexual ideas and practices.[26] American colonists paid close attention
to the sexual behavior of individuals, not to eliminate sexual expression but to
channel it into what they thought was its proper setting and purpose, namely,

as a "duty and a joy within marriage, and for purposes of procreation."[27] More recently, the election of conservative Republican Ronald Reagan in 1980 emboldened the Christian Right to advance a fundamentalist family values discourse. Resembling the colonial discourse from the 1600s, the contemporary family values position argues (1) all sexual practices should occur only within the confines of heterosexual marriage; (2) the fundamental purpose of sexuality is procreation; and (3) children should be protected from all sexual information with the exception of abstinence as the preferred form of birth control before marriage.

This historical and contemporary agenda that has suppressed and often censored a range of ideas concerning human sexuality has made it difficult to have open, candid, and fact-based public debates. This censorship not only affects public dialogues but it also influences research on human sexuality.[28] Heterosexism, with its ideas about what constitutes normal and deviant sexuality holds sway to the point where significant gaps exist in the social science literature on human sexuality. Despite the conservative thrust since 1980, the suppression of a range of ideas about human sexuality is not new. Research done in the 1950s by Alfred Kinsey and his colleagues at Indiana University provides a textbook case of sexual censorship. Kinsey's work treated all sexual practices, including homosexuality and bisexuality, as inherently "normal" and defined the array of sexual practices reported by study participants as benign indicators of human difference. But Kinsey's work virtually ground to a halt when funding for this line of scientific research dried up.

It has taken the field some time to recover from this censorship. In essence, heterosexism and its accompanying assumptions of heterosexuality operate as a hegemonic or taken-for-granted ideology that has influenced research on human sexuality. Societal norms that install heterosexuality as the only way to be normal still hold sway.[29] For example, the term *sexuality* itself is used so synonymously with *hetero*sexuality that schools, churches, and other social institutions treat heterosexuality as natural, normal, and inevitable. Studying sexual practices that stray too far from prevailing norms, for example, sex outside of marriage, adolescent sexuality, homosexuality, and formerly taboo sexual practices such as anal and oral sex, become situated within a social problems framework. This approach not only stigmatizes individuals and groups who engage in alternative sexual practices but it also reinforces views of human sexuality itself as being a problem that should not be discussed in public. Alternately, research on human sexuality is often annexed to bona fide social problems, for example, adolescent pregnancy and people living with HIV/AIDS. Sexuality seems to be everywhere, but research that investigates variations in human sexuality outside of a social problems framework has only recently come to the forefront.

The treatment of sex education in American public schools illustrates how a sexually repressive culture strives to render human sexuality invisible. Sex education remains a hot topic, with students receiving spotty information at best. Topics that are important to adolescents have been difficult to include within sex education programs. Despite high student interest and a growing recognition that comprehensive sex education might save lives, programs tend to shy away from discussing sexuality before marriage, the use of contraception, homosexuality, and other controversial topics. Ironically, the checkered pattern of research on human sexuality offers a good case for how heterosexism operates as a system of power that negatively affects straight and lesbian, gay, bisexual, and transgendered (LGBT) students alike. Because adolescents of all sexual orientations are in the process of forming sexual identities, they are especially affected by heterosexism. For example, despite a high adolescent pregnancy rate, worrisome increases in the rate of HIV infection among American adolescents, and emerging research demonstrating that high school students grappling with LGBT identities are more prone to depression and suicide, the reluctance to talk openly about human sexuality within U.S. schools places students at risk. Similarly, a special report on adolescent sexuality points to the difficulties of collecting data on adolescent conceptions of abstinence.[30] Anecdotal reports suggest that many adolescents who engage in oral sex think that they are practicing abstinence because they are refraining from genital sexual intercourse. These practices may protect them from pregnancy, but they also expose adolescents to risks of sexually transmitted diseases, including HIV.[31]

Despite these repressive practices, on the other hand, sexual ideas and images within contemporary U.S. society enjoy a visibility that would have been unheard of in Kinsey's 1950s America. Recognizing that sex sells, corporations increasingly use it to sell cars, toothpaste, beer, and other consumer goods. This media saturation has made sexual spectacles highly visible within American popular culture. Soap operas, prime time television, billboards, music videos, movies, and the Internet all contain explicit sexual material. Making sex highly visible in marketplace commodity relations becomes important to maintaining profitability within the U.S. capitalist political economy. The goal is neither to stimulate debate nor to educate, but to sell products.

In the absence of other forums, talk shows on network television provide one important public medium for gaining sexual information. Unfortunately, such shows foster the commodification of sexuality. Stressing sexually explicit conversations that titillate rather than instruct, talk shows illustrate how marketplace relations profit from sexual spectacles. By the early 2000s, this market had segmented into a variety of shows, each carving out its specific identity, often based on distinctive norms regarding race, class, gender, and sexuality.[32] For example, *The Montel Williams Show* routinely trumpets the benefits of the heterosexual family, primarily by extolling the role of fathers in their children's lives. By itself, this message is fairly innocuous. However, the show's format creates sexual spectacles that function as modern-day morality plays about race, gender, and sexuality. Mr. Williams, an African American, routinely conducts paternity tests for women who are not "sure" who fathered their babies. The potential fathers are invited to hear the results of the paternity test on the air, with a stern talk by Mr. Williams concerning their "responsibility" to those branded as fathers by DNA evidence. This family drama is played out repeatedly, with Mr. Williams readying himself to deliver the message to wayward young men—if you take it out of your pants, you need to take care of your babies. Moreover, as an African American man married to a White woman, on his show Mr. Williams repeatedly brings on working-class, interracial couples in which young White mothers try to get their sexually irresponsible Black boyfriends to claim paternity. If this weren't enough, Mr. Williams also devotes shows to the pain experienced by biracial children in search of their wayward parents.

The Maury Povich Show also trades in this racial family drama, but with more emphasis on race and sexuality. Not only does Mr. Povich, a White American, present shows in which White women seek paternity tests for their Black male partners, Mr. Povich presents Black women and Black men in an especially stark light. One show, for example, featured a Black woman who brought on nine Black men as candidates for her six-month-old daughter's "baby daddy."[33] All nine failed the paternity test.

After the revelation, with cameras rolling in search of the all-important "money shot,"[34] Mr. Povich followed the distraught young mother backstage, and volunteered to keep working with her until she had tracked down the Black deadbeat dad. Like Mr. Williams, Mr. Povich delivers a message about responsibility to the DNA-branded fathers. Via the choice of topic, and showing the African American woman whose sexuality was so out of control that she had no idea who had fathered her child, Mr. Povich panders to longstanding societal beliefs about Black sexuality.

The crying and raw emotion solicited on Mr. Williams's and Mr. Povich's shows pales in comparison to the staged sexual spectacles of *The Jerry Springer Show*. Reminiscent of the London freak shows of Sarah Bartmann's time, Mr. Springer's shows routinely combine sexuality and violence, two sure-fire audience builders. Here participants are invited to come on the air and reveal "secrets" to seemingly unsuspecting spouses, lovers, and friends. The "secrets" routinely involve cheating, lying, and false paternity. By his choice of guests, Mr. Springer's show also takes sexual spectacles to an entirely new level. Morbidly obese women parade across the stage in bikinis, verbally taunting the audience to comment on their appearance. In a context in which women's bodies are routinely sexualized, displaying seemingly hideous female bodies is designed to shock and solicit ridicule. These confessional talk shows also routinely conduct paternity tests, show pictures of babies who lack legal fathers, discuss sexual infidelity, and display audience members in sexually explicit clothing (or lack thereof). For many Americans, these shows substitute for public discussions of sexuality because few other outlets are available.

African Americans are well represented in the public spectacles provided by Mr. Williams's, Mr. Povich's, and Mr. Springer's talk shows. Guests on all three programs are clearly working-class, with many of them Black and Latino. These shows are not just about sexuality; they also signal clear messages about race and class. They depict the challenges of explaining a new, interracial class structure that can no longer rely on biological notions of race to differentiate poor people (assumed to be Black) from middle-class people (assumed to be White). In the new multicultural America, Blacks can be middle class (the hugely popular *Cosby Show* broke that barrier in the 1980s) and, in fact, a certain degree of Black middle-class visibility is needed to buttress arguments of equal opportunity (Oprah Winfrey and Montel Williams both exemplify this need for visible, accomplished Blacks). But how does one explain the persistence of poverty among *White* Americans if poverty has long been attributed to Black biological inferiority? They are not biologically Black, but their poverty and downward mobility can be explained if they are seen as being culturally or socially Black. Whites who embrace Black culture become positioned closer to Blacks and become stigmatized. In the context of the new racism, cultural explanations for economic success and poverty substitute for biological arguments concerning intelligence or genetic dispositions for immorality or violence.

Viewing stories about historically taboo interracial sexuality between White women and Black men becomes the new sexual spectacle, where working-class White women become "darkened" by their sexual relationships with irresponsible working-class Black men.[35] When accused of paternity by these "trashy" White women, Black men are depicted as proud of their irresponsible sexual behavior. Certainly White men are given paternity tests on these shows, but typically these are working-class or poor White men who are hauled in by working-class White mothers of their alleged children. In contrast to the White women who point the finger of paternity at both Black and White men, Black women rarely identify White men as the potential fathers of their babies. Given the history of interracial, institutionalized rape of Black women by White men, White fathers of Black children would hardly be newsworthy. Instead, Black women are presented as being so reckless that they do not know who fathered their children or, sharing a common fate with their White sisters, they point the finger at irresponsible Black men. Despite similarities that link all three shows, they do offer different scripts for solving the problems of these sexual spectacles. Part of the appeal of *The Montel Williams Show* lies in his role in this family drama—Williams plays the part of the caring yet stern Black patriarch who provides the fatherly discipline that so many of his guests seemingly lack. In contrast, Mr. Povich presents himself as a kindly White father, showing concern for his emotional albeit abnormal guests. Mr. Springer is merely a ringmaster—he doesn't get near his guests, preferring instead to watch the cursing and chair throwing from a safe distance. Discipline them, listen to them, or dismiss them—all three solutions apply to working-class and poor guests. Apparently, middle-class Americans (even Black ones) have little difficulty identifying which sexual partner conceived their children. Affluent, thirty-something White women awaiting the results of paternity tests for their biracial babies just do not appear on any of these shows.

Much more is at stake here than the accuracy of the depictions of African American women and men within talk shows and other forms of mass media. African Americans and Black culture are highly visible within the American movies, music, sports, dance, and fashion that help shape contemporary ideologies of race, gender, sexuality, and class in a global context. Sexual spectacles travel, and they matter. Historical context disappears, leaving seemingly free-floating images in its wake that become the new vocabulary that joins quite disparate entities. Terms such as "primitive," "backward," "jungle," "wild," and "freak" uncritically cycle through contemporary global culture, leaving undisturbed the pejorative historical meanings associated with this vocabulary. But history hides in the shadows of these terms, because these concepts are incomprehensible without a social context to give them meaning. For example, the pervasive use of animal imagery persists within some expressions of contemporary Black popular culture, as suggested by the decision to clothe Destiny's Child in animal-skin bikinis on their album cover. These depictions eerily resemble past practices of associating Africans with animals, particularly apes, monkeys, and chimpanzees. The choice of animal may change—no longer apes, Black men have taken on new identities as "dogs" energetically engaged in chasing the (kitty) "cat"—but associating Black men and women with lusty, animal sexual practices apparently has not. Although different meanings may be associated with animal imagery, Snoop Doggy Dog, Little Bow Wow, and the classic phrase "you my main dog" all invoke this same universe of animal imagery. Moreover, representations of Black men as "dogs" who have replaced the cool "cats" of prior eras of African American jazzmen, as well as the video "hos" who populate rap music videos suggest the emergence of an increasingly sophisticated gender-specific expression of ideas about Blackness sold in the global marketplace. Josephine Baker's banana dance and Destiny's Child's "bootylicious" would be meaningless without this history, even if those enjoying the images do not consciously see the connections.

African American theorist Cornel West identifies the paradox of a sexually repressive culture that, on the one hand, seems saturated with sexuality, but that, on the other hand, suppresses education and open dialogue concerning human sexuality. To West, race matters: "the paradox of the sexual politics of race in America is that, behind closed doors, the dirty, disgusting, and funky sex associated with Black people is often perceived to be more intriguing and interesting, while in public spaces talk about Black sexuality is virtually taboo."[36] Black sexuality is routinely invoked within American society, namely, the alleged sexual prowess of the Black men accused of fathering babies with White women, but analyzing it is discouraged. The result is a society fraught with contradictions. For example, well-off White teenagers can drive expensive cars to racially segregated high schools and college campuses that admit only a few handpicked African Americans, all the while booming the latest sexually explicit lyrics of their favorite Black hip-hop artist. American viewers can sit in their living rooms viewing talk shows that censure the African American man accused of fathering three out-of-wedlock children with two different White women, yet still be intrigued by his sexual prowess. Legions of young American men can wonder what it would be like to get Beyoncé Knowles from Destiny's Child or Jennifer Lopez in bed.

Like other Americans, African Americans must make sense of this curious sexual climate that accompanies the new racism. This task is made even more difficult by the fact that African Americans are included in these debates, often serving as examples of what *not* to be or, alternately, as icons of sexual freedom served up as the antidote to American sexual repression. As part of the color-blind racism that has accompanied the erasure of the color line, the ubiquitous *inclusion* of images of Black sexuality that permeate contemporary movies, television shows, and music videos can replicate the power relations of racism today just as effectively as the *exclusion* of Black images did prior to the 1960s. Thus, Cheryl Clarke's observation that African Americans live in a sexually repressive culture speaks less to the prominence of representations of Black sexuality within an increasingly powerful mass media than to the *function* of these images in helping to construct a "limited sexual system."

GENDER, SEXUALITY, AND AFRICAN AMERICAN POLITICS

African Americans typically think that gender relations are a private concern, mainly reflecting the love relationships between heterosexual men and women. Those who see the harmful effects of gender oppression on African Americans still wish to define issues of gender and sexuality solely within the context of Black community politics, a domestic issue among Black people. Place the "public" issue of race first, they counsel, and leave the more "private" issues of gender and sexuality for us to work out among ourselves. Relying on ideas about family to construct ideas about race, this approach sees African Americans as participating in a large, imagined racial family. In service to the race, each individual African American should put on a good face for the critical White public that sits in judgment outside African American communities. The adage "don't air dirty laundry in public" speaks to this African American community norm of keeping these and other family problems hidden.[37]

What these approaches fail to grasp is that commonsense notions about differences of gender and sexuality that allegedly distinguish Whites (carriers of "normal" gender ideology and sexual practices) from Blacks (carriers of "deviant" gender ideology and sexual practices) have long served as the fulcrum for constructing racial difference. Within white/black binary thinking, ideas about racial normality and deviancy draw heavily upon ideas about gender and sexuality for meaning. Moreover, because racial normality has been defined in gender-specific terms, African American progress or lack thereof in achieving the gender norms attributed to Whites has long been used as a marker of racial progress. Stated differently, African Americans have been evaluated within the context of a sex role theory that by its very nature disadvantages Black people.[38] Within a Western sex role ideology premised on ideas of strong men and weak women, on active, virile masculinity and passive, dependent femininity, the seeming role reversal among African Americans has been used to stigmatize Black people.[39] This ideology not only identifies a reversed, damaged gender ideology as a sign of racial difference, it further claims that flawed ideas concerning Black masculinity and Black femininity reflect equally problematic conceptions of sexuality.

Because African Americans are in many ways quintessentially American, individual African Americans as well as African Americans as a collectivity can have just as much difficulty as everyone else in understanding these broader U.S. sexual politics. But, because African Americans have historically been harmed by these contradictory sexual politics, the stakes are much higher to develop a critical consciousness. The refusal to discuss *in public* the profound influence of Western constructions of a deviant Black sexuality on African American men and women leaves a vacuum in contemporary African

American politics. Major Black civil rights organizations, for example, the National Association for the Advancement of Colored People (NAACP) and the Urban League continue to skirt issues associated with gender and sexuality.[40] Black Christian churches constitute the most important African American community organizations, and yet they continue to preach a conservative gender ideology, and shun controversial topics, especially sexuality.[41] Gender politics that deny African American women the pulpit when close to 70 percent of churchgoing members are female speak to the need for engagement on these issues. Louis Farrakhan, the head of the Nation of Islam (NOI), called a very successful Million Man March on Washington, D.C. in 1995, yet the NOI's gender politics are grounded in the bedrock of the patriarchal nuclear family and, in many ways, are indistinguishable from those of mainstream Black Christian denominations as well as the sexually repressive culture discussed earlier.[42]

African American politics of the post–civil rights era seems to be between a rock and a hard place. Racial segregation as the legal mechanism for racial oppression has been struck down and the racial ideologies that justified it have been forcefully challenged. Few would offer biological explanations for African American joblessness, poor school performance, higher rates of pregnancy out of wedlock, and higher rates of incarceration. But the changing legal climate and the muting of racial theories rooted in biology neither means that new forms of racism are absent nor that cultural arguments are replacing biology as the reason given for African American disadvantage.[43]

This new racism does present some formidable puzzles for African American politics. In prior periods in which biological theories were used to justify racist practices, racism and antiracism had a seemingly organic and oppositional relationship. One could either be *for* racism by believing that Blacks were biologically inferior and deserved the treatment that they received or one could be *against* it by rejecting these beliefs and pointing to racial prejudice and institutional discrimination as more important in explaining Black disadvantage. These distinctions no longer hold for many White and Black Americans. Under the new color-blind racism that erases the color line, racism itself seems to have disappeared. As French sociologist Michel Wieviorka points out, "this clear-cut polarity between racists and anti-racists no longer exists."[44] With the exception of largely discredited right-wing groups, few American organizations openly advocate theories of Black inferiority based on outdated racial biology. As a result, groups holding vastly different perspectives on what constitutes antiracist political activism can claim that they are the true antiracists.

Taking Martin Luther King, Jr.'s advice to heart that "people should be judged by the content of their character, and not by the color of their skin," for example, one group believes that treating everyone the same, regardless of color, moves American society toward equality. Within this assimilationist, color-blind version of antiracism, recognizing racial differences, or, in some versions, even using the term *race*, fosters racism. In contrast, another group argues that recognizing racial differences is an essential first step in unpacking racial meanings that continue to shape social relations. They see a color-conscious, multicultural diversity as the future of American democracy. Ironically, individuals and groups holding these disparate views can now accuse one another of perpetuating racism itself.[45] Both appropriate the symbols of the civil rights and Black power movements for their own ends. In this context, it becomes possible for conservative Supreme Court Justice Clarence Thomas and Black Nationalist filmmaker Spike Lee *both* to admire and to claim the legacy of Malcolm X. If all of the actual racists in the United States have curiously disappeared, it becomes much more difficult to argue that racism persists. After all, if George W. Bush, Louis Farrahkan, Bill Clinton, Colin Powell, and Molefi Asante can all claim the mantle of being antiracists, how does one recognize racism?[46]

African American politics is buffeted by the same trends that afflict antiracist practices overall. In the context of new U.S. racial formations and of conflicting approaches to Black empowerment and social justice, African American antiracist politics seems stuck between two ineffective ideological options. On one side stands a threadbare civil rights agenda that continues to preach racial integration to an African American population so incarcerated in extensive inner-city ghettos that few Whites are left to integrate schools, neighborhoods, and public facilities.[47] Whites have voted with their feet and their pocketbooks, and few attend the annual Martin Luther King Day rally anymore. On the other side stands a largely symbolic Black Nationalist agenda that shapes the gender politics of controversial organizations such as the Nation of Islam. Black nationalist ideology also appears as a faux radical politics in some hip-hop culture, for example, in the work of Public Enemy or Ice T, primarily because African American youth quite rightly perceive few other options. Neither choice has been especially effective in addressing the social problems of the inner cities or in fostering a broader social justice agenda within the United States.

Black Americans must figure out how to deal with the contours of the new racism and must do so with an increased sensitivity to issues of gender and sexuality. In this regard, political theorist Cathy J. Cohen's schema of consensus and crosscutting political issues provides a useful model for understanding current African American antiracist politics. Consensus issues affect all identifiable group members, in this case, all who claim or are assigned a Black identity. Consensus issues may affect all group members, but they may not take the same form for all group members. In contrast, crosscutting issues disproportionately and directly affect only certain segments of a group. Cohen suggests that current African American politics treat race as a consensus issue while assigning gender and sexuality a secondary status as crosscutting issues. Within this thinking, Black women are affected by gender and Black men are not, and lesbian, gay, bisexual, and transgendered Black people are affected by sexuality and heterosexual Blacks are not.

The new social relations of the post–civil rights era mandate new understandings of how race, class, gender, and sexuality operate as consensus and crosscutting issues within African American politics and how they might be differently configured for what lies ahead. Race continues to be a compelling consensus issue for African Americans because the vast majority of Blacks are either directly affected by racial discrimination or know someone who is or has been affected. For most, middle–class Black achievement is only one generation away from the racism of the past, and its effects are still felt. This racial consensus has political effects in that African American voting behavior demonstrates a commitment to racial solidarity. Despite the growth of a new Black middle class, African Americans are more likely to vote as a racial bloc than they are to vote their social class interests.[48] Claims from William Julius Wilson notwithstanding,[49] most African Americans recognize that class differences *among* African Americans are now more pronounced. But when it comes to electoral politics, they continue to choose race over class, that is, when they perceive that they have a choice at all.

Both gender and sexuality have historically been crosscutting issues within the framework of an overarching antiracist political project. This has been a problem because, within Black political arenas, crosscutting issues are often deemed to be secondary to the greater good of the group.[50] In a context in which gender has been associated with Black women and in which sexuality has been the province of Black (LGBT) people, these groups have often been encouraged to take a back seat for the greater good of racial solidarity. Many have not gone willingly. The explosion of Black feminism since the 1970s has been spurred on, in large part, by the refusal of Black women activists to take a back seat to men within both the civil rights and the Black Nationalist political movements. Similar catalysts stimulated the increasing visibility of Black lesbians and gays. These groups point out that, without serious attention to contemporary Black sexual politics, African Americans may uncritically circulate ideas about race, class, gender, and sexuality that bear striking resemblance to those long advanced by White elites.

An antiracist politics that does not reframe the consensus issue of race in terms of class, gender, sexuality, and age will remain incapable of responding to the complexities of the new racism. Take, for example, the pressing issue of violence that confronts people of African descent. African Americans are all affected by violence, but by different manifestations. Regardless of social class, Black men are more likely to encounter state-sanctioned violence at the hands of police whereas Black women are more likely to experience intimate violence of battering and rape at the hands of fathers, brothers, spouses, boyfriends, and men in their neighborhoods. Black youth and children witness this violence and are profoundly affected by it. Black LGBT people encounter hate crimes of verbal and physical harassment that stem from homophobia. Young Black men often kill one another, a form of internecine violence that reflects the significance of age. Poor and working-class Black people are more vulnerable to certain types of violence than their more affluent counterparts. Violence represents a potentially divisive issue if one form of violence is deemed to be more important than others because the segment of Black people who experience it are deemed more worthy of attention and help. Rather than viewing violence as a crosscutting issue, each group member would recognize the importance of all forms of antiviolence political action, even if particular forms of violence, for example, police harassment or wife battering or rape, did not directly affect him or her.

The issue for African American political agendas is to see the interconnectedness of consensus and crosscutting issues in crafting African

American political agendas. Gender, sexuality, class, and age need not be crosscutting issues within the consensus issue of race but instead are crucial for developing effective racial politics. As the discussion of crafting antiviolence initiatives suggests, the real consensus issue is how to keep race, class, gender, sexuality, and age in dialogue with one another in crafting an antiracist African American politics. Not only are gender, sexuality, and class critical for internal African American politics, developing a more complex analysis creates possibilities for coalitions with other groups who are engaged in similar social justice projects. For example, African Americans cannot address violence alone because the violence against Black women also affects women in a global context. The forms of state violence that concern African American men also affect Latino men and poor and working-class White American men. State violence is not unique to the United States, as numerous cases of state-sanctioned violence in Central and South America and in Africa, Eastern Europe, and Asia suggest. The environmental justice movement pays attention to violence against children from dumping, pesticides, and pollution. These are all broad-based social justice projects, and a robust Black politics would be prepared to engage in coalitions such as these.

Given these challenges, it is vital that the notion of antiracist politics be expanded beyond more traditional notions of political parties, social movements, and grassroots political organizations. Political anthropologist James C. Scott uses the term "infrapolitics" to describe the hidden behaviors of everyday resistance. Despite appearances of consent, people challenge inequalities of race, class, gender, and sexuality through conversations, jokes, songs, folklore, theft, foot-dragging, and a multitude of everyday behaviors.[51] As African American historian Robin D. G. Kelley points out, "the political history of oppressed people cannot be understood without reference to infrapolitics, for these daily acts have a cumulative effect on power relations."[52] Everyday life contains many opportunities for resistance, if individual thoughts and actions can be conceptualized in this fashion. Infrapolitics provide important insights concerning the political possibilities for oppressed groups that seemingly lack political options. For example, within African American communities, men and women have different degrees of access to formal power. Men are more likely to engage in traditional politics of officeholding whereas women have been more involved in the day-to-day infrapolitics of community organizing.

Moreover, because infrapolitics and traditional politics are interdependent, neither is sufficient as the sole form of political resistance.

In a new global context, both the organizational politics of formal political arenas and the infrapolitics of everyday African American life are ground zero for issues that go far beyond the happenings in Black inner-city neighborhoods, city politics, or within the United States itself. Given the visibility of African Americans within a global popular culture, African American reactions to these new social relations are highly important. In mapping Black responses to the new racism with an eye toward developing a progressive Black sexual politics adequate for broader antiracist initia-tives, African Americans respond in often contradictory ways. Twenty years ago, Cheryl Clarke saw silences and self-censorship. Now, however, these silences are being supplemented by growing numbers of African American men and women who seem ever ready to replicate these images in full public view. Discourses such as the references to Jennifer Lopez's butt sell because they allude to a certain kind of sexuality long associated with people of African descent. Seemingly unaware of this history, or per-haps exploiting it, some African American artists capitalize on a situation in which everyone knows on some level what gives ideas about Black sexu-ality their meaning but no one is ultimately responsible. It's one thing if Jennifer Lopez and Beyoncé Knowles from Destiny's Child profit from their own images and present themselves in performance as "bootylicious." It's entirely another if adolescent girls tap into this message of female power and head off to their eighth grade classrooms decked in the same "bootylicious" apparel, all the while purchasing the clothes required to achieve this image with money they don't have. The theme here is not cen-sorship of Black girls, but rather to question whether they can "handle it" if they are so woefully uninformed about the legacy of Sarah Bartmann.

Contemporary forms of oppression do not routinely force people to submit. Instead, they manufacture consent for domination so that we lose our ability to question and thus collude in our own subordination. Images of J-Lo, Destiny's Child, and Montel Williams are all part of this process of reproduction and contestation. In this context of oppressions occurring through the normal structures of society, within contemporary nation-states such as the United States, oppression becomes expressed as a rou-tinized violence or normalized war within one society. Within the United States, oppression now takes a new form, one where society itself is saturated with the relations of warfare against selected members of society itself. Routinized violence can break through into open conflict (1992 in Los Angeles and 2001 in Cincinnati), but more often, this normalized war also operates through the infrapolitics of everyday life, through a series of mini-assaults that convince each one of us to stay in our place.[53] Black people are under assault, and the racial and gender meanings assigned to Black bodies as well as the social meanings of Black sexuality in American society overall constitute sites of contestation in an uncivil civil war against Black people.

DEVELOPING A PROGRESSIVE BLACK SEXUAL POLITICS

African Americans express quite diverse and often contradictory responses to the challenges raised by prevailing Black sexual politics. How can Jennifer Lopez and Destiny's Child be independent women and bootylicious at the same time? If Sarah Bartmann, Josephine Baker, Destiny's Child, and Jennifer Lopez can be convinced to perceive themselves solely in terms of the value of their bootys in marketplace relations, then oppression may be complete. If African American men accept the images of themselves as sexually irresponsible boys as depicted on the Montel Williams, Maury Povich, and Jerry Springer shows, then they too participate in structuring their own oppression. But is anyone ever without agency to this degree?

The antidote to a gender-specific racial oppression that advances controlling images of deviant Black sexuality does not lie in embracing a conservative politics of respectability that mimics the beliefs of those responsible for the sexually repressive culture in the first place. Rather, in the context of a new racism, men and women who rescue and redefine sexuality as a source of power rooted in spirituality, expressiveness, and love can craft new understandings of Black masculinity and Black femininity needed for a progressive Black sexual politics. When reclaimed by individuals and groups, redefined ideas about sexuality and sexual practices can operate as sources of joy, pleasure, and empowerment that simultaneously affirm and transcend individual sexual pleasure for social good.

Black feminist poet Audre Lorde certainly knew this when, almost thirty years ago, she identified the power of the erotic as an important source of energy for resisting gender oppression.[54] Lorde redefined the erotic as the deep feelings within each of us in search of love, affirmation, recognition, and a spiritual and/or physical connection to one another. Lorde argued that impoverished notions of love of self and others lie at the heart of oppression. Reclaiming the erotic as a domain of exploration, pleasure, and human agency is thus vital to individual empowerment. Lorde associated erotic power with women and with female sexuality. But the power of the erotic need not be reserved for women, nor is it synonymous with physical sexual expression. Such power is available to all human beings.

For women and men alike, and for individuals from diverse racial, ethnic, sexual, age, and national backgrounds, claiming such power remains easier said than done. Expressing individual agency and challenging the Black sexual politics that shape everyday life is complicated; linking the *individual* agency expressed in these social locations to a *collective* group politics may seem unattainable. The dialectical relationship between oppression and activism makes all politics difficult, including this one. A fundamental contradiction lies at the juncture where intersecting oppressions grounded in dominance confront a resistance nourished by expansive notions of care, eroticism, spirituality, and politicized love. On the one hand, perverting the power of the erotic by manipulating ideas about sexuality has been and continues to be an important dimension of oppressions of race, gender, class, and sexuality. For African Americans, these manipulations take myriad forms and continue to affect contemporary Black sexual politics. On the other hand, because deeply held feelings, especially those that have bodily expression, constitute one of the most important sources of energy available to human beings, people who are able to reclaim the power of the erotic gain a crucial weapon in resisting these intersecting oppressions. Despite these challenges, for African Americans, the struggle is essential.

TWO

THE PAST IS EVER PRESENT
Recognizing the New Racism

It's just me against the world, baby, me against the world.
I got nothin' to lose—it's just me against the world.
                                        —Tupac Shakur

Black youth born after the great social movements of the 1950s and 1960s should have faced a bright future. Social movements of the past fifty years celebrated victories over historical forms of racism, perhaps naively believing that they were creating a new foundation for this new generation. The end of colonialism and dismantling of racial apartheid within the United States and in South Africa signaled the possibilities for antiracist, democratic societies in which Blackness would no longer serve as a badge of inferiority. Yet the actual social conditions that confront this global cohort and their responses to it have turned out to be quite different. When it comes to Black youth, poor housing, inferior education, precarious health status, and dwindling job prospects reoccur across diverse societies. Whether in newly democratic nation-states such as South Africa, African nation-states that have had formal independence for over thirty years, advanced industrial societies such as the United States, Great Britain, France, and Germany, or historically independent states of the Caribbean and Latin America, youth who are noticeably of African descent fare worse than their lighter-skinned counterparts. For many, Tupac Shakur's words, "I got nothin' to lose—it's just me against the world," ring true.

Victory over one form of racism has not, apparently, ensured triumph over others. How is it that social conditions can change so dramatically yet still relegate Black youth to the bottom of the social hierarchy?[1] As hip-hop social critic Bakari Kitwana points out, "now more than ever . . . divided generations must begin to understand the ways that the new Black youth culture both empowers and undermines Black America. As brilliant a moment in history as the civil rights and Black power eras were, the older generation must realize they cannot claim any real victory if the hip-hop generation cannot build significantly on those gains."[2] The emergence of new Black youth culture in the United States that simultaneously empowers and undermines African American progress signals a new phase in the contours of racism itself as well as antiracist initiatives that will be needed to counter it.

What's new about this new racism? First, new patterns of corporate organization have made for an increasingly global economy. In particular, the concentration of capital in a few corporations has enabled them to shape many aspects of the global economy. One outcome is that, on a global scale, wealth and poverty continue to be racialized, with people of African descent disproportionately poor.[3] Second, local, regional, and national governmental bodies no longer yield the degree of power that they once did in shaping racial policies. The new racism is transnational.[4] One can now have racial inequality that does not appear to be regulated by the state to the same degree. For example, the legal support given racial segregation in the United States has been abandoned yet African Americans remain disproportionately at the bottom of the social hierarchy. Third, the new racism relies more heavily on the manipulation of ideas within mass media. These new techniques present hegemonic ideologies that claim that racism is over. They work to obscure the racism that does exist, and they undercut antiracist protest.[5] Globalization, transnationalism, and the growth of hegemonic ideologies within mass media provide the context for a new racism that has catalyzed changes within African, Black American, and African-Diasporic societies. From one society to the next, Black youth are at risk, and, in many places, they have become identified as problems to their nation, to their local environments, to Black communities, and to themselves.[6]

This new racism reflects the juxtaposition of old and new, in some cases a continuation of long-standing practices of racial rule and, in other cases, the development of something original. In the United States, the persist-ence of poor housing, poor health, illiteracy, unemployment, family upheaval, and social problems associated with poverty and powerlessness all constitute new variations of the negative effects of colonialism, slavery, and traditional forms of racial rule. The new racism reflects sedimented or past-in-present racial formations from prior historical periods.[7] Some elements of prior racial formations persist virtually unchanged, and others are trans-formed in response to globalization, transnationalism, and the proliferation of mass media. Each racial formation reflects distinctive links among char-acteristic forms of economic and political exploitation, gender-specific ide-ologies developed to justify Black exploitation, and African American men's and women's reactions both to the political economy and to one another. Each also generated distinctive African American political responses that aimed to provide a better life for each generation of Black youth.

THE POLITICAL ECONOMY OF CHATTEL SLAVERY

Chattel slavery was crucial to the founding of U.S. capitalism because the buying and selling of human beings of African descent formed a template for the economic and racial oppression of Black Americans. Under chattel slavery, people of African descent occupied a particular place in class rela-tions—their bodies and all that was contained in those bodies (labor, sexu-ality, and reproduction) were objectified and turned into commodities that were traded in the marketplace. Dehumanizing Black people by defining them as nonhuman and as animals was a critical feature of racial oppres-sion. Enslaved Africans who were owned, traded, and sold as part of capi-talist marketplace relations were clearly exploited. Once held as slaves, Black people gained no income from their labor. The objectification of people of African descent as chattel, the commodification of objectified Black bodies as property, and the exploitation of Black people as property and as workers are all closely linked.[8]

Chattel slavery also relied upon gender oppression. Within the politi-cal economy of chattel slavery, this process of objectification, commodifi-cation, and exploitation took different forms for African American women and men. Black women were workers like men, and they did hard manual labor. But because they were women, Black women's sexuality and repro-ductive capacity presented opportunities for forms of sexual exploitation and sexual slavery (ultimate submission of the master/slave relationship). Barbara Omolade describes this gender-specific commodification as one in which the White master used "every part" of the enslaved African woman: "to him she was a fragmented commodity whose feelings and choices were rarely considered: her head and her heart were separated from her back and her hands and divided from her womb and vagina."[9] To mask these relationships, supporters of slavery created controlling images whose effects persist even today. For example, objectifying Black women agricultural workers as mules justified working them as if they were animals. The institutionalized rape of enslaved Black women spawned the controlling image of the jezebel or sexually wanton Black woman. This representation redefined Black women's bodies as sites of wild, unrestrained sexuality that could be tamed but never completely subdued. The image of the breeder woman emerged to defend the reproductive policies of slavery that encouraged enslaved Black women to have many children. Sexuality and fertility were neither designed for Black women's pleasure nor subject to their control. The system was designed to stamp out agency and annex Black women's bodies to a system of profit.[10]

For African American men, the economic and racial oppression of chattel slavery also took gender-specific forms. Because Black men did hard manual labor, justifying the harsh conditions forced upon them required objectifying their bodies as big, strong, and stupid. White elites apparently found men of African descent to be more threatening than women because they believed that Black men were naturally violent. Men allegedly possessed the wildness attributed to Blacks as a race, but they carried the additional characteristic of being prone to violence. This combination of violence and sexuality made Black men inherently unsuitable for work until they were trained by White men and placed under their discipline and control. To explain these relations, White elites created the controlling image of the buck. Unlike images of African natives who roam their wild homelands like beasts untamed by civilization (colonialism), the representation of the buck described a human animal that had achieved partial domestication through slavery. This image depicted Black men as being intellectually inferior to Whites and reinforced the political status of enslaved African men as chattel. Taming the beast in order to produce the buck involved domesticating Black men's predilection for violence, placing their brute strength in service to productive manual labor, and directing their natural albeit deviant sexuality toward appropriate female partners. In this fashion, White elites reduced Black men to their bodies, and identified their muscles and their penises as their most important sites.[11]

Because the vast majority of enslaved African women and men did agricultural labor, these controlling images of the mule, jezebel, breeder woman and the buck justified Black economic exploitation. But chattel slavery also produced another class of Black workers who allegedly formed a better class of Negroes. House servants worked in close proximity to Whites. Their exploitation not only was organized differently from those who worked in agriculture, but the representations developed for domestic servants foreshadowed contemporary understandings of assimilation and the skills needed for racial integration. In essence, domesticated African Americans were the ones who had been stripped of their predilection for unrestrained sexuality and violence (in other words, their stereotypical Blackness). These were the slaves who exhibited behaviors that made them suitable to serve Whites. To justify the exploitation of domestic servants, White elites created controlling images of Uncle Tom and Mammy as prototypes of asexual, safe, assimilated, and subordinated Black people. Whatever actual enslaved Africans felt about this pantheon of controlling images, the distinctive sets of images used to explain differences among African Americans also served the purpose of justifying a preliminary class system within African American civil society.

Because chattel slavery was clearly unjust, the threat of Black resistance was omnipresent, and periodic slave uprisings illustrated that this threat was not unfounded.[12] White elites demonstrated an obsession with fears of Black revolt and instituted practices designed to quell rebellions. In essence, chattel slavery did not need the night riders, hooded K. K. K., and cross burnings that came to full fruition in the postemancipation period that followed. Killing Black people, while it may have made bad business sense, was legal. Enslaved African women and men alike could be whipped, beaten, and killed with no legal recourse. As long as a master killed his own slaves, he was within his rights. If, however, he killed the slave of someone else, property rights came into play. Ironically, their value in the marketplace saved many Black people's lives—no profit could be realized from a dead slave. With slaves seen not as human beings but as an investment, it is easy to see why selling a recalcitrant slave was a better option than beating one to death.

Gender also mattered among White elites. White men and women had different rights, with propertied White men claiming a White masculinity that granted them control over their wives and legal children as well as their property (slaves). Masculinity became defined in patriarchal terms, namely, their performance as "masters" at home and in public activities of commence and government. Under patriarchal assumptions, maintaining a family (e.g., a wife and dependent children) and having material wealth (land and/or slaves) were essential to (White) masculinity.[13] Chattel slavery marked the emergence of a hegemonic White masculinity rooted in a dual relationship of the White gentleman/White lady so celebrated in Southern folklore, and in a racialized master/slave relationship. Violence was central for maintaining this hegemonic White masculinity. It also laid the foundation for forms of masculinity that installed propertied White men at the top of the social hierarchy, Black men at the bottom, and landless working-class White men somewhere in between. The ability of White men to whip and kill Black men at will and force them to witness violence against their female partners and children served not just as a tool of racial control, but violence also became deeply embedded in the very definition of masculinity. Because enslaved African men were denied the patriarchal power that came with family and property, they claimed other markers of masculinity, namely, sexual prowess and brute strength. Foreshadowing contemporary images of Black masculinity that celebrate hypersexuality and athletic ability, Black men were permitted dimensions of masculinity that most benefited Whites.[14]

Black women were also targets of violence within this system of racial rule that relied upon violence as an important dimension of masculinity. Black women were subject to additional violence. Institutionalized rape, a form of sexual violence whose aim is to dominate or control its female (and male) victims, permeated chattel slavery. Rape served the specific purpose of political and/or economic domination of enslaved African women, and by extension, African Americans as a collectivity.[15] Rape was not the only attack on Black women's bodies—medical experimentation and repeated childbearing also took their toll.[16] Hortense Spillers describes the importance of property relations to this entire situation: "Under conditions of captivity, the offspring of the female does not 'belong' to the Mother, nor is s/he 'related' to the 'owner,' though the latter 'possesses' it, and in the African American instance, often fathered it."[17] Sexual stereotypes of women of African descent as jezebels not only justified rape, medical experimentation, and unwanted childbearing inflicted upon Black women but it covered up Black women's protests as well.

The economic exploitation that produced a fledgling social class system among Blacks, the gender-specific use of violence for political domination, and the use of gender-specific controlling images to justify these practices are, by now, fairly well known. In contrast, African American men's and women's thoughts and actions in response to their enslavement and to one another remain more controversial. Clearly many Black people chose the option of flight, and ran away when they could. A few organized visible rebellions erupted, indicating that people of African descent have always resisted.[18] But most could not publicly protest, and they hid their resistance behind the mask of seeming acceptance. Did Mammy really love her White charges more than her own? Was the buck happy in the fields because he sang to pass the time? How did Black lovers feel about one another in such harsh conditions that produced such distorted pictures of Black people?

Because there really is no way definitively to answer these questions, scholarly evaluations of Black gender relations under chattel slavery diverge dramatically and change over time. Prior to the 1970s, scholarship of American chattel slavery often upheld a "weak man, strong woman" thesis, arguing that African American men in particular had been irreparably damaged by their inability to establish patriarchy within African American families and communities.[19] In response, revisionist scholarship refuted this thesis of Black gender pathology. Arguing that enslaved men and women tried desperately to marry and maintain families, such scholarship suggested slavery advanced a fundamental if unrecognized and undervalued gender equality.[20] Because neither men nor women could be installed as "masters" or "matriarchs" within Black families, Black gender ideology was thought to be more egalitarian. Taking a cue from contemporary cross-cultural research on the African Diaspora that demonstrates substantial African cultural continuities within music, dance, art, and funeral practices, one strand of this revisionist history suggested that African American families were not irreparably damaged by slavery. Rather, they were organized around African-derived conceptions of Black extended family networks that resemble those of other African-influenced groups.[21]

More recently, some scholars have returned to the "irreparable dam-age" thesis to claim yet again that the damage done by slavery persists into the present. For example, sociologist Orlando Patterson, a prominent scholar of slavery, argues that "Afro-American gender relations, and con-sequently their marital and familial relations, have always been in crisis" and that "this crisis is the major internal source of the wider problems of Afro-Americans. It is the main means by which the group ends up victim-izing itself."[22] After presenting a depressing array of statistics on African American marital rates, Patterson sees contemporary economic factors as necessary but insufficient influences on contemporary Black gender rela-tions. Arguing that some other cause must be present, Patterson resurrects the "weak male, strong female" thesis: "something else must be at play. Something that runs deep into the peculiarities of the Afro-Americans' own past. In searching for it, we are inevitably led back to the centuries-long holocaust of slavery and what was its most devastating impact: the ethnocidal assault on gender roles, especially those of father and husband, leaving deep scars in the relations between Afro-American men and women."[23] Sadly, because he persists in elevating male suffering above that of Black women, Patterson cannot envision a situation in which African American women and men are differently and equally harmed by the "holocaust of slavery."

Because historical and social science evidence cannot definitively gauge enslaved Black men's and women's perceptions of how slavery affected their ideas about gender and one another, fictional works provide another angle of vision. The works of Black women's fiction constitute an especially rich site for exploring Black women's agency and reclaiming the voices of the oppressed. For example, Shirley Anne Williams's *Dessa Rose* examines the complicated question of interracial sexual desire under slav-ery and its effects of interracial women's relationships. Toni Morrison's much-acclaimed *Beloved* directly confronts the issue of how slavery impoverished the ability to love and how reclaiming love constituted an essential step toward freedom.

The debates continue, but several facts remain. Chattel slavery estab-lished the economic, political, and ideological framework for the treatment of Black people. The rudimentary form of the Black social class system was established under slavery, as were the gender-specific forms of its over-all organization. The effects of being denied economic opportunities and citizenship rights, and of being plagued by violence and images that justified poverty and powerlessness, continue to be felt under the new racism.

RACIAL SEGREGATION AND THE RURAL SOUTH

Racial oppression did not disappear in 1865 when chattel slavery legally ended. Rather, African Americans encountered a new form of racism that also economically exploited them in gender-specific ways. Landowners still needed African American labor for Southern agriculture, and they searched for ways to get Blacks to work for minimal compensation. Emancipated African Americans were "free" to sell their labor and compete for work, just as poor Whites had done before them or they were "free" to starve.[24] Politically, Black men gained the right to vote. This enfranchisement presented White elites with a new challenge. How would they assure a supply of cheap Black agricultural workers if Black people were no longer politically subordinate? During Reconstruction (1865–1877), African Americans made major political gains, and they succeeded in electing Black public officials to state office. White backlash challenged this new, multiracial democracy by passing laws that mandated racial segregation of Blacks and Whites.

In 1892, Homer Plessy defied a Louisiana law that required railroad companies to provide equal but separate accommodations for White and Black Americans. Fully aware of the law and intending to challenge this expression of the color line, Plessy took a seat in a passenger car designated for Whites. Refusing to pass for White, Plessy announced to the conductor that he was a Negro and refused to move to the car reserved for "coloreds." He was promptly arrested. In its 1896 review of Plessy's case, the U.S. Supreme Court upheld the Louisiana law, and by declaring the idea of "separate but equal" acceptable, legalized racial segregation. *Plessy v. Ferguson* stood as the law of the land until 1954. After many years of litigation by the NAACP Legal Defense Fund, the U.S. Supreme Court revisited the "separate but equal" doctrine and, in *Brown v. Topeka Board of Education*, declared it inherently damaging to African American children. In this changing legal context, and fully aware that she was breaking the laws of Montgomery, Alabama, on December 1, 1955, Rosa Parks took a seat in the White section of a Montgomery bus. Unable to pass as White, Mrs. Parks had little need to announce her "real" racial classification. Like

Homer Plessy, she too was promptly arrested. Following Mrs. Parks's arrest, the African American citizens of Montgomery boycotted the bus system for almost one year before gaining their legal rights to sit anywhere on the bus that suited them, an event that marked the beginning of the civil rights movement and the end of legal segregation.

During the period when racial segregation was legally sanctioned, the political economy of racism mandated the separation of Black and White Americans in all spheres of social interaction. Whereas all African Americans lived under a political, legal, and social system that installed racial segregation into the very fabric of American society, Southern states achieved this separation through laws whereas Northern states relied more heavily on customs.[25] Laws and customs required that Blacks and Whites occupy separate and unequal spaces in housing, neighborhoods, job categories, schools, and, in the South, transportation, movie theaters, restaurants, shops, amusement parks, and other public institutions. Supplementing earlier religious justifications for Black inferiority, scientific ideas about race that emerged during this period used biology to explain racial difference between Blacks and Whites, and then used racial differences to justify racial segregation. Enforcing the rigid system of segregation required maintaining clear boundaries between racial groups to ensure that some African Americans would not "pass" as White and thus illegally enjoy the privileges reserved for Whites. An obsession with racial classification, racial identity, and monitoring interracial sexual contact became central to the edifice of racial meanings.

Those Blacks who remained in the South during this period faced hard times. Economically, the conditions that African Americans experienced in the rural South, especially during the fifty-year period after emancipation, set the stage for intergenerational Black poverty that continues to this day. Upon emancipation, the vast majority of African Americans remained in the South, primarily because they had nowhere else to go. Most continued to work in Southern agriculture, but not as an undifferentiated mass of workers. Varying combinations of landownership and education meant that African Americans were economically exploited in different ways. Emancipated domestic workers and skilled workers (e.g., carpenters, blacksmiths, iron workers, etc.) constituted one class of Blacks. Black agricultural workers subdivided into two groups, one a class of Black landowners who were able to establish family farms, and the other, a class of land renters who became the laborers for sharecropping systems. Black landowners fared far better than landless African Americans, many of whom continued to sharecrop well into the twentieth century. This distinction between landowners and renters was virtually impossible under slavery. But upon emancipation, this distinction between owners and renters would become an increasingly important dimension of Black social class in the South.

The effects of relationship to the land, social class distinctions, and timing of Black migration out of the South (if it occurred at all) persist into the present. For example, in the early 1990s, journalist Leon Dash spent several years interviewing Rosa Lee Cunningham, her eight children, and five of her grandchildren, all grappling with the realities of urban poverty in Washington, D.C. Rosa Lee's parents had migrated in the 1930s, seeking refuge from harsh lives as sharecroppers in North Carolina. Rosa Lee's background sheds light on the class system among Southern rural African Americans. Her father's side of the family were "piney woods" Blacks, descendents of slaves and sharecroppers who lived in the woods. This group was able to procure some sort of education for their children. In contrast, her mother's side of the family was at the bottom of the Black social class hierarchy. They were sharecroppers known as "river" or "swamp" Blacks who were descendents of slaves who had lived and worked on the same plantations since emancipation. Receiving virtually no education, the swamp Blacks were cut off from the larger world. Neither group of sharecroppers was able to leave farming because neither possessed the education and/or skills needed. In contrast to these uneducated and/or landless groups, better-educated African Americans who had skills but who lacked land, typically the children of landowners or the renters who were fortunate enough to go to school, were most likely to migrate out of the area when urban factory jobs opened up for African Americans during World War I.[26]

Politically, Jim Crow segregation introduced mechanisms of social control that built upon those established during chattel slavery. Lynching and rape emerged as two interrelated, gender-specific forms of sexual violence. Perceptions of Black hypersexuality occupied an increasingly prominent place in American science, popular culture, religious traditions, and state policies.[27] These beliefs in a deviant Black sexuality in turn sparked gender-specific controlling images of African American men as potential rapists who deserved to be lynched, and African American women as so morally loose that they were impossible to rape. These gender-specific forms of sexualized violence were essential tools in maintaining economic exploitation and the political subordination of racial segregation. Ironically, even though Black people were also murdered and raped under chattel slavery, these crimes were not labeled lynching or rape. Because lynching and rape only apply to *human* beings who possess legal freedom and citizenship rights, these terms simply did not apply to enslaved Africans. Just as animals can be killed at will and sex with animals is perceived as a deviant sexual practice but not rape, Africans without rights could not be lynched or raped. In contrast, these forms of sexualized violence were designed to force legally free African American men and women into their prescribed places under racial segregation.

Black men negotiated new understandings of Black masculinity in this economic and political climate. On the one hand, African men were routinely denied the "40 acres and a mule" that would enable them to support their families. Moreover, the political disenfranchisement associated with Jim Crow meant that all Black men were placed in the position of being unable to protect the women they loved from sexual assault. Because they failed to "fight fire with fire" by violently resisting the rapists of their daughters, sisters, wives, and mothers, such men relinquished claims to hegemonic White masculinity and were relegated to a subordinated Black masculinity. Ironically, at the same time, these seemingly emasculated men were depicted as being naturally hyper-heterosexual. Black men were also seen as being potentially violent, primarily a retaliatory violence against White men. The myth of the Black rapist emerged in this context. According to this controlling image, Black men were naturally sexually violent, primarily through the potential use of the penis as a weapon of violence against White women. African American men were simultaneously accused of having a natural sexual desire for White women that grew in part from their now untamed buck status as sexual animals, and in part from ideas about White womanhood as beautiful, the most desirable and irresistible women, lacking agency in sexual matters, and in need of White male protection from dangerous "free" Black men.[28]

This period ushered in a different set of experiences for African American women. Although they had legal freedom, they did not possess the vote. Black women also needed to work, and their labor in agricultural work and in domestic service exposed them to sexual harassment and rape at work and in public places. Ironically, the property relations of chattel slavery that exposed Black women to sexual assault by the males in their master's family also protected them from sexual assault by White men from other families or by White males as a group. Black women were the "private" property of their masters and, as such, enjoyed the "protections" afforded private property in the United States. Under slavery, Black women were raped, but similar to marital rape, their victimization was not perceived as rape because they were chattel, not humans. In contrast, emancipation and the gaining of individual rights ushered in a new series of vulnerabilities because such women lacked the so-called protection provided by elite White men. No longer the property of a *few* White men, African American women became sexually available to *all* White men. As free women who belonged to nobody except themselves and in a climate of violence that meted out severe consequences for their either defending themselves or soliciting Black male protection, Black women could be raped.

Social practices such as lynching and institutionalized rape that became so deeply embedded in the fabric of American society required powerful ideological justifications. The growth of mass media enabled ideas about Black sexuality to spread more rapidly beyond the reading public. In 1915, the film *Birth of the Nation* told the story of the origins of the Ku Klux Klan through a three-hour film drama filled with now-familiar Black stereotypes. In *Birth of the Nation*, we see a Southern, White propertied family brought to ruin after the Civil War, with hordes of unruly Black people running through the streets of their idyllic small town, and eventually breaking into the family "home" and destroying property. In response to this treatment by enfranchised but clearly uncivilized Black citizens, Whites fight back. They form the Ku Klux Klan, depicted as a noble nationalist organization whose purpose is to save the American nation (and its White daughters) from a reign of Black terror. To this day, *Birth of the Nation* stands as a pivotal work in mass media, and it is used to illustrate early cinematographic techniques to film students. Unfortunately, *Birth of the Nation* also serves as a template for representations of Black people that also persist today.

The character of Gus, the freed Black man who cannot help lusting after the White daughter of a prominent Southern family, is important for understanding how racial ideologies are created and disseminated. Rather than submit to Gus, the White heroine protects her honor by jumping off a cliff to her death. It is important to remember that Black men may have been depicted as rapists, but this controlling image also depended on parallel ideas about Black women. African American historian Paula Giddings discusses how depicting Black women as immoral jezebels helped create representations of Black men as rapists: "often overlooked is the fact that Black men were thought capable of these sexual crimes *because* of the lascivious character of the women of the race in a time when women were considered the foundation of a group's morality."[29] In his book, *The Plantation Negro As Freeman*, Philip Bruce describes the thinking of the day:

> The rape of a negress by the male of her own color is almost unheard of [because the Black male] is so accustomed to the wantonness of the women of his own race that it is not strange that his intellect, having no perception of the personal dignity or the pangs of outraged feeling, should be unable to gauge the terrible character of this offense against the integrity of virtuous womanhood.[30]

In brief, jezebels couldn't be raped.

Gaining Black male protection certainly helped defend Black women against interracial rape. Yet in a context of state-sanctioned lynching of Black men under the guise of protecting White womanhood from rape, the costs were high for Black men who pursued this path to manhood.[31] The climate of lawlessness that accompanied lynching also meant that Black women had little recourse against Black men who raped Black women. Until the challenges raised by the Black Women's Club Movement in the late nineteenth century, African American women largely suffered in silence. The results of interracial rape were visible. After emancipation, a period of time when Black/White interracial marriages were banned, the number of biracial African Americans *increased*.[32] Under rigid rules of Jim Crow's *de jure* racial segregation, the one-drop rule categorized mulatto children as Black. Because the children of these interracial unions were born free and no longer benefited their White fathers, their biological fathers refused to pay for them. Instead, the care and feeding became the sole province of their Black mothers, often in partnership with African American men who claimed paternity and raised the children as their own.

As economic opportunities shrank, political rights disappeared, and in a context of escalating violence, many African American men and women who had the education, skills, and/or means to do so responded by voting with their feet. Expressing outrage with Black people's treatment in Memphis, Ida B. Wells-Barnett urged its African American citizens to "save our money and leave a town that will neither protect our lives and property, nor give us a fair trial in the courts, when accused by white persons."[33] This scenario was repeated across the South. Beginning in the early twentieth century, many Blacks simply left the rural South, moving to rural areas of the West, to cities of the South, and with large numbers continuing on to cities in the North.

During this period, many African Americans migrated from rural areas of the South to territories in the West. Throughout African American communities in Arkansas, Louisiana, and Tennessee, rumors spread that Oklahoma might provide escape from the harsh conditions in states in the Deep South. Anita Hill's family left the Deep South in 1913 and migrated to Oklahoma. There they found "sundown" towns, White towns with ordinances or de facto rules that prohibited Blacks from their boundaries after dark. Southern Black migrants, especially those who were able to acquire land, also founded all-Black townships and a rural life as farmers that shielded them from the harshest aspects of racial segregation. African Americans realized that the first line of defense in such harsh conditions lay in renewed self-reliance and commitment to family, church, and their African American communities.

Anita Hill provides an important perspective on rural life among African American landowners. Migration enabled Hill's family to acquire land and establish a family farm. These Southern rural families had continuity from one generation to the next. As Hill describes it, "my parents' early lives were remarkably similar to my grandparents'. My mother, like hers, gave birth to thirteen children. And the rural and racially segregated conditions under which each raised her children were much the same."[34] Work, church, school, and community all provided additional protective layers around Black children. The youngest of thirteen children, Hill identifies her family as the center of her life:

> At home, I came into the world surrounded by family—people of all ages—and as only a child can conceive, they all belonged to me, and I

to them. And this marvelously rich world of human interaction more than made up for what we lacked in cultural experience. We did not travel, we did not take vacations or go to the movies. We were farm people. Our family outings consisted of going to church and prayer meetings, visiting nearby relatives, the yearly all-black rodeo, and the segregated, until I was six fair.[35]

Within the tight confines of all-Black communities, gender operated in distinctive ways. For one, women had many children. In the case of Hill's family, the children came like clockwork, every two years. Lone Tree Missionary Baptist Church was the center of family spiritual and social life. As Hill recalls,

The women of Lone Tree were my role models. Most were farmers and homemakers who came out of the fields to clean their homes and the church building. The lessons they taught, both religious and social, are the most valuable to me. They were not "feminists," in the modern sense of the word. They worshiped in a service which prohibited women from preaching or leading. When women and men sat separately in church, it was most likely out of this denigration of women's roles. Yet they were essential to the operation of the church and voiced their opinions. Importantly, they expected just as much from the girls in the church as from the boys. Even more important, by example, they taught me about concern for the collective—the community.[36]

Hill's reflections provide an important window on a way of life in which gender mattered, but in which racism mattered even more. Her retrospective allows a view of how African American landowners who remained in Southern communities were able to carve out lives with dignity within the belly of the beast.

Because other African American families lacked land, education, and/or marketable skills, they were not as fortunate as the Hill family. Like Rosa Lee's family, they were stuck until the growth of mechanized farm machinery and agribusiness finally pushed many off the land in the 1930s and 1940s. By moving to the North and trying to find jobs, they hoped to join the Black urban working class that preceded them. Early-arriving migrants who arrived in Northern cities before the 1930s fared much better than their later-arriving counterparts. Beginning in the early twentieth century, large numbers of African Americans left rural areas of the South and moved to Southern and Northern cities, creating new Black urban populations in Southern cities like Birmingham, Alabama and Washington, D.C., as well as in Northern cities such as New York, Chicago, Detroit, and Cleveland.[37]

Collectively, these migrations set the stage for a new Black consciousness that developed among migrants who were no longer living among family and friends in small, rural communities. These waves of migration in conjunction with ongoing shifts from agricultural work to industrial capitalism set the stage for the growth of an industrial, urban working class, for new forms of Black community politics, and for the reorganization of gender and sexuality within African American communities.

RACIAL SEGREGATION AND URBAN GHETTOIZATION

The Northern migrations enabled two important trends to unfold. On the one hand, cities became racially segregated and this resegregation fostered new forms of African American economic exploitation. Racial segregation in Northern cities routinely exploited Black people by keeping them confined to the worst jobs, locked up in the worst neighborhoods, and, as was the case with the "sundown" towns of Oklahoma, generally restricted from movement in White areas. Black men were relegated to the dirtiest jobs in industry, when they could get those jobs at all. The majority of Black women remained in domestic service, this time doing day work instead of the live-in work prevalent in the South. Wages were better than in the rural South, but wage discrimination meant that African Americans were underpaid. Because Black families had limited options in a context of racially segregated housing, landlords raised rents and pushed families into overcrowded and unhealthy housing conditions. Limited job opportunities and residential segregation combined to produce a new form of prison, racially segregated Black urban neighborhoods that became known as "ghettos" and that are the precursors to the contemporary "hood."[38]

On the other hand, Black people within these new urban ghettos gained new tools for fighting back. Despite police mistreatment and *de jure* discrimination, Northern Blacks clearly had more political rights than their Southern counterparts. African Americans from many different

places who found themselves squeezed together in new Black urban neighborhoods founded churches, fraternal organizations, social clubs, and
other new Black organizations that fostered a cross-fertilization of ideas.
Urbanization marked the emergence of major African American political
organizations. Some like the NAACP (1909) and the Urban League (1910)
became crucial elements during the civil rights era that lasted until the
1954 *Brown v. Board of Education* decision outlawed racial segregation.
Other organizations relied on Black Nationalist ideology that preached
self-reliance, economic development, and separate development. For
example, The United Negro Improvement Association founded by
Marcus Garvey contained a large, working-class constituency of Black
immigrants from the Caribbean and Black migrants from the rural South.

African American antiracist politics reflected the contradictions created by migrations to cities, the ghettoization that African Americans
encountered, and social movements that arose in response to Black political, economic, and social disenfranchisement. The 1920s constitute a
watershed decade within Northern urban Black communities such as New
York, Detroit, Chicago, and other large cities. During this crucial period of
Black community development, one characterized by "ideological, political, and cultural contestation between an emergent Black bourgeoisie and
an emerging Black working class,"[39] ideas about race, class, sexuality, gender, and African American politics were reworked in a variety of ways. The
establishment of multifaceted urban Black communities enabled women,
gays and lesbians, and Black workers to organize and to become more visible and vocal on their own behalf. In essence, urbanization enabled formerly submerged Black subpopulations to emerge and fostered the
visibility of a preexisting Black heterogeneity concerning gender, sexuality,
class, and immigrant status. As a result, the complex processes of urbanization had gender and class specific consequences for African American
community organization, for Black cultural institutions, and for the emergence of Black popular culture.[40]

One of the most noteworthy effects of Black urbanization was the
migration of Black single women and its effects on African American
women and their families. Freed from the responsibilities of perpetual
childbearing and church attendance, Black women migrants found new
lives in the cities. Not everyone welcomed these changes. Resembling
postemancipation fears about Black men who had been "freed" from the

domesticating influence of slavery, Black women who were "freed" from the domesticity of rural Southern families were often seen as threatening the social order. Three fears of the early twentieth century that were associated with African American women included: (1) rampant and uncontrolled female sexuality; (2) fear of miscegenation; and (3) independent Black female desire.[41] Just as Black men's sexuality had been made the focus of the changes brought about by emancipation in the rural South, Black women's sexuality became an important measure of African American progress in Northern cities.

Both middle-class and working-class Black women challenged the prevailing ideology of Black women's sexual immorality, yet they did so from distinctive vantage points. Middle-class Black women, especially those in the Black Baptist Church and within the Black Women's Club Movement, refuted the controlling image of the jezebel by advocating a "politics of respectability" characterized by cleanliness of person and property, temperance, thrift, polite manners, and sexual purity.[42] In this context, many middle-class Black women viewed the behavior of Black women migrants as socially dangerous and engaged in reform efforts to help their disadvantaged sisters. Black middle-class female reformer Jane Edna Hunter's description of the sexuality of dance halls and nightclubs draws heavily upon Western discourses of deviant Black sexuality and eerily foreshadows some contemporary condemnations of hip-hop culture[43]: "Here, to the tune of St. Louis voodoo blues, half-naked Negro girls dance shameless dances with men in Spanish costumes. . . . The whole atmosphere is one of unrestrained animality, the jungle faintly veneered with civilized trappings."[44] From the vantage point of middle-class Black reformers, the positive influence of the home and church could counterbalance the dance halls and jazz clubs signaling the dangers of the street. By claiming respectability through their manners and morals, poor and working-class Black women might define themselves outside the parameters of prevailing racist discourse.

Evelyn Brooks Higginbotham describes how, in the early twentieth century, notions of respectability for working-class Blacks were intertwined with perceptions of Black urban space:

> The church played the single most important role in influencing normative values and distinguishing respectable from non-respectable

behavior among working-class Blacks . . . the competing images of the
church and the street symbolized cultural divisions within the mass of
the black working poor. . . . The street signified male turf, a public
space of worldly dangers and forbidden pleasures. Churches and households, both rejecting the worldly attractions of male social space, signified fame and also sacred space. Women who strolled the streets or
attended dance halls and cheap theaters promiscuously blurred the
boundaries of gender.[45]

Those who embraced a politics of respectability aimed to provide dignity
for working-class African American women migrants who led hard lives,
yet the actual programs targeted toward working-class women clearly
advised them to emulate the respectability of middle-class female role
models. Despite being embedded in racially segregated communities, the
politics of respectability basically aimed for White approval. Achieving
respectability pivoted on adhering to standards of White femininity inherited from the tradition of Southern chivalry. Not only were these standards
difficult for Black female industrial and domestic workers to achieve, to the
dismay of middle-class reformers, many working-class women rejected
them.

Working-class Black women in urban areas wanted respect but saw the
contradictions that plagued this version of respectability. Sexuality was
one of the few realms in which masses of African American women could
exercise autonomy, and thus tangibly distinguish themselves as free women
both from the sexual exploitation of slavery as well as the demands of having thirteen babies in insular Southern rural families. In her study of Black
women's blues, Angela Davis points out that "denial of sexual agency was
in an important respect the denial of freedom for working-class Black
women."[46] Mammy and jezebel may have remained installed in White
minds as archetypes of Black womanhood, but working-class Black women
resisted and reworked these images differently from middle-class Black
women. Primarily through a blues culture that gave voice to their concerns,
they too rejected jezebel as the icon of a debased Black female sexuality, yet
they refused to jettison a Black women's sexuality grounded in sensuality
and desire. Respectability was too high a price. Instead, they defined their
sexual selves in terms much closer to erotic sensibilities about Black female
expressiveness, sensuality, and sexuality. Angela Davis reports how urban-

ization allowed a Black women's blues to emerge that brought voice to emergent Black working-class women's consciousness and sexuality. Women's blues provided a cultural space for community-building among working-class Black women, and it was a space in which "the coercions of bourgeois notions of sexual purity and 'true womanhood' were absent."[47]

The growth of Black women's blues paralleled another dimension of the greatly expanded discourse on sexuality in the 1920s that also rejected "bourgeois notions of sexual purity." Urbanization also fostered the increased visibility of lesbian, gay, and bisexual (LGB) African Americans.[48] Collectively, the demands of rural agricultural life, Jim Crow laws, and a conservative Black church that saw homosexuality as a sin combined to stigmatize all seemingly deviant sexualities, heterosexual and gay alike. Because migration to cities enabled formerly isolated LGB African Americans to find one another and to create a critical mass within the confines of Black ghettos, urbanization catalyzed the emergence of a gay, lesbian, and bisexual presence within urban African American communities. Harlem, in particular, housed the development of a Black gay and lesbian, presence that challenged the tenets of heterosexism.[49] Black artists used their art to grapple with ideas of sex, gender, and race. Black men, many of them like Langston Hughes, closeted gay men, sparked a Harlem Renaissance with varying subtexts on Black sexuality. A Black lesbian presence remained closeted, but revisionist work on Black urbanization suggests that Black lesbians in urban areas were also able to craft a communal, albeit submerged, existence.[50] By their presence, gay, lesbian, and bisexual African men and women challenged prevailing codes of Black masculinity and Black femininity.

Then as is the case now, heterosexual Black men found it far more difficult to challenge hegemonic ideas of femininity or masculinity than did working-class Black women and African American gays, lesbians, and bisexuals living in big cities. Instead, many Black men either ran away from responsibility for their families (the precursor "migration" out of Black domestic space that set the stage for today's female-headed households) or they tried to refute subordinated Black masculinity by living their own versions of a politics of respectability. Under the strictures of racial segregation, many middle-class African American men, in particular, paid a high price for trying to show that Black men could be just like White men.[51] Unlike working-class Black women and men immersed in blues culture, or

gay, lesbian, or bisexual Black people exploring new forms of eroticism, Jill
Nelson describes how her father lost the ability to show love as one casualty of trying to be a "real" man:

> For him and many fathers of his generation, the price of navigating the
> segregated road to success in the 1940s and 50s was defensiveness, a
> constant, smoldering rage, the loss of the ability to communicate love in
> any way but through material things. The closing of that opening, the
> soft spot in the soul. That allows us to give and receive love. I know this
> had much to do with being black and male, that sense that black men
> have of always moving through a world that is hostile, of constantly hav-
> ing to prove themselves as non-threatening, intelligent, finally worthy of
> some small chance, while holding on to some sense of manhood.[52]

Nelson identifies the costs to her father and to his loved ones of his decision to hold onto widely accepted definitions of manhood that some argue
continue today as part of a contemporary politics of respectability. As
Devon Carbado points out, "the 'innocent' or 'respectable' Black male
image is considered to be essential to Black civil rights agendas,"[53] yet it is
an image that is difficult to maintain because it requires such self-censorship
and denial. Moreover, just as such a politics may provide limited relief
from being a direct target, because it fails to directly challenge the system
of ideas itself, such respectability provides only partial relief.

Despite the strictures of limited job opportunities and racially segregated housing, migration from the South to Northern cities prior to the
1960s enabled many working-class African Americans to improve their
lives. The children of Northern working-class Black families, especially
those who had access to education and who came of age in the 1950s and
1960s, were positioned to benefit from the better job opportunities and
new legislative climate catalyzed by Black political struggle. Migrants may
have been poor, but, like recent immigrants to the United States, Black
migrants still had hope that moving to cities would provide a better life, if
not for them then for their children. The struggles of the civil rights movement in the South in the 1950s and 1960s and the dramatic legislative victories that changed the legal context for African Americans fostered a
belief among African Americans in the North that Black activism would
yield tangible political and economic benefits.

Born in 1971 to a mother deeply involved in Black Nationalist politics, Tupac Shakur exemplified the future of Black political struggle. He was born after the passage of unprecedented civil rights legislation and should have benefited from the accomplishments of both the civil rights and Black power movements. Instead, Shakur spent his childhood living in poverty and witnessed firsthand the devastation of Black urban neighborhoods struggling with drugs, crime, and violence. When, in 1995, one year before he was murdered, Tupac rapped, "I got nothin' to lose—it's just me against the world," his words spoke to a growing recognition among African Americans of how Black politics had failed. By 1995, Tupac was surrounded by many highly visible media images of successful African Americans but saw little connection between his life and theirs. In explaining this situation, African American social critic Randall Robinson points out: "Take no comfort from what you may see as examples of conspicuous black success. It has closed no economic gap and is statistically insignificant. It is the children of the black poor, the bulk legatees of American slavery, that we must salvage—or, in our time, we will have marked time but accomplished nothing."[54]

THE CLOSING DOOR: THE POST-CIVIL RIGHTS ERA

Many accounts of the vanishing color line make little room for the Tupac Shakurs among contemporary Black youth. Instead, they celebrate a new multicultural America that seems bent on sweeping Tupac's nihilism under the rug and relegating racism to the dustbins of the past. For example, in *Love's Revolution*, Maria Root points to increased rates of interracial marriage, especially for Black men, as evidence of a "revolution" in values that is ushering in a new nonracial America.[55] Identifying the growth of a new Black middle class as evidence of racial uplift, well-respected social scientist William Julius Wilson argues that racism diminishes the further up the economic ladder African Americans climb.[56] In this regard, he joins other scholars who view the racial ideologies and practices of Latin American nations where "money whitens" as applicable for American race relations. All of these factors matter—mass media, marital rates, and a changing social class structure all indicate that former patterns of racial segregation have given way to something new. But what?

For all Americans, the political, economic, and social reorganization of American society that began in the 1970s and took shape during the 1980s and 1990s suggested that a more democratic, multicultural America was at hand. Politically, much changed in the United States. Social movements by Blacks, Latinos, women, and gays and lesbians, among others, catalyzed a changing legal climate in the United States. In a span of less than twenty-five years, legal reforms set the stage for the erosion of a wide array of mechanisms for reproducing social inequality in American society. In addition to the 1954 *Brown v. Board of Education* Supreme Court decision, in the decades that followed, the Civil Rights Act of 1964 prohibited discrimination on the basis of race, color, religion, sex, age, ethnicity, or national origin; the Fair Housing Law of 1968 prohibited discrimination against people seeking housing on the basis of race, color, religion, or national origin; and the Voting Rights Act of 1965 repealed local discriminatory practices against African American voters, an act amended in 1975 and 1982 to include linguistic minorities. The Immigration Act of 1965 removed barriers to immigration for people from primarily non-White nations. The 1967 *Loving v. Virginia* Supreme Court decision removed all legal barriers to interracial marriage. In 2003, in *Lawrence and Garner v. Texas*, the Supreme Court struck down an antisodomy law that made it illegal for same sex partners to engage in sexual conduct that was allowed for different sex partners. In essence, the court ruled that the sexual practices of LGBT people were covered under privacy laws. Collectively, this new legal infrastructure provided a legal context for challenging deep-seated customs across virtually all segments of American society.

In contrast to the victories in the legal system, the changing contours of residential racial segregation during the twenty-year period from 1980 to 2000 suggested that, for many African Americans, this new multicultural America would remain elusive. In 1999, African Americans (55.1 percent) were far more likely than non-Hispanic Whites (21.7 percent) to live inside the central city boundaries of metropolitan areas.[57] This overarching framework of disproportionately Black central cities and disproportionately White greater metropolitan areas produced new patterns of residential racial segregation. While residential racial segregation declined overall, for large segments of the Black population, especially poor and working-class African Americans, residential racial resegregation within urban areas persisted.[58] The concentration of poor and working-class Black people in racially segregated neighborhoods has been so severe in metropolitan areas with large Black populations, that it is often described as "hypersegregation."[59]

By the 2000 census, the African American population numbered 36.4 million people and was characterized by clear social class differences that took geographic form within patterns of racial segregation.[60] For middle-class African Americans and for those working-class African Americans who were able to move into the middle class, the Black political movements of the 1960s and 1970s delivered tangible, albeit tenuous, gains. The proportion of African Americans in the middle class clearly grew in this new legal climate, spurred by new opportunities that allowed many African Americans to join the middle class for the first time.[61] Women and men who acquired jobs as managers in corporations and government agencies, as well as certain staff and line positions in these sectors, benefited from the changed political climate. African American physicians, lawyers, teachers, university professors, engineers, journalists, and other professionals typically procured sufficient job security, job autonomy, decision-making power, and good salaries and benefits that enabled them to move into or up within a growing Black middle class.[62]

An increasingly heterogeneous Black middle class emerged, based in part on the paths that they followed to get there.[63] Some well-off African Americans were positioned to take advantage of the opportunities created by the civil rights movement. Their families had been middle-class for generations, had participated in Black community politics, and had functioned as a Black bourgeoisie or leadership class.[64] Far more African Americans arrived via the route of individual social mobility from the working class. This upward mobility typically required access to higher education; the protections provided by strong antidiscrimination and affirmative action programs in education and employment; the assimilation of White norms and values, including those concerning gender and sexuality; as well as the social skills needed to handle increasing contact with White people as colleagues and friends. No matter how they arrived in the Black middle class, many well-off Blacks engaged in yet another migration, this time out of African American inner-city neighborhoods into racially integrated urban and suburban neighborhoods. The Census Bureau reports that from 1980 to 2000 residential racial segregation declined for African Americans (although it was still higher than any other group).[65] Although these communities routinely resegregated and often became all-Black enclaves, they did provide better housing, schools, and facilities for African American children.[66]

Ideally, African American children growing up in middle-class neighborhoods would retain the class benefits provided by their parents. There is some evidence that passing on middle-class economic gains in the post–civil rights era may be far more difficult than originally thought, in part, due to the proximity of Black middle-class neighborhoods to working-class and poor Black communities. Mary Patillo-McCoy's study of the difficulties faced by Black youth in the fictional Chicago neighborhood of Groveland illustrate the pressures facing middle-class Black youth. For one, they are often mistaken for delinquents by security guards and other officials because they mimic the dress, walk, and talk of working-class Black youth. In this way, stylistic choices often have tangible material consequences. For another, in a community in which the influences of ghetto life permeate everyday life, embracing ghetto styles takes on different meaning than for youth who are in predominantly White middle-class neighborhoods: "sometimes, when you dress like a gangsta, talk like a gangsta, and rap like a gangsta, soon enough you *are* a gangsta."[67]

Many poor and working-class African Americans need not assume the trappings of gangstas—the lack of economic options in their neighborhoods pressures them to become gangstas. For Black youth who feel they have "nothin' to lose" because they lack access to the housing, education, health care, and jobs needed for upward social mobility, the political victories of the civil rights and Black power movements failed to produce the promised economic development envisioned by civil rights activists. The hope was that the opportunities for Black working-class children would continue after the victories of the civil rights and Black power movements. But four back-to-back recessions in the 1970s, a growing White backlash against equal opportunity, and the ascendancy of conservative Republican administrations under Ronald Reagan (1980–1988) and George Bush (1988–1992) as well as the election of George W. Bush to the presidency in 2000 combined to shatter this expectation. In the 1980s, Republican administrations set about dismantling enforcement efforts for equal opportunity, cutting funding for urban programs, incarcerating growing numbers of African Americans in the burgeoning prison industry, shrinking the social welfare budget through punitive measures, and endorsing historical labor market patterns.[68] Fearful of losing conservative White voters who had traditionally supported the Democratic Party, party leaders shifted the party to the right. For example, in 1996, Democratic president Bill Clinton signed the Personal Responsibility and Work Opportunity Reconciliation Act, a law that, despite its lofty title, effectively shifted social welfare programs back to the states and signaled a retrenchment from federal social welfare programs.[69]

Participants in civil rights and Black Nationalist struggles saw their activism as providing opportunities for the next generation of Black youth to live better lives. They reasonably expected that, as did earlier generations of African Americans, Black youth living in inner-city areas might use routes for upward social mobility to better themselves. Instead, as the music of Tupac Shakur and other hip-hop artists reminds us, the door of economic opportunity closed and routes for upward social mobility seem distant memories. For far too many Black youth, inner-city neighborhoods have become dumping grounds, as one observer describes it, "jobless, crime-ridden ghettos [that] have become glorified, modern-day concentration camps."[70] Within inner-city neighborhoods, public schools are dilapidated, teachers are underpaid and overwhelmed, guns and the informal drug economy have made African American neighborhoods dangerous, and jobs have vanished.[71] Gone are the sports programs, music, debate clubs, and other elements of public school education that helped poor and working-class youth stay in school.

Poor and working-class Black youth who grew up in the 1980s and 1990s, often within racially segregated, inner-city neighborhoods, encountered markedly different economic, political, and social conditions than those that faced their parents or those provided to middle-class youth of all races. Despite coming of age during a time of unprecedented social change, regardless of gender, opportunities for poor Black youth eroded. For example, for children under age eighteen the poverty rate is consistently three times higher for Black children than for White children—in 1998, it was 37 percent for Black children versus 11 percent for non-Hispanic White children.[72] When it comes to poverty among Black children, gender did not make a significant difference. Black males under age eighteen had a poverty rate of 36 percent and Black females a rate of 37.3 percent.[73] With over one-third of all Black youth living in poverty, mainly in inner-city, racially segregated neighborhoods, young Black men and women *both* face limited prospects for quality education, well-paid employment, and stable family life. At the same time, poor and working-class Black youth also face gender-specific challenges in two main areas: (1)

eroding work and family structures within urban Black working-class neighborhoods; and (2) the changing contours of Black working-class culture assaulted by drugs, crime, and guns.

The most noteworthy structural changes within African American working-class neighborhoods in the post–World War II period concern work and family.[74] Joblessness fosters family disruption for both men and women, and the effects on each have taken gender-specific forms. In this regard, the rapid growth of a criminal justice system that ensnares large numbers of young, working-class, urban African American men has separated them from their families and left many with slim prospects for stable family life. There appears to be no place for young Black men in urban labor markets, but there is one in jails and prisons. Since 1980, whatever measures are used—rates of arrest, conviction, jail time, parole, or types of crime—African American men are more likely than White American men to encounter the criminal justice system. For example, in 1990, the non-profit Washington, D.C. based Sentencing Project released a survey suggesting that, on an average day in the United States, one in every four African American men aged 20–29 was either in prison, jail, or on probation/parole.[75] Incarcerating young Black men is profitable. The privatized prison industry capitalizes on the growth of prisons. This industry consists of a network of private corporations that provide every service imaginable to prisons and inmates, from prison construction and operation to telecommunications services, food, clothing, and medicine. Corporations also capitalize on cheap prison labor.[76] Jobless Blacks collecting unemployment insurance are unprofitable. In contrast, "the inroads that have been made in privatizing the prison industry have created a profit motive for keeping young Blacks locked up."[77]

In this context, women are left to head families, a structural change with great implications for African American youth and for Black working-class neighborhoods. By 1999, less than one-half (47 percent) of all Black families were married-couple families, 45 percent were maintained by women with no spouses present, while only 8 percent were maintained by men with no spouses present.[78] Families maintained by Black women are not inherently worse than those maintained by married couples but a sizeable majority of Black families that are maintained by women live in poverty.[79] Family income, however, is greatly affected by having a male earner in the household, primarily because men on average earn far more than women when they are able to find work. Family composition affects family income. For example, in 1998, 20.8 percent of Black families maintained by married couples had incomes less than $25,000. The corresponding percentage for Black families maintained by men with no spouse present was 43.1 percent and by Black women with no spouse present was 66.8 percent.[80] The lowest percentage of families with income under $25,000 was found among married couple families (20.8), the highest among families headed by single mothers (66.8), and the middle by single fathers heading families (43.1).

These structural changes in work and family affected the quality of life in Black urban neighborhoods, and they catalyzed changes within Black working-class culture. During the onslaught of drugs and guns in the 1980s, Black working-class neighborhoods simply became more dangerous. Residents of working-class, urban Black communities increasingly beset by drugs and crime used the terms "decent" and "street" families to distinguish stable yet vulnerable working-class families from working-class families in crisis.[81] In this context, the "decent" families, those where members had some connection to traditional jobs in the formal blue-collar labor market or the secondary labor markets, struggled to get by. Plagued by chronic unemployment, these families confronted uncertain industrial jobs, underpaid clerical work, and low-paid service work. Such families may move in and out of the social welfare system and individuals within these "decent" families may have difficulties with the police. In contrast, "street" families, those who have largely fallen out of the formal labor market and whose fate is linked to the informal economy of the global drug industry, have more tenuous connections to school, employment, and other markers of citizenship. They too may move in and out of the social welfare and penal systems, but they hold little hope of ever being "decent" or even wanting to become "decent."

Gender matters in this working-class variation of the tension between Black respectability and Black authenticity, between being "decent" and "street." The growth of the prison culture in the 1980s greatly influenced African American social organization, especially for young African American men. In particular, the arrest and imprisonment of Black street gangs in the 1970s and 1980s fostered more pronounced and organized gang structures within prisons that became conduits for hierarchies of masculinity. Prison gangs inevitably became connected to their street gang

counterparts (in fact, many join gangs while in prison, primarily for protection). As the line between street gangs and prison gangs blurred, so did
the distinctions between prison culture, street culture, and some aspects of
Black youth culture. More important, this growing interconnectedness of
prison, street, and youth culture, with the importance given to hierarchies
of masculinity, affects African American neighborhoods and families. The
valorization of thug life within Black youth culture, the growing misogyny
within heterosexual love relationships, and the increased visibility (and
some would say the increased virulence) of homophobic violence targeted
to gay, lesbian, and bisexual African Americans all seem to be casualties of
the incarceration of African American men and the ceaseless need to prove
one's "manhood."[82]

Black women have often found themselves on the front line in dealing
with issues that affect Black men. As girlfriends and wives, Black women
are often the ones who bear the brunt of Black men's anger at a racism that
has and continues to operate so thoroughly through gendered practices and
ideologies. Reflecting the realities of street culture, some forms of rap
music may serve the purpose of political expression concerning racism,
but they also now operate as an important site for the spread of sexism and
homophobia. Male artists who refer to Black girls and women as "bitches,"
"hos," "freaks," "skeezers," "gold diggers," and "chickenheads" malign
Black women, "decent" and "street" alike. Protesting this misogyny in rap,
Johnnetta Cole and Beverly Guy-Sheftall contend: "We are concerned
because we believe that hip-hop is more misogynist and disrespectful of
Black girls and women than other popular music genres. The casual references to rape and other forms of violence and the soft-porn visuals and
messages of many rap music videos are seared into the consciousness of
young Black boys and girls at an early age."[83]

Despite the misogyny that takes the form of Black women-blaming
that permeates American culture, Black mothers who struggle to retain
"decent" families remain justifiably worried about the effects of "street
culture" on their sons. Black daughters often misunderstand this concern
until they become mothers. Several African American autobiographies,
especially those written by Black women, identify this theme of Black
mothers who treat their sons differently from their daughters. For example, in her memoir *An American Story*, journalist Debra Dickerson
describes her childhood as one of five siblings, four girls and one boy.

Despite her academic achievements, her mother ignored her whereas her brother, who routinely did poorly, was repeatedly forgiven for his misdeeds.[84] In her aptly titled volume, *Mama's Girl*, Veronica Chambers reports similar differential treatment: "my brother . . . was the only person I ever met who almost flunked kindergarten. He was smart—eventually he would test better in math than I did—but he was badly behaved. As he got older, his behavior got worse, until it reached the point where he was always talking back to the teachers and never bothered to do any of the work."[85] Chambers's mother was so worried about her son that his actions formed the subject of many conversations with her women friends. Chambers felt neglected: "there was never any talk about me or what I needed. I was just a quick rest stop in their marathon conversations."[86]

Dickerson and Chambers viewed their mothers' behavior through the lens of childhood, and they came to the conclusion that a certain inequality stemmed from this differential treatment. But Black mothers who worry about the fate of their sons because they are single parents living in dangerous neighborhoods may also be reacting to bona fide threats to their sons' well-being. African American women are often particularly afraid for their sons, fearing that their son's race and size might get them killed for no reason. Marita Golden captures this fear for her son Michael growing up in Washington, D.C.:

> My son careened into adolescence. I heard the deepening of Michael's voice, witnessed the growth spurts that propelled him to a height that echoed his father's, saw the sudden appearance of muscles. . . . I was flushed with trepidation. Soon Michael would inhabit that narrow, corrupt crawl space in the minds of whites and some black people too, a space reserved for criminals, outcasts, misfits, and black men. Soon he would become a permanent suspect.[87]

Golden knows that her son must leave boyhood behind, but she sees all too clearly the costs of doing so. She does not want to join the legions of Black women who attend funerals, burying children who are far younger than they are.

These new social relations that disrupt Black families, incarcerate young men, leave Black women as single mothers, and foster new forms of Black working-class culture constitute yet another racial formation that builds upon and changes those of the past. Chattel slavery as a distinct form of bondage, the labor exploitation of rural Southern agriculture, and urban industrialization and the racial segregation of Black populations through ghettoization have all left their mark on today. These three racial formations may have peaked during specific periods of African American history, but now they overlap, draw strength from one another, and continue to contribute to the new racism. For example, reflecting this past-in-present racism, pockets of rural poverty in the contemporary American South are a direct consequence of sharecropping and other agricultural policies and technologies of the postemancipation South. Similarly, African American hyper-ghettos in Baltimore, Philadelphia, Detroit, Chicago, and other large metropolitan areas as well as urban/suburban housing patterns that make many cities *de facto* Black ghettos, are direct descendents of policies of *de facto* racial segregation developed during the height of urban industrialization. Even slavery persists, but not in the form of chattel slavery experienced by enslaved Africans in the American South. If one defines slavery as "the total control of one person by another for the purpose of economic exploitation,"[88] children and young women and men involved in prostitution and the situation of illegal immigrants held in debt bondage to pay off the cost of their passage constitute reworked versions of slavery.

Just as emerging structures of the new racism constitute a reformulation of former racial formations, the closing door of racial opportunity of the post–civil rights era also invokes ideas and practices about class, gender, and sexuality associated with those prior periods. All three past-in-present racial formations have effects that endure into the present and are likely to persist, regardless of changes in ideology. In *The Debt*, African American social critic Randall Robinson describes the legacy of these prior racial formations: "No nation can enslave a race of people for hundreds of years, set them free bedraggled and penniless, pit them, without assistance in a hostile environment, against privileged victimizers, and then reasonably expect the gap between the heirs of the two groups to narrow. Lines, begun parallel and left alone, can never touch."[89]

The contemporary closing door of opportunity must be judged in the context of prior racial formations dedicated to maintaining the "parallel lines" of separate and unequal opportunities and outcomes. Legal changes are necessary, but they are far from sufficient in responding to a new seemingly color-blind racism where the past is ever present. Contemporary ideas about race, gender, and sexuality did not drop from the sky. In this context, neither Black men nor women can win an oppression contest, because both face different challenges raised by the new racism. Both suffer from different expressions of the disappearing hope that the closing door of opportunity represents.

THREE

PRISONS FOR OUR BODIES, CLOSETS FOR OUR MINDS
Racism, Heterosexism, and Black Sexuality

> White fear of black sexuality is a basic ingredient of white racism.
>
> —Cornel West

For African Americans, exploring how sexuality has been manipulated in defense of racism is not new. Scholars have long examined the ways in which "white fear of black sexuality" has been a basic ingredient of racism. For example, colonial regimes routinely manipulated ideas about sexuality in order to maintain unjust power relations.[1] Tracing the history of contact between English explorers and colonists and West African societies, historian Winthrop Jordan contends that English perceptions of sexual practices among African people reflected preexisting English beliefs about Blackness, religion, and animals.[2] American historians point to the significance of sexuality to chattel slavery. In the United States, for example, slaveowners relied upon an ideology of Black sexual deviance to regulate and exploit enslaved Africans.[3] Because Black feminist analyses pay more attention to women's sexuality, they too identify how the sexual exploitation of women has been a basic ingredient of racism. For example, studies of African American slave women routinely point to sexual victimization as a defining feature of American slavery.[4] Despite the important contributions of this extensive literature on race and sexuality, because much of the literature assumes that sexuality means *hetero*sexuality, it ignores how racism and heterosexism influence one another.

In the United States, the assumption that racism and heterosexism constitute two separate systems of oppression masks how each relies upon the other for meaning. Because neither system of oppression makes sense without the other, racism and heterosexism might be better viewed as sharing one history with similar yet disparate effects on all Americans differentiated by race, gender, sexuality, class, and nationality. People who are positioned at the margins of both systems and who are harmed by both typically raise questions about the intersections of racism and heterosexism much earlier and/or more forcefully than those people who are in positions of privilege. In the case of intersections of racism and heterosexism, Black lesbian, gay, bisexual, and transgendered (LGBT) people were among the first to question how racism and heterosexism are interconnected. As African American LGBT people point out, assuming that all Black people are heterosexual and that all LGBT people are White distorts the experiences of LGBT Black people. Moreover, such comparisons misread the significance of ideas about sexuality to racism and race to heterosexism.[5]

Until recently, questions of sexuality in general, and homosexuality in particular, have been treated as crosscutting, divisive issues within antiracist African American politics. The consensus issue of ensuring racial unity subordinated the allegedly crosscutting issue of analyzing sexuality, both straight and gay alike. This suppression has been challenged from two directions. Black women, both heterosexual and lesbian, have criticized the sexual politics of African American communities that leave women vulnerable to single motherhood and sexual assault. Black feminist and womanist projects have challenged Black community norms of a sexual double standard that punishes women for behaviors in which men are equally culpable. Black gays and lesbians have also criticized these same sexual politics that deny their right to be fully accepted within churches, families, and other Black community organizations. Both groups of critics argue that ignoring the heterosexism that underpins Black patriarchy hinders the development of a progressive Black sexual politics. As Cathy Cohen and Tamara Jones contend, "Black people need a liberatory politics that includes a deep understanding of how heterosexism operates as a system of oppression, both independently and in conjunction with other such systems. We need a black liberatory politics that affirms black lesbian, gay, bisexual, and transgender sexualities. We need a black liberatory politics that understands the roles sexuality and gender play in reinforcing the oppression rooted in many black communities."[6] Developing a progressive Black sexual politics requires examining how racism and heterosexism mutually construct one another.

MAPPING RACISM AND HETEROSEXISM: THE PRISON AND THE CLOSET

> We regarded the struggle in prison as a microcosm of the struggle
> as a whole. We would fight inside as we had fought outside. The
> racism and repression were the same; I would simply have to fight
> on different terms.
>
> —Nelson Mandela

Like Nelson Mandela's view, when it comes to racism in the United States, life for African American women and men can be compared to being in prison.[7] Certainly the metaphor of the prison encapsulates the historical placement of African Americans in the U.S. political economy. The absence of political rights under chattel slavery and Jim Crow segregation and the use of police state powers against African Americans in urban ghettos have meant that Black people could be subjugated, often with little recourse. Moreover, prisons are rarely run solely by force. Routine practices such as strip searches, verbal abuse, restricting basic privileges, and ignoring physical and sexual assault among inmates aim to control prisoners by dehumanizing them. Visiting his brother Robbie, who was incarcerated on a life sentence in a Pennsylvania prison, author John Wideman describes this disciplinary process:

> The visitor is forced to become an inmate. Subjected to the same sorts
> of humiliation and depersonalization. Made to feel powerless, intimi-
> dated by the might of the state. Visitors are treated like both children
> and ancient, incorrigible sinners. We experience a crash course that
> teaches us in a dramatic, unforgettable fashion just how low a prisoner
> is in the institution's estimation. We also learn how rapidly we can

descend to the same depth. . . . We suffer the keepers' prying eyes, prying machines, prying hands. We let them lock us in without any guarantee the doors will open when we wish to leave. We are in fact their prisoners until they release us. That was the idea. To transform the visitor
into something he despised and feared. A prisoner.[8]

As direct recipients of the anti–civil rights agenda advanced under conservative Republican administrations, contemporary African Americans living
in inner cities experienced the brunt of punitive governmental policies that
had a similar intent.[9] Dealing with impersonal bureaucracies often subjected
them to the same sorts of "humiliation and depersonalization" that
Wideman felt while visiting his brother. Just as he was "made to feel powerless, intimidated by the might of the state," residents of African American
inner-city neighborhoods who deal with insensitive police officers, unre-
sponsive social workers, and disinterested teachers report similar feelings.

African American reactions to racial resegregation in the post–civil
rights era, especially those living in hyper-segregated, poor, inner-city
neighborhoods, resemble those of people who are in prison. Prisoners that
turn on one another are much easier to manage than ones whose hostility
is aimed at their jailers. Far too often, African Americans coping with racial
segregation and ghettoization simply turn on one another, reflecting
heightened levels of alienation and nihilism.[10] Faced with no jobs, crumbling public school systems, the influx of drugs into their neighborhoods,
and the easy availability of guns, many blame one another. Black youth are
especially vulnerable.[11] As urban prisoners, the predilection for some Black
men to kill others over seemingly unimportant items such as gym shoes,
jewelry, and sunglasses often seems incomprehensible to White Americans
and to many middle-class Black Americans. Privileged groups routinely
assume that all deserving Americans live in decent housing, attend safe
schools with caring teachers, and will be rewarded for their hard work with
college opportunities and good jobs. They believe that undeserving Blacks
and Latinos who remain locked up in deteriorating inner cities get what
they deserve and do not merit social programs that will show them a future.
This closing door of opportunity associated with hyper-segregation creates
a situation of shrinking opportunities and neglect. This is the exact climate
that breeds a culture of violence that is a growing component of "street
culture" in working-class and poor Black neighborhoods.[12]

Given this context, why should anyone be surprised that rap lyrics often tell the stories of young Black men who feel that they have nothing to lose, save their respect under a "code of the street."[13] Ice Cube's 1993 rap "It Was a Good Day," describes a "good" day for a young Black man living in Los Angeles. On a "good" day, he didn't fire his gun, he got food that he wanted to eat, the cops ignored him and didn't pull him over for an imaginary infraction, and he didn't have to kill anyone. Is this art imitating life, or vice versa? Sociologist Elijah Anderson's ethnographic studies of working-class and poor Black youth living in Philadelphia suggests that, for far too many young African American males, Ice Cube's bad days are only too real.[14] Just as male prisoners who are perceived as being weak encounter relentless physical and sexual violence, weaker members of African American communities are preyed upon by the strong. Rap artist Ice T explains how masculinity and perceived weakness operate:

> You don't understand anyone who is weak. You look at gay people as prey. There isn't anybody in the ghetto teaching that some people's sexual preferences are predisposed. You're just ignorant. You got to get educated, you got to get out of that jail cell called the ghetto to really begin to understand. All you see is a sissy. A soft dude. A punk.[15]

Women, lesbian, gay, bisexual, and transgendered people, children, people living with HIV, drug addicts, prostitutes, and others deemed to be an embarrassment to the broader African American community or a drain upon its progress or simply in the wrong place at the wrong time become targets of silencing, persecution, and or abuse. This is what prisons do—they breed intolerance.

The experiences of people in prison also shed light on the myriad forms of African American resistance to the strictures of racial oppression. No matter how restrictive the prison, some prisoners find ways to resist. Often within plain sight of their guards, people who are imprisoned devise ingenious ways to reject prison policies. Nelson Mandela recounts the numerous ways that he and his fellow prisoners outwitted, undermined, tricked, and, upon occasion, confronted their captors during the twenty-seven years that he spent as a political prisoner in South African prisons. Craving news of the political struggle outside, prisoners communicated by writing in milk on blank paper, letting it dry to invisibility and, once the note was passed on, making the words reappear with the disinfectant used to clean their cells. They smuggled messages to one another in plastic wrapped packages hidden in food drums.[16] In the case of solitary confinement where an inmate could be locked up for twenty-three hours a day in a dark cell, just surviving constituted an act of resistance. As Mandela observes, "Prison is designed to break one's spirit and destroy one's resolve. To do this, the authorities attempt to exploit every weakness, demolish every initiative, negate all signs of individuality—all with the idea of stamping out that spark that makes each of us human and each of us who we are."[17] Mandela and his fellow prisoners recognized the function of actual prisons under racial apartheid and of apartheid policies as an extension of prison.

Recognizing that their everyday lives resemble those of prison inmates often politicizes individuals. Autobiographies by African Americans who were imprisoned because of their political beliefs, for example, Angela Davis and Assata Shakur, or who became politicized during their imprisonment, for example, Malcolm X or George Jackson, point to the significance of actual incarceration as a catalyst for resistance. In the 1980s, many poor and working-class African American youth who were locked up in urban ghettos and facing the closing door of opportunity refused to turn their rage upon one another. Instead, many chose to rap about the violence and intolerance around them and, in the process, created an influential hip-hop culture that reached youth all over the world. Crafted in the South Bronx, an urban landscape that had been abandoned by virtually everyone, African American, Latino, and Afro-Caribbean youth created rap, break dancing, tagging (graffiti), fashions and other cultural creations.[18] Ice Cube's rap about his good day represents the tip of an immense hip-hop iceberg. With few other public forums to share their outrage at a society that had so thoroughly written them off, Black youth used rap and hip-hop to protest the closing door of opportunity in their lives and to claim their humanity in the face of the dehumanization of racial segregation and ghettoization. Without strategies of noncooperation such as those exhibited by Mandela and his colleagues and without developing new forms of resistance such as hip-hop, Black people simply would not have survived.

What is freedom in the context of prison? Typically, incarcerated people cannot voluntarily "come out" of prison but must find a way to "break out." Under chattel slavery, the history of the Underground Railroad certainly reflected the aspirations of enslaved Africans to break out of the prison of slavery and to flee to the quasi freedom offered by Northern states. But just as gender, age, skin color, and class affect the contours of oppression itself, these very same categories shape strategies of resistance. As African American women's slave narratives point out, men and young people could more easily break out by running away than women, mothers, and older people. Then as now, African American women are often reluctant to leave their families, and many sacrifice their own personal freedom in order to stay behind and care for children and for others who depend on them. Under Jim Crow segregation, very light-skinned African Americans faced the difficult choice of "passing" and leaving their loved ones behind. More recently, as prime beneficiaries of the antidiscrimination and affirmative action policies of the civil rights movement, many middle-class and affluent African Americans have moved to distant White suburbs. Such actions certainly reflect a desire to escape the problems associated with poor and working-class Black neighborhoods. If one can "buy" one's freedom, as Nike ads proclaim, why not exercise personal choice and "just do it"?

In other situations, African Americans have recognized the confines of the prison and, through unruly, spontaneous uprisings or through organized political protests, have turned upon their jailers. A series of urban uprisings in cities such as New York, Detroit, Miami (1980), Los Angeles (1992), and Cincinnati (2001) typify the explosive reactions of many poor and working-class African Americans to bad schools, terrible housing, no jobs, little money, and dwindling prospects. The catalyst is usually the same—police brutality against unlucky African American citizens. More organized Black protests also reflect this process of turning upon the jailers of racism and refusing to cooperate with unjust laws and customs. Historically, social formations that kept African Americans impoverished and virtually powerless—chattel slavery, labor exploitation of the Jim Crow Southern agriculture, and the continuing growth of urban ghettos— all sparked organized African American political protest. The abolitionist movement, the formation of the NAACP (1909) and the Urban League (1910), the size of Marcus Garvey's Black Nationalist United Negro Improvement Association (1920s), the many organizations that participated in the civil rights and Black Power movements, and the increased visibility of Black youth through hip-hop culture reflect resistance to racism.

Racism may be likened to a prison, yet sexual oppression has more often been portrayed using the metaphor of the "closet."[19] This metaphor is routinely invoked to describe the oppression of lesbian, gay, bisexual, and transgendered people. Historically, because religion and science alike defined homosexuality as deviant, LGBT people were forced to conceal their sexuality.[20] For homosexuals, the closet provided some protection from homophobia that stigmatized LGBT sexual expression as deviant. Being in the closet meant that most hid their sexual orientation in the most important areas of their lives. With family, friends, or at work, many LGBT people passed as "straight" in order to avoid suspicion and exposure. Passing as straight fostered the perception that few gays and lesbians existed. The invisibility of gays and lesbians helped normalize heterosexuality, fueled homophobia, and supported heterosexism as a system of power.[21]

Because closets are highly individualized, situated within families, and distributed across the segregated spaces of racial, ethnic, and class neighborhoods, and because sexual identity is typically negotiated later than social identities of gender, race, and class, LGBT people often believe that they are alone. Being in the private, hidden, and domestic space of the closet leaves many LGBT adolescents to suffer in silence. During the era of racial segregation, heterosexism operated as smoothly as it did because hidden or closeted sexualities remained relegated to the margins of society *within* racial/ethnic groups. Staying in the closet stripped LBGT people of rights. The absence of political rights has meant that sexual minorities could be fired from their jobs, moved from their housing, have their children taken away in custody battles, dismissed from the military, and be targets of random street violence, often with little recourse. Rendering LGBT sexualities virtually invisible enabled the system of heterosexism to draw strength from the seeming naturalness of heterosexuality.[22]

Since the 1980s, gay, lesbian, bisexual, and transgendered people have challenged heterosexism by coming out of the closet. If the invisibility of sexual oppression enabled it to operate unopposed, then making heterosexism visible by being "out" attacked heterosexism at its core. Transgressing sexual borders became the hallmark of LGBT politics. The individual decision to come out to one's family or friends enabled formerly closeted LGBT people to live openly and to unsettle the normalization of heterosexuality. Transgression also came to characterize one strand of gay group politics, moving from the gay and lesbian identity politics of the first phase of "gay liberation" to more recent queer politics.[23] Gay pride marches that embrace drag queens, cross-dressers, gay men who are flamboyantly dressed, individuals with indeterminate gender identities, and mannish lesbians push the envelope beyond accepting the LGBT people who are indistinguishable from everyone else, save for this one area of sexual orientation. Through public, visible, and often outrageous acts, "queering" normal sexuality became another hallmark of LGBT politics. The phrase, "we're queer, we're here, get used to it" embraces a clear stance of defiance. At the same time, another strand of gay politics strives to be seen as "good gay citizens" who should be entitled to the same rights as everyone else. Practices such as legitimating gay marriages and supporting adoptions by gay and lesbian couples constitute another expression of transgression. By aiming for the legitimacy granted heterosexual couples and families, gay and lesbian couples simultaneously uphold family yet profoundly challenge its meaning.[24]

Racism and heterosexism, the prison and the closet, appear to be separate systems, but LGBT African Americans point out that *both* systems affect their everyday lives. If racism and heterosexism affect Black LGBT people, then these systems affect *all* people, including heterosexual African Americans. Racism and heterosexism certainly converge on certain key points. For one, both use similar state-sanctioned institutional mechanisms to maintain racial and sexual hierarchies. For example, in the United States, racism and heterosexism both rely on segregating people as a mechanism of social control. For racism, segregation operates by using race as a visible marker of group membership that enables the state to relegate Black people to inferior schools, housing, and jobs. Racial segregation relies on enforced membership in a visible community in which racial discrimination is tolerated. For heterosexism, segregation is enforced by pressuring LGBT individuals to remain closeted and thus segregated from one another. Before social movements for gay and lesbian liberation, sexual segregation meant that refusing to claim homosexual identities virtually eliminated any group-based political action to resist heterosexism. For another, the state has played a very important role in sanctioning both forms of oppression. In support of racism, the state sanctioned laws that regulated where Black people could live, work, and attend school. In support of heterosexism, the state maintained laws that refused to punish hate crimes against LGBT people, that failed to offer protection when LGBT people were stripped of jobs and children, and that generally sent a message that LGBT people who came out of the closet did so at their own risk.[25]

Racism and heterosexism also share a common set of practices that are designed to discipline the population into accepting the status quo. These disciplinary practices can best be seen in the enormous amount of attention paid both by the state and organized religion to the institution of marriage. If marriage were in fact a natural and normal occurrence between heterosexual couples and if it occurred naturally within racial categories, there would be no need to regulate it. People would naturally choose partners of the opposite sex and the same race. Instead, a series of laws have been passed, all designed to regulate marriage. For example, for many years, the tax system has rewarded married couples with tax breaks that have been denied to single taxpayers or unmarried couples. The message is clear—it makes good financial sense to get married. Similarly, to encourage people to marry within their assigned race, numerous states passed laws banning interracial marriage. These restrictions lasted until the landmark Supreme Court decision in 1967 that overturned state laws. The state has also passed laws designed to keep LGBT people from marrying. In 1996, the U.S. Congress passed the Federal Defense of Marriage Act that defined marriage as a "legal union between one man and one woman." In all of these cases, the state perceives that it has a compelling interest in disciplining the population to marry and to marry the correct partners.[26]

Racism and heterosexism also manufacture ideologies that defend the status quo. When ideologies that defend racism and heterosexism become taken-for-granted and appear to be natural and inevitable, they become hegemonic. Few question them and the social hierarchies they defend. Racism and heterosexism both share a common cognitive framework that uses binary thinking to produce hegemonic ideologies. Such thinking relies on oppositional categories. It views race through two oppositional categories of Whites and Blacks, gender through two categories of men and women, and sexuality through two oppositional categories of heterosexuals and homosexuals. A master binary of normal and deviant overlays and bundles together these and other lesser binaries. In this context, ideas about "normal" race (whiteness, which ironically, masquerades as racelessness), "normal" gender (using male experiences as the norm), and "normal" sexuality (heterosexuality, which operates in a similar hegemonic fashion) are tightly bundled together. In essence, to be completely "normal," one must be White, masculine, and heterosexual, the core hegemonic White masculinity. This mythical norm is hard to see because it is so taken-for-granted. Its antithesis, its Other, would be Black, female, and lesbian, a fact that Black lesbian feminist Audre Lorde pointed out some time ago.[27]

Within this oppositional logic, the core binary of normal/deviant becomes ground zero for justifying racism and heterosexism. The deviancy assigned to race and that assigned to sexuality becomes an important point of contact between the two systems. Racism and heterosexism both require a concept of sexual deviancy for meaning, yet the form that deviance takes within each system differs. For racism, the point of deviance is created by a *normalized White heterosexuality* that depends on a *deviant Black hetero-sexuality* to give it meaning. For heterosexism, the point of deviance is created by this very same *normalized White heterosexuality* that now depends on a *deviant White homosexuality*. Just as racial normality requires the stigmatization of the sexual practices of Black people, heterosexual normality relies upon the stigmatization of the sexual practices of homosexuals. In both cases, installing White heterosexuality as normal, natural, and ideal requires stigmatizing alternate sexualities as abnormal, unnatural, and sinful.

The purpose of stigmatizing the sexual practices of Black people and those of LGBT people may be similar, but the content of the sexual deviance assigned to each differs. Black people carry the stigma of *promis-cuity* or excessive or unrestrained heterosexual desire. This is the sexual deviancy that has both been assigned to Black people and been used to construct racism. In contrast, LGBT people carry the stigma of *rejecting* heterosexuality by engaging in unrestrained homosexual desire. Whereas the deviancy associated with promiscuity (and, by implication, with Black people as a race) is thought to lie in an *excess* of heterosexual desire, the pathology of homosexuality (the invisible, closeted sexuality that becomes impossible within heterosexual space) seemingly resides in the *absence* of it.

While analytically distinct, in practice, these two sites of constructed deviancy work together and both help create the "sexually repressive culture" in America described by Cheryl Clarke.[28] Despite their significance for American society overall, here I confine my argument to the challenges that confront Black people.[29] Both sets of ideas frame a hegemonic discourse of *Black sexuality* that has at its core ideas about an assumed promiscuity among heterosexual African American men and women and the impossibility of homosexuality among Black gays and lesbians. How have African Americans been affected by and reacted to this racialized system of heterosexism (or this sexualized system of racism)?

AFRICAN AMERICANS AND THE RACIALIZATION OF PROMISCUITY

Ideas about Black promiscuity that produce contemporary sexualized spectacles such as Jennifer Lopez, Destiny's Child, Ja Rule, and the many young Black men on the U.S. talk show circuit have a long history. Historically, Western science, medicine, law, and popular culture reduced an African-derived aesthetic concerning the use of the body, sensuality, expressiveness, and spirituality to an ideology about *Black sexuality*. The distinguishing feature of this ideology was its reliance on the idea of Black promiscuity. The possibility of distinctive and worthwhile African-influenced worldviews on anything, including sexuality, as well as the heterogeneity of African societies expressing such views, was collapsed into an imagined, pathologized Western discourse of what was thought to be essentially African.[30] To varying degrees, observers from England, France, Germany, Belgium, and other colonial powers perceived African sensuality, eroticism, spirituality, and/or sexuality as deviant, out of control, sinful, and as an essential feature of racial difference.[31]

Western religion, science, and media took over 350 years to manufacture an ideology of Black sexuality that assigned (heterosexual) promiscuity to Black people and then used it to justify racial discrimination. The racism of slavery and colonialism needed ideological justification. Toward this end, preexisting British perceptions of Blackness became reworked to frame notions of racial difference that, over time, became folded into a broader primitivist discourse on race. Long before the English explored Africa, the terms "black" and "white" had emotional meaning within England. Before colonization, white and black connoted opposites of purity and filthiness, virginity and sin, virtue and baseness, beauty and ugliness, and God and the devil.[32] Bringing this preexisting framework with them, English explorers were especially taken by Africans' color. Despite actual variations of skin color among African people, the English described them as being *black*, "an exaggerated term which in itself suggests that the Negro's complexion had powerful impact upon their perceptions."[33] From first contact, biology mattered—racial difference was embodied. European explorers and the traders, colonists, and settlers who followed were also struck by the differences between their own cultures and those of continental Africans. Erroneously interpreting African cultures as being inferior to their own, European colonial powers redefined Africa as a "primitive" space, filled with Black people and devoid of the accoutrements of more civilized cultures. In this way, the broad ethnic diversity among the people of continental Africa became reduced to more generic terms such as "primitive," "savage," and "native." Within these categories, one could be an Ashanti or a Yoruba, but each was a savage, primitive native all the same. The resulting primitivist discourse redefined African societies as inferior.[34]

Western natural and social sciences were deeply involved in constructing this primitivist discourse that reached full fruition in the nineteenth and early twentieth centuries.[35] Through laboratory experiments and field research, Western science attempted to understand these perceived racial differences while creating, through its own practices, those very same differences. For example, Sarah Bartmann's dissection illustrates this fascination with biological difference as the site of racial difference, with sexual difference of women further identified as an important topic of study.[36] Moreover, this perception of Africa worked with an important idea within nineteenth-century science, namely, the need to classify and rank objects, places, living things, and people. Everything had its place and all places were ranked.[37] With its primitiveness and alleged jungles, Africa and its peoples marked the bottom, the worst place to be, and a place ripe for colonial conquest. Yet at the same time, Africa was dangerous, different, and alluring. This new category of primitive situated Africans just below Whites and right above apes and monkeys, who marked this boundary distinguishing human from animals. Thus, within Western science, African people and apes occupied a fluid border zone between humans and animals.

With all living creatures classified in this way, Western scientists perceived African people as being more natural and less civilized, primarily because African people were deemed to be closer to animals and nature, especially the apes and monkeys whose appearance most closely resembled humans. Like African people, animals also served as objects of study for Western science because understanding the animal kingdom might reveal important insights about civilization, culture, and what distinguished the human "race" from its animal counterparts as well as the human "races" from one another. Donna Haraway's study of primatology illustrates Western scientists' fascination with identifying how apes differed from humans: "the study of apes was more about humans. Moreover, the close proximity to apes and monkeys that Africans occupied within European derived taxonomies of life such as the Great Chain of Being worked to link Africans and animals through a series of overlapping constructs. Apes and Africans both lived in Africa, a place of wild animals and wild people. In both cases, their source of wildness emerged from their lack of culture and their acting out of instinct or bodily impulses."[38] This family resemblance between African people and animals was not benign—viewing Africans and animals alike as embodied creatures ruled by "instinct or bodily impulses" worked to humanize apes and dehumanize Black people.

In this context, studying the sexual practices of African people and animals took on special meaning. Linking African people and animals was crucial to Western views of Black promiscuity. Genital sexual intercourse or, more colloquially, the act of "fucking," characterized animal sexuality. Animals are promiscuous because they lack intellect, culture, and civilization. Animals do not have erotic lives; they merely "fuck" and reproduce. Certainly animals could be slaughtered, sold, and domesticated as pets because within capitalist political economies, animals were commodities that were owned as private property. As the history of animal breeding suggests, the sexual promiscuity of horses, cattle, chickens, pigs, dogs, and other domesticated animals could be profitable for their owners. By being classified as proximate to wild animals and, by analogy, eventually being conceptualized as being animals (chattel), the alleged deviancy of people of African descent lay in their sexual promiscuity, a "wildness" that also was believed to characterize animal sexuality. Those most proximate to animals, those most lacking civilization, also were those humans who came closest to having the sexual lives of animals. Lacking the benefits of Western civilization, people of African descent were perceived as having a biological nature that was inherently more sexual than that of Europeans. The primitivist discourse thus created the category of "beast" and the sexuality of such beasts as "wild." The legal classification of enslaved African people as chattel (animal-like) under American slavery that produced controlling images of bucks, jezebels, and breeder women drew meaning from this broader interpretive framework.[39]

Historically, this ideology of Black sexuality that pivoted on a Black heterosexual promiscuity not only upheld racism but it did so in gender-specific ways. In the context of U.S. society, beliefs in Black male promiscuity took diverse forms during distinctive historical periods. For example, defenders of chattel slavery believed that slavery safely domesticated allegedly dangerous Black men because it regulated their promiscuity by placing it in the service of slave owners. Strategies of control were harsh and enslaved African men who were born in Africa or who had access to their African past were deemed to be the most dangerous. In contrast, the controlling image of the rapist appeared after emancipation because Southern Whites' feared that the unfettered promiscuity of Black freedmen constituted a threat to the Southern way of life. In this situation, beliefs about White womanhood helped shape the mythology of the Black rapist. Making White women responsible for keeping the purity of the White race, White men "cast themselves as protectors of civilization, reaffirming not only their role as social and familial 'heads,' but their paternal property rights as well."[40]

African American women encountered a parallel set of beliefs concerning Black female promiscuity. White Americans may have been repulsed by a Black sexuality that they redefined as uncivilized "fucking," but the actions of White men demonstrated that they simultaneously were fascinated with the Black women who they thought engaged in it. Under American slavery, all White men within a slave-owning family could treat enslaved African women within their own families as sexual property. The myth that it was impossible to rape Black women because they were already promiscuous helped mask the sexual exploitation of enslaved Black women by their owners. Using enslaved Black women for medical experimentation constituted another form of control. As individuals who are trained to watch, dissect, and cast a critical eye on biological and social phenomena, scientists became voyeurs *extraordinaire* of Black women's bodies. For example, between 1845 and 1849, Marion Sims, now remembered variously as the Father of American Gynecology, the Father of Modern Gynecology, and the Architect of the Vagina, conducted surgical experiments on slave women in his backyard hospital in Montgomery, Alabama. Aiming to cure vaginal fistulas resulting from hard or extended childbirth, Sims discovered a way to peer into Black women's vaginas. Placing Lucy, a slave woman into knee-chest position for examination, Sims inserted a pewter spoon into her vagina and recounts, "introducing the bent handle of the spoon I saw everything, as no man had ever seen before. The fistula was as plain as the nose on a man's face."[41]

The events themselves may be over, but their effects persist under the new racism. This belief in an inherent Black promiscuity reappears today. For example, depicting poor and working-class African American inner-city neighborhoods as dangerous urban jungles where SUV-driving White suburbanites come to score drugs or locate prostitutes also invokes a history of racial and sexual conquest. Here sexuality is linked with danger, and understandings of both draw upon historical imagery of Africa as a continent replete with danger and peril to the White explorers and hunters who penetrated it. Just as contemporary safari tours in Africa create an imagined Africa as the "White man's playground" and mask its economic exploitation, jungle language masks social relations of hyper-segregation that leave working-class Black communities isolated, impoverished, and dependent on a punitive welfare state and an illegal international drug trade. Under this logic, just as wild animals (and the proximate African natives) belong in nature preserves (for their own protection), unassimilated, undomesticated poor and working-class African Americans belong in racially segregated neighborhoods.

This belief in Black promiscuity also continues to take gender-specific forms. African American men live with the ideological legacy that constructs Black male heterosexuality through images of wild beasts, criminals, and rapists. A chilling case was provided in 1989 by the media coverage of an especially brutal crime that came to be known as the "Central Park Jogger" panic. In this case, a White woman investment banker jogging in Central Park was raped, severely beaten, and left for dead. At the time, the police believed that she had been gang-raped by as many as twelve Black and Latino adolescents. The horror of the crime itself is not in question, for this attack was truly appalling. But as African American cultural critic Houston A. Baker points out, what was also noteworthy about the case was the way in which it crystallized issues of race, gender, class, and sexuality in the mass media. The assault occurred during a time when young Black men and hip-hop culture were becoming increasingly visible in urban public space. Lacking spacious basement recreation rooms and well-tended soccer fields, African American and Latino youth set up their equipment on streets and in public parks, creating public hip-hop theaters. Graffiti, breakdancing, and enormous boom boxes blasting the angry lyrics of gangsta rap effectively "blackened" urban spaces. Baker describes how public space became a site of controversy: "Urban public space of the late twentieth-century [became] . . . spaces of audiovisual contest. It's something like this: 'My billboards and neon and handbills and high-decibel-level television advertising are purely for the public good. Your boom boxes and graffiti are evil pollutants. Erase them, shut them down!'"[42]

The attack in Central Park occurred in this political, social, and cultural context. The "park panic" that followed the incident drew upon this fear of young Black men in public space, as evidenced by their loudness, their rap music, and their disrespect for order (graffiti). In doing so, it referenced the primitivist ideology of Blacks as animalistic. Media phrases such as "roving bands" and "wolf pack" that were used to describe young urban Black and Latino males during this period were only comprehensible *because* of long-standing assumptions of Black promiscuity. Drawing upon the historical discourse on Black promiscuity, the phrase "to go buck wild" morphed into the new verb of "wilding" that appeared virtually overnight. Baker is especially insightful in his analysis of how the term "wilding" sounded very much like rapper Tone-Loc's hit song "Wild Thing," a song whose content described sexual intercourse. "Wilding" and "Wild Thing" belong to the same nexus of meaning, one that quickly circulated through mass media and became a plausible (at least as far as the media was concerned), explanation for the brutality of the crime.[43] Resurrecting images of Black men as predatory and wild, rape and "wilding" became inextricably linked with Black masculinity.

The outcome of this case shows how deeply entrenched ideologies can produce scenarios that obscure the facts. Ironically, twelve years after five young Black males were convicted of the crime, doubts arose concerning their guilt. A convicted murderer and serial rapist came forward, confessed to the rape, and claimed he had acted alone. After his story was corroborated by DNA testing, the evidence against the original "wolf pack" seemed far less convincing than in the climate created by "wilding" as the natural state of young Black men. In 2003, all of the teenagers originally convicted of the crime were exonerated, unfortunately, after some had served lengthy jail terms.[44]

African American women also live with ideas about Black women's promiscuity and lack of sexual restraint. Reminiscent of concerns with

Black women's fertility under slavery and in the rural South, contempo-rary social welfare policies also remain preoccupied with Black women's fertility. In prior eras, Black women were encouraged to have many chil-dren. Under slavery, having many children enhanced slave owners' wealth and a good "breeder woman" was less likely to be sold.[45] In rural agricul-ture after emancipation, having many children ensured a sufficient supply of workers. But in the global economy of today, large families are expen-sive because children must be educated. Now Black women are seen as pro-ducing too many children who contribute less to society than they take. Because Black women on welfare have long been seen as undeserving, long-standing ideas about Black women's promiscuity become recycled and redefined as a problem for the state.[46]

In her important book *Killing the Black Body: Race, Reproduction, and the Meaning of Liberty*, legal scholar Dorothy Roberts claims that the "sys-tematic, denial of reproductive freedom has uniquely marked Black women's history in America."[47] Believing the unquestioned assumption of Black female promiscuity influences how poor and working-class Black women are treated. The inordinate attention paid to the sexual lives of adolescent Black women reflects this ongoing concern with an assumed Black female promiscuity.[48] Rather than looking at lack of sex education, poverty, sexual assault, and other factors that catalyze high rates of preg-nancy among young Black women, researchers and policy makers often blame the women themselves and assume that the women are incapable of making their own decisions. Pregnancy, especially among poor and work-ing-class young Black women, has been seen as evidence that Black women lack the capacity to control their sexual lives. As a visible sign of a lack of discipline and/or immorality, becoming pregnant and needing help exposes poor and working-class women to punitive state policies.[49] Arguing that Black women have been repeatedly denied reproductive autonomy and control over their own bodies, Roberts surveys a long list of current viola-tions against African American women. Black women are denied repro-ductive choice and offered Norplant, Depo-Provera, and similar forms of birth control that encourage them to choose sterilization. Pregnant Black women with drug addictions receive criminal sentences instead of drug treatment and prenatal care. Criticizing two controversial ways in which the criminal justice system penalizes pregnancy, Roberts identifies the impossible choice that faces women in these situations. When a pregnant woman is prosecuted for exposing her baby to drugs in the womb, her crime hinges on her decision to have a baby. If she has an abortion she can avoid prosecution, but if she chooses to give birth, she risks going to prison. Similarly, when a judge imposes birth control as a condition of probation, for example, by giving a defendant the choice between Norplant or jail, incarceration becomes the penalty for her choice to remain fertile. These practices theoretically affect all women, but, in actuality, they apply primarily to poor and working-class Black women. As Roberts points out, "prosecutors and judges see poor Black women as suitable subjects for these reproductive penalties because society does not view these women as suitable mothers in the first place."[50]

AFRICAN AMERICANS AND THE WHITENING OF HOMOSEXUALITY

Depicting people of African descent as symbols of embodied, natural sexuality that "fucked" like animals and produced babies installed Black people as the essence of nature. Moreover, the concern with Black fertility linked perceptions of promiscuity to assumptions of heterosexuality. Within this logic, homosexuality was assumed to be impossible among Black people because same-sex sexual practices did not result in reproduction:

> Among the myths Europeans have created about Africa, the myth that homosexuality is absent or incidental is the oldest and most enduring. For Europeans, black Africans—of all the native peoples of the world— most epitomized "primitive man." Since primitive man is supposed to be close to nature, ruled by instinct, and culturally unsophisticated, he had to be heterosexual, his sexual energies and outlets demoted exclusively to their "natural" purpose: biological reproduction. If black Africans were the most primitive people in all humanity—if they were, indeed, human, which some debated—then they had to be the most heterosexual.[51]

If racism relied on assumptions of Black promiscuity that in turn enabled Black people to "breed like animals," then Black sexual practices that did not adhere to these assumptions challenged racism at its very core. Either

Black people could not be homosexual or those Blacks who were homosexual were not "authentically" Black.[52] Black people were allegedly not threatened by homosexuality because they were protected by their "natural" heterosexuality. In contrast, Whites had no such "natural" protection and thus had to work harder at proving their heterosexuality. By a curious twist of logic, these racist assumptions about an authentic Blackness grounded in a promiscuous heterosexuality helped define Whiteness as well. In this context, homosexuality could be defined as an internal threat to the integrity of the (White) nuclear family. Beliefs in a naturalized, normal hyper-heterosexuality among Black people effectively "whitened" homosexuality. Within a logic that constructed race itself from racially pure families, homosexuality constituted a major threat to the White race.[53]

Contemporary African American politics confront some real contradictions here. A discourse that constructs Black people as the natural essence of hyper-heterosexuality and White people as the source of homosexuality hinders developing a comprehensive analysis of Black sexuality that speaks to the needs of straight and gay Black people alike. Those African Americans who internalize racist ideologies that link Black hyper-heterosexuality with racial authenticity can propose problematic solutions to adolescent pregnancy, rape, sexual violence, and the troubling growth of HIV/AIDS among African Americans. Such beliefs generate strategies designed to regulate tightly the sexual practices of Black people as the fundamental task of Black sexual politics. This position inadvertently accepts racist views of Blackness and advocates an antiracist politics that advocates copying the heterosexist norms associated with White normality. Such beliefs also foster perceptions of LGBT Black people as being less authentically Black. If authentic Black people (according to the legacy of scientific racism) are heterosexual, then LGBT Black people are less authentically Black because they engage in allegedly "White" sexual practices. This entire system of sexual regulation is turned on its head when heterosexual African Americans reject promiscuity yet advocate for a Black eroticism.

In a similar fashion, visible, vocal LGBT Black people who come out and claim an erotocism that is not predicated upon heterosexuality also profoundly challenge the same system. The historical invisibility of LGBT African Americans reflects this double containment, both within the prison of racism that segregates Black people in part due to their alleged sexual deviancy of promiscuity and within the closet of heterosexism due to the alleged sexual deviancy of homosexuality. The closets created by heterosexism were just as prominent within Black communities as outside them. For example, the Black Church, one of the mainstays of African American resistance to racial oppression, fostered a deeply religious ethos within African American life and culture.[54] The Black Church remains the linchpin of African American communal life, and its effects can be seen in Black music, fraternal organizations, neighborhood associations, and politics.[55] As religious scholar C. Eric Lincoln points out, "for African Americans, a people whose total experience has been a sustained condition of multiform stress, religion is never far from the threshold of consciousness, for whether it is embraced with fervor or rejected with disdain, it is the focal element of the black experience."[56]

At the same time, the Black Church has also failed to challenge arguments about sexual deviancy. Instead, the Black Church has incorporated dominant ideas about the dangers of promiscuity and homosexuality within its beliefs and practices.[57] Some accuse the Black Church of relying on a double standard according to which teenaged girls are condemned for out-of-wedlock pregnancies but in which the men who fathered the children escape censure. The girls are often required to confess their sins and ask for forgiveness in front of the entire congregation whereas the usually older men who impregnate them are excused.[58] Others argue that the Black Church advances a hypocritical posture about homosexuality that undercuts its antiracist posture: "Just as white people have misused biblical texts to argue that God supported slavery, and that being Black was a curse, the Bible has been misused by African Americans to justify the oppression of homosexuals. It is ironic that while they easily dismiss the Bible's problematic references to Black people, they accept without question what they perceive to be its condemnation of homosexuals."[59]

One reason that the Black Church has seemed so resistant to change is that it has long worried about protecting the community's image within the broader society and has resisted *any* hints of Black sexual deviance, straight and gay alike. Recognizing the toll that the many historical assaults against African American families have taken, many churches argue for traditional, patriarchal households, and they censure women who seemingly reject marriage and the male authority that creates them. For women, the babies who are born out of wedlock are irrefutable evidence for women's sexual transgression. Because women carry the visible stigma of sexual transgression—unlike men, they become pregnant and cannot hide their sexual histories—churches more often have chastised women for promiscuity. In a sense, Black churches historically preached a politics of respectability, especially regarding marriage and sexuality because they recognized how claims of Black promiscuity and immorality fueled racism. In a similar fashion, the Black Church's resistance to societal stigmatization of all African Americans as being sexually deviant limits its ability to take effective leadership within African American communities concerning all matters of sexuality, especially homosexuality. Black Churches were noticeably silent about the spread of HIV/AIDS among African Americans largely because they wished to avoid addressing the sexual mechanisms of HIV transmission (prostitution and gay sex).[60]

Within Black churches and Black politics, the main arguments given by African American intellectuals and community leaders that explain homosexuality's presence within African American communities show how closely Black political thought is tethered to an unexamined gender ideology. Backed up by interpretations of biblical teachings, many churchgoing African Americans believe that homosexuality reflects varying combinations of: (1) the loss of male role models as a consequence of the breakdown of the Black family structure, trends that in turn foster weak men, some of whom turn to homosexuality; (2) a loss of traditional religious values that encourage homosexuality among those who have turned away from the church; (3) the emasculation of Black men by White oppression; and (4) a sinister plot by White racists as a form of population genocide (neither gay Black men nor Black lesbians have children under this scenario).[61] Because these assumptions validate only one family form, this point of view works against both Black straights and gays alike. Despite testimony from children raised by Black single mothers, families headed by women alone routinely are seen as "broken homes" that somehow need fixing. This seemingly pro-family stance also works against LGBT African Americans. Gay men and lesbians have been depicted as threats to Black families, primarily due to the erroneous belief that gay, lesbian, and bisexual African Americans neither want nor have children or that they are not already part of family networks.[62] Holding fast to dominant ideology, many African American ministers believe that homosexuality is unnatural for Blacks and is actually a "white disease." As a result, out LGBT African Americans are seen as being disloyal to the race.

Historically, this combination of racial segregation and intolerance within African American communities that influenced Black Church activities explains the deeply closeted nature of LBGT Black experiences. The racial segregation of Jim Crow in the rural South and social institutions such as the Black Church that were created in this context made living as openly gay virtually impossible for LGBT African Americans. In small town and rural settings of the South, it made sense for the majority of LBGT Black people to remain deeply closeted. Where was the space for out Black lesbians in Anita Hill's close-knit segregated community of Lone Tree in which generations of women routinely gave birth to thirteen children? Would coming out as gay or bisexual Black men make any difference in resisting the threat of lynching in the late nineteenth century? In these contexts, Black homosexuality might have further derogated an already sexually stigmatized population. Faced with this situation, many African American gays, lesbians, and bisexuals saw heterosexual passing as the only logical choice.

Prior to early-twentieth-century migration to Northern cities, Black gays, lesbians, and bisexuals found it very difficult to reject heterosexuality outright. Cities provided more options, but for African Americans residential housing segregation further limited the options that did exist. Despite these limitations, gay and lesbian Black urban dwellers did manage to carve out new lives that differed from those they left behind. For example, the 1920s was a critical period for African American gays, lesbians, and bisexuals who were able to migrate to large cities like New York. Typically, the art and literary traditions of the Harlem Renaissance have been analyzed through a race-only Black cultural nationalist framework. But LGBT sexualities may have been far more important within Black urbanization than formerly believed. Because the majority of Harlem Renaissance writers were middle-class, a common assumption has been that their response to claims of Black promiscuity was to advance a politics of respectability.[63] The artists of the Harlem Renaissance appeared to be criticizing American racism, but they also challenged norms of gender and sexuality that were upheld by the politics of respectability.

Contemporary rereadings of key texts of the Harlem Renaissance suggest that many had a homoerotic or "queer" content. For example, new analyses locate a lesbian subtext within Pauline Hopkins's novel *Contending Forces*, a homoerotic tone within the short stories of Black life detailed in

Cane, and an alternative sexuality expressed in the corpus of Langston Hughes's work.[64] British filmmaker Isaac Julien's 1989 prizewinning short film *Looking for Langston* created controversy via its association of Hughes with homoeroticism. Julien's intent was not to criticize Hughes, but rather, to "de-essentialize black identities" in ways that create space for more progressive sexual politics. At a conference on Black popular culture, Julien explains this process of recognizing different kinds of Black identities: "I think blackness is a term used—in the way that terms like 'the black community' or 'black folk' are usually bandied about—to exclude others who are part of that community . . . to create a more pluralistic interreaction [*sic*] in terms of difference, both sexual and racial, one has to start with de-essentializing the notion of the black subject."[65] Basically, rejecting the erasure of gay Black male identities, Julien's project creates a space in which Hughes can be both Black and queer.

Middle-class African Americans may have used literary devices to confront gendered and sexual norms, but working-class and poor African American in cities also challenged these sexual politics, albeit via different mechanisms. During this same decade, working-class Black women blues singers also expressed gendered and sexual sensibilities that deviated from the politics of respectability.[66] One finds in the lyrics of the blues singers explicit references to gay, lesbian, and bisexual sexual expression as a natural part of lived Black experience. By proclaiming that "wild women don't get no blues," the new blues singers took on and reworked longstanding ideas about Black women's sexuality. Like most forms of popular music, Black blues lyrics talk about love. But, when compared to other American popular music of the 1920s and 1930s, Black women's blues were distinctive. One significant difference concerned the blues' "provocative and pervasive sexual—including homosexual—imagery."[67] The blues took on themes that were banished from popular music—extramarital affairs, domestic violence, and the short-lived nature of love relationships all appeared in Black women's blues. The theme of women loving women also appeared in Black women's blues, giving voice to Black lesbianism and bisexuality.

When it came to their acceptance of Black gays, lesbians, and bisexuals, urban African American neighborhoods exhibited contradictory tendencies. On the one hand, Black neighborhoods within large cities became areas of racial and sexual boundary-crossing that supported more visible lesbian and gay activities. For example, one community study of the lesbian community in Buffalo, New York, found racial and social class differences among lesbians. Because Black lesbians were confined to racially segregated neighborhoods, lesbians had more house parties and social gatherings within their neighborhoods. In contrast, White working-class lesbians were more likely to frequent bars that, ironically, were typically located near or in Black neighborhoods.[68] In her autobiography *Zami*, Audre Lorde describes the racial differences framing lesbian activities in New York City in the 1950s where interracial boundaries were crossed, often for the first time.[69] These works suggest that African American lesbians constructed sexual identities within African American communities in urban spaces. The strictures placed on all African American women who moved into White-controlled space (the threat of sexual harassment and rape) affected straight and lesbian women alike. Moreover, differences in male and female socialization may have made it easier for African American women to remain closeted within African American communities. Heterosexual and lesbian women alike value intimacy and friendship with their female relatives, their friends, and their children. In contrast, dominant views of masculinity condition men to compete with one another. Prevailing ideas about masculinity encourage Black men to reject close male friendships that come too close to homoerotic bonding.

On the other hand, the presence of Black gay, lesbian, and bisexual activities and enclaves within racially segregated neighborhoods did not mean that LGBT people experienced acceptance. Greatly influenced by Black Church teachings, African Americans may have accepted homosexual individuals, but they disapproved of homosexuality itself. Relations in the Black Church illustrate this stance of grudging acceptance. While censuring homosexuality, Black churches have also not banished LGBT people from their congregations. Within the tradition of some Church leaders, homosexuality falls under the rubric of pastoral care and is not considered a social justice issue. Ministers often preach, "love the sinner but hate the sin."[70] This posture of "don't be too out and we will accept you" has had a curious effect on churches themselves as well as on African American antiracist politics. For example, the Reverend Edwin C. Sanders, a founding pastor of the Metropolitan Interdenominational Church in Nashville, describes this contradiction of accepting LGBT Black people, just as long as they are not too visible. As Reverend Sanders points out: "the unspoken message . . . says it's all right for you to be here, just don't say anything, just play your little role. You can be in the choir, you can sit on the piano bench, but don't say you're gay."[71] Reverend Sanders describes how this policy limited the ability of Black churches to deal with the spreading HIV/AIDS epidemic. He notes how six Black musicians within Black churches died of AIDS, yet churches hushed up the cause of the deaths. As Reverend Sanders observes, "Nobody wanted to deal with the fact that all of these men were gay black men, and yet they'd been leading the music for them."[72]

The dual challenges to racism and heterosexism in the post–civil rights era have provided LGBT Black people with both more legal rights within American society (that hopefully will translate into improved levels of security) and the potential for greater acceptance within African American communities. As a result, a visible and vocal Black LGBT presence emerged in the 1980s and 1990s that challenged the seeming separateness of racism and heterosexism in ways that unsettled heterosexual Black people and gay White people alike. Rejecting the argument that racism and heterosexism come together solely or even more intensively for LGBT African Americans, LGBT African American people highlighted the connections and contradictions that characterize racism and heterosexism as mutually constructing systems of oppression. Working in this intersection between these two systems, LGBT African Americans raised important issues about the workings of racism and heterosexism.

One issue concerns how race complicates the closeting process and resistance to it. Just as Black people's ability to break out of prison differed based on gender, class, age, and sexuality, LGBT people's ability to come out of the closet displays similar heterogeneity. As LGBT African Americans point out, the contours of the closet and the costs attached to leaving it vary according to race, class, and gender. For many LGBT Whites, sexual orientation is all that distinguishes them from the dominant White population. Affluent gay White men, for example, may find it easier to come out of the closet because they still maintain many of the benefits of White masculinity. In contrast, in part because of a multiplicity of identities, African American gay, lesbian, bisexual, and transgendered individuals seem less likely than their White counterparts to be openly gay or to consider themselves completely out of the closet.[73] Race complicates the coming-out process. As Kevin Boykin recalls, "coming out to my family members, I found, was much more difficult than coming out to my friends. Because my family had known me longer than my friends had, I thought they at least deserved to hear the words 'I'm gay' from my own lips. . . . On the other hand, precisely because my family had known and loved me as one person, I worried that they might not accept me as another. Would they think I had deceived them for years?"[74] Gender and age add further layers of complexity to the coming-out process, as the difficulties faced by African American lesbians and gay African American high school youth suggest.[75]

Another related issue concerns the endorsement of "passing" and/or assimilation as possible solutions to racial and sexual discrimination. Black LGBT people point to the contradictions of passing in which, among African Americans, racial passing is routinely castigated as denying one's true self, yet sexual passing as heterosexual is encouraged. Barbara Smith, a lesbian activist who refused to remain in the closet, expresses little tolerance for lesbians who are willing to reap the benefits of others' struggles, but who take few risks themselves:

> A handful of out lesbians of color have gone into the wilderness and
> hacked through the seemingly impenetrable jungle of homophobia. Our
> closeted sisters come upon the wilderness, which is now not nearly as
> frightening, and walk the path we have cleared, even pausing at times to
> comment upon the beautiful view. In the meantime, we are on the other
> side of the continent, hacking through another jungle. At the very least,
> people who choose to be closeted can speak out against homophobia. . . .
> [Those] who protect their closets never think about . . . how their
> silences contribute to the silencing of others.[76]

Even if the "wilderness" is not nearly as frightening as it once was, the seeming benefits of remaining closeted and passing as straight may be more illusory than real. Because of the ability of many LGBT individuals to pass as straight, they encounter distinctive forms of prejudice and discrimination. Here racism and heterosexism differ. Blackness is clearly identifiable, and in keeping with assumptions of color blindness of the new racism, many Whites no longer express derogatory racial beliefs in public, especially while in the company of Blacks. They may, however, express such beliefs in private or behind their backs. In contrast, U.S. society's assumption of heterosexuality along with its tolerance of homophobia imposes no such public censure on straight men and women to refrain from homophobic comments in public. As a result, closeted and openly LGBT people may be exposed to a much higher degree of interpersonal insensitivity and overt prejudice in public than the racial prejudice experienced by Blacks and other racial/ethnic groups.[77]

Black churches and African American leaders and organizations that held fast in the past to the view of "don't be too out and we will accept you" faced hostile external racial climates that led than to suppress differences among African Americans, ostensibly in the name of racial solidarity. This version of racial solidarity also drew upon sexist and heterosexist beliefs to shape political agendas for all Black people. For example, by organizing the historic 1963 March on Washington where Martin Luther King, Jr. gave his legendary "I Have a Dream Speech," African American civil rights leader Bayard Rustin played a major role in the civil rights movement. Yet because Rustin was an out gay man, he was seen as a potential threat to the movement itself. Any hint of sexual impropriety was feared. So Rustin stayed in the background, while Martin Luther King, Jr. maintained his position as spokesperson and figurehead for the march and the movement. But the question for today is whether holding these views on race, gender, and sexuality makes political sense in the greatly changed context of the post–civil rights era. In a context where out-of-wedlock births, poverty, and the spread of STDs threatens Black survival, preaching abstinence to teens who define sexuality only in terms of genital sexual intercourse or encouraging LGBT people to renounce the sin of homosexuality and "just be straight" simply miss the mark. Too much is at stake for Black antiracist projects to ignore sexuality and its connections to oppressions of race, class, gender, and age any longer.

RACISM AND HETEROSEXISM REVISITED

On May 11, 2003, a stranger killed fifteen-year-old Sakia Gunn who, with four friends, was on her way home from New York's Greenwich Village. Sakia and her friends were waiting for the bus in Newark, New Jersey, when two men got out of a car, made sexual advances, and physically attacked them. The women fought back, and when Gunn told the men that she was a lesbian, one of them stabbed her in the chest.

Sakia Gunn's murder illustrates the connections among class, race, gender, sexuality, and age. Sakia lacked the protection of social class privilege. She and her friends were waiting for the bus in the first place because none had access to private automobiles that offer protection for those who are more affluent. In Gunn's case, because her family initially did not have the money for her funeral, she was scheduled to be buried in a potter's grave. Community activists took up a collection to pay for her funeral. She lacked the gendered protection provided by masculinity. Women who are perceived to be in the wrong place at the wrong time are routinely approached by men who feel entitled to harass and proposition them. Thus, Sakia and her friends share with all women the vulnerabilities that accrue to women who negotiate public space. She lacked the protection of age—had Sakia and her friends been middle-aged, they may not have been seen as sexually available. Like African American girls and women, regardless of sexual orientation, they were seen as approachable. Race was a factor, but not in a framework of interracial race relations. Sakia and her friends were African American, as were their attackers. In a context where Black men are encouraged to express a hyper-heterosexuality as the badge of Black masculinity, women like Sakia and her friends can become important players in supporting patriarchy. They challenged Black male authority, and they paid for the transgression of refusing to participate in scripts of Black promiscuity. But the immediate precipitating catalyst for the violence that took Sakia's life was her openness about her lesbianism. Here, homophobic violence was the prime factor. Her death illustrates how deeply entrenched homophobia can be among many African American men and women, in this case, beliefs that resulted in an attack on a teenaged girl.

How do we separate out and weigh the various influences of class, gender, age, race, and sexuality in this particular incident? Sadly, violence against Black girls is an everyday event. What made this one so special? Which, if any, of the dimensions of her identity got Sakia Gunn killed? There is no easy answer to this question, because *all* of them did. More important, how can any Black political agenda that does not take *all* of these systems into account, including sexuality, ever hope adequately to address the needs of Black people as a collectivity? One expects racism in the press to shape the reports of this incident. In contrast to the 1998 murder of Matthew Shepard, a young, White, gay man in Wyoming, no massive protests, nationwide vigils, and renewed calls for federal hate crimes legislation followed Sakia's death. But what about the response of elected and appointed officials? The African American mayor of Newark decried the crime, but he could not find the time to meet with community activists who wanted programmatic changes to retard crimes like Sakia's murder. The principal of her high school became part of the problem. As one activist described it, "students at Sakia's high school weren't allowed to hold a vigil. And the kids wearing the rainbow flag were being punished like they had on gang colors."[78]

Other Black leaders and national organizations spoke volumes through their silence. The same leaders and organizations that spoke out against the police beating of Rodney King by Los Angeles area police, the rape of immigrant Abner Louima by New York City police, and the murder of Timothy Thomas by Cincinnati police said nothing about Sakia Gunn's death. Apparently, she was just another unimportant little Black girl to them. But to others, her death revealed the need for a new politics that takes the intersections of racism and heterosexism as well as class exploitation, age discrimination, and sexism into account. Sakia was buried on May 16 and a crowd of approximately 2,500 people attended her funeral. The turnout was unprecedented: predominantly Black, largely high school students, and mostly lesbians. Their presence says that as long as African American lesbians like high school student Sakia Gunn are vulnerable, then every African American woman is in danger; and if all Black women are at risk, then there is no way that any Black person will ever be truly safe or free.

PART II

RETHINKING BLACK GENDER IDEOLOGY

FOUR

GET YOUR FREAK ON
Sex, Babies, and Images
of Black Femininity

2001: Established songwriter, producer, rapper, and singer Missy Elliott's smash hit "Get Your Freak On" catapults her third album to the top of the charts. Claiming that she can last 20 rounds with the "Niggahs," Missy declares that she's the "best around" because she has a "crazy style." In tribute to and in dialogue with Elliott, singer Nelly Furtado also records her version of "Get Your Freak On." Describing Elliott, Furtado sings "she's a freak and I'm a chief head banger." In case listeners might think Furtado is not as down as Elliott, Furtado sings "Who's that bitch? Me!" Elliott's song becomes so popular that a series of websites offer its mesmerizing sitar tones as ringers for cell phones. They ring in Burger King. "Get your freak on" . . . "Hello?"

2001: At the height of his career in 1981, the "King of Funk" Rick James hits it big with "Superfreak." Describing the kind of girls who wait backstage with their girlfriends in the hopes of landing a rock star, "Superfreak" portrays a "very kinky girl" who is "never hard to please." She's "pretty wild," he loves to "taste her," but she is not the kind of girl that he can take home to his mother. James's hit catapults the term "freak" into popular culture. Midnight Star sing "I'm Your Freakazoid, come on and wind me up." Whodini proclaims the "freaks come out at night." In the 1990s, M. C. Hammer samples "Superfreak" for his million-seller album *Can't Touch This*. Ironically, by the 2001 debut of Missy Elliott's "Get Your Freak On," Rick James's main claim to fame lies in his place on a comedy website titled *The Funny Pages: List of Penises*. Situated in a taxonomy of penises that includes the "American Express Penis" (don't leave home without it), the McDonald's Penis (over 8 billion served), and the Uncle Sam Penis (we want you), there it is—the Rick James Penis (it's *superfreaky*).[1]

Missy Elliott's "Get Your Freak On" may have appeared to come from nowhere, but the differing meanings associated with the term *freak* are situated at the crossroads of colonialism, science, and entertainment. Under colonialism, West African people's proximity to wild animals, especially apes, raised in Western imaginations the specter of "wild" sexual practices in an uncivilized, inherently violent wilderness.[2] Through colonial eyes, the stigma of biological Blackness and the seeming primitiveness of African cultures marked the borders of extreme abnormality. For Western sciences that were mesmerized with body politics,[3] White Western normality became constructed on the backs of Black deviance, with an imagined Black hyper-heterosexual deviance at the heart of the enterprise. The treatment of Sarah Bartmann, forced medical experimentation on slave women during gynecology's early years, and the infamous Tuskegee syphilis experiment illustrate how Western sciences constructed racial difference by searching the physiology of Black people's bodies for sexual deviance.[4] Entertainment contributed another strand to the fabric enfolding contemporary meanings of freak. In the nineteenth century, the term *freak* appeared in descriptions of human oddities exhibited by circuses and sideshows. Individuals who fell outside the boundaries of normality, from hairy women to giants and midgets, all were exhibited as freaks of nature for the fun and amusement of live audiences.

When Elliot sang "Get Your Freak On," she invoked a term with sedimented historical meaning. But there's more. During the twenty-year period spanning James's "Superfreak" and Elliott's "Get Your Freak On," the term *freak* came to permeate popular culture to the point at which it is now intertwined with ideas about sexuality, sexual identities, and sexual practices. "Freaky" sex consists of sex outside the boundaries of normality—the kind of "kinky" sexuality invoked by Rick James and other popular artists. As boundaries of race, gender, and sexuality soften and shift, so do the meanings of *freaky* as well as the practices and people thought to engage in them. The term initially invoked a sexual promiscuity associated with Blackness, but being freaky is no longer restricted to Black people. As Whodini raps, "freaks come in all shapes, sizes and colors, but what I like about 'em most is that they're real good lovers." James, Elliott, and other African American artists may have led the way, but the usages of *freak* have traveled far beyond the African American experience. The term has shown a stunning resiliency, migrating onto the dance floor as a particular dance (*Le Freak*) and as a style of dancing that signaled individuality, sexual abandon, craziness, wildness, and new uses of the body. "Get your freak on" can mean many things to many people. To be labeled a freak, to be a freak, and to freak constitute different sites of race, gender, and sexuality within popular culture.

How do we make sense of the meanings, use, and speed with which the term *freak* travels in the new racism? This term is not alone. Joining *freak*, terms such as *nigger*, *bitch*, and *faggot* also reappear in everyday speech. Collectively, these terms signal a reworking of historical language of racism, sexism, and heterosexism, all played out in the spectacles offered up by contemporary mass media. On one level, *freak*, *nigger*, *bitch*, and *faggot* are just words. But on another level, these terms are situated at an ideological crossroads that both replicates and resists intersecting oppressions. Because the new racism requires new ideological justifications, these terms help shape changing social conditions. People also resist systems of oppression often by taking offensive words and changing their meaning; the case, for example, of African American men whose use of the term *nigger* challenges the derogatory usages of White America.[5]

What seems different today under the new racism is the changing influence of Black popular culture and mass media as sites where ideas concerning Black sexuality are reformulated and contested.[6] In modern America where community institutions of all sorts have eroded, popular culture has increased in importance as a source of information and ideas. African American youth, in particular, can no longer depend on a deeply textured web of families, churches, fraternal organizations, school clubs, sports teams, and other community organizations to help them negotiate the challenges of social inequality. Mass media fills this void, especially movies, television, and music that market Black popular culture aimed at African American consumers. With new technologies that greatly expand possibilities for information creation and dissemination, mass media needs a continuing supply of new cultural material for its growing entertainment, advertising, and news divisions. Because of its authority to shape perceptions of the world, global mass media circulates images of Black femininity and Black masculinity and, in doing so, ideologies of race, gender, sexuality, and class.

In the 1990s, Black popular culture became a hot commodity. Within mass media influenced social relations, African American culture is now photographed, recorded, and/or digitalized, and it travels to all parts of the globe. This new commodified Black culture is highly marketable and has spurred a Black culture industry, one that draws heavily from the cultural production and styles of urban Black youth. In this context, representations of African American women and African American men became increasingly important sites of struggle. The new racism requires new ideological justifications, and the controlling images of Black femininity and Black masculinity participate in creating them.[7] At the same time, African American women and men use these same sites within Black popular culture to resist racism, class exploitation, sexism, and/or heterosexism.

Because racial desegregation in the post–civil rights era needed new images of racial difference for a color-blind ideology, class-differentiated images of African American culture have become more prominent. In the 1980s and 1990s, historical images of Black people as poor and working-class Black became supplemented by and often contrasted with representations of Black respectability used to portray a growing Black middle class. Poor and working-class Black culture was routinely depicted as being "authentically" Black whereas middle- and upper-middle class Black culture was seen as less so. Poor and working-class Black characters were portrayed as the ones who walked, talked, and acted "Black," and their lack of assimilation of American values justified their incarceration in urban ghettos. In contrast, because middle- and upper-middle-class African American characters lacked this authentic "Black" culture and were virtually indistinguishable from their White middle-class counterparts, assimilated, propertied Black people were shown as being ready for racial integration. This convergence of race and class also sparked changes in the treatment of gender and sexuality. Representations of poor and working-class authenticity and middle-class respectability increasingly came in gender-specific form. As Black femininity and Black masculinity became reworked through this prism of social class, a changing constellation of images of Black femininity appeared that reconfigured Black women's sexuality and helped explain the new racism.

"BITCHES" AND BAD (BLACK) MOTHERS: IMAGES OF WORKING-CLASS BLACK WOMEN

Images of working-class Black women can be assembled around two main focal points. The controlling image of the "bitch" constitutes one representation that depicts Black women as aggressive, loud, rude, and pushy. Increasingly applied to poor and/or working-class Black women, the representation of the "bitch" constitutes a reworking of the image of the mule of chattel slavery. Whereas the mule was simply stubborn (passive aggressive) and needed prodding and supervision, the bitch is confrontational and actively aggressive. The term *bitch* is designed to put women in their place. Using *bitch* by itself is offensive, but in combination with other slurs, it can be deadly. Randall Kennedy reports on the actions of a 1999 New Jersey state court that removed a judge, in part, for his actions in one case. The judge had attempted to persuade the prosecutor to accept a plea bargain from four men indicted for robbing and murdering a sixty-seven-year-old African American woman. The judge told the prosecutor not to worry about the case since the victim had been just "some old nigger bitch."[8]

Representations of Black women as bitches abound in contemporary popular culture, and presenting Black women as bitches is designed to defeminize and demonize them. But just as young Black men within hip-hop culture have reclaimed the term *nigger* and used it for different ends, the term *bitch* and the image of Black women that it carries signals a similar contestation process. Within this representation, however, not all bitches are the same. Among African American Studies undergraduate students at the University of Cincinnati, the consensus was that "bitch" and "Bitch" referenced two distinctive types of Black female representations. All women potentially can be "bitches" with a small "b." This was the negative evaluation of "bitch." But the students also identified a positive valuation of "bitch" and argued (some, vociferously so) that only

African American women can be "Bitches" with a capital "B." Bitches with a capital "B" or in their language, "Black Bitches," are super-tough, super-strong women who are often celebrated.

They may be right. During the early 1970s, when films such as *Shaft* and *Superfly* presented African American women as sexual props for the exploits of Black male heroes, Pam Grier's films signaled the arrival of a new kind of "bitch." As a "Black Bitch," Grier's performances combined beauty, sexuality, and violence. For example, in *Sheba, Baby* (1975), Grier is routinely called a "bitch" by the bad guys, a derisive appellation that does not seem to phase her. In other places in the same film when she is called a "Bitch" the term seems to signal admiration. She becomes a "Bad Bitch" (e.g., a good Black woman), when she puts her looks, sexuality, intellect, and/or aggression in service to African American communities. By contemporary standards, the violence in most of Grier's films seems tame. But her films did contain violence and Grier was often the one engaging in it. Despite her long hair, facial features, and full-figured body that granted her femininity under Western standards of beauty, Grier's height made her taller than most men, a size that granted her the power of potentially dominating them. This she did in several films, from slapping her brother for capitulating to drug dealers in *Foxy Brown* (1974) to putting a headlock on a Black male gangster and stuffing his face in a bucket of flour in *Sheba, Baby*. Grier may have been called a "bitch," but in *Sheba, Baby* and *Foxy Brown* she got revenge on the loan sharks and drug dealers that preyed upon poor and working-class African Americans. Moreover, her actions routinely drew admiration and praise from the African American men in these films, as well as those who were in the audience. Film critic Donald Bogle describes audience reaction to an especially memorable scene in *Foxy Brown* that he calls "enjoyably perverse." Prior to the scene, Grier's lover and brother were both killed by two drug kingpins, a corrupt White man and his White girlfriend. Grier's Foxy Brown catches up with the man and has her boys unzip his pants. He is then castrated. Bogle describes what happened next:

> Pam pays a visit to the man's ladyfriend—carrying a jar that contains the poor man's most valuable parts. Grier then throws the jar at the white woman; it falls on the floor, its contents apparently rolling this way and that (mercifully, the audience doesn't see this; it's left to the

imagination), all to the horror of the woman who, upon recognizing what is before her eyes, screams out the name of the man she has loved. It's her poor Steve! Audiences howled over this one![9]

Apparently, in 1974, Black men were not intimidated by Grier's depiction of a strong Black woman, as long as she was on their side.[10]

Grier may have established a template for a new kind of "Black bitch," but contemporary Black popular culture's willingness to embrace patriarchy has left the "Black bitch" as a contested representation. Ironically, Black male comedians have often led the pack in reproducing derisive images of Black women as being ugly, loud "bitches." Resembling Marlon Riggs' protestations about the "sissy" and "punk" jokes targeted toward Black gay men, "bitches" are routinely mocked within contemporary Black popular culture. For example, ridiculing African American women as being like men (also, a common representation of Black lesbians) has long been a prominent subtext in the routines of Redd Foxx, Eddie Murphy, Martin Lawrence, and other African American comedians. In other cases, Black male comedians dress up as African American women in order to make fun of them. Virtually all of the African American comics on the popular show *Saturday Night Live* have on occasion dressed as women to caricature Black women. Through this act of cross-dressing, Black women can be depicted as ugly women who too closely resemble men (big, Black, and short hair) and because they are aggressive like men, become stigmatized as "bitches." As Jill Nelson points out:

> Whatever the genre, black women are fair game. It is a tradition among
> many black male comedians to dress up as black women, transforming
> themselves into objects of revulsion and ridicule. From Flip Wilson in
> the 1970s in drag playing loud, crass, unattractive 'Geraldine' . . . to the
> . . . situation comedy 'Martin,' starring Martin Lawrence, whose drag
> alter ego is an ignorant, loud, sexual predator named Sheneneh, the way
> to elicit a guaranteed laugh is to put on a dress and play the unattrac-
> tive, dominating, sexually voracious black woman.[11]

Nelson then speculates why this situation exists: "Black male comedians have encased black women in a negative stereotype, the basis of which is self-hatred projected on the handiest target: black women"[12]

In the universe of Black popular culture, the combination of sexuality and bitchiness can be deadly. Invoking historical understandings of Black women's assumed promiscuity, some representations of the "bitch" draw upon American sexual scripts of Black women's wildness. Here, the question of who controls Black women's sexuality is paramount. One sign of a "Bitch's" power is her manipulation of her own sexuality for her own gain. Bitches control men, or at least try to, using their bodies as weapons. In her novel *The Coldest Winter Ever*, Sister Souljah presents one of the few book-length treatments of hip-hop culture's materialistic "bad bitch." Souljah tells the story of Winter Santiago, the oldest of four daughters of a New York City drug dealer, whose three sisters bear the names Porsche, Mercedes, and Lexus. A coming-of-age story, the novel traces Winter's grooming through her opulent adolescence to be a "bad bitch," only to learn how quickly wealth and power were stripped away when her father was put in prison. Souljah's depiction of Winter Santiago provides one of the best descriptions of a "bad bitch":

> A bad bitch is a woman who handles her business without making it
> seem like business. Only dumb girls let love get them delirious to the
> point where they let things that really count go undone. For example,
> you see a good-looking nigga walking down the avenue, you get excited.
> You wet just thinking about him. You step to him, size him up, and you
> think, Looks good. You slide you eyes down to his zipper, check for the
> print. Inside you scream, Yes, it's all there! But then you realize he's not
> wearing a watch, ain't carrying no car keys, no jewels, and he's sporting
> last month's sneakers. He's broke as hell.[13]

Winter then continues to identify the two options that are available to a "bad bitch" faced with this situation. She can either take him home and "get her groove on just to enjoy the sex and don't get emotionally involved because he can't afford her" or she can walk away and "leave his broke ass standing right there."[14] Having a relationship is out.

This theme of the materialistic, sexualized Black women has become an icon within hip-hop culture. The difficulty lies in telling the difference between representations of Black women who are sexually liberated and those who are sexual objects, their bodies on sale for male enjoyment. On the one hand, the public persona of rap star Lil' Kim has been compared to that of a female hustler. Resembling representations of her male counterpart who uses women for financial and sexual gain, the public performance of Lil' Kim brings life to the fictional Winter Santiago. An exposé in *Vibe* magazine describes Kim's public face: "Lil' Kim's mythology is about pussy, really: the power, pleasure, and politics of it, the murky mixture of emotions and commerce that sex has become in popular culture. . . . She is, perhaps, the greatest public purveyor of the female hustle this side of Madonna, parlaying ghetto pain, pomp, and circumstances into mainstream fame and fortune."[15] But should we think that Lil' Kim is shallow, the article goes on to describe her "soft center": "Kim's reality, on the other hand is about love. It is her true currency . . . the entirely of her appeal has much to do with the fact that love—carnal, familial, self-destructive, or spiritual—is the root of who Kim is. Pussy is just the most marketable aspect of it."[16] What do we make of Lil' Kim? Is she the female version of misogynistic rappers? If so, her performance is what matters. To be real, she must sell sexuality as part of working-class Black female authenticity.

On the other hand, many African American women rappers identify female sexuality as part of women's freedom and independence. Being sexually open does not make a woman a tramp or a "ho." When Salt 'n Pepa engage in role reversal in their video "Most Men Are Tramps," they contest dominant notions that see as dangerous female sexuality that is not under the control of men. Lack of male domination creates immoral women. Salt 'n Pepa ask, "have you even seen a man who's stupid and rude . . . who thinks he's God's gift to women?" The rap shows a group of male dancers wearing black trench coats. As Salt 'n Pepa repeat "tramp," the men flash open their coats to reveal outfits of tiny little red G-strings. The video does not exploit the men—they are shown for just a second. Rather, the point is to use role reversal to criticize existing gender ideology.[17] In their raps "Let's Talk about Sex," and "It's None of Your Business," the group repeats its anthem of sexual freedom.

This issue of control becomes highly important within the universe of Black popular culture that is marketed by mass media. Some women are bitches who control their own sexuality—they "get a freak on," which remains within their control and on their own terms. Whether she "fucks men" for pleasure, drugs, revenge, or money, the sexualized bitch constitutes a modern version of the jezebel, repackaged for contemporary mass media. In discussing this updated jezebel image, cultural critic Lisa Jones distinguishes between gold diggers/skeezers (women who screw for status) and crack hoes (women who screw for a fix).[18] Some women are the "hos" who trade sexual favors for jobs, money, drugs, and other material items. The female hustler, a materialistic woman who is willing to sell, rent, or use her sexuality to get whatever she wants constitutes this sexualized variation of the "bitch." This image appears with increasing frequency, especially in conjunction with trying to "catch" an African American man with money. Athletes are targets, and having a baby with an athlete is a way to garner income. Black women who are sex workers, namely, those who engage in phone sex, lap dancing, and prostitution for compensation, also populate this universe of sexualized bitches. The prostitute who hustles without a pimp and who keeps the compensation is a bitch who works for herself.

Not only do these images of sexualized Black bitches appear in global mass media, Black male artists, producers, and marketing executives participate in reproducing these images. As cultural critic Lisa Jones points out, "what might make the skeezer an even more painful thorn in your side is that, unlike its forerunners, this type is manufactured primarily by black men."[19] If the cultural production of some African American male artists is any indication, Jones may be on to something.

In the early 1990s, and in conjunction with the emergence of gangsta rap, a fairly dramatic shift occurred within Black popular culture and mass media concerning how some African American artists depicted African American women. In a sense, the *celebration* of Black women's bodies and how they handled them that had long appeared in earlier Black cultural production (for example, a song such as "Brick House" within a rhythm and blues tradition) became increasingly replaced by the *objectification* of Black women's bodies as part of a commodified Black culture. Contemporary music videos of Black male artists in particular became increasingly populated with legions of young Black women who dance, strut, and serve as visually appealing props for the rapper in question. The women in these videos typically share two attributes—they are rarely acknowledged as individuals and they are scantily clad. One Black female body can easily replace another and all are reduced to their bodies. Ironically, displaying nameless, naked Black female bodies had a long history in Western societies, from the display of enslaved African women on the auction block under chattel slavery to representations of Black female bodies in contemporary film and music videos. Describing the placement and use of primitive art in Western exhibits, one scholar points out, "'namelessness' resembles 'nakedness': it is a category always brought to bear by the Westerner on the 'primitive' and yet a phony category insofar as the namelessness and nakedness exist only from the Euro-American point of view."[20]

Not only can the entire body become objectified but also parts of the body can suffer the same fate. For example, music videos for Sir Mix A Lot's "Baby Got Back," the film clip for "Doing Da Butt" from Spike Lee's film *School Daze*, and the music video for 2LiveCrew's "Pop That Coochie" all focused attention on women's behinds generally, and Black women's behinds in particular. All three songs seemingly celebrated Black women's buttocks, but they also objectified them, albeit differently. "Baby Got Back" is more clearly rooted in the "Brick House" tradition of celebrating Black women's sexuality via admiring their bodies—in his video, Sir Mix A Lot happily wanders among several booty swinging sisters, all of whom are proud to show their stuff. "Doing Da Butt" creates a different interpretive context for this fascination with the booty. In Lee's party sequence, being able to shake the booty is a sign of authentic Blackness, with the Black woman who is shaking the biggest butt being the most authentic Black woman. In contrast, "Pop That Coochie" contains a bevy of women who simply shake their rumps for the enjoyment of the members of 2LiveCrew. Their butts are toys for the boys in the band. Ironically, whereas European men expressed fascination with the buttocks of the Hottentot Venus as a site of Black female sexuality that became central to the construction of White racism itself, contemporary Black popular culture seemingly celebrates these same signs uncritically.

Objectifying Black women's bodies turns them into canvases that can be interchanged for a variety of purposes. Historically, this objectification had a clear racial motive. In the post–civil rights era, however, this use of Black women's bodies also has a distinctive gender subtext in that African American men and women participate differently in this process of objectification. African American men who star in music videos construct a certain version of manhood against the backdrop of objectified nameless, quasi naked Black women who populate their stage. At the same time, African American women in these same videos often objectify their own bodies in order to be accepted within this Black male-controlled universe.

Black women now can get hair weaves, insert blue contact lenses, dye their hair blond, get silicone implants to have bigger breasts, and have ribs removed to achieve small waists (Janet Jackson) all for the purpose of appearing more "beautiful."[21]

Whether Black women rappers who use the term *bitch* are participating in their own subordination or whether they are resisting these gender relations remains a subject of debate. Rap and hip-hop serve as sites to contest these same gender meanings. The language in rap has attracted considerable controversy, especially the misogyny associated with calling women "bitches" and "hos."[22] First popularized within rap, these terms are now so pervasive that they have entered the realm of colloquial, everyday speech. Even White singer Nelly Furtado proudly proclaims, "Who's that bitch? Me!" Yet because rap is a sphere of cultural production, it has space for contestation. For example, in 1994 Queen Latifah's "U.N.I.T.Y." won a Grammy, a NAACP Image Award, and a Soul Train Music Award. Latifah claims that she did not write the song to win awards, but in response to the verbal and physical assaults on women that she saw around her, especially in rap music. As one line from her award-winning song states, "Every time I hear a brother call a girl a bitch or a ho. Trying to make a sister feel low, You know all of that's got to go."[23]

Black bitches are one thing. Black bitches that are fertile and become mothers are something else. In this regard, the term *bitch* references yet another meaning. Reminiscent of the association of Africans with animals, the term *bitch* also refers to female dogs. Via this association, the term thus invokes a web of meaning that links unregulated sexuality with uncontrolled fertility. Female dogs or bitches "fuck" and produce litters of puppies. In a context of a racial discourse that long associated people of African descent with animalistic practices, the use of the term bitch is noteworthy. Moreover, new technologies that place a greater emphasis on machines provide another variation on the updated bitch. In contrast to Black female bodies as animalistic, Black female bodies become machines built for endurance. The Black superwoman becomes a "sex machine" that in turn becomes a "baby machine." The thinking behind these images is that unregulated sexuality results in unplanned for, unwanted, and poorly raised children.

The representation of the sexualized bitch leads to another cluster of representations of working-class Black femininity, namely, controlling images of poor and working-class Black women as bad mothers. Bad Black Mothers (BBM) are those who are abusive (extremely bitchy) and/or who neglect their children either in utero or afterward. Ironically, these Bad Black Mothers are stigmatized as being inappropriately feminine because they reject the gender ideology associated with the American family ideal.[24] They are often single mothers, they live in poverty, they are often young, and they rely on the state to support their children. Moreover, they allegedly pass on their bad values to their children who in turn are more likely to become criminals and unwed teenaged mothers.

Reserved for poor and/or working-class Black women, or for women who have fallen into poverty and shame as a result of their bad behavior, a constellation of new images describes variations of the Bad Black Mother. The image of the crack mother illustrates how controlling images of working-class Black femininity can dovetail with punitive social policies. When crack cocaine appeared in the early 1980s, two features made it the perfect target for the Reagan administration's War on Drugs. Crack cocaine was primarily confined to Black inner-city neighborhoods, and women constituted approximately half of its users. In the late 1980s, news stories began to cover the huge increase in the number of newborns testing positive for drugs. But coverage was far from sympathetic. Addicted pregnant women became demonized as "crack mothers" whose selfishness and criminality punished their children in the womb. Fictional treatments followed soon after. For example, in the feature film *Losing Isaiah*, Academy Award–winning actress Halle Berry plays a woman on crack cocaine who is so high that she abandons her baby. A kindly White family takes Isaiah in, and they patiently deal with the host of problems he has due to his biological mother's failures.

Representations such as these contributed to a punitive climate in which the criminal justice system increasingly penalizes pregnancy by prosecuting women for exposing their babies to drugs in the womb and by imposing birth control as a condition of probation. Between 1985 and 1995, thirty states charged approximately 200 women with maternal drug use. Charges included distributing drugs to a minor, child abuse and neglect, reckless endangerment, manslaughter, and assault with a deadly weapon.[25] In virtually all of these cases, the women prosecuted were poor and African American. As legal scholar Dorothy Roberts points out, "prosecutors and judges see poor Black women as suitable subjects for these reproductive penalties because society does not view these women as suitable mothers in the first place."[26]

Drug use is one sure-fire indicator used to create the BBM representation, but simply being poor and accepting public assistance is sufficient. In the 1960s, when African American women successfully challenged the racially discriminatory policies that characterized social welfare programs, the generic image of the "bad Black mother" became crystallized into the racialized image of the "welfare mother." These controlling images underwent another transformation in the 1980s as part of Reagan/Bush's efforts to reduce social welfare funding for families. Resembling the practice of invoking the controlling image of the Black rapist via the Bush campaign's use of Willie Horton in 1988, the Reagan/Bush administrations also realized that racializing welfare by painting it as a program that unfairly benefited Blacks was a sure-fire way to win White votes. This context created the controlling image of the "welfare queen" primarily to garner support for refusing state support for poor and working-class Black mothers and children. Poor Black women's welfare eligibility meant that many chose to stay home and care for their children, thus emulating White middle-class mothers. But because these stay-at-home moms were African American and did not work for pay, they were deemed to be "lazy." Ironically, gaining rights introduced a new set of controlling images. In a political economy in which the children of poor and working-class African Americans are unwanted because such children are expensive and have citizenship rights, reducing the fertility becomes critical.[27]

These images of bitches and bad Black mothers came at a time when African American children and youth became expendable. Simply put, in the post–civil rights era, poor Black children became superfluous as workers. Under chattel slavery and Jim Crow segregation of the rural South, the need for cheap, unskilled labor and African American political powerlessness fostered population policies that encouraged Black women to have many children. Since African Americans themselves absorbed the costs attached to raising children, a large, disenfranchised, and impoverished Black population matched the perceived interest of elites. Black children cost employers little because children did unskilled labor and were ineligible for existing social welfare benefits. The post-civil rights era that required a more highly educated workforce and that increased Black children's eligibility for social welfare benefits made them more expensive to train and to hire. In this political and economic context, poor and working-class African American women were encouraged to have fewer children, often through punitive population control policies.[28]

Beyond the efforts to criminalize the pregnancies of crack-addicted women, a series of public policies have been introduced that aim to shrink state and federal social welfare budgets, in part by reducing Black women's fertility.[29] Despite its health risks and unpleasant side effects, Norplant was marketed to poor inner-city Black teenagers.[30] As a coercive method of birth control, users found that they had little difficulty getting their physicians to insert the contraceptive rods into their bodies but, since only physicians were qualified to remove the rods, getting them out was far more difficult. Depo Provera as a birth control shot was also heavily marketed to women who seemingly could not control their fertility and needed medical intervention to avoid motherhood.[31] Finally, welfare legislation that threatens to deny benefits to additional children is designed to discourage childbearing. In a context in which safe, legal abortion is difficult for poor women to obtain, the "choice" of permanent sterilization makes sense. Representations of Bad Black Mothers help create an interpretive climate that normalizes these punitive policies.[32]

Controlling images of working-class Black women pervade television and film, but rap and hip-hop culture constitute one site where misogyny is freely expressed and resisted. Given this context, African American women's participation in rap and hip-hop as writers, producers, and as performers illustrates how African American women negotiate these representations. In a sense, Black female rappers who reject these representations of working-class Black women follow in the footsteps of earlier generations of Black blues women who chose to sing the "devil's music."[33] The 1990s witnessed the emergence of Black women who made music videos that were sites of promotion, creativity, and self-expression. For example, hip-hop artists Salt 'n Pepa, Erykah Badu, Lauryn Hill, and Missy Elliott depict themselves as independent, strong, and self-reliant agents of their own desire. Because rap revolves around self-promotion, female rappers are able to avoid accusations of being self-centered or narcissistic when they use the form to promote Black female power. Rap thus can provide an important forum for women.[34]

Black women's self-representation in rap results in complex, often contradictory and multifaceted depictions of Black womanhood.[35] One study of representations of Black women in popular music videos found that controlling images of Black womanhood occurred simultaneously with resistant images. On the one hand, when music videos focused on Black women's bodies, presented one-dimensional womanhood by rarely depicting motherhood, and showcased women under the aegis of a male sponsor, they did re-create controlling images of Black womanhood. On the other hand, the music videos also contained distinctive patterns of Black women's agency. First, in many videos, Blackness did not carry a negative connotation, but instead served as a basis for strength, power, and a positive self-identity. Second, despite a predominance of traditional gender roles, Black women performers were frequently depicted as active, vocal, and independent. But instead of exhibiting the physical violence and aggression found in men's videos, the music videos sampled in the study demonstrate the significance of verbal assertiveness where "speaking out and speaking one's mind are a constant theme."[36] Another theme concerns achieving independence—Black women may assert independence, but they look to one another for support, partnership, and sisterhood. Black women's music videos may be situated within hip-hop culture, but they reflect the tensions of negotiating representations of Black femininity: "what emerges from this combination of agency, voice, partnership, and Black context is a sense of the construction of Black woman-centered video narratives. Within these narratives, the interests, desires, and goals of women are predominant. . . . Black women are quite firmly the subjects of these narratives and are able to clearly and unequivocally express their points of view."[37]

Representations of Black women athletes in mass media also replicate and contest power relations of race, class, gender, and sexuality. Because aggressiveness is needed to win, Black female athletes have more leeway in reclaiming assertiveness without enduring the ridicule routinely targeted toward the bitch. Black female athletes provide a range of images that collectively challenge not only representations of the bitch and the bad mother but are also beginning to crack the financial gender gap separating men's and women's sports. Whereas men have been able to use athletics, most recently college and professional basketball, for upward social mobility and financial security, women lacked this social mobility route until the passage of Title IX. This legislation helped generate opportunities for girls and women who wish to benefit from athletics in ways that have been long

available to boys and men. Because Black women have not typically participated in the women's sports of figure skating, gymnastics, and until the
Williams sisters, women's tennis, they have not been the image of the
female athlete. The entry of Black women into basketball and tennis has
changed this situation. Black women athletes' bodies are muscular and athletic, attributes historically reserved for men, yet their body types also represent new forms of femininity.

Take, for example, the dilemma that the tennis world faced with the
success of African American sisters Venus and Serena Williams. The
achievements of the Williams sisters are unprecedented. Standing at
6–foot-1 ½ inches and with a 127 mph serve that once set a women's world
record, Venus Williams has held the Wimbledon title twice (2000 and 2001)
and at the Sydney Olympics was the first woman to win a gold medal in
singles and doubles (with sister Serena) since 1924. Winning 3.9 million
dollars in prize money, Serena Williams surged ahead in 2002, winning
three Grand Slam titles to take the number one ranking away from Venus.
In 2002, the Williams sisters were ranked number one (Venus) and number
two (Serena) in the world, a first ever for siblings. Unlike Althea Gibson,
Zina Garrison, and other African American female tennis stars whose
demeanor and style of play resembled the White women dominating the
sport, the Williams sisters basically reject tennis norms. They are exceptionally strong and play power games like men. They rebuff tennis
"whites" in favor of form-fitting, flashy outfits in all sorts of colors. They
play with their hair fixed in beaded, African-influenced cornrows that are
occasionally died blond. The tennis world cannot remove them because the
Williams sisters win. Their working-class origins mean that they don't fit
into the traditional tennis world and they express little desire to mimic
their White counterparts. Yet their achievements force issues of excellence
and diversity to the forefront of American politics.

The danger for Black women athletes does not lie in being deemed less
feminine than White women because, historically, Black women as a group
have been stigmatized in this fashion. Rather, for all female athletes and for
Black women athletes in particular, the danger lies in being identified as
lesbians. The stereotype of women athletes as "manly" and as being lesbians and for Black women as being more "masculine" than White women
converge to provide a very different interpretive context for Black female
athletes. In essence, the same qualities that are uncritically celebrated for

Black male athletes can become stumbling blocks for their Black female counterparts. Corporate profits depend on representations and images, and those of Black female athletes must be carefully managed in order to win endorsements and guarantee profitability.

With its high percentage of African American women athletes, and of non-Black athletes who identify positively with Blackness, the Women's National Basketball Association (WNBA) realized that its profitability might suffer if the league was perceived as dominated by lesbian ballplayers. In order to ensure that the "mannish" label applied to lesbians, female athletes, and Black women as a group would not come to characterize the WNBA, the League pursued at least two strategies.[38] For one, WNBA players are sexualized in the media in ways that never apply to men. Their sexuality helps sell basketball, yet it must be a certain kind of sexuality that simultaneously avoids images of the muscled woman or the sports dyke and that depicts the women as sexually attractive to men (in other words, as heterosexual). For example, during its first season in 1997, early marketing of the league featured Lisa Leslie and Rebecca Lobo, two women whose facial features, long hair, and body types (Leslie was a model) both invoked traditional images of femininity. Over the years, much was made of Lisa Leslie's modeling career. Still struggling to contain the image of women as dykes, during the 2002 season, one series of advertisements focused on individual players who each gave a vignette about her life and likes. The ads followed a common pattern—the athlete would face the camera, often holding a basketball, and would say a few words. Interspersed throughout her narrative were action shots of her playing basketball, still shots of her childhood, and other visuals that presented her accomplishments. However, the ads all shared another feature—unlike their basketball uniforms that provide more than adequate coverage for their breasts and buttocks, each woman was dressed in fitted sweat pants, and in a form-fitting top that, for some, exposed a hint of their midriffs and an occasional navel. In essence, the advertisements aimed simultaneously to celebrate and "feminize" their athleticism by showing women in action and showing their navels.

The second strategy aims to feminize the women by positioning them within traditional gender ideology concerning motherhood and the family. For example, to strengthen the association between the women players and ideas of motherhood and family, the league recruits children to its games and routinely showcases families and children on its television coverage. Pre-taped interview segments aired during games often focus on the family life of the players. Cynthia Cooper and Sheryl Swoops, two marquee players, both have been shown in this fashion. In some cases, television shots show the male partner of the player cheering on his love interest, often babysitting their child. Another strategy lies in presenting teams themselves as "families." Shots of teams during time-outs focus on the players' closeness, showing an emphasis on hand holding and group hugs. These dual strategies of treating the women as sexual objects and repositioning them within domestic family settings both work to contain the lesbian sexual threat of Black female basketball players. As one critic observes, "we can read the familial narratives that populate discussions of the WNBA as more than simply attempts to recontextualize muscular women within the space of domesticity. . . . The familial discourse also helps stabilize the player's sexuality as heterosexuality even as it locates femininity in a muscular, physically active corporeality: tough, yes; dykes, no."[39]

Images of working-class Black femininity all articulate with the social class system of the post–civil rights era. Depicting African American women as bitches; the sexual use of African American women's bodies by circulating images of Black women's promiscuity; derogating the reproductive capacities of African American women's bodies; and efforts to refashion images of Black female athletes in order to erase lesbianism all work to obscure the closing door of racial opportunity in the post–civil rights era. On the surface, these interconnected representations offer a plausible explanation for poor and/or working-class African American women's class status: (1) too-strong, bitchy women are less attractive to men because they are not feminine; (2) to compensate, these less-attractive women use their sexuality to "catch" men and hopefully become pregnant so that the men will marry them; and (3) men see through this game and leave these women as single mothers who often have little recourse but to either try and "catch" another man or "hustle" the government. But on another level, when it comes to poor and working-class African American women, this constellation of representations functions as ideology to justify the new social relations of hyper-ghettoization, unfinished racial desegregation, and efforts to shrink the social welfare state. Collectively these representations construct a "natural" Black femininity that in turn is central to an "authentic" Black culture.

Aggressive African American women create problems in the imperfectly desegregated post–civil rights era, because they are less likely to accept the terms of their subordination. In this context, Black "bitches" of all kinds must be censured, especially those who complain about bad housing, poor schools, abusive partners, sexual harassment, as well as their own depiction in Black popular culture. They and their children must be depicted as unsuitable candidates for racial integration. Take, for example, the resistance to poor and working-class single mothers who aim to move into White neighborhoods. Resistance to racial housing desegregation can be palpable, primarily because poor and working-class Black children are stigmatized as being aggressive, undisciplined, unruly, and unsuitable playmates for White children of any social class. The prevailing logic suggests that, in the absence of strong fathers, their too strong mothers could not teach them properly so the children repeat the cycle of inappropriate gender behavior. In this sense, the term *bitch* becomes a way of stigmatizing poor and working-class Black women who lack middle-class passivity and submissiveness. Their undesirable, inappropriate behavior justifies the discrimination that they might experience in housing, jobs, schools, and public accommodations.

The social welfare state is not alone in punishing Black women who are deemed to be too aggressive. Within African American communities, women who fail to negotiate the slippery border that has distinguished the independent Black woman from the controlling Black bitch can find themselves ridiculed, isolated, abandoned, and often in physical danger. The 2003 murder of fifteen-year-old Sakia Gunn shows what can happen to Black women who are seen as being out of their place.[40] But more important, the silence of major African American organizations concerning not just media images of poor and working-class Black women but their actual treatment by government officials, the men in their lives, and strangers on the street also contributes to Black women's oppression.

MODERN MAMMIES, BLACK LADIES, AND "EDUCATED BITCHES": IMAGES OF MIDDLE-CLASS BLACK WOMEN

Images of working-class Black femininity that pivot on a Black women's body politics of bitchiness, promiscuity, and abundant fertility also affect middle-class African American women. In essence, the controlling images associated with poor and working-class Black women become texts of what *not* to be. To achieve middle-class status, African American women must reject this gender-specific version of authenticity in favor of a politics of respectability. They must somehow figure out a way to become Black "ladies" by avoiding these working-class traps. Doing so means negotiating the complicated politics that accompany this triad of bitchiness, promiscuity, and fertility.

Middle-class African American career women encounter a curious repackaging of the controlling images generated for poor and working-class Black femininity, now reformulated for middle-class use. Images of middle-class Black femininity demonstrate a cumbersome and often contradictory link between that of modern mammy and Black lady. The Black lady image is designed to counter claims of Black women's promiscuity. Achieving middle-class status means that Black women have rejected the unbridled "freaky" sexuality now attributed primarily to working-class Black women. At the same time, because middle-class Black women typically need to work in order to remain middle class, they cannot achieve the status of lady by withdrawing from the workforce. Images of the Black lady are designed to resolve these contradictions.

Claire Huxtable's role on the hugely popular 1980s *Cosby Show* (played by actress Phylicia Rashad) helped shape the contours of the middle-class Black lady.[41] Each week, American families tuned their sets for a glimpse into the inner workings of the upper-middle-class, African American Cosby family. The Cosby family consisted of a professional married couple, their five children, and grandparents who visited from time to time. The Huxtables lived far better than the vast majority of Americans of all racial backgrounds. Their home was filled with paintings, they demonstrated a mastery of standard American English, and they seemed deeply committed to their college alma maters. The Huxtables also escaped and provided an escape from social problems then plaguing large numbers of Americans. On *The Cosby Show*, drugs, crime, teenage pregnancy, unemployment, discrimination happened to other people. The family itself was immune.

The character of Claire Huxtable exemplifies the new Black lady invented for middle- and upper-middle-class African American women. As a wife and mother, the character of Claire Huxtable was beautiful, smart, and sensuous. No cornrows, gum chewing, cursing, miniskirts, or plunging necklines existed for the character of Claire Huxtable. Despite the fact that she was a lawyer, the show never showed her actually at her place of employment. Doing so would introduce the theme of her sexuality into the workplace, and exploring these contradictions apparently were beyond the skills of the show's writers. Instead, she was allowed to be a sexual being, but only within the confines of heterosexual marriage and family. Occasionally, she and her husband would cuddle under the covers, until they were typically interrupted by one of their five children. Despite this commitment to hearth and home, Claire Huxtable somehow managed to make law partner in record time.[42] Black women's sexuality was safely contained to domestic space, and within the confines of heterosexual marriage.

More recent images of Black professional women also negotiate the slippery terrain of distancing Black women from the assumptions of aggression and sexuality attributed to working-class Black women while not making middle-class Black women unsuitable for hard work. To address this dilemma, the image of Mammy, the loyal female servant created under chattel slavery, has been resurrected and modernized as a template for middle-class Black womanhood. Maneuvering through this image of the modern mammy requires a delicate balance between being appropriately subordinate to White and/or male authority yet maintaining a level of ambition and aggressiveness needed for achievement in middle-class occupations. Aggression is acceptable, just as long as it is appropriately expressed for the benefit of others. Aggression and ambition for oneself is anathema. Modern mammies must be aggressive, especially if they expect to achieve within the male-defined ethos of corporations, government, industry, and academia. To get ahead, they must in some fashion be "bitchy," often with a capital "B." Yet because these same qualities simultaneously defeminize Black middle-class women and mark them with the trappings of working-class, authentic Blackness that is anathema in desegregated settings, middle-class Black female aggression must be carefully channeled.

The post–civil rights era has generated its share of representations of modern mammies, many of who also function as Black ladies. This combination of Black lady and modern mammy seems most evident on network television, a medium that reaches a broad audience. Unlike Claire Huxtable, who was almost always shown at home, these modern mammies are almost exclusively shown in the workplace. Many apparently either have no family life or such lives are clearly secondary to the requirements of their jobs. These women are tough, independent, smart, and asexual. But they are also devoted to their organizations, their jobs, and, upon occasion, their White male bosses. They are team players and their participation on the team is predicated upon their willingness to lack ambition for running the team and never to put family ahead of the team.

Despite the pressures to depict undying loyalty to the job, several representations of modern mammies do manage to raise but not resolve the contradictions associated with this representation. For example, the character of Ella Farmer (eloquently played by the late actress Lynn Thigpen) on the network television show *The District*, works for the Washington, D.C. Police Department as a high-level data analyst. Ella's commitment to African Americans is clear—she takes in an orphaned nephew and displays qualities of care and competence that are refreshing after decades of traditional, familyless mammies. She is clearly a Black lady. She uses standard American English, dresses impeccably, and always has a dignified demeanor. Her character is also staunchly devoted to the "Chief," her White boss. Ella is loyal, and this is an important quality in depictions of modern mammies. One incredible episode shows the extent of Ella's loyalty. Unlike other modern mammies who are destined to remain single, Ella not only managed to meet an available professional African American man (e.g., he had no criminal record, he had a good job, he was interested in neither men nor White women, and he had no apparent child support payments), but he asked her to marry him. The night before her wedding, Ella receives a call from the "Chief" that he and her coworkers are under quarantine because a deadly virus may have infected them. Ella leaves her groom-to-be and her orphaned nephew and rushes to headquarters. Apparently oblivious to putting her own life in danger, she tries to enter the building in order to be with the Chief and other quarantined staff members and is restrained by police officers. Even more remarkably, Ella expressed this devotion hatless in a raging snowstorm, sporting a stylish hairstyle that was freshly done in anticipation of her wedding. The message is clear: job first, marriage second.

The character of Anita Van Buren (played by S. Epatha Merkerson), a lieutenant in the New York City Police Department on the long-running show *Law and Order*, provides another image of a strong Black female professional that is developed within the strictures of the Black lady and the modern mammy. Unlike the undying loyalty expected of a modern mammy, this character reveals the cracks in the ideology. Lieutenant Van Buren supervises two men, both of whom respect her judgment. She also has a family. They are discussed in the workplace, but this character, like virtually all of the characters on the show, is never shown at home. But Lieutenant Van Buren's troubles become apparent when she refuses to be too subservient, a problem within a police department that is patterned on the military. Her loyalty is questioned when she files a discrimination suit against the department because she has not been promoted. The characters of Ella Farmer and Lieutenant Anita Van Buren both break new ground in depicting strong Black women who are in charge. But despite the transgressive elements of their characters, neither *The District* nor *Law and Order* unseats one main criterion of modern mammies. Ella Farmer and Lieutenant Anita Van Buren both remain loyal to social institutions of law and order that are run by White men.

Despite the considerable attention paid to Anita Hill in Black feminist theorizing, Oprah Winfrey has had a far greater impact within American culture than any other living African American woman.[43] Oprah is one of the richest women in the world. In 2003, Winfrey became the first Black woman on *Forbes* magazine's list of billionaires, two years after Black Entertainment Television's founder Robert Johnson became the first Black billionaire. A good deal of Winfrey's success lies in her ability to market herself within the familiar realm of the mammy, not violate the tenets of being a Black lady, yet reap the benefits of her performance for herself. Following in the footsteps of Hattie McDaniel, Winfrey's career seemingly echoes McDaniel's reply to those who criticized her acceptance of stereotypical roles. McDaniel once said, "Why should I complain about making seven thousand dollars a week playing a maid? If I didn't, I'd be making seven dollars a week actually being one!"[44] Winfrey constitutes the penultimate successful modern mammy whom African American and, more amazingly, White women should emulate. Winfrey markets herself in the context of the synergistic relationship among entertainment, advertising, and news that frame contemporary Black popular culture. Winfrey began in soft news reporting, a format that positioned her to assume a local Chicago talk show and learn the ropes of delivering the all-important "money shot."[45] Her success in Chicago grew into the hugely popular *Oprah Winfrey Show*. Winfrey's corporate power is impressive. Her show mixes a winning combination of news and entertainment, or infotainment. She instructs and raises general consciousness on a list of important social issues ranging from child abuse to wife battering to rape. Almost single-handedly, Winfrey got America to read, an impressive accomplishment in a mass-media-saturated society that balks at funding libraries and public education. Having a book listed on her "Oprah's Book Club" ensured overnight success. Winfrey entertains, makes money, and instructs, a stunning fusion of entertainment, advertising, and news. Winfrey's immense success provides a stamp of endorsement to any philosophy that she might endorse that goes far beyond any expertise she might possess on any given topic.

Yet Winfrey reinforces an individualistic ideology of social change that counsels her audiences to rely solely on themselves. Change yourself and your personal problems will disappear, advises Winfrey. If we each took personal responsibility for changing ourselves, social problems in the United States would vanish. On the surface, this advice appears to reinforce the themes of a changed self and personal responsibility as constituting important criteria for Black women's arrival in the middle class. These themes are recognizable to many Black women who struggle on a daily basis to make ends meet (media figure Iyanla Vanzant also built a large following among African American women with basically the same advice). Yet Winfrey's message stops far short of linking such individual changes to the actual resources and opportunities that are needed to escape from poverty, stop an abusive spouse from battering, or avoid job discrimination. The organizational group politics that helped create the very opportunities that Winfrey herself enjoys are minimized in favor of a message of personal responsibility that resonates with the theme of "personal responsibility" used by elites to roll back social welfare programs. Even *Law and Order*'s fictional Lieutenant Anita Van Buren found that individual effort was not enough to ensure her promotion on merit. When she sued, she was punished.

When African American middle-class women stray too far from the narrow confines of the Black lady and the modern mammy, the price can be high. Anita Hill's treatment during the 1992 Senate confirmation hearings of now Supreme Court Justice Clarence Thomas is instructive in this regard. Hill demonstrated all of the qualities of the assimilated, acceptable middle-class African American woman. Hill exemplified a politics of respectability—she stayed in school, got good grades, spoke standard

American English, and believed in the traditional American values of family, faith, and hard work. She never married, remained childless, and was devoted to her job. Yet because Hill was the target of sexual harassment, she was called upon to testify about her experiences years later. Virtually overnight, Hill as exemplary Black career woman became derogated as a dangerous, out of control threat to the social order. Given the lack of scandal in Hill's personal history, her demeanor as a witness, and her basic credibility, Hill's veracity was challenged. Her reliability as a witness was disputed on the grounds that she was acting out a fantasy of unrequited love for Thomas, a man who was her superior and who might be an ideal future husband who would protect her and allow her to share in his power. Thomas apparently rejected her and married a White woman, behavior that sparked a deep desire for revenge. Amazingly, this version of events actually fostered the rediscovery of *erotomania*, a medical disorder that first officially appeared 1987 as a subcategory of Delusional Disorder that was used as a political weapon against her.[46] In brief, Hill was accused of being crazy.

Hill's race and gender made this fabricated story plausible. Positioning Hill within the controlling image of the single, frustrated, ambitious Black woman who, unlike Mammy, did not show loyalty to her boss, contributed to the perception of Hill as crazy. Her physical appearance as a dark-skinned Black woman, one that allegedly rendered her less attractive than Thomas's White wife, also added plausibility to this diagnosis of erotomania. Hill's efforts to counter these accusations by bringing her family with her to the hearings did not prevail. Moreover, the core idea that emerged from this event was not solely that Black women can and will use false charges of sexual harassment. The barrier to success for ambitious Black men no longer consisted solely of White men (and women). A more insidious enemy had appeared, namely, Black women in close proximity to Black men who use Black men's trust to betray them.[47] Moreover, this theme of betrayal feeds into a broader community norm that sees independent Black women as somehow failing to support Black men. These are the women who "don't know how to treat a brother."

Hill's story illustrates the contradictions that face middle-class African American women who become judged within the confines of modern mammies and Black ladies. In Hill's case, the mammy and the lady collided head-on, with Hill herself left as the casualty. As modern mammies, such women are expected to put everyone else's wishes ahead of their own needs; in fictional Ella Farmer's case, her own wedding and personal happiness in favor of the "Chief's" predicament and, in Hill's case, Clarence Thomas's alleged desires for sexual favors as the cost of keeping her job. But succumbing to his demands would have meant that Hill no longer fell within the equally confining image of Black ladyhood. Rejecting his demands eventually exposed Hill to the charge of aggression and bitchiness. Being the ultimate corporate, academic, or government mammy yields a lifetime of faithful service that can border on exploitation. These representations depict Black women professionals as women alone, either because their dedication to their careers has meant that they have not devoted sufficient time to their personal lives or because they have some sort of negative trait that makes them less desirable as marital partners, in Hill's case, a latent case of erotomania.

More recently, the stricture of the Black lady and the modern mammy are making room for a new image, namely, the educated Black bitch. These women have money, power, and good jobs. But they are beautiful and, in some ways, they invoke Pam Grier's persona as "Bad Bitches" that control their own bodies and sexuality. For example, in the 1992 film *Boomerang*, Marcus Graham (played by Eddie Murphy) is a young, successful marketing executive within a Black-run firm who treats women as conquests. As a ladies' man, Graham has no trouble finding women until he meets Jacqueline (Robin Givens), a powerful executive whose values concerning power, money, and sexuality closely resemble his own. Jacqueline turns the tables by treating Graham in the same way that he has treated others. By the end of the film, Jacqueline has been demonized and installed as the archetypal educated Black bitch, Graham has been humbled and humanized by her abuse, and he is then able to see the beauty in another educated Black woman (played by Halle Berry), who has supported him all along. She is educated, but, unlike Jacqueline, she is appropriately subordinate. In a more playful and muted version of the educated Black bitch representation, Vivica Fox's depiction of the memorable character Lysterine in the 1997 film *Booty Call* also shows an educated, middle-class Black woman who is not searching for a committed relationship but who wants men for the sex they can provide. In contrast to Jacqueline, who is demoted in her job, Lysterine shows no such passion—she's in search of good booty. Both characters raise important questions about the migration of representations of working-class "bad bitches" to the terrain of middle-class Black professional women who earned their own money.

Together, representations of Black ladies, modern mammies, and educated Black bitches help justify the continued workplace discrimination targeted toward many middle-class African American women. They lack loyalty (refuse to go out in a snowstorm in their wedding night to save their bosses), they are not ladylike enough (Anita Hill's alleged erotomania that surfaced when Thomas rejected her advances), or they are so cutthroat and ruthless that they cannot be trusted (Jacqueline's turning the tables and Lysterine's values concerning the booty call). These representations also are used to explain why so many African American women fail to find committed male partners—they allegedly work too hard, do not know how to support Black men, and/or have character traits that make them unappealing to middle-class Black men. Only rarely do the families, friendships, and love relationships that African American women actually have find media validation. For example, the numbers of Black women who, through separation, divorce, or the decision to have children without male partners, live as single parents are routinely seen as having a lesser form of family life. Even more rarely are relationships that fall outside the scope of acceptable societal norms validated in mass media space. For example, with the exception of the HBO series *The Wire* that debuted in 2002, representations of Black lesbians in committed coupled relationships remain rare. This show is unusual in that, unlike the characters of Ella Farmer and Lieutenant Van Buren who also work on behalf of law and order, the character of Shakima Greggs, an African-American/Korean-American female narcotics detective (played by Sonja Sohn), is in an openly lesbian relationship. Culturally Black, Kima is shown on the job, often engaged in everyday chitchat with her male colleagues about her "woman." She is also shown at home with all of the conflicts that were denuded from characters such as Claire Huxtable. Kima argues with her Black lesbian partner Cheryl, who fears for Kima's safety on dangerous narcotics details and wishes that she would place more emphasis on her law school studies. Kima and Cheryl are shown in sexual situations, a rarity in mass media. On *The Wire*, the committed love relationship of this Black lesbian couple is treated as no different than any other relationship on the series. This ordinary treatment thus provides a mass media depiction of middle-class Black women that remains highly unusual.

* * *

In essence, the mass media has generated class-specific images of Black women that help justify and shape the new racism of desegregated, color-blind America. Because presenting African American culture as being indistinguishable from other cultures is not necessarily entertaining, news-worthy, or marketable, depictions of Black culture needed to be *different* from White norms, yet still supportive of them. This media constructed Blackness took class-specific forms that mirrored changes in actual social class formations among African Americans. The arrival of middle-class "Black" respectability, as evidenced by the strictures of the Black lady and the modern mammy, helped shape a discourse about racial integration and African American women's place in it. For example, the Cosby family was definitely "Black" because they had Black cultural referents in their home (artwork, they listened to jazz, etc.), yet their values allegedly matched those of White middle-class Americans. Such images participated in an "enlightened racism" whereby Whites could claim that they were not racist, primarily because they would welcome Black families like the Cosbys as neighbors, despite data on patterns of urban migration suggest-ing that Whites actually preferred racially homogeneous neighborhoods.[48] New patterns of color-blind racism needed a few acceptable, assimilated Blacks who could meet the high standards set by the Cosby family and, for Black women, those of modern mammies and Black ladies.

Working-class Black authenticity also became reworked in the context of color-blind racism. During this same era, the allegedly authentic Black culture associated with working-class and poor African Americans also populated mass media. Working-class Black culture also depicted ideas about difference from assumed White norms using gender-specific images; only, in this case, commodified Black culture contained elements of danger and excitement. Black hip-hop culture, with its images of urban neighbor-hoods as wild, out-of-control, criminal havens, its rap artists as self-proclaimed gangstas, and its rejection of conservative family values via young mothers with babies and no husbands also entered American homes. Invoking historical stories of Black promiscuity, depictions of Black women's sexuality were central to this sense of excitement and danger. Television enabled viewers to simulate the excitement and sense of adven-ture that prior groups of Whites accessed by going on African safari, visit-ing the naughty Harlem jazz clubs of the 1920s, or reading the travelogues of survivors of these exploits. Identifying the actual "dangers" and "excitement" of working-class Black youth culture as authentic Black culture, and selling it to audiences in a global context, satisfied the demands of the global marketplace. Gender-specific images of Black bitches and bad mothers flourished in this climate.

In this context, it is important to remember that ideologies of gender, race, class, and sexuality that produce the controlling images of Black femininity discussed here are never static. Rather, they are always internally inconsistent, reflect the experiences of the people who agree with and refute them, and thus are constantly subject to struggle.[49] As the work of Black female artists within rap and the broadening of images of Black professional women on television suggest, contemporary images of Black femininity reflect these contradictions. How do those of Black masculinity fit within this new racism? Moreover, how do gender-specific images of Black femininity and Black masculinity work together?

FIVE

BOOTY CALL
Sex, Violence, and Images
of Black Masculinity

1997: The film *Booty Call* joins the ranks of a series of Hollywood romantic comedies that explore sexuality, love, and commitment in the 1990s. By following the exploits of four African Americans on a double date, the film examines the intricacies of the booty call, namely, the act of calling or contacting a person for the sole purpose of having sex. Rushon and Bunz, two men with conflicting views on commitment, differ on how Black men should treat Black women. Bunz believes in making booty calls and sees women as good for little else. Rushon has long followed Bunz's advice. But now that Rushon has been dating Nikki, his girlfriend of seven weeks, he questions the logic of the booty call. Nikki and Lysterine, the potential sex partners of the two men, both insist upon safe sex, yet they also differ in their perceptions of sexuality, love, and commitment. Nikki's search for a commitment from Rushon before having sex is far removed from Lysterine's views that booty calls can go both ways. During the evening, Nikki's resistance softens and Lysterine becomes enamored with Bunz. The women are ready, but they will only have safe sex. Thus begins the comedy—the seemingly endless search by Rushon and Bunz for condoms that turn into one disaster after another. Will these men ever get the booty?

Virtually overnight, the term *booty* came to permeate contemporary popular culture. Jennifer Lopez's booty is such an important asset to her career that she allegedly insures her buttocks. To help women who are less well endowed, advertisements sell booty enhancement surgery. A 1992 *Newsweek* article on "Buzzwords" among teenagers identifies *punk* (bad, not hip, uncool), *White* (someone who's bad at basketball), and *booty* (sex) as widely used teenage lingo. MTV shows an hour-long documentary devoted to the history of the booty. Who can forget the impact of hip-hop artist Sisquo's "Thong Song," the soundtrack for a fashion style that had women in the early 2000s proudly showing hints of their thong underwear (covering booty cleavage) under low-cut jeans? The term *booty call* also entered popular vernacular well before the 1997 film of the same name. It is now installed on many college campuses as a term for sex. Like urban legends, stories about African American men who seek booty calls (men who use women for sex and who reject commitment) circulate among African American women. On one campus, an African American female student who worked the front desk of a large dormitory regaled her class with stories of Black men who repeatedly signed in and out on the same night, visiting different women for booty calls. Should we erroneously think that only men make booty calls, women engage in booty calls as well. In this usage, a woman will call a man to come over in the middle of the night for sex (booty).

Two sets of meanings of the term *booty* provide an interpretive context for explaining this fascination with the booty. The first set reflects ideas about property and masculinity. This strand defines booty as plunder taken from an enemy in times of war. The actual booty is a valuable prize, award, or gain that cannot be given away—it must be taken. Thus, because this usage applies to goods or property seized by force, an element of violence is part of this very definition of *booty*. Because men historically have been soldiers, this characterization reflects ideas about masculinity, property, and violence. These meanings of *booty* draw upon images of conquest, warfare, and property that install the term *booty* within a staunchly masculine frame.[1]

The second set of meanings of *booty* reflects ideas about sexuality and race. The 2000 edition of the *American Heritage Dictionary of the English Language* provides the following meanings: 1. *Slang* The buttocks. 2. *Vulgar slang* a. The vulva or vagina. b. Sexual intercourse. Moreover, the dictionary speculates on the origins of this usage of *booty*. Describing the etymology of the term, it points out that *booty* may be from African American vernacular English, from the obsolete Black English *booty*, and perhaps may be an alternation of the term *body*. What an interesting series of connections—buttocks, women's genitalia, sexual intercourse, and the body overall—all drawn from Western perceptions of Black people and culture. The constellation of terms that surround the term *booty* not only suggests that women of African descent are ground zero for the meanings associated with the term *booty* but also that historical meanings of Black promiscuity are alive and well in contemporary popular culture. A simple Google search of the term *booty* should dispel doubts—many of the websites clearly link Blackness, sexuality, and African American women.

When combined, these meanings of the term *booty* form a backdrop for contemporary mass media–generated gender ideology, with special meaning for Black masculinity.[2] In the context of the new racism in which miseducation and unemployment have marginalized and impoverished increasing numbers of young Black men, aggression and claiming the prizes of urban warfare gain in importance. Being tough and having street smarts is an important component of Black masculinity.[3] When joined to understandings of booty as sexuality, especially raw, uncivilized sexuality, women's sexuality becomes the actual spoils of war. In this context, sexual prowess grows in importance as a marker of Black masculinity. For far too many Black men, all that seems to be left to them is access to the booty, and they can become depressed or dangerous if that access is denied. In this scenario, Black women become reduced to sexual spoils of war, with Black men defining masculinity in terms of their prowess in conquering the booty.

Mass media's tendency to blur the lines between fact and fiction has important consequences for perceptions of Black culture and Black people. Images matter, and just as those of Black femininity changed in tandem with societal changes, those of Black masculinity are undergoing a similar process. As is the case for controlling images of Black femininity, representations of Black masculinity reflect a similar pattern of highlighting certain ideas, in this case, the sexuality and violence that crystallizes in the term booty, and the need to develop class-specific representations of Black masculinity that will justify the new racism. In this context, some representations of Blackness become commonsense "truths." For example,

Black men in perpetual pursuit of booty calls may appear to be more authentically "Black" than Black men who study, and the experiences of poor and working-class Black men may be established as being more authentically Black than those of middle- and upper-middle class African American men.

ATHLETES AND CRIMINALS:
IMAGES OF WORKING-CLASS BLACK MEN

In 1997, professional basketball player Latrell Sprewell choked P. J. Carlesimo, his coach on the Golden State Warriors. Almost overnight, this three-time all-star became a symbol of what many saw as the worst of basketball. He instantly stood for how skewed professional sports had become, an "indictment of a generation of jocks seen not only as too black but too pampered, too lawless, too greedy."[4] For many, Sprewell's actions also symbolized the contradictions of how Western ideologies depict Black men's bodies. The combination of physicality over intellectual ability, a lack of restraint associated with incomplete socialization, and a predilection for violence has long been associated with African American men. Because Sprewell and similar "bad boy athletes" were "blackening" the sport, their behaviors reflected changing race relations in the wider society. In some ways, the Sprewell incident also marked a turning point in masculine gender politics. Influenced by a White male military model that often defined discipline in terms of the legitimate authority of father figures, Carlesimo's coaching tradition was in decline. Sprewell was at the forefront of a generation of players who, raised on rap, "see any type of disrespect as an assault on their manhood and a stifling of their creativity."[5] In short, Carlesimo was not Sprewell's daddy, and because both were now in the pros, the father-son coaching style of college basketball no longer applied.

Sprewell, other Black basketball players, and Black people in hip-hop culture signal a reworking of historical representations of Black masculinity, ironically, by using those very same representations in new ways. Historically, African American men were depicted primarily as bodies ruled by brute strength and natural instincts, characteristics that allegedly fostered deviant behaviors of promiscuity and violence. The buck, brute, the rapist, and similar controlling images routinely applied to African American men all worked to deny Black men the work of the mind that routinely translates into wealth and power. Instead, relegating Black men to the work of the body was designed to keep them poor and powerless. Once embodied, Black men were seen as being limited by their racialized bodies.

In the current context of commodified Black popular culture, the value attached to physical strength, sexuality, and violence becomes reconfigured in the context of the new racism. In some cases, the physical strength, aggressiveness, and sexuality thought to reside in Black men's bodies generate admiration, whereas in others, these qualities garner fear. On the one hand, the bodies of athletes and models are admired, viewed as entertaining, and used to sell a variety of products. For example, Keith Harrison, an African American male model for the Polo clothing line, never speaks but symbolizes a Black male body that should be admired. Similarly, the hip-hop magazine *Vibe* relies heavily on Black male models and athletes to sell gym shoes, clothes, CDs, and other trappings of hip-hop culture. On the other hand, the image of the feared Black male body also reappears across entertainment, advertisement, and news. As any Black man can testify who has seen a purse-clutching White woman cross the street upon catching sight of him, his physical presence can be enough to invoke fear, regardless of his actions and intentions. This reaction to Black men's bodies emboldens police to stop motorists in search of drugs and to command Black youth to assume the position for random street searches. Racial profiling is based on this very premise—the *potential* threat caused by African American men's bodies. Across the spectrum of admiration and fear, the bodies of Black men are what matters.

In this context, the contested images of Black male athletes, especially "bad boy" Black athletes who mark the boundary between admiration and fear, speak to the tensions linking Western efforts to control Black men, and Black men's resistance to this same process. Athletics constitutes a modern version of historical practices that saw Black men's bodies as needing taming and training for practical use. Given the small numbers of Black men who actually make it to professional sports, the visibility of Black male athletes within mass media speaks to something more than the exploits of actual athletes. Instead, the intense scrutiny paid to sports in general, and to basketball players in particular, operates as a morality play about American masculinity and race relations. Black athletes, and their varying degrees of acceptance and rejection of the types of social scripts held out by Carlesimo, become important visual stages for playing out the new racism. In essence, the myth of upward social mobility though sports represents, for poor and working-class Black men, a gender-specific social script for an honest way out of poverty. Its rules are clear—submit to White male authority in order to learn how to become a man.

Spectacle is an important component of the depiction of Black athletes, especially in the current climate of mass media entertainment and advertising.[6] Boxing has long provided this type of spectacle for American audiences. Black boxers in particular are seen as inherently violent and in need of "trainers" who can focus their talent toward victory in the ring. Whereas a string of seemingly violent Black men have provided brutal spectacles for boxing fans, boxer Mike Tyson elevated the image of the Black brute to new levels. Ironically, Tyson also became a hero within hip-hop, representing, according to Nelson George, "a bare-chested, powerful projection of the dreams of dominance that lay thwarted in so many hearts."[7] As a result of his physical prowess in the ring and because his force and irreverence earned respect, Tyson is mentioned in scores of rap records. At the same time, Tyson's behavior in the ring after serving a prison term (for biting off part of another boxer's ear) makes him a suspect hero. Moreover, Tyson's history of domestic violence and his rape conviction suggest that the spectacle Tyson provides for White and Black audiences alike may be as much about gender and sexuality as about race.[8]

African American professional athletes reveal varying degrees of acceptance and rejection of this morality play that constructs Black men by their physicality and then markets images of boxers, basketball players, and football lineman (less so, quarterbacks) to a seemingly insatiable public. Black male athletes in high school and college sports, especially those from poor and working-class backgrounds, often have little recourse but to follow the rules. But professional players who are the focus of media spectacles have far more options. Not only do these athletes signal changes in American race relations, superstar athletes are valuable commodities. Todd Boyd describes the new social context for superstar athletes that contributes to this new attitude of defiance:

> It is important to understand that Black men, especially young Black men, are held in the highest contempt by a large segment of society. This has always been the case, and this contempt has always been

exposed through sport. Yet, in modern society, these same Black men are often entertainment for the masses. Though it is acceptable for these men to entertain, they are held in contempt for the money they make because of their entertainment.[9]

Black men who earn large salaries but who are deferential and appear to uphold American values are acceptable. The problems arise when players realize their value, their significance to the game, and try to capitalize on their accomplishments. Then they are often held in the highest contempt.

Black male athletes playing professional sports have worked within these politics and have used them to upset both the images themselves as well as the financial arrangements that underlie the exploitation of Black men's bodies. For example, Julius Erving played professional basketball when the NBA had an image problem. On the court, he was a model of propriety, yet his style of play legitimated Black playground ball (primarily dunking). Moreover, his acquisition of a Coca Cola bottling plant in the early 1980s established him as an entrepreneur. Following Erving's lead, Magic Johnson became an icon in the symbolic battles between the LA Lakers and his counterpart Larry Bird on the Boston Celtics. Their careers marked a rivalry that persisted into the 1980s and that set the stage for a new era in basketball.[10] Johnson was not just a player; he used his basketball earnings to invest in inner-city theaters and community development.

The rise of hip-hop and its relationship to basketball signals a new set of social relations concerning Black athletes and their unwillingness to put up with the political and economic arrangements of the past. Like Latrell Sprewell, Black basketball players are often described as insolent, unruly, and in need of punishment.[11] Sprewell has not been alone in this pantheon of African American athletes that American sports fans simultaneously admire and hate. Sprewell may have choked his coach, but his lucrative contract with the Knicks and his performance on the court bought him respect. Apparently being insolent and unruly is not a problem if a Black man can play. In some cases, the bad boy image may enhance a player's reputation. Take, for example, how Alan Iverson's career progressed after he joined the Philadelphia 76ers in 1996. To Iverson's way of thinking, he was an entertainer, and his quick crossover dribble thrilled fans and helped revitalize the sport. His image, however, made him an antihero. By retaining his cornrows and continuing to hang out with his friends from the hood, his run-ins with the law provided much bad press. "He was . . . a walking reminder that the days of *cultural* crossover, when black stars such as Julius Erving and Michael Jordan sought and won white acceptance, were over. Iverson was leading a new generation of ballplayers, kids much less interested in acquiescing to white, mainstream taste. . . . It is a constant theme in rap music: Selling out and forgetting where you come from is anathema."[12]

In this context, Black male athletes who refuse to bow down to abusive coaches unsettle prevailing norms of race and gender. They reject the family drama script that says that players should view their coaches as father figures, and that fans should emulate athletes as role models. When basketball great Charles Barkley retired from the NBA in 2000 after sixteen years of professional basketball, he left behind more than impressive statistics—more than twenty thousand points, ten thousand rebounds, and four thousand assists.[13] Barkley became the first athlete since Muhammad Ali and Bill Russell to question the media's insistence on conferring role model status on Black athletes who modeled deferential behavior. Barkley advised youth not to use him as a role model, but to follow their parents and teachers instead. Breaking ranks with commonsense patriarchal beliefs that young Black men were lost without the firm hand of older men, Barkley pointed out, "My mother and grandmother were two of the hardest-working ladies in the world, and they raised me to work hard."[14] Should there be any confusion, Barkley even made a Nike commercial in which he proclaimed, "I am not a role model." In one interview, he vowed, "I'm a strong black man—I don't have to be what you want me to be."[15]

Unfortunately, Barkley became caught up in a media-generated morality play in which he was routinely pitted against other Black male athletes who were far more deferential to White authority. Whereas Michael Jordan refused to condemn the exploitative labor practices used to make the gym shoes that bore his image and from which he profited, Barkley routinely spoke his mind. Take, for example, his comments to the press in a Philadelphia locker room in which Barkley reputedly said: "just because you give Charles Barkley a lot of money, it doesn't mean I'm not going to voice my opinions. Me getting twenty rebounds ain't important. We've got people homeless on our streets and the media is crowding around my locker. It's ludicrous."[16] Barkley also injured his own cause by inadvertently spitting on a little girl while aiming for a courtside heckler who was yelling racial epithets. As one writer points out, "in the soap opera narrative of sports, Barkley's 'badness' was set against Jordan's 'goodness,'" leaving little room for the complicated, multifaceted Charles Barkley.[17]

The father-figure thesis assumes that young Black men need tough coaches who will instill much-needed discipline in the lives of fatherless and therefore unruly Black boys. For example, an incident at Indiana University that led to the subsequent firing of coach Bobby Knight for physically attacking an African American player was not uniformly censured. Many believed that young Black players, lacking male role models in their lives, need the strong hand of a coach, even an abusive one such as Knight. The role model thesis also suggests that Black male youth in general need images of successful, professional Black male athletes as positive role models. Little mention is made of the fact that basketball and sports confine young Black boys to achievements of the body and not of the mind. Most Black American boys will never achieve the wealth and fame of their athletic role models through sports. Keeping them mesmerized with sports heroes may actually weaken their ability to pursue other avenues to success. Moreover, the role-model thesis underestimates the motivation of legions of Black boys who work hard at things for which they think they have a future. Theses of natural Black athletic ability notwithstanding, NBA players rarely get as far as they do without hard work. For example, at 6'4" Charles Barkely is short by NBA standards. He developed his skill through practice. In tenth grade he shot baskets every night, sometimes all night if he could get away with it, and mastered his leaping skills by jumping back and forth over a four-foot chain-link fence.[18] The summer before his senior year in college, Latrell Sprewell made himself into a perimeter shooter by, every day, taking nearly five hundred shots from twelve feet. Then he'd take five hundred shots from thirteen feet, and then fourteen feet, moving a foot at a time until he improved his three-point shooting range.[19]

The bottom line for professional Black athletes is that they can reject people who would reject them because their wealth enables them to do so. Todd Boyd describes the new attitude:

> When you reject the system and all that goes along with it, when you say, "I don't give a fuck," you then become empowered, liberated, controller of your own destiny. This is certainly the case in basketball,

because the players make enough money to be able not to give a fuck, as
money is the ultimate source of liberation in capitalist America.[20]

For Boyd, athletes with money are in a position to critique the very sys-
tem that allegedly rewards them. This is one reason why figures like
Iverson, Sprewell, and Barkley are so hated and revered by Whites and
Blacks alike.

Some Black men's bodies may be admired, as is the case for athletes,
but other Black male bodies symbolize fear. Historical representations
of Black men as beasts have spawned a second set of images of that center
on Black male bodies, namely, Black men as inherently violent, hyper-
heterosexual, and in need of discipline. The controlling image of Black
men as criminals or as deviant beings encapsulates this perception of Black
men as inherently violent and/or hyper-heterosexual and links this representation to poor and/or working-class African American men. Again, this
representation is more often applied to poor and working-class men than
to their more affluent counterparts, but all Black men are under suspicion
of criminal activity or breaking rules of some sort.

This image of Black male deviancy crystallized in criminality is far
from benign—the United States incarcerates more Black men than any
other country. Whereas Black men constitute 8 percent of the U.S. population, they comprise approximately 50 percent of the prison population.
By any measure, the size of the U.S. inmate population is enormous—the
rate of incarceration in the United States is about 727 prisoners per
100,000 people. The vast majority of other countries incarcerate far fewer
people. Most European countries, for example, imprison fewer than 100
people per 100,000 residents, a rate more than seven times lower than that
of the United States.[21]

Covering up incarceration on such a mass scale requires powerful
media images that reward poor and working-class Black youth who submit
to White male authority by using athletics for honest upward social mobility, and punish others who do not. When it comes to representations of
Black male deviance, several important variations exist. The thug or
"gangsta" constitutes one contemporary controlling image. The thug is
inherently physical and, unlike the athlete, his physicality is neither
admired nor can it be easily exploited for White gain. The "gangsta" may
be crafty, but the essence of his identity lies in the inherent violence asso-

ciated with his physicality. Media representations of African American men as thugs grew in the post–civil rights era. Alan Iverson basically took the "thug" images out of the ghetto and inserted it onto the basketball court.

Mass media marketing of thug life to African American youth diverts attention away from social policies that deny Black youth education and jobs. It also seems designed to scare Whites and African Americans alike into thinking that racial integration of seemingly poor and working-class Black boys (the allegedly authentic Blacks) is dangerous. Who wants to live next door to a thug or sit next to one in school? In this context, the phenomenon in which young African Americans seemingly celebrate elements of thug life seems counterintuitive because looking and/or acting like a thug attracts discriminatory treatment.[22] Yet the depiction of thug life in hip-hop remains one of the few places Black poor and working-class men can share their view of the world in public. Raps about drugs, crime, prison, prostitution, child abandonment, and early death may seem fabricated, but these social problems are also a way of life for far too many Black youth.[23]

In this context, the work of artists like Tupac Shakur simultaneously affirms the realities of thug life yet critiques its existence and continuation. Tupac symbolized the contradictions of the hip-hop generation. He is routinely pegged as a gangsta rapper, yet his work ranged over several genres of rap.[24] Moreover, Tupac symbolized the tensions of an era. "What did it mean to be a child of the Black Panthers, to have a postrevolutionary childhood?" asks cultural critic Michael Dyson.[25] Dyson's book-length monograph examines the complexities of Tupac's life, his straddling of the ideals of revolutionary politics, and the materialism that forms the down side of hip-hop culture. Using Tupac's life and death as emblematic of an era, Dyson provides a provocative analysis of the difference between thugs and revolutionaries. Arguing that Tupac lives the "tension between revolutionary ambition and thug passion," Dyson suggests that revolutionaries and thugs alike share a worldview in which flipping the economic order is the reason for social rebellion.[26] They both see problems and they both want change. Yet thug logic undermines the society that the revolutionary seeks to change. "Thug ambition is unapologetically predatory, circumventing the fellow feeling and group solidarity demanded of revolutionaries," Dyson contends.[27]

In the political economy of hip-hop culture, as a genre, gangsta rap reflects these tensions between actual thug life and a commodified thug persona that was marketed and sold in the global marketplace. Tupac Shakur's career came to an end when gangsta reality and representation converged. Following a Mike Tyson fight, an unknown assailant gunned him down. In contrast, other gangsta rappers keep a tight rein on separating their personal and professional lives. Take, for example, the contradictions that define the career of gangsta rapper Ice Cube. Ice Cube promoted the Nation of Islam's ideology of self-help and self-respect but also made a bundle "hustling St. Ides Malt liquor in the ghetto."[28] His racial politics seem inextricably linked with a dangerous gender ideology that profits from the marketability of rebellious Black masculinity. His 1990 debut solo album *Amerikkka's Most Wanted* deals with racism in law enforcement, sexual irresponsibility, and other social issues, yet the vulgarity and misogyny of his subsequent work is legendary. Despite his protestations that he only uses vulgarities to communicate with people who would otherwise tune him out, he derogates women by counseling his listeners "you can't trust no bitch."[29] Ironically, despite this ghetto persona, Ice Cube, actually named O'Shea Jackson, lives in a wealthy White neighborhood, in a gated home, with his wife and three children. He was raised in a two-parent family in a middle-class residential area of south central Los Angeles, has never been in prison, and graduated from the wealthiest high school in Los Angeles.[30] Unlike Tupac, whose childhood poverty and ongoing problems with the law exposed him not just to the representations but to the realities of his gangsta persona, apparently Ice Cube knew what a convincing gangsta performance could buy.

In a mass media context that blurs fiction and reality, the effectiveness of attempts by Tupac, Ice Cube, and other Black men to seize the power of the media in order to unsettle representations of Black criminality have come under close scrutiny. Given the potential power of mass media, the language in rap has attracted considerable controversy, especially negative reactions to the widespread use of the term *niggah*. As legal scholar Randall Kennedy points out, the term *nigger* has long been featured in African American folk humor. Before the 1970s, it rarely appeared in the routines of professional comedians and was extremely rare in shows performed before racially integrated audiences. With live shows and a string of albums, Richard Pryor changed all of this. Pryor's political humor defied social conventions that accepted Black comedians as clowns but rejected them as satirists. Pryor opened the door for those who followed, both in comedy (Chris Rock) and the now ubiquitous use of the term *niggah* within hip-hop culture in ways that contest historical views of Black men as weak and subordinate.[31] In essence, many Black men aim to do with the term *nigger* what members of other oppressed groups have done with similar slurs. They throw the slur back at the oppressor by changing its meaning. They have added a "positive meaning to *nigger*, just as women, gays, lesbians, poor whites, and children born out of wedlock have defiantly appropriated and revalued such words as *bitch, cunt, queer, dyke, redneck, cracker,* and *bastard.*"[32]

Western traditions of presenting Black men as embodied, sexualized beings foster another variation of seeing Black men's bodies of sites of inherent deviance. Because sexuality has been such an important part of the depiction of Black masculinity, Black men's bodies remain highly sexualized within contemporary mass media. Images of Black men often reduce them not only to bodies (the case of the athletes) but also to body parts, especially the penis. In analyzing the depiction of Black men in *Hustler* magazine, a popular periodical whose primary readership consists of working-class White men, Gail Dines found ample representations of Black male promiscuity. Dines argues that in movies and magazines that feature Black men, the focus of the camera and plot is often on the size of the Black penis and on Black men's allegedly insatiable sexual appetite for White women. Searching for a similar pattern in *Hustler*, Dines found that Black men were most often found in cartoons in which they could be caricatured, and that a major feature of the humor presented centered on the size and deployment of the Black male penis. Using the depiction of King Kong as a frame of reference, Dines observes: "whereas the original Kong lacked a penis, the *Hustler* version had, as his main characteristic, a huge black penis that is often wrapped around the 'man's' neck or sticking out of his trouser leg. The penis, whether erect or limp, visually dominates the cartoon and is the focus of humor. This huge penis is depicted as a source of great pride and as a feature that distinguishes Black men from White men."[33] In this sense, the penis becomes the defining feature of Black men that contributes yet another piece to the commodification of Black male bodies.[34]

Hustlers or "players" constitute benign versions of the rule breaking associated with gangstas and objectifying Black men's bodies as sex objects.

More refined, the hustler has one foot on either side of the law. The hustler can be a simple "player," one who uses people to trick them out of something that he wants. Players often target women, trading sexuality for economic gain. The image of the Black male hustler works with historical notions of African American men as too lazy to work and in need of the domesticating influences of slavery, sharecropping, boot camp, and prison. Representations of hustlers suggest that African American men would rather live off of other people, very often women, than go to work. The theme of charisma is paramount here, the notion of style that a hustler brings to his endeavor. The prevalence of representations of Black men as pimps speaks to this image of Black men as sexual hustlers who use their sexual prowess to exploit women, both Black and White. Ushered in by a series of films in the Blaxploitation era, the ubiquitous Black pimp seems here to stay. Kept alive through HBO-produced quasi documentaries such as *Pimps Up, Hos Down*, African American men feature prominently in these media constructions. Professional pimps see themselves more as businessmen than as sexual predators, with slapping their sex workers around the cost of doing business. For example, the men interviewed in the documentary *American Pimp* all discuss the skills involved in being a successful pimp. One went so far as to claim that only African American men made really good pimps. Thus, the controlling image of the Black pimp combines all of the elements of the more generic hustler, namely, engaging in illegal activity, using women for economic gain, and refusing to work.

Tying the concept of Black men as sexual predators so closely with ideas about normative Black masculinity raises the stakes dramatically within Black heterosexual relationships. Despite the fact that the film *Booty Call* is a romantic comedy with likable characters, it draws upon these sedimented historical meanings by focusing on promiscuity as a defining feature of Black masculinity. Moreover, it casts the struggle to redefine Black masculinity in class-specific terms, one in which the sexual practices of the working-class character become juxtaposed to those of the middle-class character. The images of working-class Bunz and middle-class Rushon serve as touchstones for a reworking of ideas about sexuality, violence, and Black masculinity in the post–civil rights era. It's no accident that Bunz and Rushon are cast as originating in the same social class, but now belonging to different ones. Bunz wears running clothes and Rushon wears suits. When Bunz finds out that Rushon has not yet had sex with

Nikki, he criticizes Rushon for failing to score. "College has got you too sensitive," states Bunz. "Sensitive?" asks Rushon. "You ain't got no player left in you," answers Bunz. Via his ridicule, Bunz relies on dominant ideas that associate authentic Black masculinity with a hyper-heterosexuality thought to characterize working-class Black men. He uses these ideas to accuse middle-class Rushon of being less authentically Black and therefore less masculine.

Booty Call is situated within a specific historical moment that reflects the convergence of two meanings of booty in which men (and sometimes women) aim to capture the booty (property or spoils of war) via sexual conquest. This placement, however, does not mean that it uncritically replicates these historical meanings. On the one hand, by its very title, *Booty Call* draws upon entrenched historical meanings concerning race, gender, and sexual property. As was the case with the term *freak*, the film invokes ideas about Black promiscuity and the film would be meaningless without this history. One might ask whether this film could even be made with White American actors cast in the starring roles? But on the other hand, *Booty Call* aims to disrupt these very same historical meanings. Here, Black women take the lead in demanding a different kind of Black masculinity from their partners. Nikki, Rushon's love interest, clearly rejects the prevailing association of African American women's bodies with perceptions of Black female sexuality as wild and "freaky." She is not a sexual prude, but her demand for safe sex and commitment speaks to Black women's agency and self-determination. Nikki insists on using condoms because she realizes that "unsafe" sex might leave her with a STD and/or a baby. Although Nikki's friend Lysterine (who is Bunz's blind date) is sexually adventurous, after Nikki's prodding, she too insists upon condoms. She's sexually daring, but her classic line "no glove, no love" draws a line in the sand. These women demand a new kind of Black masculinity in which sexual norms around the booty call and around love relationships merit renegotiation.

One striking element of this film is that, despite their differences, both Black men in *Booty Call* listen to Black women. Neither tries to dominate the women and neither resorts to threats or violence. Rushon has waited seven long weeks to have sex with Nikki, but when she demands that he wear a condom, he gets dressed and goes to the convenience store in search of one. Bunz may be, in the words of Lysterine, a "hoodrat," but when she demands a condom, he joins Rushon in the middle of the night shopping

trips for these essential items. The act of booty call is not a foregone conclusion in this film. Rather, the need to renegotiate the terms of booty calls
is debated. In a similar fashion, the reality of gender ideology and dominant ideas about Black masculinity is not the issue. Rather, the terms of
Black masculinity are at stake.

The real drama in *Booty Call* does not lie in reconfiguring Black femininity but in challenging prevailing notions of a sexualized Black masculinity. Nikki and Lysterine symbolize versions of middle-class Black
femininity of the Black Lady and the Educated Bitch. Neither character
has a real internal dilemma in the course of the film. They say what they
want and stick to it. However lovable, Bunz also seems incapable of
change—he is the timeless, nonhistorical representation of Black male
promiscuity. Rushon is the character who faces the dilemma of crafting a
new form of Black masculinity that will spare him Bunz's ridicule, but that
will also enable him to commit to Nikki. Thus, despite the association of
the term *booty* with Black women, the core question of *Booty Call* concerns which version of Black masculinity will win out? Will the working-
class version of Black authenticity symbolized by Bunz's incessant search
for the booty triumph? Or will Rushon's fledgling efforts to claim a middle-class politics of respectability prevail?

Poor and working-class Black men are also depicted more often as perpetrators of violence. The use of the phrase "black-on-black" violence to
describe violence within African American urban neighborhoods invokes
images of poor and working-class Black men, not those respectable men
from the Black middle class. The phrase also illustrates how the political
economy of production, primarily the convergence of entertainment,
news, and advertising, converge to produce a racial ideology that circulates
in a global context. This phrase originated not in the United States but as
part of the end of apartheid in South Africa.[35] First used in a 1986 speech
to Parliament by then-president P. W. Botha who described "black-on-
black" violence as being "brutal murders by radical Black people," the
term appeared in the U.S. press as a frame for reporting on the end of
apartheid. In the South African press, Zulus were repeatedly described as
"tribes" and the ANC with its Xhosa ethnicity (of Mandela) became redefined as another tribe. Print and broadcast media made little use of politics
or economics to explain the violence, choosing instead to install a racial
frame of interethnic violence. The term was picked up by the American

press, and it has been used in a similar fashion. As the authors point out, "Labeling all violence among Black people as factional, internecine, and part of 'blood feuds' implies a natural cohesiveness or unity among Black people because they are black. The terms used suggest a fight among family members, calling up a long-standing Western image of the tribe as a naturally occurring, familial social structure."[36] "Black-on-black" violence is the site at which the U.S. news media reconstruct Black Africa as "tribal," threatening, savage, and incapable of self-government and democracy and also Black urban neighborhoods as sites equally incapable of controlling their children and being self-governing.[37]

The arguments that recast Black people and violence as an inevitable outcome of either biological nature or cultural backwardness are remarkably similar in both locations. In both the South African and U.S. media, news of "black-on-black" violence centers on one type of perpetrator, typically a young, Black male. The struggle against apartheid or against a punitive urban police force, then, is reduced to a "self-perpetuating" rebellion of youth against bona fide authority."[38] In an interpretation of social change that sounds eerily reminiscent of how the end of slavery unleashed the controlling image of the Black rapist, within media accounts of "black-on-black" violence, it is the *end* of apartheid that has "unleashed the violence." Within the South African discourse, Black male youth, inherently violent, moving in gangs, "schooled [by the anti-apartheid movement] only in the struggle," are said by September 1990 to have discovered that "liberation might yield few benefits for them without the education they eschewed for the flames of revolution."[39] The conditions under which they live, then, are of their own choosing and are the cause, rather than the result, of South Africa's troubles. Black men are transformed from being victims and heroes to being—along with the anti-apartheid movement itself—the root cause of the violence.[40]

Similarly, the gangs that have taken over African American urban neighborhoods represent the outcome of Black youth freed of discipline, primarily that of the punitive father, and of strong social institutions that kept them in place. Within this interpretive context, legitimated White state violence—in the case of South Africa, the apartheid government and for the United States, an occasionally "out of control" police force—although it is often condemned in media texts as "excessive" is also redeemed by its promise to restore order.[41] News stories about violence are about transgressions of social boundaries, the consequences of those transgressions, and the reestablishment of social order.

Representations that reduce Black men to the physicality of their bodies, that depict an inherent promiscuity as part of authentic Black masculinity, that highlight the predatory skills of the hustler, and that repeatedly associate young Black men in particular with violence converge in the controlling image of Black men as booty call-seeking rapists. Initially, the myth of the Black male rapist who lusted after White women emerged during postemancipation Jim Crow segregation as a tool for controlling Black men who were prematurely freed from the civilizing influences of slavery. While not as necessary to contemporary relations of rule as those during the Jim Crow era, apparently the image of the Black rapist can be revived when the need arises. For example, during the 1988 Republican presidential campaign, George Bush's campaign staff made the behavior of Willie Horton, a convicted African American male rapist who raped a White woman while participating in an early release program, central to his stance on crime. As George Cunningham points out, "George Bush's deployment of the figure of 'Willie' Horton as a black male rapist helped to manufacture the majority that elected him as heir to the conservative Ronald Reagan."[42] Like Gus, the archetypal Black rapist first seen in D. W. Griffith's 1915 classic film *The Birth of a Nation*, Horton came to symbolize the Black man who was freed *prematurely* not from slavery but from the necessary strictures of prison. As a result, the public needed protection from African American men like Horton whose excessive booty calls placed society at risk.[43]

SISSIES AND SIDEKICKS:
IMAGES OF MIDDLE-CLASS BLACK MEN

In the 1980s, *The Cosby Show* was one of the most popular shows on American television. Bill Cosby played the role Heathcliff Huxtable, a physician and father of five children, who was married to Claire, his beautiful lawyer-wife. In the uncertainties of the 1980s, when African Americans experienced increased access to schools, jobs, and neighborhoods long reserved for Whites, Cosby offered a reassuring image to Whites. He was the Black buddy, friend, or Black sidekick that everyone wanted. Resurrecting an image of Black masculinity in service to Whites,

Cosby's image was marketable, nonthreatening, entertaining, and eminently likable. In contrast to the derogated images of working-class Black masculinity, Cosby's squeaky clean image as America's Black buddy or sidekick provided one social script for the types of African American men who would find acceptance in a desegregating America.

The image of Cosby's character set the template for middle-class Black masculinity—he was friendly and deferential; he was loyal both to dominant societal values such as law and order as well as to individuals who seemingly upheld them; he projected a safe, nonthreatening Black identity; and he was defined neither by his sexual prowess nor by any hint of violence. Collectively, each of these features of representations of the Black buddy and Black sidekick intersected with changes in American society. For one, Black buddies typically achieve acceptance through their friendly demeanors and clear deference to White authority. In this regard, Black buddies constitute representations of Black masculinity whose origins lie in that of Uncle Tom, the Negro servant who was domesticated under slavery, and in Uncle Ben, his commercial counterpart developed to sell rice and other consumer goods. Cosby's image drew upon both of these traditions. His role on *The Cosby Show* provided White families with images of a friendly African American who visited their living rooms to entertain them. If the show became too controversial, that is, too closely associated with racial issues, it could be dismissed by turning off the television. Like Uncle Tom, Black buddies are useful only if they are clearly committed to the American way of life.

Within capitalist marketplace relations, just as representations of Uncle Ben were used to sell rice, images of Bill Cosby helped sell products. Cosby was not alone. In this commodified climate, athletes who can be repackaged as Black buddies receive lucrative endorsement packages, make lots of money, and join the ranks of wealthy Americans.[44] Michael Jordan's clear rejection of any hint of political controversy enabled him to become one of the most successfully managed idols and icons of media culture. Through activities such as appearing with cartoon character Bugs Bunny in the 1996 film *Space Jam*, Jordan carefully constructed a kid-friendly demeanor. At one time, he was the leading candidate on a children's list of the person whom they would most want to invite to a birthday party. Golfer Tiger Woods's mixed-race background and his rejection of a "Black" identity contributed to his success as a marketable commodity.

Part of Jordan's and Woods's success in reaching so many American fans can be attributed to the path blazed by Cosby's image. Cosby's role as a spokesperson for Jello products, especially the numerous advertisements that he made with multiracial groups of children, positioned him as non-threatening and safe. Who could have guessed that one Jello ad could modernize images of Uncle Tom and Uncle Ben by repackaging historical images of Black masculinity to meet the needs of a desegregating America?

Loyalty is another characteristic feature of the controlling image of the Black buddy. As depicted in mass media, there is little danger of Black buddies stealing the silverware, reverting to Black English, or raping the wife. Instead, Black buddies are typically shown as stripped of the seemingly dangerous parts of Blackness, leaving the useful parts as sufficient markers of difference to satisfy the tastes of a multicultural America. Within Hollywood films, for example, the image of the Black sidekick, a specific rendition of the Black buddy image that characterized films in the 1980s, reflects a loyalty that resembles that depicted by the image of the modern mammy. Often portrayed within film by an African American actor whose loyalty to his White male friend rivaled that of the mythical Uncle Tom, the Black sidekick typically lacked an independent Black male identity. Instead, his sense of self stemmed from his relationship to his White friend or work partner. A series of White heroes and their Black sidekicks set the tone in television and film. From Bill Cosby's stint as Robert Culp's buddy in the television drama *I Spy* to Danny Glover playing Mel Gibson's reluctant buddy in the *Lethal Weapon* films to Eddie Murphy who served as Nick Nolte's sidekick in *48 Hours* as well as the sidekick to a cadre of White police officers in *Beverly Hills Cop*, "Hollywood . . . put what is left of the Black presence on the screen in the protective custody . . . of a White lead or co-star, and therefore in conformity with dominant, White sensibilities and expectations of what Black people should be like."[45]

Apparently, what "Black people should be like" is being physically Black so that racial integration can be seen but not culturally Black, for example, display any of the behaviors of an assumed authentic Blackness. Thus, being seen as being physically Black yet lacking a racial identity constitutes another feature of the Black buddy image. Michael Jordan's phenomenal success points to the lucrative benefits for those Black buddies who manage to develop personas as "raceless" individuals. Jordan became a cultural icon and worshiped as a hero in large part because his clean-cut image was markedly different from the cornrowed, tattooed, trash-talking demeanor of "bad boy" ball players. Alan Iverson, Latrell Sprewell, Dennis Rodman, and Charles Barkley cannot be mistaken as anybody's subordinate buddies or sidekicks—Sprewell tried to choke his coach. In the postintegration era, Black men like Cosby and Jordan are accepted with open arms as White America's buddies precisely because they are not like the bad boy athletes, criminals, or other representations of working-class (authentic) Black masculinity. Television shows like *The Cosby Show* and sports provide mass media arenas in which these ideas about race are worked through. Race, especially Blackness, increasingly informs contemporary racial politics, yet, at the same time, race is rendered largely invisible within the fabric of film, television, and sports. Jordan's appeal may be often defined as "raceless," yet as a Black buddy, he projects a certain kind of race, a certain kind of Black masculinity that will be accepted.[46]

Another distinguishing feature of the representation of the Black buddy pivots on mechanisms of containing his sexuality. Like the character of Heathcliff Huxtable on *The Cosby Show*, Black buddies are often depicted as asexual Black men. Less emphasis is placed on Black men's bodies within representations of middle-class Black men than characterizes representations of working-class Black men. For example, on *The Cosby Show*, the ability of Cosby's character to dance, shoot hoops, model chiseled abs, or perform in the sack was irrelevant. Moreover, Heathcliff Huxtable's sexuality was safely contained within the sanctity of heterosexual marriage. Occasionally, the show provided shots of Heathcliff and Claire cuddling under the covers, hinting at a safe sexuality but never showing it. Because Cosby's character was presented in a family setting, his children had a role model to emulate. The Cosby kids were not conceptualized as sexual beings either. Everyone was definitely straight.

Appearing on network television during a time of transition, Cosby's character not only was asexual but it was also nonviolent. But if the image of masculinity is one that requires a combination of sexuality and violence for "manly" men, how can one present a film with a White hero who is masculine whose sidekick seems to be too "feminine"? Buddy films must be careful not to emasculate the Black buddy because feminizing Black male images to this degree would detract from male bonding and leave the audience wondering what the White hero saw in his Black buddy. Although there are films in which this emasculation has occurred (Richard Pryor's stint as a "toy" for a spoiled White boy in the 1982 film *The Toy* comes to mind), most Black buddies are not emasculated to this degree. One way of resolving this dilemma is to eliminate all aspects of the Black buddy's life that would compete with the Black buddy's loyalty to his partner. Many Black buddies are depicted as not having families or any type of relationships, sexual or otherwise, that might distract them from their main purpose of being loyal to the White protagonist or to their jobs. Unlike the Cosby image of the Black buddy who was stripped of these qualities, images of these decontextualized Black buddies can be strong and virile on screen, as long as these qualities are placed in service to the needs of the White hero and, more recently, to legitimate social institutions, especially, the criminal justice system.

In this context, representations of Black buddies may render Black masculinity nonthreatening because expressions of violence and sexuality are placed under White authority. A fine line exists between using the image of the Black buddy to tame the threat of Black male promiscuity and violence and feminizing the Black male image to the point at which it cannot be respected. But how does the interracial buddy drama resolve the issue of the emotional relationships among men so that it does not transform male bonding into homoerotic relationships?

In order to resolve this tension, the Black buddy template often draws upon the family as a frame for explaining appropriate social relationships. This frame can be used in several ways. For one, showing either member of the buddy team in a heterosexual relationship with a woman, especially in a marriage with children, effectively challenges any homoerotic subtext between the two men. Having a wife and children at home takes on special meaning for the character of the Black buddy, for his ability to commit to one heterosexual relationship within a family unit is a sign of his ability to assimilate. Another use of the family frame defines the relationship between White hero and his Black buddy. Film critic Jacquie Jones suggests that, in mainstream cinema, the subordinate roles that Black buddies accept have traditionally been the province of women, children, and/or pets. Explaining these patterns, Jones suggests that many of these films replicate family relations in that "the Black male assumes the role of the boy; the Black women, the mother; and, of course, the White male, the father."[47] Hazel Carby takes a different view. Analyzing Danny Glover's participation within contemporary films, Carby sees not father/son bonding, but an imagined brother-to-brother bonding created in the White male imagination. Using films in which the actor Danny Glover played Black buddies or sidekicks, Carby analyzes the nature of support that the buddy provides to his White hero. In films like *Grand Canyon* and *Lethal Weapon*, Glover acts as "father confessor and psychological counselor to white men. . . . Glover has become identified as the one who manages to persuade white men to recognize, understand, and express the truth about themselves to themselves."[48] Finally, because the men enter into a fictive kin relationship as brothers, they are not sexual competitors for the same women. Here American assumptions that heterosexual relationships should occur between people of the same race effectively leave the White hero and the Black buddy confined to White and Black women, respectively. No fights over women as booty will tarnish the brotherhood. This theme of African Americans having the emotions and expressiveness to help Whites get in touch with their better selves is a recurring theme in American cinema. Typically, this emotional nurturing was done by the mammy figure, but selected men could also do this expressive caring function. Whatever the family scenario, whether they are cast as immature boys or as appropriately subordinate yet caring younger brothers, Black buddies perform the emotional labor long associated with women. This placement feminizes them.

Representations of Black buddies have been joined by yet another non-violent, asexual image of middle-class Black masculinity, namely, the "sissy." Standing in contrast to the seemingly authentic Black masculinity of the criminal, the Black athlete, and even middle-class Black buddies (who may have been subordinate, but at least they were heterosexual), representations of Black masculinity of the "punk," the "sissy," or the "faggot" offer up an effeminate and derogated Black masculinity. Representations of gay African American men depict them as peripheral characters, often in comedic roles that border on ridicule. Often the representation of the gay character works to support the heterosexuality of other males. For example, *Car Wash* (1976) introduced Lindy, an openly gay character. Dramatized as a "queen," Lindy was swishy, limp-wristed, and exhibited an exaggerated, affected feminine style. Around him, all of the other male characters were not just heterosexual, but emphatically heterosexual. To frame Black male heterosexuality, the other characters were married, had girlfriends, dated women, hired prostitutes, or flirted with the women customers. As one analyst points out, "Lindy is tolerated as part of the public world but only because he reinforces the purity of heterosexuality by presenting homosexuals as defiled and deviant."[49] Black gay men depicted in feature films continue to serve as humorous foils for the exploits of other more important characters, background characters that lend "color" to the film.

Analyzing contemporary media, Marlon Riggs identifies how Black manhood has become juxtaposed to the Negro faggot in contemporary Black cultural production:

> I am a Negro faggot, if I believe what movies, TV, and rap music say of me. My life is game for play. Because of my sexuality, I cannot be black. A strong, proud, "Afrocentric" black man is resolutely heterosexual, not *even* bisexual. Hence, I remain a Negro. My sexual difference is considered of no value; indeed, it's a testament to weakness, passivity, and the absence of real guts—balls. Hence, I remain a sissy, punk, faggot. I cannot be a black gay man because, by the tenets of black macho, black gay man is a triple negation. I am consigned, by these tenets, to remain a Negro faggot. And, as such, I am game for play, to be used, joked about, put down, beaten, slapped, and bashed, not just by illiterate homophobic thugs in the night but by black American culture's best and brightest."[50]

This "punk," "sissy," or "faggot" may have its roots in an emasculated Uncle Tom, but it also operates as a new representation in the post–civil rights era.

Given the virtual absence of representations of gay Black men in the past, these new representations enjoy a visibility within contemporary Black popular culture that is surprising. Representations of "sissies" and "Negro faggots" suggest a deviancy that lies not in Black male promiscuity but in a seeming emasculation that is chosen. Avowedly heterosexual African American men routinely deride gay Black men, primarily through ridicule (the running skit "Men on Film" on the popular television show *In Living Color* that poked fun at two Black male "sissies") or through outright homophobic comments (comedic routines by Eddie Murphy and other Black male comedians that border on homophobic vitriol). A running joke throughout movies concerns the theme in which a very large Black male prisoner threatens a boy with rape. In one memorable scene from *House Party*, a 1990 feature film by African American brothers Reginald and Warrington Huddlin, the teenaged protagonist lands in a jail cell with a big Black man who wants him to be his girlfriend. The audience is encouraged to laugh at the possibility of an adolescent boy being raped or "punked" by a Mike Tyson–esque character. Within straight Black male culture, special derision is saved for Black representations of "punks," the males who were sexually conquered by other men.

In contrast to representations of Black gay men in contexts with Black heterosexual men, images of Black gay men in settings with African American women present a very different picture. In these films, Black gay men become surrogate women, with the benefits and liabilities that this implies. As opposed to the derogated "punks," they become depicted as nonthreatening, lovable "sissies." For example, African American director John Singleton's 1993 film *Poetic Justice* contains the stereotypical gay Black male hairdresser who provides comic relief for the real heterosexual drama. This theme of gay Black buddy to women, a part that helps Black women gain insight into Black masculinity, is a recurring theme.[51] Placing Black gay men in female settings creates space for this stereotypical foil; the gay Black buddy/sidekick typically helps African American women and is routinely accepted by them and liked.

Because images of Black gay men as "punks" often are used to justify male violence upon identifiably gay Black men, such images do foster homophobia and hate crimes. But this is the tip of the iceberg because the impact of these representations goes further. Many Black men who are gay or bisexual hide their sexual orientation, preferring to pass as straight. There have always been Black men who passed, but what is different now is the emergence of a new subculture among Black gay men. Benoit Denizet-Lewis describes this phenomenon: "Rejecting a gay culture they perceive as white and effeminate, many black men have settled on a new identity, with its own vocabulary and customs and its own name: Down Low. There have always been men—black and white—who have had secret sexual lives with men. But the creation of an organized, underground sub-culture largely made up of black men who otherwise live straight lives is a phenomenon of the last decade."[52] Most of the Black men who are on the Down Low (DL) date or marry women and engage sexually with men that they meet in bathhouses, parks, the Internet, or other anonymous settings. Most DL men do not identify themselves as gay or bisexual, but primarily as Black.

On the one hand, the sexual practices attributed to the Black "sissy" do not constitute a credible threat to White heterosexual men because the presence of Black gay sexuality constitutes a feminized and therefore non-threatening Black masculinity. Representations of Black gay sexuality operate as further evidence that Black men are "weak," emasculated, and "feminized" in relation to White men. Black gay sexuality is depicted as reflecting male submission or capitulation, especially those men who are penetrated like women. When joined to the broader theme of the Black buddy or sidekick, "faggots, "punks," and "sissies" constitute the extension of the seeming symbolic emasculation of middle-class Black men associated with images of Uncle Tom and Uncle Ben. "Sissies" can be accommodated within the norms of Black assimilation because Black buddies pave the way for them.

On the other hand, Black gay sexuality might present a threat to Black heterosexual men for this exact same reason. Within the universe of Black masculinity, gay Black men pose a threat to a beleaguered Black male heterosexuality that strives to claim its place at a table dominated by representations of White-controlled masculinity. Within Black popular culture, the widespread caricature of Black gay men, thus making this sexuality visible, works to uphold constructions of authentic Black masculinity as being hyper-heterosexual. The stigma attached to Black gay sexuality is less about depicting this form of sexuality than it is in using an emasculated Black gay sexuality to establish the boundaries of both White masculinity (which is assumed to be heterosexual) and Black male heterosexuality. Thus, representing Black gay sexuality as Black male emasculation simultaneously threatens heterosexual African American men, upholds Black male hyper-masculinity (the invisibility of DL Black men and their redefinition as Black heterosexuals), and protects hegemonic White masculinity. Ironically, Black gay men can simultaneously gain acceptance, provide humor, be erased, and pose a threat.

Despite considerable pressure to use the image of the faggot or sissy for ridicule and humor, some films and television shows do dispute these representations of Black gay men. For example, the original Showtime movie *Holiday Heart* (2000) is one of the few films that try to depict gay Black men in a nonstereotypical fashion. Directed by African American director Robert Townsend, actor Ving Rhames plays the title character of Holiday—a church-loving, flamboyant gay drag queen. After Holiday's longtime lover passes away, Holiday is left alone and grieving. So when a homeless drug addict, Wanda (Alfre Woodard), and her young daughter, Niki (Jessika Quynn Reynolds), require Holiday's help, he moves them into the apartment next door to his own. The three form an unconventional family until Wanda brings home a new drug dealer boyfriend who changes everything for the worse. Wanda's inability to avoid drugs threatens to further break the trio apart. The character of Holiday helps heal the damaged Black family. This film moves depictions of Black gay men away from extreme stereotypes, yet it still positions Black gay sexuality within the framework of being the emotional ballast for the sufferings of others.

Some media contestations are more confrontational. For example, through comedy, the four Black and Latino gay men in the 2001 play *Punks* strive to disrupt the negative associations of the term itself. Because it is less subject to the strictures of programming for a mass audience, cable television has also broken from the stereotypical depiction of Black gay men. For example, in its 2001 season, the HBO series *Six Feet Under* introduced the character of Keith Charles (played by actor Mathew St. Patrick), a gay Black male cop whose White male lover David Fisher was one of the main characters. Resisting the temptation to portray Keith as the sexual Black "buddy" for David as White hero, the series instead focuses on their stormy relationship in negotiating different approaches to homosexuality. In addition to its depiction of a Black lesbian couple, the first season of HBO's original series *The Wire* introduced the character of Omar, a gay Black male gangsta who seeks revenge on the drug dealers who brutally murdered Brandon, his gay Black lover. Again, the treatment on *The Wire* breaks with stereotypes. Omar is dark-skinned, violent, and in no way appears to be the stereotypical "sissy." Moreover, the gay Black male relationship is between two working-class Black men, thus challenging the association of gay sexuality with Whiteness and/or with middle-class men.

As was the case for representations applied primarily to working-class and poor Black men, collectively, the representations for middle-class Black men also help justify the political economy of the new racism. All seem designed to exert political control on those African American men who do achieve middle-class status and to discourage far larger numbers of African American men from aspiring for social mobility into the middle class. The complex and narrow representational space saved for middle-class African American men speaks to the ways in which ideas about buddies and sidekicks, punks and sissies coalesce within discourses of Black male assimilation in the post–civil rights era. Assimilated, middle-class Black men are somehow seen as being less manly, as subordinates. Their place is assured at the middle-class table, just as long as they recognize their place of serving the needs of White-run organizations. Moreover, the deference needed to become a Black buddy takes its cues from discourses of emasculation, the popular discourse on the sissy.

When combined, images of the buddy and the sissy both construct middle-class Black men as less manly—the former because he has been emasculated by the White world, the latter because he exhibits a sexual identity that symbolizes a chosen emasculation. When presented with this narrow frame of images by institutions of formal education, Black boys of all social class often reject school. In the universe of many African American boys, studying not only identifies them as "White-identified, sellouts," excellent school performance is the domain of "girls" or "punks." Masculinity is associated with use of the body, not the mind. Girls and "fag-gots" are the ones who submit to the will of the teacher, the principal, and avowedly heterosexual boys. In this context and without developing some alternative frameworks, the more educated Black boys become, the less manly they may feel. The alternative of becoming "bad boys" in school may seem like a more realistic option. One study of fifth and sixth grade Black boys found that many were labeled troublemakers and written off by school personnel as early as age ten.[53] When combined with the competing code of the street within African American working-class urban culture, staying in school and doing well is a real accomplishment.

Ironically, holding up educated African American men as role models to Black male youth may actually aggravate this situation. The thesis of role modeling assumes that young Black men lack role models that will show them their possibilities and how to behave to get there. Working-class disadvantage is routinely seen as an outcome of the absence of middle-class Black role models. But what if working-class Black boys are familiar with these representations of middle-class Black men and simply reject them?

Through Black working-class eyes, Black elected officials, busi-nesspersons, corporate executives, and academics may resemble "academic sidekicks" or "intellectual punks." These are the men who increasingly fail to defend African American interests because they fail to defy White male power. Instead, they tolerate and in many cases collude in reproducing the conditions in the inner city. Staying in school and studying hard moves them closer to images of Bill Cosby selling Jello or Michael Jordan talking to Bugs Bunny or Tiger Woods refusing to claim Blackness at all. If the "academic sidekick" or "intellectual sissy" becomes seen by African American boys and young men as the price they have to pay for racial integration, it should not be surprising that increasing numbers of young Black men reject this route to success.[54] With a vacuum of images of Black men of whatever sexual orientation who stand up to White officials, who take principled positions on social problems that affect African Americans, and who clearly have the interests of African Americans at heart, why should poor and working-class Black boys emulate middle-class Black men? In their eyes, when Latrell Sprewell choked his coach, he stood up to White power. In Todd Boyd's words, "When you reject the system and all that goes along with it, when you say, 'I don't give a fuck,' you then become empowered, liberated, controller of your own destiny."[55] This stance may work for rich Black professional athletes, but it is a dangerous posture for Black boys with no degrees, no skills, and a whole lot of attitude. Charles Barkley may not be a role model, but neither are these representations of middle-class African American men.

CLASS-SPECIFIC GENDER IDEOLOGY AND THE NEW RACISM

Under the new racism, these class-specific representations of Black masculinity and Black femininity serve several purposes. First, these representations speak to the importance that ideologies of class and culture now have in justifying the persistence of racial inequality. Within the universe of these representations, authentic and respectable Black people become constructed as class opposites, and their different cultures help explain why poor and working-class Black people are at the bottom of the economic hierarchy and middle-class Black people are not. Authentic Black people must be contained—their authentic culture can enter White-controlled spaces, but they cannot. Representations of athletes and criminals, bitches and bad mothers refer to the poor and/or working-class African American men and women who allegedly lack the values of hard work, marriage, school performance, religiosity, and clean living attributed to middle-class White Americans. In essence, these representations of Black masculinity and Black femininity assail unassimilated Black people, point-ing out the ways in which such poor Black people are "untamed" and in need of strict discipline. In contrast, representations of sidekicks, sissies, and modern mammies describe the space of respectability for newly accepted Black people. These Black people are different from middle-class Whites, but these representations of middle-class Black people are not a threat to power relations. Social mobility, or lack thereof, becomes recast in terms of the unwillingness of poor and/or working-class Black people to shed their Blackness and the willingness of middle-class Black people to assimilate. These respectable Black people must be denuded of Blackness—they should be seen but not necessarily heard.

Under the color-blind ideology of the new racism, Blackness must be *seen* as evidence for the alleged color blindness that seemingly characterizes contemporary economic opportunity. A meritocracy requires evidence that racial discrimination has been eliminated. The total absence of Black peo-ple would signal the failure of color blindness.[56] At the same time that Blackness must be visible, it also must be contained and/or denuded of all meaning that threatens elites. Rejecting traditional racist discourse that sees racial difference as rooted in *biology*, these representations of crimi-nals and bad mothers, of sidekicks and modern mammies work better in a context of desegregation in which cultural difference has grown in impor-tance in maintaining racial boundaries. Poor and working-class African American men are not *inherently* inclined to crime, such images suggest. Rather, the *culture* in which they grow up, the authentic Black culture so commodified in the media, creates images of criminality that explains the failures of racial integration by placing the blame on the unassimilability of African Americans themselves. The joblessness, poor schools, racially seg-regated neighborhoods, and unequal public services that characterize American society vanish, and social class hierarchies in the United States, as well as patterns of social mobility within them, become explained solely by issues of individual values, motivation, and morals.

Second, when combined, these class-specific images create a Black gender ideology that simultaneously defines Black masculinity and Black femininity in relation to one another and that also positions Black gender ideology as the opposite of normal (White) gender ideology. Providing a mirror image for mainstream gender ideology of dominant men and sub-missive women, the Black gender ideology advanced by these representations depicts Black men as being inappropriately weak and Black women as being inappropriately strong. This hypothesis of weak men and strong women takes class-specific form. For example, representations of Black men reinforce ideas about Black male immaturity, irresponsibility, and, until domesticated, unsuitability for full citizenship rights, yet does so in class-specific ways. The cluster of representations for Black working-class men deems them less manly than White men and therefore weaker. Because these men do not participate appropriately in society (absent fathers, criminals, etc.), they weaken it. They are also deemed less capable of undertaking the tasks of strong men, for example, exhibiting the self-discipline to study hard in school, work in low-paying jobs, save their money, and support their children. Their strength lies in their violence and sexual prowess, but only if these qualities can be harnessed to the needs of society. In contrast to this site of weakness, representations of middle-class Black men who may be doing well but who pose little threat to White society present another dimension of weakness. Because they fail to confront the new racism, the sidekicks and sissies represent emasculated and feminized versions of Black masculinity. In contrast, class-specific images of Black femininity reinforce notions of an inappropriate, female strength. Whether working-class "bitches" who are not appropriately submissive, bad mothers who raise children without men, or "educated bitches" who act like men, this Black female strength is depicted and then stigmatized. Not even the modern mammies and Black ladies escape this frame of too-strong Black women. Such women may receive recognition for their strength on the job, but it is a strength that is placed in service to White power and authority.

This Black gender ideology constructs this thesis of weak men and strong women by drawing upon heterosexism for meaning. Representations of the Black male "sissy" that mark the boundaries of Black male hetero-sexuality and those of the "manly" Black lesbian that fulfills a similar function for Black female heterosexuality constitute an outer ring around the heterosexual family drama of weak men and strong women. Unless these ideas are challenged, they can aggravate homophobia within African American communities. As Harlon Dalton points out:

> My suspicion is that openly gay men and lesbians evoke hostility
> in part because they have come to symbolize the strong female

and the weak male that slavery and Jim Crow produced. . . .
Lesbians are seen as standing for the proposition that "Black
men aren't worth shit." More than even the "no account" men
who figure prominently in the repertoire of female blues singers,
gay men symbolize the abandonment of Black women. Thus, in
the Black community homosexuality carries more baggage than
in the larger society.[57]

If Dalton is correct, this excess baggage of homosexuality helps explain
patterns of homophobia within African American communities.

Finally, this Black gender ideology helps justify racial inequality to
White Americans and suppress resistance among African Americans.
Depicting and demonizing "weak men and strong women" enables White
Americans to point to the damaged values and relationships among Black
people as the root cause of Black social disadvantage. At the same time,
when internalized by African Americans themselves, this same Black gender ideology works to erase the workings of racial discrimination by keeping Black men and Black women focused on blaming one another for
problems. Within this logic, class-specific gender ideology becomes a convenient explanation both for the persistence of Black poverty and for
deeply entrenched racial discrimination. By demonizing poor and working-class African Americans, these representations quell long-standing
political threats that African American citizenship raises for White elites.
African Americans are blamed for their poverty and powerlessness. At the
same time, representations of middle-class Blacks discourage them from
using their literacy, visibility, and money to support African American
interests. Weak Black men who are willing to accept subordinate roles and
strong Black women who place their strength in service to White-controlled
institutions become the gold standard for measuring Black middle-class
acceptability. Together, class-specific representations of Black masculinity
and Black femininity aim to counter the threats posed by Black men and
women who have too much freedom and too many opportunities in the
post–civil rights era, at least, defined as such by those in power.

SIX

VERY NECESSARY
Redefining Black Gender Ideology

2002: African Americans were well represented at the 74th annual Academy Awards ceremony. Hostess Whoopee Goldberg returned for her fourth highly successful stint hosting the event. Winning Best Actor in 1963 for his role in *Lilies of the Field*, seventy-four-year-old actor Sidney Poitier received an honorary award for his extraordinary performances in over fifty years in the business. But the main event came when actress Halle Berry became the first African American woman to win for Best Actress and actor Denzel Washington followed in Poitier's footsteps to become the second African American man to win Best Actor. Despite the glitz of the media spectacle, some lingering doubts remained about both Berry's and Washington's awards. Halle Berry's career had included many fine films, yet she won best actress for *Monster's Ball*, a film in which Berry engaged in a torrid interracial sex scene with actor Billie Bob Thornton. Denzel Washington also had impeccable credentials as an accomplished actor. Despite his stellar performances in heroic roles in numerous films (e.g., *Malcolm X* and *John Q*), Washington won his Oscar for his depiction of a violent, corrupt police officer in *Training Day*. No one doubted Berry's talent or Washington's virtuosity as an actor. But one lingering question remained. Of all of the actresses and films that might have been selected, why *Monster's Ball* with its depiction of Black female sexuality? Of all the films in which Washington appeared, why did he win an Oscar for such a violent part?

In her 1970 essay "On the Issue of Roles," African American author Toni Cade Bambara argued: "It seems to me you find your Self in destroying illusions, smashing myths, laundering the head of whitewash, being responsible to some truth, to the struggle. That entails at the very least cracking through the veneer of this sick society's definition of 'masculine' and 'feminine.'"[1] As a foot soldier in the civil rights and Black power struggles, Bambara saw firsthand how damaging the uncritical acceptance of traditional gender ideology could be. Prevailing gender norms that assign some attributes to men and others to women see men and women as complementing one another and as incomplete and imperfect without the other. These norms of gender complementarity disadvantage many groups, African Americans disproportionately so. Bambara not only challenged these assumptions concerning appropriate behavior for men and women but she also linked this logic to issues of African American empowerment: "I am beginning to see . . . that the usual notions of sexual differentiation in roles is an obstacle to political consciousness, that the way those terms are generally defined and acted upon in this part of the world is a hindrance to full development."[2] Bambara laid it on the line—for African Americans, dominant society's ideas about masculinity and femininity were at best stifling, and, at worst, dangerous for antiracist struggles and social justice projects.

More than thirty years after Bambara's groundbreaking essay, African Americans still struggle with questions of gender within African American antiracist politics, now supplemented by a growing recognition that questions of sexuality may be equally important. Now as then, scientific discourse, mass media, and public policy all depict African Americans as either less able and/or willing to achieve dominant gender ideology. Instead, the images of Black masculinity and Black femininity in contemporary mass media suggest that a reversed and therefore deviant gender ideology hinders African American advancement. The message is simple—African American communities are populated by men who are "too weak" and by women who are "too strong."[3]

Until recently, many African American leaders have argued that Black men and women would be just like middle-class White Americans if they assimilated dominant values (especially those concerning gender) and pursued a politics of respectability.[4] Because the Black Church, one of the mainstays of African American resistance to racial oppression, generally supports conservative analyses of gender and sexuality, it has upheld this line of thought.[5] As the linchpin of African American communal life, the effects of the Black Church can be seen in Black music, fraternal organizations, neighborhood associations, and politics.[6] From its position of authority, the Black Church has shown strong support for the patriarchal family, claiming that men should be the heads of the Church, that women should not be preachers, and that men should rule their families. The Black Church has also been particularly reluctant to challenge Western arguments about sexuality and, instead, has incorporated dominant ideas about the dangers of promiscuity and homosexuality within its beliefs and practices.[7] In this context, American Americans are counseled to accept traditional gender ideology's prescription of complementary gender roles for men and women (strength and weakness), and to believe that, although these gender roles may be more difficult for African Americans to attain, such roles are nonetheless natural and normal.

African Americans who accept the thesis that Black men's and women's failure to achieve normal complementary gender roles adequately explains joblessness, poor school performance, poverty, poor housing, and other social problems often point to the commonsense solution of fixing Black heterosexual relationships and families. Black community norms often back them up by suggesting that strengthening "weak" Black men is the best way to fight racism and to reverse African American poverty. The equally obvious commonsense solution is less often discussed, but lingers under the surface. Within this logic, African American progress also requires weakening "unnaturally strong" Black women.[8] By using Black people's ability to achieve White gender norms as a sign of racial progress, upward social class mobility is increasingly hitched to the wagon of helping Black men gain "strength" within African American families and communities. This view establishes the goal of fixing Black masculinity in the center of a political agenda designed to address Black masculinity's assumed weakness. At the same time, Black women are told that their assertiveness is holding African Americans back, especially men. Sadly, a history of Black female financial independence from men and economic contributions to Black families and communities is increasingly devalued and recast as a problem.

In the context of the new racism, using these arguments to explain African American economic and political disadvantage diverts attention from structural causes for Black social problems and lays the blame on African Americans themselves. Pandering to misogyny within African American communities, new versions of Black gender ideology evolve into one of perpetrator and victim in which African American men are "too weak" *because* African American women are "too strong." Because Black women allegedly have too much strength, they are counseled to "let" Black men lead. Ironically, as Hortense Spillers suggests, "the African-American female's 'dominance' and 'strength' came to be interpreted by later generations—both Black and White, oddly enough—as a 'pathology,' as an instrument of castration."[9] Helping to deflect attention away from the major structural changes of the new racism, African American men and women are encouraged to blame one another for economic, political, and social problems within African American communities.

In the context of the post–civil rights era in which new variations of the "weak men, strong women" thesis have catalyzed gender conflict among African Americans, it is important to stress that African American women and men have a range of choices as to how to respond to dominant gender ideology. Mass media images of Black femininity and Black masculinity present but one social script among many that encourages certain behaviors and discourages others. If Black boys and girls think that being gangstas, athletes, sidekicks, bitches, bad mothers, and mammies are their only options, then this Black gender ideology can foster internalized oppression. Alternately, if African Americans design new conceptions of Black femininity and Black masculinity that reject sexism and heterosexism and that are sensitive to economic, political, and social contours of the new racism, a new and hopefully more progressive Black sexual politics might follow.

In order to develop alternatives to the internal victim-blaming stance advanced within both dominant society and antiracist Black politics, African Americans need to critique the prevailing Black gender ideology. But replacing existing ideas with more progressive conceptions of Black masculinity and Black femininity will be difficult because elite groups have a vested interest in perpetuating ideologies of Black deviancy, including the gendered one analyzed here. Halle Berry and Denzel Washington both won Oscars, but the parts they played drew upon a historical Black gender ideology of Black female sexual promiscuity and Black male corruption and violence. These are the contradictions of the new racism—images of change (winning the Oscars) and stability (the parts they played). White supremacy requires Black subordination, and ideologies that challenge existing power relations will be staunchly resisted.

HEGEMONIC MASCULINITY AND BLACK GENDER IDEOLOGY

Since the 1912 publication of *Tarzan of the Apes*, the first Tarzan novel, the Tarzan myth has not only been immensely popular but it has been a central feature in disseminating ideas about White masculinity. Twenty-four Tarzan novels in all were published, primarily from the 1910s through the 1930s. Over fifty Tarzan films appeared after the first Tarzan movie was released in 1917. As late as 1963, one out of every thirty paperbacks sold was a Tarzan novel.[10] With one infamous yell, Tarzan subdued all the beasts of the jungle and ruled fictional natives who, unlike actual colonized Africans, appeared to welcome colonialism with a smile on their faces. Although Tarzan was a fictional character, his image helps frame ideas about masculinity: "Tarzan has defined himself as a 'man' by his difference from the apes, from blacks, and from females. . . . He needs now to preserve his 'manliness,' his aloneness, figuratively if not literally. He does this through establishing power hierarchies in which all others—and especially blacks and women—are subordinate to him."[11]

Tarzan constitutes one well-known example of how mass media shapes White masculinity within U.S. society. The construction of White masculinity is not confined to fictional images. Whether the composition of the U.S. Senate or executives of global corporations or an American literary canon that glorifies the exploits of pioneers and patriots, elite White men run America. It doesn't matter that, to paraphrase the title of a Hollywood film of the same name, "White men can't jump," because they can make others jump for them. Moreover, because this group so dominates positions of power and authority, the view of masculinity patterned on Tarzan, U.S. senators, corporate executives, and cowboys is well known and is often taken as normal, natural, and ideal. It becomes hegemonic in that the vast majority of the population accepts ideas about gender complementarity that privilege the masculinity of propertied, heterosexual White men as natural, normal, and beyond reproach.[12] In this fashion, elite White men control the very definitions of masculinity, and they use these standards to evaluate their own masculine identities and those of all other men, including African American men.

Hegemonic masculinity is fundamentally a dynamic, relational construct.[13] Because it is constantly tested by the behaviors of others, such masculinity must always be achieved. These relations are not merely interconnected; they reflect the hierarchal power relations of a racialized system of sexism that frames the multiple expressions of masculinity and femininity available to African American men and women, as well as all other groups. In the American context, hegemonic masculinity becomes defined through its difference from and opposition to women, boys, poor and working class men of all races and ethnicities, gay men, and Black men.[14] In other words, hegemonic masculinity is a concept that is shaped by ideologies of gender, age, class, sexuality, and race. Ideas about groups formed within these ideologies, for example, women or LGBT people, constitute an important benchmark for defining a hegemonic masculinity that must constantly construct itself. Without these groups as ideological markers, hegemonic masculinity becomes meaningless.

In the United States, hegemonic masculinity is installed at the top of a hierarchical array of masculinities. All other masculinities, including those of African American men, are evaluated by how closely they approximate dominant social norms. Masculinity itself becomes organized as a three-tiered structure: those closest to hegemonic masculinity, predominantly wealthy White men, but not exclusively so, retain the most power at the top; those men who are situated just below have greater access to White male power, yet remain marginalized (for example, working-class White men and Latino, Asian, and White immigrant men); and those males who are subordinated by both of these groups occupy the bottom (for example, Black men and men from indigenous groups). Moreover, hegemonic masculinity *requires* these marginalized and subordinated masculinities.

Men from varying races, classes, and sexualities jockey for position within this hierarchy of masculinities. For example, like African American men, the vast majority of Latino and Asian American men are excluded from the category of hegemonic masculinity. Instead, they are assigned social scripts of marginalized masculinities, the former because of dedication to family and the latter due to representations of hard work and being a "model minority." Those Latino and Asian American men who falter can be demoted to the subordinated masculinity reserved for African American men. Those who manage to approximate the norms of hegemonic masculinity may enter the inner circle, often as "honorary" elite White men. Not surprisingly, this hierarchy of successful and failed manhood matches up to the White normality/Black deviancy framework that accompanies racism; the heterosexual/homosexual binary that supports heterosexism; structures of age that grant seniority to older males over younger ones; and a class system that grants propertied individuals more power and status than those who lack it.

It is important to stress that *all* women occupy the category of devalued Other that gives meaning to *all* masculinities. Yet, just as masculinities are simultaneously constructed in relation to one another and hierarchically related, femininities demonstrate a similar pattern. Within these crosscutting relationships, Latina, Asian, and Black women routinely inherit social scripts of marginalized and/or subordinated femininities. For example, one study of representations of Latina and Black women in fiction and of Latinas and Blacks who had careers in Hollywood films finds similarities in treatment that illuminate how marginalized and subordinated femininities are constructed.[15] Latinas are routinely presented as members of a conquered people whereas Black women appear as slaves. In this regard, both groups of women symbolize subordinated femininities and share the status of sexual outlaws: "the Latina of conquest fiction is portrayed as the half-breed harlot whose purpose is to pique the male sexual appetite and whose mixed blood elicits similar behavior to that of her Black counterpart, the mulatto."[16] Thus, within hierarchies of femininity, social categories of race, age, and sexual orientation also intersect to produce comparable categories of hegemonic, marginalized, and subordinated femininities.

Black femininity is constructed in relation to the tenets of hegemonic masculinity that subordinates all femininities to masculinity. At the same time, the social power granted to race and class in the United States means that sexism is not an either/or endeavor in which all men dominate all women. Rather, gender norms that privilege men typically play out *within* racial/ethnic and/or social class groups as well as *between* such groups. For example, working-class Latino men may expect obedience from working-class Latinas, yet when both arrive at their jobs, they may be deferential to White employers, male and female. In one sense, Black femininity is the ultimate "other" juxtaposed to hegemonic White masculinity, with poor, young Black lesbians such as fifteen-year-old murder victim Sakia Gunn saddled with an intensified version of costs attached to Black femininity.[17] In contrast, George W. Bush can be a "C" student at Yale University, have a drinking problem, and get elected president of the United States in 2000. He benefits from an intensified version of the privileges of hegemonic masculinity, namely, the privileges of Whiteness, family ties, heterosexuality, and the power that money can buy. Varying combinations of race, class, sexuality, and gender create intermediate positions between these two poles for working-class Black men, middle-class Latinas, poor gay White men, Haitian immigrants, and other groups. As a group, Black men fall between these two poles and many of the contradictions that affect Black manhood reflect this intermediate location. It is important to keep this overarching frame in mind because everyday lived experience is not this neat. Selected individual African American women such as Oprah Winfrey and Condaleezza Rice may wield considerable power and, as individuals, are definitely not oppressed. But for Black women as a class, the concept of a subordinated Black femininity holds sway. Despite the massive media attention given to African American men and women who seem to be exceptions to the rules, Black masculinity and Black femininity thus are both constructed in relation to hegemonic masculinity, a situation that also shapes their relation to one another.

Keeping It "Real": African American Men and Hegemonic Masculinity

Hegemonic masculinity in the United States has several benchmarks. For one, "real" men are primarily defined as *not* being like women. Real men are expected to be forceful, analytical, responsible, and willing to exert authority, all qualities that women seemingly lack. The use of women in the construction of masculinity is so widespread that this dimension of hegemonic masculinity seems hidden in plain sight. For example, boys on American sports teams are routinely ridiculed for "playing like girls." Boys are discouraged from crying "like girls." A major insult hurled at men is that they are "soft" like women. Within this ideological framework, simply being unlike women is not enough. For this version of masculinity to be plausible, men require female validation as constant reminders of male superiority. Otherwise, how would men know that they are not like women if only in the company of men? The irony is that, whereas dependency is typically seen as a female attribute, femininity does not *depend* on males staying in their place. In contrast, men who accept this dimension of dominant gender ideology require control over women (which takes many forms) in order to know that they are "real" men.

Within this logic, men who seem too closely aligned with women, who lack authority with the women of their racial ethnic group and/or social class, or, worst yet, who seem to be dominated by women suffer a loss of manhood. In other words, male dominance occurs within racial/ethnic categories and is one marker of male power. The legacy of seeing women as property or "booty," the spoils of warfare, establishes this theme of needing to exert male authority over at least one woman, typically a girlfriend, wife, or daughter. Representations of Black masculinity within mass media that depict working-class Black men as aggressive thugs or as promiscuous hustlers seem designed to refute accusations that Black men are "weak" because they cannot control Black women. If "real" men are those who can control women, then these representations suggest that Black men can shake the stigma of weakness by dominating unnaturally strong Black women. Being strong enough to "bring a bitch to her knees" becomes a marker of Black masculinity. Moreover, trying to exert male dominance over women places African American men and women in an adversarial relationship. Women who do not let men be men become blamed for Black male behavior. Abusive men routinely blame their partners for their own violent behavior—if she had been more of a woman (submissive), she would have let him be more of a man.[18]

Another dimension of hegemonic masculinity is that "real" men exercise control not just over women but also over their own emotions, in leadership positions, and over all forms of violence. In other words, exercising male authority is a vital component of masculinity. Yet men's access to the apparatuses of authority and violence differs depending on their social location within race and social class hierarchies. White men exercise violence within a wide array of social settings and possess legitimate authority over the mechanisms of violence. For example, elite White men run military and police forces—they have the authority to set policies concerning the legitimate use of force while erasing their own culpability for wars and other violent outcomes. Propertied White males also control the forums of symbolic violence within U.S. society, for example, sports and mass media (television, film, and music).[19] From the Revolutionary War to the 2003 War in Iraq, poor and working-class White men have joined or been drafted into military service. These men may carry the guns, but they also enforce policies that often were made without their input.

In contrast, because so many African American men lack access to the forms of political and economic power that are available to elite White men, the use of their bodies, physicality, and a form of masculine aggressiveness become more important. Black men experience violence, often at the hands of other Black men. Working-class and poor Black men have access to street weapons and their own bodies as weapons. Rather than expressing masculine authority by running corporations or holding high-level government positions, Black men search for respect from marginal social locations. Sociologist Elijah Anderson suggests that in economically depressed neighborhoods affected by drugs and crime, interpersonal violence among young African American men reflects a desperate search for respect. Possession of respect—an indicator of male authority and manhood—is highly valued. As Anderson points out, "the code of the street emerges where the influence of the police ends and personal responsibility for one's safety is felt to begin, resulting in a kind of 'people's law,' based on 'street justice.' . . . In service to this ethic, repeated displays of 'nerve' and 'heart' build or reinforce a credible reputation for vengeance that works to deter aggression and disrespect, which are sources of great anxiety on the inner-city street."[20] In the context of the closing door of opportunity of the post–civil rights era, the often-explosive interactions among African American men on the street become more comprehensible.

Boys constitute yet another benchmark used to construct hegemonic masculinity. "Real" men do not resemble or behave like immature, irresponsible males (boys) who have not yet been properly socialized into the responsibilities and benefits of adult masculinity. Physical appearance distinguishes men from boys. Men are muscular and have facial and body hair. In contrast, boys are still hairless and physically weaker. Boys are quasi women. Moreover, unlike men who have had sexual intercourse with adult women, primarily by genital penetration, boys remain sexual virgins.

Sexual intercourse with a woman initiates them into manhood. Boys are also financially dependent on others—they do not hold jobs and are not expected to support any dependents. Moreover, just as less powerful men are pressured to submit to dominant ones (e.g., criminals to cops and factory workers to managers), boys are expected to submit to adult male authority, most notably, their fathers. Within this age-stratified male drama, boys become men by submitting to adult male authority and by trying to become like their fathers. Conversely, men who lack fathers or access to male authority organized through patriarchy suffer a distinct disadvantage in hierarchies of masculinity.

Viewing people of African descent as being like children has a long history within Western culture, and, within the United States, treating African American men as boys constitutes a gender-specific manifestation of it. The use of the term *boy* in the segregated South to humiliate and demean adult Black men gave voice to this portion of hegemonic masculinity that needed Black boys to give it meaning. Western colonialism and slavery contain numerous examples of efforts to infantalize men of African descent. The Tarzan novels and movies provide one of the most visible and enduring examples of how ideologies of hegemonic masculinity needed and were constructed on the backs of men of African descent conceptualized as "boys" or "boy servants." From images of Uncle Tom and Uncle Ben to the sidekicks within contemporary popular culture, Black men have been depicted as immature men, if not actual boys.

Recognizing this history, African American men have responded with various strategies, with varying degrees of success. Black men's visibility within basketball, rap, and hip-hop culture has provided a new and highly visible cultural arena for reasserting an adult Black masculinity and rejecting the traditional "boy" status reserved for Black men. The "bad boys" of basketball are so "bad" that they can self-define as "boys" with little fear of being mistaken for them. The media spectacles of Latrell Sprewell choking his coach, Charles Barkley refusing to be a role model, Mike Tyson biting off part of an opponent's ear, and legions of crotch-grabbing young rappers who glare angrily at the camera, proclaiming their manhood, seemingly reject any efforts to treat them like children. They reject the discourse of Black sidekicks and sissies as the route for White acceptance and as a path to adult masculinity and claim media space to argue that there is another way to be Black, male, and adult.

Possessing property and the power that it commands operates as yet another benchmark of hegemonic masculinity. There are definite social class dimensions to hegemonic masculinity—"real" men are not financially dependent on others, but instead support others. They take responsibility for their families by getting married and financially supporting their wives and children. They are neither sexual renegades running from one woman to another nor pimps and hustlers who expect women to support them. Historically, working-class men lobbied for an adequate "family wage" that would enable them to support their wives and children.[21] Unemployed and underemployed working-class and poor men who fail to meet these criteria of masculinity are depicted as irresponsible, and the number of children they father with their unmarried partners provides evidence for their sexual irresponsibility and refusal to grow up. Talk shows operate as contemporary morality plays to showcase and censure poor and working-class men, many of whom are Black, who refuse to assume their financial obligations. At the same time, shows like *The Cosby Show* mask how difficult it actually is for a Black man (or woman) to become a doctor and to make enough money to purchase a New York City brownstone and support a wife and five children in style.

Being heterosexual constitutes another important benchmark of hegemonic masculinity—"real" men are also *not* gay or homosexual. In this construction of hegemonic masculinity, gay men mark the contradictions that plague male heterosexuality itself: "heterosexual men must deny desire except for the gendered Other, while making a hated Other of the men who desire them."[22] Gay men are belittled because they are seen as being like women, the stereotypical view of gay men as being "sissies," "faggots," or effeminate men. This relation between heterosexual and homosexual men carries heavy symbolic weight in the context of contemporary Western masculinity. To many people, because "homosexuality is a negation of masculinity . . . homosexual men must be effeminate."[23]

Heterosexual African American men are extremely protective of this dimension of their manhood, often resorting to violence if they feel threatened. Stereotyping Black gay men as effeminate and weak, even though the majority of Black gay men do not fit this profile, becomes an important factor in constantly asserting Black male heterosexuality. In essence, Black gay men become the ultimate weak men under the "weak men/strong women" thesis.[24] Their visibility symbolizes the Black community's collective weakness.

Finally, race itself plays an important part as a benchmark in constructing the hegemonic masculinity that defines "real" men in the United States. Black men, *by definition*, cannot be real men, *because they are Black*. The fact of Blackness excludes Black men from participating fully in hegemonic masculinity because, if they do so, they decenter the assumed Whiteness of those installed in the center of the definition itself. Within the father-son family drama of American masculinity, White fathers cannot or will not claim their Black sons. This interracial relationship violates the basic taboo of racial purity that has long characterized American society. The best that Black men can do is to achieve an "honorary" membership within hegemonic masculinity by achieving great wealth, marrying the most desirable women (White), expressing aggression in socially sanctioned arenas (primarily as athletes, through the military, or law enforcement), and avoiding suggestions of homosexual bonding.

Work That Body: African American Women and Hegemonic Femininity

As a group, women are subordinated to men, yet a pecking order among women also produces hegemonic, marginalized, and subordinated femininities. This ideology proscribes behavior for *all* women based on these assumptions, and then holds all women, including African American women, to standards that only *some* women (including many White ones) may be able to achieve. All women engage an ideology that deems middle-class, heterosexual, White femininity as normative. In this context, Black femininity as a subordinated gender identity becomes constructed not just in relation to White women, but also in relation to multiple others, namely, all men, sexual outlaws (prostitutes and lesbians), unmarried women, and girls. These benchmarks construct a discourse of a hegemonic (White) femininity that becomes a normative yardstick for all femininities in which Black women typically are relegated to the bottom of the gender hierarchy.

One benchmark of hegemonic femininity is that women *not* be like men. Maintaining an appropriately feminine demeanor invokes two standards, one physical and the other behavioral. Because women in Western societies are judged by their physical appearance more so than men, women should not resemble men. The appearance of women's bodies is subject to sustained scrutiny, and the way that women work their bodies (adorn them, carry them, use them sexually, use them to produce children, or alter them through cosmetic surgery) constitutes an important criterion for evaluating femininity. On a basic biological level, the presence of breasts, hips, a round booty, and the absense of muscles and facial hair become important indicators of womanhood that distinguish women from men, boys, and girls. Women need not actively earn femininity to the degree required of masculinity, for example, having sex with a woman, bringing home a paycheck, or demonstrating athletic prowess. Instead, women wait passively, depend on physical maturation, and hope that the adult female bodies they receive will meet social approval.[25]

Because femininity is so focused on women's bodies, the value placed on various attributes of female bodies means that evaluations of femininity are fairly clearcut. Within standards of feminine beauty that correlate closely with race and age women are pretty or they are not. Historically, in the American context, young women with milky White skin, long blond hair, and slim figures were deemed to be the most beautiful and therefore the most feminine women. Within this interpretive context, skin color, body type, hair texture, and facial features become important dimensions of femininity. This reliance on these standards of beauty automatically render the majority of African American women at best as less beautiful, and at worst, ugly. Moreover, these standards of female beauty have no meaning without the visible presence of Black women and others who fail to measure up. Under these feminine norms, African American women can never be as beautiful as White women because they never become White.

In this context of the new color-blind racism, the significance attached to skin color, especially for women, is changing. In response to the growing visibility of biracial, multiracial, Latino, Asian, and racially ambiguous Americans, skin color no longer serves as a definitive mark of racial categorization. Rejecting historical rules whereby an individual with "one drop" of "black blood" was seen as Black, the new multiracial America uses more fluid racial categories. For many Black women, Blackness can be "worked" in various ways. For example, light-skinned Halle Berry is biracial and projects a certain kind of beauty that is not purely Black. She self-identifies as an African American woman but her film career suggests that she can work her body in various ways. Berry played many Black women before her Oscar-winning performance in *Monster's Ball*. For example, in *Losing Isaiah* (1995), she plays a Black mother on crack, and in *Bulworth* (1998) she plays a streetwise confidant to a White politician. In contrast, in *Xmen* (2000) and *Swordfish* (2001) Berry plays characters in which White or Latino actresses could just as easily have been cast. In contrast to Halle Berry, who can work her biracial appearance in many ways, darker-skinned actresses such as Alfre Woodard and Angela Bassett have far fewer options.

Hair texture, a female feature that is far more malleable, also matters greatly in re-creating femininity in the context of the new color-blind racism. Because a good deal of women's beauty is associated with their hair, this aspect of women's physical appearance takes on added importance in the process of constructing hierarchies of femininity. As Banks suggests, "the 'good hair' and 'bad hair' distinction is probably the most indelible construction of hair that occupies the psyche of African Americans."[26] Some authors claim that hair texture has long been more important than skin color in racial politics. For example, in his exhaustive cross-cultural analysis of slavery, Orlando Patterson contends that dominant groups usually perform elaborate rituals on their subordinates. Shearing of hair is a key part of rituals of domination cross-culturally. Patterson points out, "it was not so much color differences as differences in hair type that become critical as a mark of servility in the Americas."[27] To explain this pattern, Patterson contends that hair provides a clearer and more powerful badge of status than skin color. Differences between Whites and Blacks were sharper in hair quality than in color and persisted much longer with miscegenation. Patterson notes, "Hair type rapidly became the real symbolic badge of slavery, although like many powerful symbols, it was disguised . . . by the linguistic device of using the term 'black,' which nominally threw the emphasis to color."[28] Raine, one of the participants in Banks's study, agrees with this position, and explains how ideas about "good hair" and "bad hair" articulate with ideas about skin color:

> Blacks are judged on their hair. I think basically the long, straight hair people are more favorable. The shorter, kinkier, nappier [the] hair, the less favoritism is shown. I've lived that, coming through school as a young girl I was dark, but I had long hair. I was put in with the little light [skin] long-haired kids. But the ones who had the short, measly, nappy hair, no matter what they looked like, they were always last, in the back.[29]

Hair increases in importance in a society where biracial, multiracial, and racially ambiguous individuals become more visible within a racially heterogeneous society. Moreover, because hair is seen as a badge of beauty for women, this physical feature becomes more central in constructing hierarchies of femininity than is the case for men.

Maintaining an appropriately feminine demeanor constitutes another dimension of trying *not* to be like men. Women can also avoid the stigma of being judged too masculine by avoiding so-called male characteristics. Women are expected to defer to men, and those women who project a submissive demeanor allegedly receive better treatment than those who do not. This theme of female submissiveness permeates the public sphere of labor market practices and government office-holding in which nurses defer to doctors, teachers to principals, and secretaries to managers. Despite a new legal structure that provides equal opportunities to girls and boys, job categories remain gender segregated. The theme of female submissiveness also shapes private, domestic sphere activities of family and community. Well-functioning families adhere to this allegedly natural authority structure that fosters female submissiveness. Women with the appropriate demeanor should remain safely sequestered in private homes and community endeavors, thus allowing men to engage in appropriately masculine behaviors of work and leadership in the public sphere.[30]

As was the case for hegemonic masculinity, there are numerous mass media examples of White women who model the art of submissiveness. The women need not have submissive personalities; they only need to recognize the boundaries of White male authority. For example, the depiction of White women in Tarzan novels and films illustrates how White women are depicted as needing (to submit to) male protection. As Tarzan's helpmate, the fictional character of Jane is an adventuresome, energetic White woman. Jane has spunk—she lives in Africa among wild animals and African natives. Jane's formal education ties her more closely to European civilization than Tarzan, and because she is a woman, she represents the civilizing influence of femininity both in the home and in the jungle itself. In the context of wild, uncivilized space, Jane keeps home and hearth functioning. She also needs White male protection. The treatment of White women like Jane in the Tarzan novels demonstrates female dependency. White women are repeatedly abducted in the Tarzan novels, on average three times per woman per novel. When the triple abduction occurs, the first abductor is usually a renegade European, the second either an Arab or an African, and the third an ape.[31]

Black women have long struggled with the behavioral dimensions of femininity whereby the very characteristics of femininity were neither possible nor desirable. African American writer Gloria Naylor encapsulates the contradictions that accompany Black women's inability to be submissive and the effects that this had on family and relationships:

> We need to speak of submissiveness. That was never in the cards for us. . . . Whether in the cotton fields of the South or the factories of the North, Black women worked side by side with men to contribute to the welfare of the family. This did not mean that men were demeaned and unloved, but it did mean that women had a voice about the destiny of their families. That independence and resiliency were admired because they aided in the collective survival when society made it difficult for Black men to find work. But when we began to internalize Euro-American values, then Black women were no longer "real" women—and of course only a real woman would love or be loved by a man.[32]

As controlling images of Black femininity, the bitch and bad Black mother both present the unassimilated, working-class Black woman as unacceptable, primarily because she lacks appropriate female qualities of submissiveness. Mass media ideologies hold out solutions to this seeming problem of working-class Black female assertiveness—either become more like the middle-class modern mammies (assertive in defense of White authority while remaining submissive to it) or aspire to become Black ladies.

Being appropriately heterosexual constitutes another important benchmark of hegemonic femininity. In a context of male dominance, heterosexual men's access to women's bodies as sexual partners constitutes an important component of hegemonic femininity. Appropriately feminine women should be married to heterosexual male partners and dedicated to sexually pleasing them. Women's actual sexual behavior within the sanctity of heterosexual marriage is less important than adhering to male-defined norms about who controls women's sexuality. Sex workers, women who control their own sexuality and who take money for sexual favors, and lesbians, women who reject heterosexual male partners, are judged as being less feminine women. When it comes to the male prerogative of access to women's bodies and sexuality, sex workers and lesbians both behave like men because they (and not men) control their own sexuality.

African American women have been stigmatized with both dimensions of seemingly deviant sexuality. Historically, Black women have been constructed as sexually immoral women, with the recurring image of the Black prostitute and, more recently, that of the Black lesbian serving as anchors for a deviant Black female sexuality that defeminizes Black women. Take, for example, how Black women are routinely typecast as prostitutes in contemporary mass media. From network television to feature films, when prostitutes are depicted, typically one or more are African American. By depicting Black lesbians as "mannish," mass media representations also show lesbians as being less feminine Black women. Queen Latifah's portrayal of Cleo in the film *Set It Off* exemplifies the "mannish" Black lesbian who exudes qualities of dominance. In the film, Cleo is big, muscular, dominates her female partner, and is physically threatening. This depiction of the "mannish" lesbian flows into perceptions of dark-skinned, big-boned Black women as being less feminine and more "mannish."[33]

Another marker of hegemonic femininity concerns the significance of work and marriage in accessing income and wealth. The higher the status of a woman, the less likely she is to work, and the more likely she is to be married and have access to income generating property. Her job is to run the family. Moreover, the behavioral norm of female submissiveness counsels married women to become mothers. Motherhood within family and male authority not only becomes another behavioral marker of whether a woman is appropriately submissive to male authority, it becomes essential to the economic survival of the heterosexual, nuclear family. Women may not earn salaries, but they produce legitimate heirs for the intergenerational transmission of property. There are definite class dimensions of hegemonic femininity—women should seek out good marriages that will provide them with economic security. Therefore, women's true femininity remains contingent on their legally sanctioned relationship to men.

Black women have had great difficulty "catching" wealthy men to marry, sharing their marital assets, and passing on marital property to their children.[34] Because the family structure of African Americans has diverged from social norms, achieving this benchmark of hegemonic femininity has been virtually impossible. The financial necessity that sent Black women to work outside the home since emancipation enabled various patterns of female authority and subordination to emerge within African American families. In essence, Black women were not financially subordinated within African American families and communities and, as a result, were deemed to be less feminine because they had to work. African American women's behavior as workers violated the assumptions of hegemonic femininity. For one, Black women did hard labor as agricultural workers or as domestic workers. The type of work that they did made it difficult to see them as fragile, ornamental, or beautiful. Because they were employed outside the home and brought home their own independent income, they seemingly usurped Black male authority within Black families. Their incomes were not supplemental—their income was essential to family survival. Black women also became mothers without benefit of marriage, and they maintained families on their own when men left.[35]

Finally, race itself plays an important part as a benchmark in constructing hegemonic femininity. Black women, by definition, cannot achieve the idealized feminine ideal because the fact of Blackness excludes them. Dominant gender ideology provides a social script for Black women whereby everyone else needs Black women to be on the bottom for everything else to make sense. Just as hegemonic White masculinity occupies the most desired social script, an equally hegemonic Black femininity organized via images of bitches, bad mothers, mammies, and Black ladies coalesce to mark the least desirable form of femininity.

REDEFINING BLACK GENDER IDEOLOGY— UNCOUPLING STRENGTH FROM DOMINANCE

Whether hegemonic masculinity or femininity, or the Black gender ideology that comprises their opposite, most African Americans try to craft meaningful lives within the confines of existing gender norms. Yet because they lack realistic opportunities to be seen as "real" men and women, the pressures Black people face to see themselves through the lens of mass media's Black sexual stereotypes affects every aspect of everyday life. Domestic violence, the decline of marriage, the spread of HIV/AIDS, substance abuse, adolescent pregnancy, and similar social issues all reflect, in large part, the damage done by prevailing Black sexual politics. Social issues such as these cannot be solved by government action alone. Each requires alternative definitions of Black masculinity and Black femininity that might spark different self-definitions, interpersonal relationships, and social practices within African American community politics.

Despite this need, for ordinary African Americans, coping with hegemonic gender ideology can be so demanding that generating alternatives can seem virtually impossible. But the importance of this task cannot be underestimated because African American survival may depend on it. One important task lies in rejecting dominant gender ideology, in particular, its use of the thesis of "weak men, strong women" as a source of Black social control. Because hegemonic masculinity equates strength with dominance, an antiracist politics must challenge this connection. Within this project, *the fundamental premise of any progressive Black gender ideology is that it cannot be based on someone else's subordination*. This means that definitions of Black masculinity that rely on the subordination of Black women, poor people, children, LGBT people, or anyone else become invalid. Definitions of Black femininity that do not challenge relations of sexism, economic exploitation, age, heterosexism, and other markers of social inequality also become suspect. Rather than trying to be strong within existing gender ideology, the task lies in rejecting a gender ideology that measures masculinity and femininity using gendered definitions of strength.

In this endeavor to craft a more progressive Black gender ideology, African American men and women face similar yet distinctive challenges. The task for African American men lies in developing new definitions of masculinity that uncouple strength from its close ties to male dominance. Good Black men need not rule their families with an iron hand, assault one another, pursue endless booty calls, and always seem to be "in control" in order to avoid the sigma of weakness. The task for African American women lies in redefining strength in ways that simultaneously enable Black women to reclaim historical sources of female power, yet reject the exploitation that has often accompanied that power. Good Black women need not be stoic mules whose primary release from work and responsibility comes once a week on Sunday morning. New definitions of strength would enable Black men and women alike to be seen as needing and worthy of one another's help and support without being stigmatized as either overly weak or unnaturally strong.

Currently, the thesis of "weak men, strong women" operates to the detriment of African Americans in three primary areas, namely, dominance in the political economy whereby wealthy White men dominate everything on a global scale; dominance in the sexual system whereby White hetero-sexual men set sexual norms and judge everyone else using these standards; and physical dominance associated with athletic prowess, aggressiveness, and violence. Redefining a Black gender ideology requires understanding how dominance operates in each of these three areas and uncoupling strength from its close association with dominance. Moreover, while the need to redefine Black gender ideology affects men and women alike, because masculinity is so intertwined with questions of dominance, Black masculinity becomes an especially important site of change.

Dominance in the Political Economy

Redefining Black gender ideology requires uncoupling the definition of strength from its current association with male dominance of jobs, wealth, and political power. Definitions of strength need to be much broader than the narrow equation of strength with financial well-being, especially, financial well-being gained through profiteering and inherited family wealth. Because neither Black men nor women control much in the global capitalist political economy, any "strength" in this area that either has is more illusory than real. With the exception of a handful of wealthy African Americans, the majority of people of African descent, regardless of gender, have been harmed by the corporate irresponsibility of globalization. Most are disproportionately poor and powerless. Given this context, it makes little sense for African American men to blame African American women for being too "strong" (holding down jobs and making money) and for women to blame men for being too "weak" (having difficulty finding jobs). The real problem and its solutions lie elsewhere.

The new racism constitutes a continuation of past-in-present forms of racial oppression, yet contemporary African Americans seem to have greater difficulty seeing how the fallacy of the "weak men, strong women" thesis compromises Black economic development strategies. For example, under conditions of Jim Crow segregation, Black men's chronic unemployment and Black women's ability to get more steady but less-well-compensated jobs were seen as one *outcome* of racial oppression. Black men were not routinely blamed for being less masculine or "weak" if their jobs paid them less than a family wage or if they were excluded altogether from the good jobs that did. If Black women found work in domestic service and/or ended up heading families on their own, they were not blamed for their self-reliance and resourcefulness and labeled as too "strong." Their efforts to provide for their families and children were valued. Clearly, *individual* African American men and women were lazy or bossy, but *collectively*, it was clear that race and gender discrimination were the root causes of African American economic and political disadvantage.[36] Black men and women did not adhere to traditional gender roles because they could not. Structural factors associated with prior forms of racism, such as discrimination in employment, housing, education, and citizenship rights helped explain the outcome.

Not much has changed under the new racism. Job flight, mechanization, poor schools, and lingering job discrimination all mean that Black men and Black women still cannot achieve the norms of hegemonic masculinity (strong men who support their families) and femininity (dependent women who rely on male income). But, because the new racism is organized differently than in the past, many African Americans cannot see the structural causes of African American disadvantage that foster disparate economic effects for men and women. For example, during the post–civil rights era, poor and working-class African American men experienced growing rates of permanent unemployment and underemployment that made it even more difficult to bring home a "family wage." Many African American men work in the informal labor market, primarily the global drug industry, as an alternative to employment in the formal labor market. Many have prison records as convicted felons, a stigma that disqualifies Black men from the franchise and thus precludes many men from invoking their voting rights as citizens to change labor laws and criminal justice procedures.[37] The convergence of these factors renders African American men less able to provide financial support for their wives and children. As a result, Black men can be viewed as irresponsible "boys" who do not fulfill their obligations as men whereas White men are "real" men because they do.

These same social conditions pressure poor and working-class African American women to take up the slack by finding work in low-paying, often dead-end service sector jobs and/or by demanding that the state provide them with the same benefits afforded to White women. For women who cannot make a living wage, social welfare policies have been as intrusive in their lives as have those of the criminal justice system in the lives of Black men. Moreover, Black women who take up the slack can be perceived as masculinized because their financial independence (albeit in poverty) is seen as usurping a masculine prerogative. Finding themselves as single parents, often at a young age, they cannot become the submissive partners trumpeted within dominant gender ideology. Instead, they become labeled as "bitches," "bad mothers," "matriarchs," and "welfare mothers," terms that blame them for taking responsibility. Such women are also vulnerable to economic exploitation by Black male hustlers. Because they do not have a man in the house and are women alone, some men expect them to pay for male company. The circle is complete—bad mothers produce irresponsible boys; adult men behaving as if they were irresponsible boys make poor romantic partners and absent fathers; and this dysfunctional Black family yields unruly, undisciplined Black children.

The fallacy of the "weak men, strong women" thesis is that it counsels Black men and women to embrace unrealistic strategies for dealing with the economic exploitation and political disempowerment of dominance. Confronted with a barrage of opinion that counsels men to look for work, it becomes difficult to see how elusive good jobs are in the postindustrial economy. This idea of African American men as inherently lazy and unwilling to work is so deeply ingrained within American culture that, as recently as 1997, a major sociology journal published an article titled "Are Young Black Men Really Less Willing to Work?"[38] The arguments that the author advances in the article make sense only in the context of a public that assumes Black male malingering to be a plausible thesis to investigate. On the one hand, the obvious answer of "no, they are not less willing to work" fits within the pseudo-liberal framework of American sociology. The obverse idea, namely, that young Black men are so culturally damaged that they don't want to work would have been unacceptable. However, at the same time, the author clearly identifies the White public as the reference group who would believe such ideas in the first place: "according to survey data, a growing number of Whites believe that discrimination is no longer a salient issue and that the persistence of racial inequality is due rather to Blacks' disposition," he observes.[39] Only in the United States could a paper whose thesis is "Black men aren't lazy" get published, primarily because it challenges dominant ideas that they are.

Black men's inability to find well-paying work that would allow them to support their families encourages far too many to leave. They may be saving their pride, but the children and female partners that they leave behind sorely miss them. Historically, many Black men worked at jobs that were beneath them—the college-educated Pullman porters come to mind—because they valued their partners and their families more than their pride. Why should today be any different? Definitions of masculinity that would enable Black men to see their worth in more than a steady paycheck would create space for new ideas for Black male strength. "Weak" Black men are those who desert their families, as opposed to the "strong" ones who stay, even if they cannot earn a living wage. Economic contributions to a family's well-being take many forms that go beyond bringing home a big paycheck.

Ironically, Black gender ideology that explains father absence through this victim-blaming model misses how Black men are doubly victimized when they become disconnected from family networks, all in the name of saving male pride. Despite the fact that families headed by Black women are not inherently inferior, the absence of men in the lives of their children constitutes a real loss for African American families. Male children may express this loss more forcefully (at least in the media), but its effects are profound for girls as well. The meaning of father absence for Black boys circulates throughout Black popular culture. From the television show *Good Times* through works as disparate as the choreography of Bill T. Jones and the music of Tupac Shakur, African American men comment on the pain that many feel at their inability to be fathers to their own children (beyond biological coupling) and not having had fathers of their own when they were young. Only by acknowledging this loss and by beginning to take responsibility for each and every child that they father, can they start the healing process.[40] Those who don't remain trapped in a derogated space of irresponsible, deadbeat dads.

The "weak men, strong women" thesis can also have equally insidious financial implications for African American women. High rates of Black poverty that leave one-third of African Americans impoverished and close to one-half of Black children officially classified as poor are unlikely to decline if Black women decided not to work. Becoming submissive and more feminine will not put food on the table. For African American women, the problem with strength coupled with dominance lies less in their needing to work than in how their "unnatural strength" has been derogated within existing gender ideology. Black women who carry a heavy load can end up being exploited by those who are closest to them. The depiction of Black women as tireless workers, both in the paid labor market and the unpaid reproductive labor of the family, reinforces views of African American women as the Strong Black Woman (SBW). As one of the few positive images used to describe Black femininity, the valorization of women's strength in African American communities makes it difficult for Black women to reject exploitative work and simply walk away from responsibility, especially from their families.

This valorization of strength coupled with the economic exploitation of Black women's paid labor and unpaid labor for their families sets up a curious set of relationships. Black men may desire those Black women who make them feel more "manly," that is, whose appearance and demeanor more closely approximate that of pretty White women. Yet these same men were often raised by strong Black mothers and also may depend on their girlfriends and mothers of their children for financial support. They *need* these strong Black women to ensure their physical survival, yet neither value them nor see them as feminine.[41] This establishes a dangerous situation that encourages Black men to become abusive toward the women who many see as controlling their lives. As hustlers who live off of women's money, these irresponsible boys develop hyper-masculine identities and use a Black male promiscuity to economically exploit Black and White women.

An alternative gender ideology that took seriously African American men's and women's placement in the global capitalist political economy would challenge these relations. If anything, heterosexual African American men and women might consider pooling their resources, no matter who earned them, in support of relationships and family units. Any family form that provided economic support for African American children, for example, gay and lesbian families, families that incorporated grandparents, cousins, and "fictive" kin, and heterosexual women or men who teamed up to purchase property together, would be valued, not maligned because it failed to measure up to some predetermined gender norms.

Economic dependency would be neither glorified for women nor demonized for men. Such dependency would not be a state of being, permanently assigned either to women who feel more feminine when they have access to a man's income or men who feel more masculine when women take care of them because they control women and their money. Men and women alike need to know that receiving support is not the same as being weak, submissive, or failing to support African American children, families, or communities. Dependency and vulnerability would not be gender specific. Those who could, would lead. Those who needed support would get it. Talent and need, not gender, would determine political and economic behavior.

When it comes to survival in the American political economy, all Black people suffer when an African American man refuses to do "women's work" or when an African American woman waits for a man to pay her bills. Everybody has to pitch in, and any gender ideology that gets in the way of collective financial success is itself part of the problem.

Sexual Dominance

A second dimension of redefining Black gender ideology requires uncoupling definitions of strength from sexual dominance and sexual exploitation. In a context that denies African American men and women access to wealth and power, sexuality can become important to both, but for different reasons. Promiscuity has been an important idea attributed to people of African descent. As the prominence of the bitches and gangstas, bad Black mothers and hustlers within Black popular culture suggests, ideas about Black sexuality have been repackaged and circulate widely. The very scope of these images implies that sexuality will serve as an important site of dominance, both racial dominance of Blacks by Whites, gender dominance of women by men, and heterosexual dominance of LGBT people by heterosexuals. Redefining Black gender ideology requires understanding and challenging how sexuality, dominance, and exploitation affect men and women differently.

For men, sexual dominance associated with the phallus becomes an important indicator of masculinity in a culture that places barriers in other areas of achievement. James Baldwin was one of the first authors to grapple with the significance of Black men's sexuality and the penis to American perceptions of Black masculinity: "I think that I know something about the American masculinity which most men of my generation do not know because they have not been menaced by it in the way that I have been. It is still true, alas, that to be an American Negro male is also to be a kind of walking phallic symbol: which means that one pays, in one's own personality, for the sexual insecurity of others."[42] The emphasis on Black men's bodies, when sexualized, becomes reduced to a focus on the Black male penis as a distillation of the essence of Black masculinity. Beliefs that reduce Black men to their penises, especially penises that are not under the control of White men, created space for the myth of the Black rapist in postemancipation Jim Crow South, and the myth of Black men's need for booty calls within contemporary Black popular culture.

This theme of reducing Black men to the penis reappears in contemporary mass media in high and low art alike. For example, cultural critic Kobena Mercer claims that the photographs of renowned photographer Robert Mapplethorpe invoke this deep taproot of Black male sexual prowess created within Western imaginations.[43] Mapplethorpe's exhibitions often raised controversy, primarily due to the depiction of gay sadomasochistic (S/M) rituals and of nude Black male bodies. Mercer notes that the photographs of gay male S/M rituals invoke an alternative sexuality that consists of *doing* something. In contrast, Black men are "confined and defined their very *being* as sexual and nothing but sexual, hence hypersexual."[44] Mapplethorpe's *Man in Polyester Suit* is especially exemplary in that the photograph eliminates all identifying features of masculinity except hands (objects to service Whites) and an exposed Black penis (sexuality).[45] In this way, the image of the man in polyester suit (itself a commodity used to sell the book of photography) reduces Black men to images of fragmented, commodified body parts.

This view of Black masculinity leaves very little room for other options. Take, for example, the emergence of a Down Low (DL) sexual subculture among Black gay and bisexual men in the last decade that fails to challenge the assumptions of hyper-heterosexuality. Black men living on the Down Low live ostensibly heterosexual lives, complete with wives and girlfriends, and also engage in secret relationships with men. As journalist Benoit Denizet-Lewis points out, "today, while there are black men who are openly gay, it seems that the majority of those having sex with men still lead secret lives, products of a black culture that deems masculinity and fatherhood as a black man's primary responsibility—and homosexuality as a white man's perversion."[46] For men on the DL, masculinity that is so intertwined with hyper-heterosexuality renders an openly gay identity impossible.

Those African American men who rely upon ideas of Black sexual prowess to define Black masculinity, especially Black heterosexual prowess, typically need women in order to actualize this type of masculinity. Whether having multiple sexual partners, dominating one partner within a domestic relationship, fathering children by many women as a mark of virility, or living a Black gay sexuality on the Down Low, men who understand their masculinity as residing in their penises require repeated reassurance that they are men. For African American men, uncoupling ideas of male strength as expressed through sexuality and virility from this system of sexual dominance is one important part of redefining Black gender ideology. Without constant struggle against these connections, Black men will continue, to paraphrase James Baldwin, to pay, through their own personalities, for "the sexual insecurity of others."

The use of ideas about Black women's promiscuity in structuring ideas about Black women's strength takes a different yet related path. On one level, the racialized battle for sexual dominance of women among men affects Black women. Historically, one mark of African American progress lay in protecting Black women from the predatory sexual advances of White men.[47] But what does protection mean in the context of the new racism? Many Black women may be shielded from the sexual harassment and assaults of White men, but they are now more vulnerable to those of Black men because hypersegregated Black ghettos are immense and Black community institutions have eroded within them.[48] In the context of the violence visited upon Black men as a collectivity, many Black women choose to support Black men at all costs. Whether granting sexual favors, ignoring Black male abuse, or caring for children with little help from their "baby's daddy," Black women have learned to become the Strong Black Woman (SBW). Being a SBW often means enduring abuse, namely, physical, emotional, and sexual harassment. Moreover, for many Black women, the institution of motherhood has become a primary site where the SBW representation holds sway. Many arrive home tired from working two jobs, only to find children and grandchildren asking for money, expecting free childcare, or looking for a place to stay. Ironically, despite mass media's negative assessment of Black motherhood for poor and working-class Black women, motherhood remains valued by the majority of Black women. Through motherhood, they exercise strength, demonstrate power, and, as a result, often suffer the consequences associated with this commitment.

A certain degree of freedom is afforded those African American women who reject traditional gender ideology of the ornamental, passive female whose sexuality should be placed in service to the men of her racial, ethnic, and/or social class group. Black hip-hop feminists' challenges to the Strong Black Woman (SBW) persona reject traditional Black gender ideology and encourage us to think differently about Black women's bodies as an important step in reclaiming Black women's sexuality as a site of agency and pleasure. Lisa Jones suggests that Black women's sense of fashion and style speaks to the freedom that can accrue to those women who realize that they are no longer confined by categories: "For black women without access to the room of one's own to make leisure-time art, our bodies, our style becomes the canvas of our cultural yearning. It has been, in recent history, not just a place or self-mutilation, but of healing."[49] Yet waiting on the other side of this freedom is a cast of sexual stereotypes that derogate free, powerful, strong women. Despite compelling reasons to do so, sometimes what is comfortable makes more sense than jumping out into the unknown. It may be even more difficult for Black women to relinquish the few hard-earned benefits that do exist simply because they are so few. The willingness of African American women to continue to claim the sexual domination and economic exploitation that can accompany the Strong Black Woman identity reflects this dilemma.

An alternative gender ideology that uncoupled strength from notions of sexual dominance and exploitation would challenge these relations. In essence, challenging dominant Black gender ideology requires developing new understandings of Black sexuality that rejects perceptions of Black promiscuity (both hyper-heterosexual and homosexual). One promising path in uncoupling strength from sexual dominance may lie in looking beyond the narrow confines of the sexually repressive culture of the United States and investigating non-Western forms of sexual expression. Unfortunately, one legacy of the colonial experience itself is that we know far less about sexualities within precolonial African societies and within indigenous societies of other non-Western peoples than we do about British, French, Portuguese, Spanish, and Dutch perceptions of such sexualities. But what can be gleaned is suggestive. Despite the common experiences of racial oppression visited upon peoples of African descent in Latin America, the Caribbean, the United States, and continental Africa, African and African-influenced societies often retained elements of

African cultures. Despite considerable heterogeneity, when it comes to African understandings of the body generally and sexuality in particular, several commonalities exist: the open expression of strong feelings and emotions; being more at ease with sensuality and eroticism as aspects of use of the body; openness about use of body both through appearance and movement; a comfort level with sexual expression both within and outside of marriage; and a commitment to spirituality that mandates its expression in everyday life.[50] The celebration of fertility has also influenced the sexual practices of African-influenced societies, fostering a strong emphasis on heterosexual genital sexuality that is seen as being critical to the survival of society. At the same time, some indigenous societies have also been tolerant of what is now seen as homosexuality. Drawing upon ideas such as these as part of the process of redefining sexuality may forge a path for redefining Black gender ideology in the American context.

Physical Dominance

Redefining Black gender ideology requires uncoupling definitions of strength from its current association with physical dominance, namely, muscular might, aggressiveness, and violence. Physical dominance and aggressiveness have become especially intertwined with contemporary ideas about Black masculinity. The use of physical force, aggression, and violence as tools of subordination creates problems within African American communities in three areas. Specifically, for African American men whose power within the broader political economy remains compromised, violence against other men (often under the guise of homophobic violence), violence against women, and violence against younger Black people, especially children (often under the guise of being authoritarian father figures) constitutes a triad of male aggression and violence that is damaging to everyone. These three areas are interconnected, and they also intersect with dominance in the political economy and with sexual dominance. Black women certainly can be aggressive and violent, especially toward Black children. But the source of physical dominance lies in ideas about Black masculinity that in turn is situated within a larger context of hegemonic masculinity. Rethinking Black gender ideology requires changing these gender-specific practices.

It is important to recognize that many of the tensions that surround Black masculinity, in this case, the aggressiveness and violence that has come to characterize Black men's relations with one another, reflect the greatly changed social environment in the 1980s and 1990s. The growth of a prison industrial complex that incarcerated large numbers of young African American men had an important influence on American and African American societies.[51] Not only is American society more violent and infused with a masculine ethos of aggressiveness and confrontation, Black men are more aggressive within this context. In particular, the arrest and imprisonment of Black street gangs, many of whose members were involved in the drug industry, fostered more pronounced and organized gang structures within prisons. Prison gangs inevitably became connected to their street gang counterparts (in fact, many join gangs while in prison, primarily for protection). As the line between street gangs and prison gangs blurred, so did the distinctions among prison culture, street culture, and some aspects of Black youth culture.[52] Multiple forms of incarceration (the racially segregated neighborhoods that constitute the prison of racism and the actual incarceration of young Black men themselves), poverty, sexual dominance, and maintaining heterosexuality at all costs become intricately intertwined. The valorization of thug life within Black youth culture, the growing misogyny within heterosexual love relationships, and the increased visibility (and some would say the increased virulence) of homophobic violence targeted to gay, lesbian, and bisexual African Americans all seem to be related to the incarceration of African American men and the ceaseless need to prove one's "manhood." This nexus of street, prison, and youth cultures generates a tremendous amount of pressure on Black men, especially young, working-class men, to avoid being classified as "weak."

Given this social context, it will be extremely difficult to convince Black men that they should renounce aggression and violence. In a predatory climate created by prison, street, and some elements of Black youth culture, being perceived as "weak" could get you killed. A more pragmatic approach might be to develop some ground rules concerning the appropriate use of that force. An important first step may lie in legitimating certain forms of Black male aggression and violence, for example, in self-defense when faced by a bona fide (as opposed to imagined) enemy or by protecting others who cannot defend themselves. Young Black women who are being harassed on the street or stalked by their boyfriends might appreciate Black male intervention to stop that violence. In the same vein, other forms of Black male aggression and violence might receive universal censure. Violence against women remains a major problem within African American communities, yet few Black organizations speak out against it. Engaging in unprovoked attacks on gay men or homosexual couples is no show of strength that makes attacker more "manly." It may be difficult to uncouple ideas about Black male strength from notions of aggression and violence, but placing Black male strength in service to community might catalyze much-needed changes.

Halle Berry and Denzel Washington may have won Oscars for their performances, but neither of the parts that they played so well unsettles prevailing Black gender ideology let alone charts new paths. Currently, we have no models that have all of the answers, only parts of a puzzle that is yet to be solved. African American director John Singleton's 2001 film *Baby Boy* provides one important piece by beginning to unpack the complexities of Black masculinity and Black femininity. Singleton's story examines why the twenty-year-old protagonist Jody (played by Tyrese Gibson) fears leaving home. Jody is still living in his thirty-six-year-old mother's house, and his ability to build an independent life for himself is profoundly constricted by a perception of Black manhood that keeps him financially dependent on his mother (her baby boy) yet claiming that, as the man of the house, he will defend her from her new live-in boyfriend. Jody exercises his "manhood" primarily through sexual dominance of Black women, primarily his relationships with the mothers of his two children. Jody is a casualty of masculine violence—his older brother was murdered and this tragedy shaped all aspects of Jody's life, including his difficulties in growing up and becoming a man. Singleton does a good job of exploring the problem—we understand how prevailing views of Black masculinity and femininity affect all of the characters in the film. However, Singleton's solution of having Jody leave boyhood behind by marrying one of his baby's mammas is far too simple. In the end, we see this new family happy, playing in the park, and awaiting the arrival of another baby. In real life, no neat formulas exist that provide the instant happy ending of *Baby Boy*. Rather, to meet the very necessary challenge of redefining Black gender ideology, we may have to find our own way.

PART III

TOWARD A PROGRESSIVE BLACK SEXUAL POLITICS

SEVEN

ASSUME THE POSITION
The Changing Contours
of Sexual Violence

At the center of the table sat a single microphone, a
glass of water, and a name card: "Professor Anita Hill."
I sat down at the lone chair at the table. . . . In front of
me, facing me and the bank of journalists, was the
Senate Judiciary Committee—fourteen white men
dressed in dark gray suits. I questioned my decision to
wear bright blue linen, though it hadn't really been a
decision; that suit was the only appropriate and clean
suit in my closet when I hastily packed for Washington
two days before. In any case, it offered a fitting
contrast.[1]

By now, the outcome of Anita Hill's 1991 testimony at the confirmation hearings of Supreme Court Justice Clarence Thomas
is well known. In a calm, almost flat manner and before a
packed room that contained twelve family members, including
both of her parents, Hill recounted how Thomas had sexually
harassed her when he headed the Equal Employment
Opportunity Commission ten years earlier. Although she
passed a lie detector test, her testimony did not affect the
upshot of the hearings. The Senate Judiciary Committee simply did not believe her. Hill was no match for the fourteen
White men in dark gray suits, many of whom had made up their
minds before hearing her testimony. Thomas's opportunistic
claim that the senators were engaged in a "high-tech lynching"

sealed the outcome. Because lynching had been so associated with the atrocities visited upon Black men, it became virtually impossible for the senators to refute Thomas's self-presentation without being branded as racists. The combination of male dominance and the need to avoid any hint of racism made the choice simple. Believing Thomas challenged racism. Doubting Thomas supported it. Thomas won. Hill lost.[2]

But was it really this simple? Certainly not for African Americans. For Black women and men, the Thomas confirmation hearings catalyzed two thorny questions. Why did so many African Americans join the "fourteen white men dressed in dark gray suits" and reject Hill's allegations of sexual harassment? Even more puzzling, why did so many African Americans who believed Anita Hill criticize her for coming forward and testifying? Critical race theorist Kimberlé Crenshaw offers one reason why the hearings proved to be so difficult: "In feminist contexts, sexuality represents a central site of the oppression of women; rape and the rape trial are its dominant narrative trope. In antiracist discourses, sexuality is also a central site upon which the repression of Blacks has been premised; the lynching narrative is embodied as its trope. (Neither narrative tends to acknowledge the legitimacy of the other)."[3]

Crenshaw joins a prestigious group of African American women and men who, from Ida B. Wells-Barnett through Angela Davis, have examined how discourses of rape and lynching have historically influenced understandings of race, gender, and sexuality within American society.[4] In American society, sexual violence has served as an important mechanism for controlling African Americans, women, poor people, and gays and lesbians, among others. In the post-emancipation South, for example, institutionalized lynching and institutionalized rape worked together to uphold racial oppression. Together, lynching and rape served as gender-specific mechanisms of sexual violence whereby men were victimized by lynching and women by rape. Lynching and rape also reflected the type of binary thinking associated with racial and gender segregation mandating that *either* race *or* gender was primary, but not both. Within this logic of segregation, race and gender constituted separate rather than intersecting forms of oppression that could not be equally important. One was primary whereas the other was secondary. As targets of lynching as ritualized murder, Black men carried the more important burden of race. In contrast, as rape victims, Black women carried the less important burden of gender.

African American politics have been profoundly influenced by a Black gender ideology that ranks race and gender in this fashion. Lynching and rape have not been given equal weight and, as a result, social issues seen as affecting Black men, in this case lynching, have taken precedence over those that seemingly affect only Black women (rape). Within this logic, lynchings, police brutality, and similar expressions of state-sanctioned violence visited upon African American men operate as consensus issues within African American politics.[5] Lynching was not a random act; instead, it occurred *in public*, was sanctioned by government officials, and often served as a unifying event for entire communities. In this sense, lynching can be defined as ritualized murder that took a particular form in the postemancipation South. In that context, through its highly public nature as spectacle, lynching was emblematic of a form of institutionalized, ritualized murder that was visited upon Black men in particular. African American antiracist politics responded vigorously to the public spectacle of lynching by protesting against it as damage done to Black men as representatives of the "race."[6] Because African American men were the main targets of this highly public expression of ritualized murder, the lynching of Black men came to symbolize the most egregious expressions of racism.

In contrast, the sexual violence visited upon African American women has historically carried no public name, garnered no significant public censure, and has been seen as a crosscutting gender issue that diverts Black politics from its real job of fighting racism. Black women were raped, yet their pain and suffering remained largely invisible. Whereas lynching (racism) was public spectacle, rape (sexism) signaled *private* humiliation. Black male leaders were not unaware of the significance of institutionalized rape. Rather, their political solution of installing a Black male patriarchy in which Black men would protect "their" women from sexual assault inadvertently supported ideas about women's bodies and sexuality as men's property. Stated differently, Black women's suffering under racism would be eliminated by encouraging versions of Black masculinity whereby Black men had the same powers that White men had long enjoyed.

By 1991, the Thomas confirmation hearings made it painfully obvious that these antiracist strategies of the past were no match for the new racism. Ranking either lynching or rape as more important than the other offered a painful lesson about the dangers of choosing race over gender or vice versa as the template for African American politics. What is needed is a progressive Black sexual politics that recognizes not only how important both lynching and rape were in maintaining historical patterns of racial segregation but that also questions how these practices may be changed and used to maintain the contemporary color-blind racism. Rather than conceptualizing lynching and rape as either race or gender-specific mechanisms of social control, another approach views institutionalized rape and lynching as *different* expressions of the *same* type of social control. Together, both constitute dominance strategies that uphold the new racism. Both involve the threat or actual physical violence done to the body's exterior, for example, beating, torture, and/or murder. Both can involve the threat of or actual infliction of violence upon the body's interior, for example, oral, anal, or vaginal penetration against the victim's will. Both strip victims of agency and control over their own bodies, thus aiming for psychological control via fear and humiliation. Moreover, within the context of the post–civil rights era's desegregation, these seemingly gender-specific forms of social control converge. Stated differently, just as the post–civil rights era has seen a crossing and blurring of boundaries of all sorts, lynching and rape as forms of state-sanctioned violence are not now and never were as gender-specific as once thought.

REVISITING THE FOUNDATION: LYNCHING AND RAPE AS TOOLS OF SOCIAL CONTROL

Lynching and rape both served the economic needs of Southern agriculture under racial segregation. In the American South during the years 1882 to 1930 the lynching of Black people for "crimes" against Whites was a common spectacle—mob violence was neither random in time nor geography. Like many other violent crimes, lynchings were more frequent during the summer months than in cooler seasons, a reflection of the changing labor demands of agricultural production cycles.[7] One function of lynchings may well have been to rid White communities of Black people who allegedly violated the moral order. But another function was to maintain control over the African American population, especially during times when White landowners needed Black labor to work fields of cotton and tobacco.

Lynching also had political dimensions. This tool of gendered, racial violence was developed to curtail the citizenship rights of African

American men after emancipation. Because Black women could not vote, Black men become targets for political repression. Explaining the power of lynching as a spectacle of violence necessary to maintain racial boundaries and to discipline populations, literary critic Trudier Harris describes the significance of violence to maintaining fixed racial group identities:

> When one Black individual dared to violate the restrictions, he or she was used as an example to reiterate to the entire race that the group would continually be held responsible for the actions of the individual. Thus an accusation of rape could lead not only to the accused Black man being lynched and burned, but to the burning of Black homes and the whipping or lynching of other Black individuals as well.[8]

This is why lynchings were not private affairs, but were public events, often announced well in advance in newspapers: "To be effective in social control, lynchings had to be visible, with the killing being a public spectacle or at least minimally having the corpse on display for all to witness. Whereas a murder—even a racially motivated one—might be hidden from public scrutiny, lynchings were not."[9]

The ritualized murders of lynching not only worked to terrorize the African American population overall but they also helped to install a hegemonic White masculinity over a subordinated Black masculinity. Lynching symbolized the type of violence visited upon African American men that was grounded in a constellation of daily micro-assaults on their manhood that achieved extreme form through the actual castration of many Black male lynch victims. Although Black women were also lynched, Black men were lynched in far greater numbers. Thus, lynching invokes ideas of Black male emasculation, a theme that persists within the contemporary Black gender ideology thesis of Black men as being "weak."[10] The myth of Black men as rapists also emerged under racial segregation in the South. Designed to contain this newfound threat to White property and democratic institutions, the sexual stereotype of the newly emancipated, violent rapist was constructed on the back of the Black buck. No longer safely controlled under slavery, Black men could now go "buck wild."

Wide-scale lynching could only emerge after emancipation because murdering slaves was unprofitable for their owners. In contrast, the institutionalized rape of African American women began under slavery and also accompanied the wide-scale lynching of Black men at the turn of the twentieth century. Emancipation constituted a continuation of actual practices of rape as well as the shame and humiliation visited upon rape victims that is designed to keep them subordinate. Black domestic workers reported being harassed, molested, and raped by their employers.[11] Agricultural workers, especially those women who did not work on family farms, were also vulnerable. In the South, these practices persisted well into the twentieth century. For example, in the 1990s, journalist Leon Dash interviewed Washington, D.C. resident Rosa Lee. It took many conversations before Lee could share family secrets of stories of sexual abuse that had occurred in rural North Carolina. Because the experiences were so painful, she herself had learned about them only in bits and pieces from stories told to her by her grandmother and aunt. Rosa Lee came to understand the harsh lives endured by her mother Rosetta and her grandmother Lugenia at the bottom of the Southern Black class structure. Describing how White men would come and look over young Black girls, Rosa Lee recounted her family's stories:

> "You could tell when they wanted something. They all would come out there. Come out there in the field while everybody was working. And they're looking at the young girls. Her mouth. Teeth. Arms. You know, like they're looking at a horse. Feeling her breasts and everything. The white men would get to whispering."
>
> "And the mothers let them men do that?" Rosa Lee asked her grandmother.
>
> "What the hell do you think they could do?" Lugenia answered. "Couldn't do nothing!"[12]

The overseers apparently preferred light-skinned Black girls, often the children of previous rapes, but dark-skinned girls did not escape White male scrutiny. In exchange for the girls, mothers received extra food or a lighter load. The costs were high for the girls themselves. Because Rosetta developed early, her mother tried to hide her when the men came. But after a while, it was hopeless. Rosetta did not escape the rapes:

> "Your mama was put to auction so many times," Lugenia told Rosa Lee. "They just kept wanting your mother." The overseers would

assign the girls they wanted sexually to work in isolated parts of the
farm, away from their families. The girls would try to get out of the
work detail. "It never worked," Lugenia said. "Those men always got
them."[13]

Lugenia continued her tale by sharing how two White overseers had raped
her when she was fourteen, and how two of her daughters, including
Rosetta, had suffered the same fate. Only one daughter was spared,
"because she was so fat," explained Lugenia. As for the children who were
conceived, they were left with their mothers. Once a girl was pregnant, she
was generally never bothered again. As Lugenia recalled: "They only
wanted virgins. . . . They felt they'd catch diseases if they fooled with any
girl that wasn't a virgin."[14]

These social practices of institutionalized lynching and institutionalized rape did not go uncontested. Ida B. Wells-Barnett's antilynching work
clearly rejected both the myth of the Black male rapist as well as the thesis
of Black women's inherent immorality and advanced her own highly controversial interpretation.[15] Not only did Wells-Barnett spark a huge controversy when she dared to claim that many of the sexual liaisons between
White women and Black men were in fact consensual, she indicted White
men as the actual perpetrators of crimes of sexual violence *both* against
African American men (lynching) *and* against African American women
(rape). Consider how her comments in *Southern Horrors* concerning the
contradictions of laws forbidding interracial marriage place blame on
White male behavior and power: "the miscegenation laws of the South
only operate against the legitimate union of the races: they leave the white
man free to seduce all the colored girls he can, but is death to the colored
man who yields to the force and advances of a similar attraction in white
women. White men lynch the offending Afro-American, not because he is
a despoiler of virtue, but because he succumbs to the smiles of white
women."[16] In this analysis, Wells-Barnett reveals how ideas about gender
difference—the seeming passivity of women and the aggressiveness of
men—are in fact deeply racialized constructs. Gender had a racial face,
whereby African American women, African American men, White women,
and White men occupied distinct race/gender categories within an overarching social structure that proscribed their prescribed place. Interracial
sexual liaisons violated racial and gender segregation.

Despite Wells–Barnett's pioneering work in analyzing sexual violence through an intersectional framework of race, gender, class, and sexuality, African American leaders elevated race over gender.[17] Given the large numbers of lynchings from the 1890s to the 1930s, and in the context of racial segregation that stripped all African Americans of citizenship rights, this emphasis on antilynching made sense. Often accused of the crime of raping White women, African American men were lynched, and, in more gruesome cases, castrated. Such violence was so horrific that, catalyzed by Ida B. Wells–Barnett's tireless antilynching crusade, and later taken up by the NAACP and other major civil rights organizations, antilynching became an important plank in the Black civil rights agenda.

In large part due to this advocacy, lynchings have dwindled to a few, isolated albeit horrific events today. This does not mean that the use of lynching as a symbol of American racism has abated. Rather, Black protest still responds quickly and passionately to contemporary incidents of lynching and/or to events that can be recast through this historic framework. For example, the 1955 murder of fourteen-year-old Emmett Till in Mississippi was described in the press as a lynching and served as an important catalyst for the modern civil rights movement. The 1989 murder of sixteen-year-old Yusef Hawkins in the Bensonhurst section of New York City also was described as a lynching. When Hawkins and three friends came to their neighborhood to look at a used car, about thirty White youths carrying bats and sticks (one with a gun) immediately approached them. Furious that the ex-girlfriend of one of the group members had invited Black people to her eighteenth birthday party, the White kids thought that Hawkins and his friends were there for the party and attacked them, shooting Hawkins dead. In 1998, three White men in Jasper, Texas, chained a Black man named James Byrd, Jr. to a pick-up truck and dragged him to his death, an event likened to a modern-day lynching. Events such as these are publicly censured as unacceptable in a modern democracy. These modern lynchings served as rallying cries for the continuing need for an antiracist African American politics.

Unfortunately, this placement of lynching at the core of the African American civil rights agenda has also minimized the related issue of institutionalized rape. Even Ida Wells-Barnett, who clearly saw the connections between Black men's persecution as victims of lynching and Black women's vulnerability to rape, chose to advance a thesis of Black women's rape through the discourse on Black men's lynching. In the postbellum period, the rape of free African American women by White men subsisted as a "dirty secret" within the *private* domestic spheres of Black families and of Black civil society. Speaking out against their violation ran a dual risk—it reminded Black men of their inability to protect Black women from White male assaults and it potentially identified Black men as rapists, the very group that suffered from lynching. The presence of biracial Black children was tangible proof of Black male weakness in protecting Black women and of Black women's violation within a politics of respectability. Because rapes have been treated as crimes against women, the culpability of the rape victim has long been questioned. Her dress, her demeanor, where the rape occurred, and her resistance all become evidence for whether a woman was even raped at all. Because Black women as a class emerged from slavery as collective rape victims, they were encouraged to keep quiet in order to refute the thesis of their wanton sexuality. In contrast to this silencing of Black women as rape victims, there was no shame in lynching and no reason except fear to keep quiet about it. In a climate of racial violence, it was clear that victims of lynching were blameless and murdered through no fault of their own.

Because the new racism contains the past-in-present elements of prior periods, African American politics must be vigilant in analyzing how the past-in-present practices of Black sexual politics also influence contemporary politics. Clarence Thomas certainly used this history to his advantage. Recognizing the historical importance placed on lynching and the relative neglect of rape, Thomas successfully pitted lynching and rape against one another for his gain and to the detriment of African Americans as a group. Shrewdly recognizing the logic of prevailing Black gender ideology that routinely elevates the suffering of Black men as more important than that of Black women, Thomas guessed correctly that Black people would back him no matter what. If nothing else comes of the Thomas hearings, they raise the very important question of how sexual violence that was a powerful tool of social control in prior periods may be an equally important factor in the new racism.

African Americans need a more progressive Black sexual politics dedicated to analyzing how state-sanctioned violence, especially practices such as lynching (ritualized murder) and rape, operate as forms of social control. Michel Foucault's innovative idea that oppression can be conceptualized as normalized war *within* one society as opposed to between societies provides a powerful new foundation for such an analysis.[18] Mass media images of a multiethnic, diverse, color-blind America that mask deeply entrenched social inequalities mean that open warfare on American citizens (the exact case that lynching Black men presented in the past), is fundamentally unacceptable. Many Americans were horrified when they saw the 1992 videotape of Rodney King being beaten by the Los Angeles police. Fictional attacks on Black men in movies are acceptable, assaults on real ones, less so. Managing contemporary racism relies less on visible warfare between men than on social relations among men and between women and men that are saturated with relations of war. In this context, rape as a tool of sexual violence may increase in importance because its association with women and privacy makes it an effective domestic tool of social control. The threat of rape as a mechanism of control can be normally and routinely used against American citizens because the crime is typically hidden and its victims are encouraged to remain silent. New configurations of state-sanctioned violence suggest the workings of a rape culture may affect not just Black women but also Black men far more than is commonly realized. Given the significance of these tools of social control, what forms of sexual violence do African American women and men experience under the new racism? Moreover, how do these forms draw upon the ideas and practices of lynching and rape?

AFRICAN AMERICAN WOMEN AND SEXUAL VIOLENCE

Racial segregation and its reliance on lynching and rape as gender-specific tools of control have given way to an unstable desegregation under the new racism. In this context, the sexual violence visited upon African American women certainly continues its historical purpose, but may be organized in new and unforeseen ways. The terms *institutionalized rape* and *rape culture* encompass the constellation of sexual assaults on Black womanhood. From the sexual harassment visited upon Anita Hill and Black women in the workplace to sexual extortion to acquaintance, marital, and stranger rapes to how misogynistic beliefs about women create an interpretive framework that simultaneously creates the conditions in which men rape women and erase the crime of rape itself to the lack of punishment meted out by the state to Black women's rapists, sexual violence is much broader than any specific acts. Collectively, these practices comprise a rape culture that draws energy from the ethos of violence that saturates American society. African American essayist Asha Bandele describes the persistent sexual harassment she experienced during her teenaged years as part of growing up in a rape culture: "although the faces may have changed, and the places may have also, some things could always be counted on to remain the same: the pulling, and grabbing, and pinching, and slapping, and all those dirty words, and all those bad names, the leering, the propositions."[19] It is important to understand how a rape culture affects African American women because such understanding may help with antirape initiatives. It also sheds light on Black women's reactions to sexual violence, and it demonstrates how this rape culture affects other groups, namely, children, gay men, and heterosexual men.

Rape is part of a system of male dominance. Recall that hegemonic masculinity is predicated upon a pecking order among men that is dependent, in part, on the sexual and physical domination of women. Within popular vernacular, "screwing" someone links ideas about masculinity, heterosexuality, and domination. Women, gay men, and other "weak" members of society are figuratively and literally "screwed" by "real" men. Regardless of the gender, age, social class, or sexual orientation of the recipient, individuals who are forcibly "screwed" have been "fucked" or "fucked over." "Freaks" are women (and men) who enjoy being "fucked" or who "screw" around with anyone. Because the vast majority of African American men lack access to a Black gender ideology that challenges these associations, they fail to see the significance of this language let alone the social practices that it upholds. Instead, they define heterosexual sex acts within a framework of "screwing" and "fucking" women and, by doing so, draw upon Western ideologies of Black hyper-heterosexuality that defines Black masculinity in terms of economic, sexual, and physical dominance. In this interpretive context, for some men, violence (including the behaviors that comprise the rape culture) constitutes the next logical step of their male prerogative.

Currently, one of the most pressing issues for contemporary Black sexual politics concerns violence against Black women at the hands of Black men. Much of this violence occurs within the context of Black heterosexual love relationships, Black family life, and within African American social institutions. Such violence takes many forms, including verbally berating

Black women, hitting them, ridiculing their appearance, grabbing their body parts, pressuring them to have sex, beating them, and murdering them. For many Black women, love offers no protection from sexual violence. Abusive relationships occur between African American men and women who may genuinely love one another and can see the good in each other as individuals. Black girls are especially vulnerable to childhood sexual assault. Within their families and communities, fathers, stepfathers, uncles, brothers, and other male relatives are part of a general climate of violence that makes young Black girls appropriate sexual targets for predatory older men.[20]

Because Black male leaders have historically abandoned Black women as collective rape victims, Black women were pressured to remain silent about these and other violations at the hands of Black men. Part of their self-censorship certainly had to do with reluctance to "air dirty laundry" in a White society that viewed Black men as sexual predators. As Nell Painter points out, "because discussion of the abuse of Black women would not merely implicate Whites, Black women have been reluctant to press the point."[21] Until recently, Black women have been highly reluctant to speak out against rape, especially against Black male rapists, because they felt confined by the strictures of traditional Black gender ideology. Describing herself and other Black women rape victims as "silent survivors," Charlotte Pierce-Baker explains her silence: "I didn't want my nonblack friends, colleagues, and acquaintances to know that I didn't trust my own people, that I was afraid of black men I didn't know. . . . I felt responsible for upholding the image of the strong black man for our young son, *and* for the white world with whom I had contact. I didn't want my son's view of sex to be warped by this crime perpetrated upon his mother by men the color of him, his father, and his grandfathers."[22] African American women grapple with long-standing sanctions within their communities that urge them to protect African American men at all costs, including keeping "family secrets" by remaining silent about male abuse.[23]

Black women also remain silent for fear that their friends, family, and community will abandon them. Ruth, a woman who, at twenty years old, was raped on a date in Los Angeles, points out: "You can talk about being mugged and boast about being held up at knife point on Market Street Bridge or something, but you can't talk about being raped. And I know if I do, I can't count on that person ever being a friend again. . . . People have one of two reactions when they see you being needy. They either take you under their wing and exploit you or they get scared and run away. They abandon you."[24] Black women recount how they feel abandoned by the very communities that they aim to protect, if they speak out. Theologian Traci West describes how the very visibility of Black female rape victims can work to isolate them: "When sexual violation occurs within their families or by any member of 'their' community, black women may confront the profound injury of being psychically severed from the only source of trustworthy community available to them. Because of the ambiguities of their racial visibility, black women are on exhibit precisely at the same time as they are confined to the invisible cage."[25]

Contemporary African American feminists who raise issues of Black women's victimization must tread lightly through this minefield of race, gender, and sex. This is especially important because, unlike prior eras when White men were identified as the prime rapists of Black women, Black women are now more likely to be raped by Black men.[26] Increasingly, African American women have begun to violate long-standing norms of racial solidarity counseling Black women to defend Black men's actions at all costs and have begun actively to protest the violent and abusive behavior of some African American men. Some African American women now openly identify Black men's behavior toward them as abuse and wonder why such men routinely elevate their own suffering as more important than that experienced by African American women: "Black women do not accept racism as the reason for sorry behavior—they have experienced it firsthand, and for them it is an excuse, not a justification."[27]

Since 1970, African American women have used fiction, social science research, theology, and their writings to speak out about violence against Black women.[28] Many African American women have not been content to write about sexual violence—some have taken to the streets to protest it. Determined not to duplicate the mistakes made during the Thomas confirmation hearings, many Black women were furious when they found out that a homecoming parade had been planned for African American boxer and convicted rapist Mike Tyson upon his release from prison. The Mike Tyson rape case catalyzed many Black women to challenge community norms that counseled it was a Black women's duty as strong Black women to "assume the position" of abuse. Within this logic, a Black woman's ability to absorb mistreatment becomes a measure of strength that can garner praise. In efforts to regulate displays of strong Black womanhood, some Black people apparently believed that prominent Black men like Mike Tyson were, by virtue of their status, incapable of sexual harassment or rape. "Many apparently felt that Washington [Tyson's victim] should have seen it as her responsibility to endure her pain in order to serve the greater good of the race," observes cultural critic Michael Awkward.[29] Rejecting this position that views sexual violence against Black women as secondary to the greater cause of racial uplift (unless, of course, sexual violence is perpetrated by White men), Black women in New York staged their own counterdemonstration and protested a homecoming celebration planned for a man who had just spent three years in prison on a conviction of rape.

ASSUME THE POSITION: BLACK WOMEN AND RAPE

Rape is a powerful tool of sexual violence because women are forced to "assume the position" of powerless victim, one who has no control over what is happening to her body. The rapist imagines absolute power over his victim; she (or he) is the perfect slave, supine, legs open, willing to be subdued or "fucked," and enjoying it. Rape's power also stems from relegating sexual violence to the private, devalued, domestic sphere reserved for women. The ability to silence its victims also erases evidence of the crime. These dimensions of rape make it a likely candidate to become an important form of social control under the new racism.

We have learned much from African American women both about the meaning of rape for women and how it upholds systems of oppression. For one, female rape victims often experience a form of posttraumatic stress disorder, a rape trauma syndrome of depression, anxiety, and despair, with some attempting suicide that affects them long after actual assaults. Women who survived rape report effects such as mistrust of men or of people in general, continued emotional distress in connection with the abuse, specific fears such as being left alone or being out at night, and chronic depression that lasted an average of five and a half years after the assault.[30] This climate harms all African American women, but the damage done to women who survive rape can last long after actual assaults. Yvonne, who was molested by an "uncle" when she was eight and raped at age twelve, describes how the rape and sexual molestation that she endured as a child affected her subsequent attitudes toward sexuality: "I didn't take pride in my body after the rape. After it happened, I became a bit promiscuous. . . . Everyone *thought* I was bad; so I thought, I should just *be* bad. After the rape it was like sex really didn't matter to me. It didn't seem like anything special because I figured if people could just take it, . . . if they just had to have it enough that they would take a little girl and put a knife to her neck and *take* it, . . . that it had nothin' to do with love."[31] Yolanda's experiences show how as an act of violence, rape may not leave the victim physically injured—emotional damage is key. The rape itself can temporarily destroy the victim's sense of self-determination and undermines her integrity as a person. Moreover, when rape occurs in a climate that already places all Black women under suspicion of being prostitutes, claiming the status of rape victim becomes even more suspect.

Black women are just as harmed by sexual assault as all women, and may be even more harmed when their abusers are African American men within Black neighborhoods. Gail Wyatt's research on Black women's sexuality provides an important contribution in furthering our understanding of Black women and rape.[32] Wyatt found little difference in the effects of rape on Black and White women who reported being rape victims. One important finding concerns the effects of *repeated* exposure to sexual violence on people who survive rape: "Because incidents of attempted and completed rape for Black women were slightly more likely to be repeated, their victimization may have a more severe effect on their understanding of the reasons that these incidents occurred, and some of these reasons may be beyond their control. As a consequence, they may be less likely to develop coping strategies to facilitate the prevention rather than the recurrence of such incidents."[33] Stated differently, African American women who suffer repeated abuse (e.g., participate in a rape culture that routinely derogates Black women more than any other group) might suffer more than women (and men) who do not encounter high levels of violence, especially sexual violence, as a daily part of their everyday lives. For example, being routinely disbelieved by those who control the definitions of violence (Anita Hill), encountering mass media representations that depict Black women as "bitches," "hoes," and other controlling images, and/or experiencing daily assaults such as having their breasts and buttocks fondled by friends and perfect strangers in school, the workplace, families, and/or on the streets of African American communities may become so routine that African American women cannot perceive their own pain.

Within the strictures of dominant gender ideology that depict Black women's sexuality as deviant, African American women often have tremendous difficulty speaking out about their abuse because the reactions that they receive from others deters them. Women may be twice victimized— even if they are believed, members of their communities may punish them for speaking out. As Yvonne points out, "where I lived in the South, any time a black woman said she had been raped, she was never believed. In my community, they always made her feel like she did something to deserve it—or she was lying."[34] Adrienne, a forty-year-old Black woman who had been raped twice, once by a much older relative when she was seven and again by her mother's boyfriend when she was twelve, observes, "Black woman tend to keep quiet about rape and abuse . . . If you talk about it, a man will think it was your fault, or he'll think less of you. I think that's why I never told the men in my life, because I've always been afraid they would not look at me in the same way. We all live in the same neighborhood. If something happens to you, *everybody* knows."[35]

One important feature of rape is that, contrary to popular opinion, it is more likely to occur between friends, loved ones, and acquaintances than between strangers. Black women typically know their rapists, and they may actually love them. Violence that is intertwined with love becomes a very effective mechanism for fostering submission. In a sense, Black women's silences about the emotional, physical, and sexual abuse that they experience within dating, marriage, and similar love relationships resembles the belief among closeted LGBT people that their silence will protect them. Just as the silence of LGBT people enables heterosexism to flourish, the reticence to speak out about rape and sexual violence upholds troublesome conceptions of Black masculinity. Within the domestic sphere, many Black men treat their wives, girlfriends, and children in ways that they would never treat their mothers, sisters, friends, workplace acquaintances, or other women. Violence and love become so intertwined that many men cannot see alternative paths to manhood that do not involve violence against women. Black feminist theologian Traci C. West uses the term "domestic captivity" to describe women who find themselves in this cycle of love and violence: "Although they are invisible, the economic, social, and legal barriers to escape that entrap women are extremely powerful. This gendered denial of rights and status compounds the breach with community. Being confined in a cage that seems invisible to everyone else nullifies a woman's suffering and exacerbates her isolation and alienation."[36]

As Barbara Omolade observes, "Black male violence is even more poignant because Black men both love and unashamedly depend on Black women's loyalty and support. Most feel that without the support of a 'strong sister' they can't become 'real' men."[37] But this may be the heart of the problem—if African American men need women to bring their Black masculinity into being, then women who seemingly challenge that masculinity become targets for Black male violence. Educated Black women, Black career women, Black women sex workers, rebellious Black girls, and Black lesbians, among others who refuse to submit to male power, become more vulnerable for abuse. Violence against "strong" Black women enables some African American men to recapture a lost masculinity and to feel like "real" men. By describing why he continued to financially exploit women, and why he hit his girlfriend, Kevin Powell provides insight into this process:

> I, like most Black men I know, have spent much of my life living in fear.
> Fear of White racism, fear of the circumstances that gave birth to me,
> fear of walking out my door wondering what humiliation will be mine
> today. Fear of Black women—of their mouths, their bodies, of their
> attitudes, of their hurts, of their fear of us Black men. I felt fragile,
> fragile as a bird with clipped wings, that day my ex-girlfriend stepped
> up her game and spoke back to me. Nothing in my world, nothing in
> my self-definition prepared me for dealing with a woman as an equal.
> My world said women were inferior, that they must, at all costs, be put
> in their place, and my instant reaction was to do that. When it was over,
> I found myself dripping with sweat, staring at her back as she ran bare-
> foot out of the apartment.[38]

Powell's narrative suggests that the connections among love, sexuality, and violence are much more complicated that the simple linear relation-ship in which African American men who are victimized by racism use the power that accrues to them as men to abuse African American women (who might then use their power as adults to beat African American chil-dren). Certainly one can trace these relations in love relationships, but the historical and contemporary interconnections of love, sexuality, violence, and male dominance in today's desegregated climate are infinitely more complex.

In these contexts, it may be possible for African American women and men to get caught up in a dynamics of love, sexuality, and dominance whereby the use of violence and sexuality resemble addiction. In other words, if Black masculinity and Black femininity can be achieved only via sexuality and violence, sexuality, violence, and domination become implicated in the very definitions themselves. Once addicted, there is no way to be a man or a woman without staying in roles prescribed by Black gender ideology. Men and women may not engage in open warfare, but they do engage in mutual policing that keeps everyone in check. As a form of sexual violence, actual rapes constitute the tip of the iceberg. Rape joins sexuality and violence as a very effective tool to routinize and normalize oppression.

The effectiveness of rape as a tool of control against Black women does not mean that they have escaped other forms of social control that have disproportionately affected Black men. Working jobs outside their homes heightens African American women's vulnerability to other forms of state-sanctioned violence. For example, Black women are vulnerable to physical attacks, and some Black women are murdered. But unlike the repetitive and ritualized form of male lynching to produce a horrific spectacle for White and Black viewers, Black women neither served as symbols of the race nor were their murders deemed to be as significant. There is evidence that forms of social control historically reserved for Black men are also impacting Black women. For example, in the post–civil rights era, African American women have increasingly been incarcerated, a form of social control historically reserved for African American men. Black women are seven times more likely to be imprisoned than White women and, for the first time in American history, Black women in California and several other states are being imprisoned at nearly the same rate as White men. Incarcerating Black women certainly shows an increasing willingness to use the tools of state-sanctioned violence historically reserved for Black men against Black women. But is there an increasing willingness to use tools of social control that have been primarily applied to women against Black men? If institutionalized rape and institutionalized lynching constitute *different* expressions of the *same* type of social control, how might they affect Black men?

AFRICAN AMERICAN MEN, MASCULINITY, AND SEXUAL VIOLENCE

African American men's experiences with the criminal justice system may signal a convergence of institutionalized rape and institutionalized murder (lynching) as state-sanctioned forms of sexual violence. Since 1980, a growing prison-industrial complex has incarcerated large numbers of African American men. Whatever measures are used—rates of arrest, conviction, jail time, parole, or types of crime—the record seems clear that African American men are more likely than White American men to encounter the criminal justice system. For example, in 1990, the nonprofit Washington, D.C.–based Sentencing Project released a survey result suggesting that, on an average day in the United States, one in every four African American men aged 20 to 29 was either in prison, jail, or on probation/parole.[39] Practices such as unprovoked police brutality against Black male citizens, many of whom die in police custody, and the disproportionate application of the death penalty to African American men certainly suggest that the state itself has assumed the functions of lynching. Because these practices are implemented by large, allegedly impartial bureaucracies, the high incarceration rates of Black men and the use of capital punishment on many prisoners becomes seen as natural and normal.

But how does one manage such large populations that are incarcerated in prison and also in large urban ghettos? The ways in which Black men are treated by bureaucracies suggests that the disciplinary practices developed primarily for controlling women can be transferred to new challenges of incarcerating so many men. In particular, the prison-industrial complex's treatment of male inmates resembles the tactics honed on women in a rape culture, now operating not between men and women, but among men. These tactics begin with police procedures that disproportionately affect poor and working-class young Black men. Such men can expect to be stopped by the police for no apparent reason and asked to "assume the position" of being spread-eagled over a car hood, against a wall, or face down on the ground. Rendering Black men prone is designed to make them submissive, much like a female rape victim. The videotape of members of the Los Angeles Police Department beating motorist Rodney King provided a mass media example of what can happen when Black men refuse to submit. Police treatment of Black men demonstrates how the command to "assume the position" can be about much more than simple policing.

Rape while under custody of the criminal justice system is a visible yet underanalyzed phenomenon, only recently becoming the subject of concern. Because rape is typically conceptualized within a frame of heterosexuality and with women as rape victims, most of the attention has gone to female inmates assaulted by male guards. Yet the large numbers of young African American men who are in police custody suggest that the relationships among prison guards and male inmates from different race and social class backgrounds constitutes an important site for negotiating masculinity. Moreover, within prisons, the connections among hegemonic and subordinated masculinities, violence, and sexuality may converge in ways that mimic and help structure the "prison" of racial oppression. Because prisons rely on surveillance, being raped in prison turns private humiliation into public spectacle. The atmosphere of fear that is essential to a rape culture as well as the mechanisms of institutionalized rape function as important tools in controlling Black men throughout the criminal justice system. Whereas women fear being disbelieved, being abandoned, and losing the love of their families, friends, and communities, men fear loss of manhood. Male rape in the context of prison signals an emasculation that exposes male rape victims to further abuse. In essence, a prison-industrial complex that condones and that may even foster a male rape culture attaches a very effective form of disciplinary control to a social institution that itself is rapidly becoming a new site of slavery for Black men.

Drawing upon a national sample of prisoners' accounts and on a complex array of data collected by state and federal agencies, *No Escape: Male Rape in U.S. Prisons*, a 2001 publication by Human Rights Watch, claims that male prisoner-on-prisoner sexual abuse is not an aberration; rather, it constitutes a deeply rooted systemic problem in U.S. prisons. They note, "judging by the popular media, rape is accepted as almost a commonplace of imprisonment, so much so that when the topic of prison arises, a joking reference to rape seems almost obligatory."[40] Prison authorities claim that male rape is an exceptional occurrence. The narratives of prisoners who wrote to Human Rights Watch say otherwise. Their claims are backed up by independent research that suggests high rates of forced oral and anal intercourse. In one study, 21 percent of inmates had experienced at least one episode of forced or coerced sexual contact since being incarcerated, and at least 7 percent reported being raped. Certain prisoners are targeted for sexual assault the moment they enter a penal facility. A broad range of factors correlate with increased vulnerability to rape: "youth, small size, and physical weakness; being White, gay, or a first offender; possessing 'feminine' characteristics such as long hair or a high voice; being unassertive, unaggressive, shy, intellectual, not street-smart, or 'passive'; or having been convicted of a sexual offence against a minor."[41]

As is the case of rape of women, prisoners in the Human Rights Watch study, including those who had been forcibly raped, reported that the *threat* of violence is a more common factor than actual rape. A rape culture is needed to condone the actual practices associated with institutionalized rape. Once subject to sexual abuse, prisoners can easily become trapped into a sexually subordinate role. Prisoners refer to the initial rape as "turning out" the victim. Rape victims become stigmatized as "punks:" "Through the act of rape, the victim is redefined as an object of sexual abuse. He has been proven to be weak, vulnerable, 'female,' in the eyes of other inmates."[42] Victimization is public knowledge, and the victim's reputation will follow him to other units and even to other prisons. In documenting evidence that sounds remarkably like the property relations of chattel slavery, Human Rights Watch reports on the treatment of male rape victims:

> Prisoners unable to escape a situation of sexual abuse may find themselves becoming another inmate's "property." The word is commonly used in prison to refer to sexually subordinate inmates, and it is no exaggeration. Victims of prison rape, in the most extreme cases, are literally the slaves of their perpetrators. Forced to satisfy another man's sexual appetites whenever he demands, they may also be responsible for washing his clothes, massaging his back, cooking his food, cleaning his cell, and myriad other chores. They are frequently "rented out" for sex, sold, or even auctioned off to other inmates. . . . Their most basic choices, like how to dress and whom to talk to, may be controlled by the person who "owns" them. Their name may be replaced by a female one. Like all forms of slavery, these situations are among the most degrading and dehumanizing experiences a person can undergo.[43]

Prison officials condone these practices, leaving inmates to fend for themselves. Inmates reported that they received no protection from correctional staff, even when they complained.

Analyzing the connections among imprisonment, masculinity, and power, legal scholar Teresa Miller points out that "for most male prisoners in long-term confinement, the loss of liberty suffered during incarceration is accompanied by a psychological loss of manhood."[44] In men's high-security prisons and large urban jails, for example, sexist, masculinized subcultures exist where power is allocated on the basis of one's ability to resist sexual victimization (being turned into a "punk"). Guards relate to prisoners in sexually derogatory ways that emphasize the prisoners' subordinate position. For example, guards commonly address male prisoners by sexually belittling terms such as *pussy, sissy, cunt,* and *bitch.*[45] Moreover, the social pecking order among male prisoners is established and reinforced through acts of sexual subjugation, either consensual or coerced submission to sexual penetration. The theme of dominating women has been so closely associated with hegemonic masculinity that, when biological females are unavailable, men create "women" in order to sustain hierarchies of masculinity.

Miller reports that the pecking order of prisoners consists of three general classes of prisoners: men, queens, and punks. "Men" rule the joint and establish values and norms for the entire prison population. They are political leaders, gang members, and organizers of the drug trade, sex trade, protection rackets, and smuggled contraband. A small class of "queens" (also called bitches, broads, and sissies) exists below the "men." A small fraction of the population, they seek and are assigned a passive sexual role associated with women. As Miller points out, "the queen is the foil that instantly defined his partner as a 'man.'"[46] However, "queens" are denied positions of power within the inmate economy. "Punks" or "bitches" occupy the bottom of the prison hierarchy. "Punks" are male prisoners who have been forced into sexual submission through actual or threatened rape. As Miller points out, "punks are treated as slaves. Sexual access to their bodies is sold through prostitution, exchanged in satisfaction of debt and loaned to others for favors."[47] In essence, "punks" are sexual property. A prisoner's position within this hierarchy simultaneously defines his social and sexual status.

Male rape culture has several features that contribute to its effectiveness as a tool of social control. For one, in the prison context, maintaining masculinity is always in play. Miller points to the fluid nature of masculine identity: "Because status within the hierarchy is acquired through the forcible subjugation of others, and one's status as a man can be lost irretrievably through a single incident of sexual submission, 'men' must constantly demonstrate their manhood through sexual conquest. Those who do not vigorously demonstrate their manhood through sexual conquest are more apt to be challenged and be potentially overpowered. Hence, the surest way to minimize the risk of demotion is to aggressively prey on other prisoners."[48] Consensual and forced sexual contact among men in prison has become more common.[49] Because masculinity is so fluid and is the subject of struggle, it is important to note that sexual relations between men does not mean that they are homosexuals. Rather, sexual dominance matters. Those men who are treated as if they were women, for example, the "queens" who voluntarily submit to the sexual advances of other men and are orally or anally "penetrated" like women, may become lesser, less "manly" men in prison but need not be homosexuals. Moreover, those men who are forcibly penetrated and labeled "punks" may experience a subordinated masculinity in prison, but upon release from prison, they too can regain status as "men." Engaging in sexual acts typically reserved for women (being penetrated) becomes the mark of subordinated masculinity. In contrast, those men who are "on top" or who are serviced by subordinate men retain their heterosexuality. In fact, their masculinity may be enhanced by a hyper-masculinity that is so powerful that it can turn men into women.

Another important feature of male rape culture in prison concerns its effects on sexual identities. Since male prisoner-on-prisoner rape involves persons of the same sex, it is often misnamed "homosexual rape" that is thought to be perpetrated by "homosexual predators." This terminology ignores the fact that the vast majority of prison rapists do not view themselves as being gay. Rather, they are heterosexuals who see their victim as substituting for a woman. Because sexual identities as heterosexual or homosexual constitute fluid rather than fixed categories, masculinity in the prison context is performed and constructed.[50] The sexual practices associated with rape—forced anal and oral penetration—determine sexual classification as "real" men or "punks," not biological maleness. In this predatory environment, it is important to be the one who "fucks with" others, not the one who "sucks dick" or who is "fucked in the ass." As one Illinois prisoner explains it: "the theory is that you are not gay or bisexual as long as YOU yourself do not allow another man to stick his penis into your mouth or anal passage. If you do the sticking, you can still consider yourself to be a macho man/heterosexual."[51] The meaningful distinction in prison is not between men who engage in sex with men and in sex with women, but between what are deemed "active" and "passive" participants in the sexual act.[52]

Installing a male rape culture in prison has the added important feature of shaping racial identities. White men rarely rape Black men. Instead, African American men are often involved in the rape of White men who fit the categories of vulnerability.[53] One Texas prisoner describes the racial dynamics of sexual assault: "Part of it is revenge against what the non-white prisoners call, "'The White Man,' meaning authority and the justice system. A common comment is, 'ya'll may run it out there, but this is our world!'"[54] Another prisoner sheds additional light on this phenomenon: "In my experience having a 'boy' (meaning white man) to a Negro in prison is sort of a 'trophy' to his fellow black inmates. And I think the root of the problem goes back a long time ago to when the African Americans were in the bonds of slavery. They have a favorite remark: 'It ain't no fun when the rabbit's got the gun, is it?'"[55] Drawing upon psychoanalytic theory, William Pinar offers one explanation for these racial patterns: "Straight black men could have figured out many kinds of revenge, could they not: physical maiming for one, murder for another. But somehow black men knew exactly what form revenge must be once they were on 'top,' the same form that 'race relations' have taken (and continues to take) in the United States. 'Race' has been about getting fucked, castrated, made into somebody's 'punk,' politically, economically, and, yes, sexually."[56]

Yet another important feature of male rape culture in prison that shows the effectiveness of this form of sexual violence concerns its effects on male victims/survivors. Men who are raped often describe symptoms that are remarkably similar to those of female rape victims, namely, a form of posttraumatic stress disorder described as a rape trauma syndrome. Men expressed depression, anxiety, and despair, with some attempting suicide.[57] Another devastating consequence is the transmission of HIV.[58] However, because male rape victims are men, they still have access to masculinity and male power, if they decide to claim it. As one Texas prisoner described his experiences in the rape culture: "It's fixed where if you're raped, the only way you [can escape being a punk is if] you rape someone else. Yes I know that's fully screwed, but that's how your head is twisted.

After it's over you may be disgusted with yourself, but you realize that you're not powerless and that you can deliver as well as receive pain."[59] Because prison authorities typically deny that male rape is a problem, this inmate's response is rational. As one inmate in a Minnesota prison points out, "When a man gets raped nobody gives a damn. Even the officers laugh about it. I bet he's going to be walking with a limp ha ha ha. I've heard them."[60]

It is important to remember that the vast majority of African American men are not rapists nor have they been raped. However, male rape in prison as a form of sexual dominance and its clear ties to constructing the masculine pecking order within prisons do have tremendous implications for African American male prisoners, their perceptions of Black masculinity, and the gendered relationships among all African Americans. First and foremost, such a large proportion of African American men are either locked up in state and federal prisons and/or know someone who has been incarcerated, large numbers of African American men are exposed to conceptions of Black masculinity honed within prison rape culture.[61] Among those African American men who are incarcerated, those who fit the profile of those most vulnerable to abuse run the risk of becoming rape victims. In this context of violence regulated by a male rape culture, achieving Black manhood requires *not* fitting the profile and *not* assuming the position. In a sense, surviving in this male rape culture and avoiding victimization require at most becoming a predator and victimizing others and, at the least, becoming a silent witness to the sexual violence inflicted upon other men.

Second, so many African American men are in prison on any given day that we fail to realize that the vast majority of these very same men will someday be released. Black men cannot be easily classified in two types, those who are "locked up" in prison and those who remain "free" outside it. Instead, prison culture and street culture increasingly reinforce one another, and the ethos of violence that characterizes prison culture flows into a more general ethos of violence that affects all Black men. For many poor and working-class Black men, prison culture and street culture constitute separate sides of the same coin. Sociologist Elijah Anderson's "code of the streets" has become indistinguishable from the violent codes that exist in most of the nation's jails, prisons, reform schools, and detention centers. Describing young Black men's encounters with the criminal justice system as "peculiar rites of passage," criminologist Jerome Miller contends: "So many young black males are now routinely socialized to the routines of arrest, booking, jailing, detention, and imprisonment that it should come as no surprise that they bring back into the streets the violent ethics of survival which characterize these procedures."[62] For middle-class Black men who lack the actual experiences of prison and street culture, mass media representations of gangstas as authentic symbols of Black masculinity help fill the void. They may not be actual gangstas, but they must be cognizant that they could easily be mistaken as criminals. Varieties of Black masculinity worked through in prisons and on the streets strive to find some place both within and/or respite from this ethos of violence.

Black men who have served time in prison and are then released bring home this ethos of violence and its culpability in shaping Black masculinity. Certainly these men are denied access to full citizenship rights, for example, having a prison record disqualifies large numbers of Black men from getting jobs, ever holding jobs as police officers, or even voting. But an equally damaging effect lies in the views of Black masculinity that these men carry with them through the revolving doors of street and prison culture, especially when being victims or perpetrators within a male rape culture frames their conceptions of gender and sexuality. One wonders what effects these forms of Black masculinity are having on African American men, as well as their sexual partners, their children, and African American communities.

As sociologist Melvin Oliver points out in *The Violent Social World of Black Men*, African American men live in a climate of violence.[63] Because the American public routinely perceives African American men as actual or potential criminals, it often overlooks the climate of fear that affects Black boys, Black men on the street, and Black men in prison. In his memoir titled *Fist, Stick, Knife, Gun: A Personal History of Violence in America*, Geoffrey Canada details how he and his brothers had to work out elaborate strategies for negotiating the streets of their childhood, all in efforts to arrive safely at school, or buy items at the grocery store. As children of a single mother, they lacked the protection of an older Black man, thus making them vulnerable in the pecking order among Black men.[64] All Black boys must negotiate this climate of fear, yet it often takes an especially tragic incident to arouse public protest about Black boys who victimize one another. For example, in 1994, five-year-old Eric Morse was dropped from a fourteenth floor apartment window to his death in the Ida B. Wells public housing project in Chicago. His tormentors allegedly threw him down a stairwell, stabbed him, and sprayed him with Mace before dropping him from the window. The two boys convicted of murdering him were ten and eleven years old.

The question of how the ethos of violence affects Black male adolescents is of special concern. In many African American inner-city neighborhoods, the presence of gang violence demonstrates a synergistic relationship between Black masculinity and violence. Research on Black male youth illustrates an alarming shift in the meaning of adolescence for men in large, urban areas. Autobiographical work by David Dawes on the Young Lords of Chicago, Nathan McCall recalling his youth in a small city in Virginia, and Sayinka Shakur's chilling autobiography that details how his involvement in gang violence in Los Angeles earned him the nickname "Monster" all delineate shocking levels of Black male violence.[65] As revealed in these works, many young Black men participate in well-armed street gangs that resemble military units in which they are routinely pressured to shoot and kill one another. In these conditions, it becomes very difficult for Black boys to grow up without fear of violence and become men who refuse to use violence against others.

Only recently have scholars turned their attention to the effects that living in fear in climates of violence might have both on the quality of African American men's lives and on their conceptions of Black masculinity. Sociologist Al Young conducted extensive interviews with young Black men who were in their twenties, with some surprising findings. The men in his study did not exhibit the swagger and bravado associated with glorified hip-hop images of gangstas, thugs, and hustlers. Instead, these men shared stories of living in fear of being victimized, of dropping out of school because they were afraid to go, of spending considerable time figuring out how to avoid joining gangs, and, as a result, becoming cut off from all sorts of human relationships.[66] Some suggest that Black men have given up hope, or as columnist Joan Morgan states: "When brothers can talk so cavalierly about killing each other and then reveal that they have no expectation to see their twenty-first birthday, that is straight-up depression masquerading as machismo."[67]

Unlike Young's work, the effects of violence on African American men, especially those with firsthand knowledge of a prison male rape culture, have been neglected within social science research. Moreover, the effects of sexual violence on African American men also generates new social problems for African American families, communities, and American society overall. As the graphic discussion of the male "slaves" as property within the penal system indicates, many Black men victimize one another and strive to reproduce the same male pecking order *within* African American communities that they learn and understand as masculine within prison. These men victimize not just women and children; they harm other men and place all in a climate of fear.

SEXUAL VIOLENCE REVISITED

The new racism reflects changes in mechanisms of social control of the post–civil rights era. Lynching and rape as forms of violence still permeate U.S. society, but because they no longer are as closely associated with the binary thinking of the logic of segregation, these seemingly gender-specific practices of sexual violence are organized in new ways. First, movies, films, music videos, and other mass media spectacles that depict Black men as violent and that punish them for it have replaced the historical spectacles provided by live, public lynchings. When combined with the criminalization of Black men's behavior that incarcerates so many men, the combination of mass media images and institutional practices justifies these gender-specific mechanisms of control. For example, as vicarious participants in spectator sports, audience members can watch as men in general, and African American men in particular, get beaten, pushed, trampled, and occasionally killed, primarily in football arenas and boxing rings. The erotic arousal that many spectators might feel from viewing violence that historically came in attending live events (the violence visited upon the lynch victim being one egregious example of this situation) can be experienced vicariously in the anonymity of huge sports arenas and privately via cable television. Films and other forms of visual media provide another venue for framing societal violence. Contemporary films, for example, the slasher horror films targeted to adolescents, produce images of violence that rival the most gruesome lynchings of the past. Lynching is no longer a live show confined to African American men, but, as is the case with other forms of entertainment, has moved into the field of representations and images. Thus, there is the same ability to watch killing, but in the safety of one's living room, with DVD technology allowing the scene to be replayed. Both of these mass media spectacles fit nicely with the lack of responsibility associated with the new racism. Viewers need not "know" their victims, and violence can be blamed on the "bad guys" in the film or on governmental or corporate corruption. Witnessing beatings, tortures, and murders as spectator sport fosters a curious community solidarity that feeds back into a distinctly American ethos of violence associated with the frontier and slavery. Black men are well represented within this industry of media violence, typically as criminals whose death should be celebrated, and often as murder victims who are killed as "collateral damage" to the exploits of the real hero.

Second, in this new context of mass media glorification of violence, rape of women (but not of men) along with the constellation of practices and ideas that comprise rape culture has been moved from the hidden place of privacy of the past and also displayed as spectacle. Whether in Hollywood feature films, independent films such as Spike Lee's *She's Gotta Have It*, or the explosion of pornography as lucrative big business, viewers can now see women raped, beaten, tortured, and killed. Clearly, the ideas of a rape culture persist as a fundamental form of sexual dominance that affects African American women. As feminists remind us, thinking about rape not as a discrete act of violence but as part of a systemic pattern of violence reveals how social institutions and the idea structures that surround rape work to control actual and potential victims. Not every women needs to be raped to have the *fear* of rape function as a powerful mechanism of social control in everyday life. Women routinely adjust their behavior for fear of being raped. The workings of a rape culture, the privacy of the act, the secrecy, the humiliation of being a rape victim, seem especially well suited to the workings of routinization of violence as a part of the "normalized war" that characterizes desegregation. Rape becomes more readily available as a public tool of sexual dominance. At the same time, prison rape of men is not taken seriously and does not routinely appear as entertainment.

Third, the mechanisms of social control associated with a rape culture and with institutionalized rape might be especially effective in maintaining a new racism grounded in advancing myths of integration that mask actual social relations of segregation. Both Black men and Black women are required to "assume the position" of subordination within a new multicultural America, and the practices of a rape culture help foster this outcome. Most Americans live far more segregated lives than mass media leads them to believe. The vast majority of men and women, Blacks and Whites, and straights and gays still fit into clearly identifiable categories of gender, race, and sexuality, the hallmark of a logic of segregation. At the same time, the increased visibility and/or vocality of individuals and groups that no longer clearly fit within these same categories have changed the political and intellectual landscape. For example, many middle-class African Americans now live in the unstable in-between spaces of racially desegregated neighborhoods; lesbian, gay, bisexual, and transgendered (LGBT) people who have come out of the closet undercut the invisibility required for assumptions of heterosexism; some working-class kids of all races now attend elite universities; and biracial children of interracial romantic relationships have challenged binary understandings of race. Crossing borders, dissolving boundaries, and other evidence of an imperfect desegregation does characterize the experiences of a substantial minority of the American population.

When it comes to African Americans, focusing too closely on these important changes can leave the impression that much more change is occurring than actually is. The record on African American racial desegregation is far less rosy. This illusion of racial integration, especially that presented in a powerful mass media, masks the persistence of racial segregation for African Americans, especially the racial hypersegregation of large urban areas. Maintaining racial boundaries in this more fluid, desegregated situation requires not just revised representations of Black people in mass media but also requires new social practices that maintain social control yet do not have the visibility of past practices. Institutionalized rape serves as a mechanism for maintaining gender hierarchies of masculinity and femininity. But institutionalized rape and the workings of rape culture can also serve as effective tools of social control within racially desegregated settings precisely because they intimidate and silence victims and encourage decent people to become predators in order to avoid becoming victims. In this sense, the lessons from a rape culture become important in a society that is saturated with relations of war against segments of its own population but that presents itself as fair, open, and without problems.

Finally, these emerging modes of social control have important implications for antiracist African American politics generally and for developing a more progressive Black sexual politics in particular. Violence constitutes a major social problem for African Americans. State violence is certainly important, but the violence that African Americans inflict upon one another can do equal if not more damage. When confronting a social problem of this magnitude, rethinking Black gender ideology, especially the ways in which ideas about masculinity and femininity shape Black politics becomes essential. As the Clarence Thomas confirmation revealed, African Americans' failure to understand the gendered contours of sexual violence led them to choose race over gender. Incidents such as this suggest that Black leaders have been unable to help either Black women or Black men deal with the structural violence of the new racism because such leaders typically fail to question prevailing Black gender ideology. What happens when men incorporate ideas about violence (as an expression of dominance) into their definitions of Black masculinity? Can they remain "real" men if they do not engage in violence? How much physical, emotional, and/or sexual abuse should a "strong" Black woman absorb in order to avoid community censure? Stopping the violence will entail much more than Black organizations who protest state-sanctioned violence by White men against Black ones. Because violence flows from social injustices of race, class, gender, sexuality, and age, for African American women and men, eradicating violence requires a new Black sexual politics dedicated to a more expansive notion of social justice.

EIGHT

NO STORYBOOK ROMANCE
How Race and Gender Matter

The thirty-five undergraduates who enrolled in the first offering of "Introduction to Black Gender Studies" were an especially brave group. Most were in their early twenties, with African American women forming a sizable minority. The class also reflected the diversity of social class, sexualities, ethnicity, and religion characteristic of a large, urban university. As the course evolved and the students became more comfortable with one another, discussions became more candid. One class session in particular stands out in my mind. On that day, I asked the following questions: "Do your parents want you to marry? If so, what kind of partner do they want for you?" Student responses were revealing. No one identified the assumption that underlay the questions, namely, that getting married constitutes a deepseated social norm. Virtually everyone agreed that their parents would like them to marry; yet, African American women in particular did not hold out much hope that they would find suitable partners. Their responses suggested that they had considered these questions more thoroughly than either African American men or White students: "a decent Black man," "a man with a job," and "a good Christian man," Black women responded, making the gender and race of their preferred partners crystal clear. After hearing the women's answers, African American men offered similar responses: "marry a Black woman," "don't disrespect your mother," "marry within the race," and "marry a woman who can make something of herself," they responded in virtual unanimity. Initially puzzled by the race-specific nature of Black students' responses, White students came to see how "White" served as a silent qualifier for their own beliefs. They too were expected to marry within their race and choose partners of the opposite gender. No one mentioned sexuality until an "out" White lesbian student broke the ice. When she quipped, "My parents would be happy if I brought home *any* man!" everyone laughed.

This class discussion illustrates how the rules that regulate love relationships in the United States pivot on varying combinations of choosing partners who are the same and/or different from oneself. One fundamental rule governs all others—marry a partner of the same race and different gender.[1] Beyond widespread social pressure to marry, this seemingly simple tenet spawns a series of minor regulations. Because the "different gender" rule installs heterosexuality as the preferred form of sexual expression, in a context that denies gay and lesbian marriages, getting married becomes a mechanism for certifying heterosexuality. In the U.S. context in which race and class are so tightly bundled together, marrying within one's race typically means maintaining existing social class arrangements. Because wealth and poverty are passed down through families, keeping families racially homogeneous virtually ensures that middle- and upper-middle class White Americans will retain family assets and that Black Americans will experience intergenerational debt, if not poverty. Religion also matters—one student's desire for a "good Christian man" points to the significance of Christianity as a civil religion in the United States, and government policy that privileges Christians over Muslims, Buddhists, and agnostics. Although age didn't even enter directly into the conversation, it too shaped student responses. Like heterosexuality, age was simply taken for granted, languishing in the category of the obvious. When pushed, however, students were fairly clear about the meaning of age. Citing a popular phrase, one young Black man joked, "ain't nothin' an old woman can do but show me the way to a young one."

Historically, these rules worked through a logic of segregation that organized all aspects of American society. Racism, sexism, heterosexism, and class exploitation as systems of oppression all draw upon varying dimensions of this logic of segregation. Segregate people into boxes of ghettos, barrios, closets, and prisons, rank the boxes as being fundamentally separate and unequal, and keep the entire system intact by forbidding individuals to get to know one another as fully human beings. In this context, laws and religious teachings that detail who people could *not* marry are fundamental in upholding social inequality. They regulate love and sexuality by mystifying segregation and keeping people alienated from one another. The Black gender ideology described in this volume is but one example of many powerful ideologies that serve this purpose. These belief systems encourage individuals to grant humanity only to those in their own segregated boxes and to dehumanize, objectify, and, upon occasion, commodify and demonize everyone else. People who are alienated from one another and from their own honest bodies become easier to rule.

The effects of official policies of segregation persist today, yet the post–civil rights era has replaced the rigid boundaries of the past with more fluid borders between groups.² Middle–class Whites and poor Blacks may live in different neighborhoods, yet their children may take classes together in college classrooms. Desegregated spaces and practices catalyze new possibilities for intimate love relationships between individuals who no longer are confined by the logic of segregation. In this context, many Americans claim that the rules of "same race, different gender" no longer fit their current realities. Americans possess the formal rights to love and, with the exception of LGBT people, marry whomever they like, but are they really free to do so? Contemporary intimate love relationships are influenced by a convergence of factors that collectively shape each individual's lived realities as well as his or her perceptions of what is possible and desirable. Love may appear to come from nowhere, but it is profoundly affected by the political, economic, and social conditions of the new racism.

How African Americans grapple with these rules has tremendous implications for African Americans as individuals as well as for antiracist Black politics. When it comes to the rules themselves, African Americans are already, in some sense, gender rebels. Some accept the rules but point to the virtual impossibility of following them. How can heterosexual African American men marry and raise families when 25 percent are arrested, incarcerated, or on parole? What are educated, heterosexual African American women to do who find themselves facing a Black male shortage that leaves them with few to no prospects of meeting and marrying African American men of similar status? With 70 percent of all college degrees awarded to African Americans going to women, how do middle-class Black women marry within the "race"? Others reject the rules out-right. What would a "same race" partner look like for African Americans who self-define as mixed race or biracial? What does "same race" mean in the context of a multiethnic America with growing populations of Latinos and Asians who have varying degrees of "African descent"? How do Black gays and lesbians negotiate the "different gender" requirement when they are forbidden to marry at all?

When it comes to resisting the manipulation of sexuality and love by systems of power, much is at stake not simply for African Americans but for all people. Oppression functions not simply by forcing people to sub-mit, as is the case with the repackaging of sexual violence to serve the needs of the new racism, but also works by rendering its victims unlovable. Once objectified in their own eyes and in those of their supporters, people police one another and all become more easily exploited and controlled. Because African Americans have been so harmed by these relations, the question of the intimate love relationships of Black men and women takes on added importance. In this context, resistance consists of loving the unlovable and affirming their humanity. Loving Black people (as distin-guished from dating and/or having sex with Black people) in a society that is so dependent on hating Blackness constitutes a highly rebellious act.

When it comes to intimate love relationships, defiant behavior occurs all around us, yet because we do not recognize it, we have difficulty sup-porting it or engaging in it ourselves. Rebellion can occur among people who seemingly follow the rules. For heterosexual African American men, *choosing to love and commit to a heterosexual relationship with a Black woman is a rebellious act.* By choosing to love women whom society has so demo-nized, Black men exhibit a form of "strength" in resisting their depictions as hustlers, bad boys, and criminals. For heterosexual African American women, demanding that their Black male sexual partners respect them for who they are constitutes a rebellious act in a society that stigmatizes Black women as unworthy of love. Rebellion also occurs by breaking the rules. African American men and women who marry outside the "race" do break the rules. Crossing the color line to marry interracially challenges deep-seated American norms, yet such relationships may not be inherently pro-gressive. Similarly, by choosing to love the same gender, especially those involved in interracial relationships, African American LGBT people are disloyal. Such love requires coming out of the closet and thus challenges the rules that frame the closet itself. Whether they appear to be following the rules or breaking them, Black love relationships of all types can uphold prevailing hierarchies of race, class, gender, and sexuality. Because hierarchy becomes intertwined with love and sexual expression, this is when oppression is more effective. But rebelling not simply against the rules but against what the rules are designed to do creates space for a very different set of individual relationships, and a more progressive Black sexual politics. What are some of the issues that confront Black people as they search for love within the confines of these rules? When it comes to love and sexuality, what does rebellion mean for straight Black people who are in same-race love relationships, heterosexual African Americans who cross the color line, and LGBT Black people who violate the same gender rule?

FOLLOWING THE RULES: MARRIAGE AND COMMITMENT

Disappearing Acts (2000), a made-for-HBO film, may typify a new phase in African American heterosexual love relationships. The film depicts the struggles of an African American woman and man to build a love relationship within the same race, different gender rule. Zora (played by Sanaa Lathan), a struggling high school music teacher who wants a career as a singer/songwriter, moves from Manhattan to Brooklyn with plans to use the money she saves on cutting a demo tape. On moving day, she meets Franklin (played by Wesley Snipes), a personable, fine-looking construction worker. They appear to be in love, become sexually intimate, yet each resists committing to the other. Finding herself pregnant, Zora wonders how she can hold fast to her dream and be a mother. Finally confessing to Zora that he has two sons from a prior relationship and he never finished high school, Franklin questions what he can bring to their relationship. Both grapple with issues of commitment and their "disappearing acts" in relation to one another speak to the complexities that frame contemporary African American heterosexual relationships.

Disappearing Acts seems to describe a sea change within African American heterosexual love relationships, one in which a sizeable proportion of African Americans remain single, and in which those Blacks who do marry are less likely to do so than Whites.[3] Despite these changing patterns within Black heterosexual partnerships, it is important to reiterate that the vast majority of the 36.4 million African Americans continue to marry or enter into committed relationships with other African Americans.[4] However, in the post–civil rights era marriage, sexuality, and parenthood have become separate and distinct experiences to the point at which long-term, committed heterosexual relationships and social activities may no longer constitute a common experience for most African Americans.[5]

Until the last few decades when African Americans gained the legal right to marry "outside the race," the pressures on African Americans concerning marriage and committed love relationships were internal to African American communities. Given the uneven patterns of desegregation, this continues today. Black popular culture has long provided a window on the passionate relationships that have bound heterosexual Black women and men together. Often described as the "love and trouble tradition," Black heterosexual partnerships have produced their own form of disappearing acts.[6] In prior periods in which residential racial segregation pushed African American men and women together, commitment was less of an issue. Survival required racial solidarity and marrying non-Blacks was legally forbidden. In contrast, the changing Black social class structure that has resulted in some residential desegregation has exposed African Americans to potential partners of the same social class. Many middle-class Black people now possess the educational credentials and the finances to live in racially desegregated neighborhoods, attend desegregated schools, and get good jobs.[7] Moreover, because so many poor and working-class African Americans in large urban areas live in large ghettos, their love relationships may more closely resemble the "love and trouble" tradition crafted in earlier periods.[8]

On the one hand, the chances for mutual recognition and understanding become greater within love relationships in which both partners recognize how the structure of racism harms both Black men and Black women, and does so through gender-specific mechanisms. Historically, understanding this shared fate was mandatory. In situations of chattel slavery and the Jim Crow South where Black men were lynched for the seeming transgression of even looking at a White woman, and where Black women were vulnerable to rape by White men with little recourse in the court system, it seemed prudent if not essential for Black men and women unconditionally to support one another. Maligning one another in public (before Whites) constituted signs of disunity, and each Black individual was afforded some degree of acceptance from African Americans as a group.

Barbara Omolade speculates as to how having a clear understanding of racial segregation affected the relations among African American women and men: "since it was blatantly clear that no one would survive alone on the land in the face of white terror, we stayed together in marriage and family to help each other survive. Courting, romance, sex, and love were all tempered and shaped by mutual need and by opposition to the system of white supremacy."[9] The shared economic, political, and cultural reality brought about by racism and the absence of a powerful mass media that marketed images of Black deviancy for entertainment encouraged solidarity across differences of gender. Black men and women were more likely to recognize one another as fully human beings within a system that dehumanized both.

On the other hand, heterosexual African American women and men who uncritically accepted prevailing Black gender ideology often ended up feeling stuck with one another. As one thinker puts it, "patriarchy is not just 'out there,' external to our relationships and experiences; it is manifested in and constituted by the ways in which we structure those relationships and experiences."[10] African American men who crafted their understanding of Black masculinity around images of bucks, Uncle Toms, and rapists could come to resent any show of strength by African American women. Conversely, African American women who wished to claim the mantle of Black respectability often erased tell-tale signs of bitchiness or bad mothering by submitting to Black male dominance. Confusing male dominance with strength, and female submission with weakness, both felt that their capitulation to prevailing norms served the interests of the "race."

The social conditions may have changed, but these same tensions operate in the post–civil rights era. Racism continues to operate in gender- and class-specific ways and seeing how this happens might revitalize Black male-female love relationships. The absence of such an analysis can lead to finger pointing and statements of blame. For example, high rates of incarceration and single parent households that affected African American men and women in the 1980s can be interpreted as gender-specific sites of racial oppression that disproportionately affect poor and working-class African Americans. However, armed with mass media images of gangstas, thugs, bitches, and welfare mothers, some commentators identified these outcomes of racial oppression to explain Black poverty itself. As evidenced by the misogyny in some segments of hip-hop culture, in which Black men and women began to blame one another for the joblessness, poor schools, inadequate housing, and other causes of Black poverty, these gender politics had a negative effect on Black love relationships.

Middle-class Black people are no less affected by the need to develop rebellious analyses of the challenges that they face that affect love relationships. In particular, the growing gap between college graduation rates of African American women and men promises to have effects that last far beyond college. Analyzing the marital histories of graduates of twenty-eight selective colleges and universities, sociologist Donna Franklin found evidence of trouble when wives were the main wage earners. The Black women surveyed were much more likely than White women to have husbands who earned less, and those who had been married were also more than twice as likely to have gotten divorced. Franklin attributes the higher divorce rate among highly educated Black women to the women's higher earnings.[11] This explanation is only plausible in a situation in which women and men accept prevailing gender ideology that grants men natural financial superiority. Black couples who reject the premise that strong men should earn more money than their wives create new opportunities for new kinds of marriages.

The absence of Black leadership that helps African Americans see how the political economy of the new racism affects love relationships leaves the majority of Black men and women adrift. Either they uncritically accept the traditional view of gender and sexuality advanced within the Black Church or they are left stitching together relationships that are unduly influenced by negative media representations of Black masculinity and Black femininity. Moreover, marketplace models of relationships, described some time ago by sociologist Robert Staples as the "finance/romance" exchange, encourage men to compete with one another for the most desirable, feminine women. Women are encouraged to market their attributes in the marketplace of potential partners, all the while searching for a complementary mate who meets the requirements of a "real" man. This capitalist value system where men "hunt" for sexual conquests and women "shop" for partners in the love marketplace elevates sexuality as a valuable commodity. As Nathan McCall points out, "in the male idiom, where men were called 'hounds' and women were dubbed 'foxes,' it required no great leap of logic to extend the realm of conquest to sex. The hunt was on, and females were the game."[12]

Black youth have not escaped these marketplace forces. But because as a group, they have come of age during deteriorating economic and political conditions in African American communities and have been so immersed within and visible in shaping contemporary Black popular culture, this cohort has been on the front line of issues of love, sexuality, and relationships. The hip-hop generation claims new ideas about personal freedom both to self-define, and in choice of one's love interests. They are seemingly rebellious in appearance, actions, and beliefs. But in a context marked by the erosion of African American community organizations, Black youth may be more influenced by Western ideologies than they think. As Bakari Kitwana points out: "an intense focus on materialism is characteristic of our generation (among both men and women) and is a critical variable in the shaping (and, at times, undoing) of our relationships."[13] Women who aspire to be "material girls" aim for men with money. Men who make their way via "hustling" search for women who have jobs, welfare checks, and/or who are willing to offer sexual favors. Within individualistic marketplace relations, holding fast to the tenets of the prevailing Black sexual politics can foster unrealistic expectations about romance and love relationships and profound disappointment when they fail to materialize.

Mass media images of Black masculinity and Black femininity can have an especially pernicious effect on how Black men and women perceive one another. African American men who see Black women as being physically unattractive, domineering, and promiscuous and African American women who see Black men as being criminally inclined, promiscuous, and dangerous evaluate the worth of their potential sexual partners and love interests through distorted lenses. In the absence of a progressive Black sexual politics that redefines Black gender ideology, African American women and men can find themselves policing one another's conformity to a Black gender ideology that did not work in the past and that definitely does not work now. Legal scholar and social critic Derrick Bell identifies the problems that this mutual policing can bring: "We trivialize ourselves when we attempt to define African American male/female relationships in terms of the prevailing culture: we attribute to black females mystical powers and strengths that become burdensome in their superficiality, and we attribute weakness and defeat to black males. . . . The result is that we disempower ourselves and imperil our capacity to love unconditionally and, through that love, to grow and create together."[14]

Within these marketplace models of shopping and hunting for suitable love interests within the confines of rules that brand certain people as off-limits, the act of "catching" the right partner takes on extreme importance. Under tenets of hegemonic masculinity, men cannot be men without women and vice versa. Each gender remains incomplete without the other to complement it. When it comes to heterosexual African American love relationships, the prevailing Black gender ideology has significant consequences because both partners are steeped in it and often cannot see its assumptions. For women, the seeming shortage of marriageable African American men becomes redefined less by analyzing the myriad social issues that African American men confront (and that contribute to this shortage), but in searching for the elusive good "catch" in a sea of Black men as an "endangered species." Joan Morgan criticizes this new identity category of the ENDANGEREDBLACKMAN (EBM) by describing how damaging this construct can be for Black love relationships:

> He's that frustrating lover whose untapped potential will never be reached 'cuz he's given up on his dreams and taken to quoting statistics instead. His failure to hold a job, get an education, or take care of his kids is everybody's fault—white people, the system, and even you "*Cuz, you know, black women got it easier because "the Man" don't consider y'all a threat.* He's that womanizing athlete, rapper, or Supreme Court judge who cries racism whenever he gets caught confusing sexual abuse with power.[15]

In a context of a shortage of "good" (heterosexual) Black men, many African American women remain silent about the exploits of EBM, despite the fact that men cause harm not only to their partners but also to themselves. Commenting on this situation, Dalton observes, "I don't need to be convinced that Black men are an endangered species. But that is no reason to compel Black women to suffer in silence."[16] Moreover, love relationships with the EBM remain problematic because such men fundamentally disrespect Black women and uphold prevailing Black sexual politics: "Love without respect is a lethal thing. It is at the heart of any dysfunctional, abusive relationship. All the unconditional love in the world does not negate the truth. The ENDANGEREDBLACKMAN is a creature black women have learned to love, but he is not one we respect."[17]

African American women search for the right man to complement them, all the while feeling as if they are in competition with other women and wary of the motives and men whom they meet. Adhering to marketplace models of love affects relationships *among* African American women, one where, the Black male shortage generates intense competition among Black females. Many Black women aim to make themselves more acceptable or desirable by endorsing traditional gender ideology. In a context in which men are intimidated if not repelled by "strong women," becoming more submissive seemingly increases a woman's chances of finding a Black male partner. But women who hide their strength and who basically prop up men who are weak do neither themselves nor the men in their lives a favor. Because such men *know* that they need women in order to feel like real men, this situation actually heightens men's sense of weakness—they do not feel stronger. Asking for help is one thing—*expecting* it as a male prerogative as an EBM is another. Take for example, the African American male undergraduates who routinely ask their Black female classmates to share lecture notes, to help them with assignments, and, in some cases, to type, edit, or occasionally write their term papers and other class assignments. These men claim a masculinity that is predicated on dominance. They exercise control over women by convincing women to do their schoolwork and to be sexual partners. But such men weaken themselves because they never develop the skills and independence required to write their own term papers and think their own original thoughts. Their masculinity remains fragile because it is predicated upon female subordination.

This perception of a marketplace mismatch between available and desirable African American men and women can affect how African American women behave within their love relationships. One study of a sample of thirty-three heterosexual Black women in Atlanta reports a significant difference in the women's perceptions that good sex was a requirement for a good or ideal relationship. Sadly, most did not consider their current or most recent relationships as ideal. Several single, middle-class women over age thirty reported that they felt used in sexual relationships. Although the older women mainly complained about men who asked them to engage in sex acts that they did not want, the younger women, both working-class and middle-class, feared that their partners would leave them if they did not cooperate. One of the younger women explained:

The guys push you around. They know it is important for a girl to hold
on to a guy . . . they use you and then tell you that some other bitch is
better. I understand a man wants to be in control, but there are limits. . . .
Jay, my boyfriend, tells me he'll leave for whoever . . . I don't want to
get pregnant and one time I mentioned condoms to him. . . . He went
off and told me that was my problem. I love him and he takes good care
of me. He is very gentle and always wants me to come . . . sometimes, I
fake an orgasm because he would feel bad. . . . I should leave him, but
he is so great. He is especially good after we have had an argument and
he wants to make up for it. . . . I know several other girls who are flirt-
ing with him all the time. They don't care he already has a woman.[18]

This young woman loves her partner, but she sees how they bring fundamentally different perceptions of one another to the relationship. This
young woman's partner would be horrified to consider himself as a user of
women, but by referring to other women as "bitches," refusing to wear a
condom that would protect both partners from unplanned pregnancies and
sexually transmitted diseases, and pressuring his partner to achieve a sexual orgasm, he does foster her objectification.

In essence, a problematic Black gender ideology coupled with an unattainable hegemonic (White) gender ideology leaves heterosexual Black men
and women struggling to develop honest, affirming love relationships. The
patently negative gender ideology reserved for African Americans certainly cannot form a foundation for loving relationships. How can seemingly "wild" women and men learn to love one another? In his discussion
of Snoop Doggie Dog's choice of "dog" as a term for Black men, Paul
Gilroy wryly observes, "the dog and the bitch belong together. They are a
couple, but their association does not bring about sexual healing."[19] Or as
Joan Morgan suggests, "Sistas are hurt when we hear brothers calling us
bitches and hos. But the real crime isn't the name-calling, it's their failure
to love us—to be our brothers in the way that we commit ourselves to being
their sistas. But recognize: Any man who doesn't truly love himself is incapable of loving us in the healthy way we need to be loved. It's extremely
telling men who can only see us as 'bitches' and 'hos' refer to themselves
only as 'niggas.'"[20]

At the same time, those African Americans who try to build their love
relationships on the foundation of traditional gender ideology reserved for

Whites often find that the economic, political, and social opportunities denied to Black people limit their chances of success. In this regard, a gender ideology that defines "real" Black men as hyper-heterosexual can compromise love relationships. Conrad R. Pegues points out how the convergence of heterosexism with racism can add another layer of unrealistic expectations, false hope, and disappointment for Black heterosexuals:

> Homophobia breeds the living of lies, causing black women angrily to say that there are not enough "good" men around. The war of the sexes in the black community fuels a lack of trust in black men in general. No one stops to ask if the definition of a man is really viable if it allows black heterosexual men to be abusive and emotionally inaccessible and causes some black homosexual men to play with black women's emotions in their attempt to live by the accepted standards of male social behavior . . . when trying to live a lie about one's sexual preference, your feelings get so wrapped up in what you're doing to hide your true self from the public that you don't develop an authentic emotional life.[21]

Moving toward more affirming intimate love relationships must involve honesty. In describing how issues of sexuality and love can alter relationships between African American men and women, Debra, a forty-five-year-old barber, wonders why Black men seem so reluctant to be fully honest:

> The thing I've come to understand about relationships is that friendship is love. Everything that draws one person to another—whether it's sexual or non-sexual, between men and women, men and men or women and women—is a type of love. And that love is content with itself. It's a good and positive thing. It's funny that black men don't seem to understand this. They know how to be friends with a woman, and they can be honest in that friendship. But in love relationships, they may be good men but they aren't honest with women about who they are and what they want. They just don't seem to be able to do this on a one-to-one basis with a black woman.[22]

If Black men encounter social pressures to define masculinity in terms of their ability to dominate women, gay men, and children, no wonder that many men will have trouble being honest with the women who love them. The openness that is so hard to develop requires African American women and African American men to see honestly who the other person really is and love them unconditionally. Rebellious relationships would recognize that "the greatest gift that can be given to someone you love is to give them the gift to see themselves as you see them."[23] Because existing gender ideology hides African American men and women from one another, it reinforces oppression in ways that become very difficult to uproot. Racism, class exploitation, sexism, and heterosexism erase the humanity of Black men and women. Returning that humanity in the context of heterosexual love relationships profoundly rocks this system.

BREAKING THE RULES: CROSSING THE COLOR LINE

The 1967 film *Guess Who's Coming to Dinner* broke one of the cardinal rules governing love relationships. Depicting the impending marriage between Dr. John Prentice, an African American physician (played by Sidney Poitier), and Joey Drayton, the young, idealistic daughter of a prominent White San Francisco publisher, the film examined parental responses to breaking the "same race" rule. As is true of many Hollywood films, the characters in this film were no ordinary people. The doctor had to be exceptionally qualified to marry a White woman—this Prentice proved by getting the monsignor of a church in San Francisco to vouch for his credentials (thus putting to rest questions of whether this Black man was *really* a doctor). Thus, only a wealthy, highly educated, and quasi famous African American man was suitable for interracial marriage. The standards applied to his future bride were far less stringent. She was physically attractive and wealthy—a good catch for any man. But her politics were more prominent than those of her future husband. Joey was a naïve, romantic White woman whose unflinching belief in the logic of color blindness made her suitable for interracial marriage. Only someone this idealistic and sheltered could fail to notice the massive Black social protests that occurred in the United States in the 1960s. As a couple, they were notoriously asexual—they are seen kissing but once in the film, and the audience views this event through a cabdriver's rearview mirror. The parental response was predictable—both fathers objected to the marriage and both mothers were more supportive. Sadly, the roles played by the two

African American women in the film both drew upon the mammy figure. The first, Poitier's long-suffering Black mother, was initially upset to see her son marry outside the race, but she is willing to put her feelings aside in order to help a string of characters work through their own reactions. Unfortunately, the second, the Black maid who raised Joey, rudely questions whether this African American man, regardless of his credentials, is really deserving of a White woman. Rolling her eyes and accusing the doctor of being a hustler, her mannerism states, "I know your game mister, and you'll have to get by me to hurt this precious little White girl."

Guess Who's Coming to Dinner presented a fictional treatment of the greatly changed legal context ushered in that same year by *Loving v. Virginia*, the landmark U.S. Supreme Court case that lifted the ban on interracial marriage.[24] By the standards of 1967, couples like that depicted in *Guess Who's Coming to Dinner* or the litigants in the *Loving* case were rebellious. They broke the rules and, in the case of the *Loving* case, got those rules overturned. But is crossing the color line still rebellious to the same degree?

In the over thirty years since the film's release, the percentage of African Americans who have crossed the color line to marry interracially has grown. But the depiction of interracial love in *Guess Who's Coming to Dinner* also foreshadowed a pronounced and, from the perspective of heterosexual Black women, troubling trend of the post–civil rights era, namely, the numbers of African American men involved in interracial love relationships with White women far outnumbers that of African American women with White men.[25] These growing rates of interracial marriage (albeit still statistically small) aggravated a long-standing double standard within African American civil society—Black men who date and marry White women are received quite differently from Black women who date and marry White men. For example, Rod, an African American man in his thirties married to a White woman, describes how his family most likely would react if his sisters married White men: "Honestly, they would probably not be accepted . . . for the men, most of the men, we have had relationships, have brought the women to a family gathering, but not my sisters. Too much negative response from the family."[26] Even though the changed legal and social climate of desegregation gave both African American women and men the right to break the "same race" rule, a constellation of social factors censured Black women from doing so while winking at Black men who did. Apparently, rebelling against the "marry the same race" rule operates differently for Black men and Black women.[27]

Traditional explanations for this double standard identify the different histories of African American women and men in the United States as a factor that greatly influences contemporary Black community norms. For African American women, acquiring legal rights meant freedom from White male persecution. Historically, good Black women were those who resisted the sexual advances of White men, not those who invited them. The history for men differed. One mark of hegemonic White masculinity lay in its ability to restrict the sexual partners available to Black men. African American men were forbidden to engage in sexual relations with all White women, let alone marry them. In this context, any expansion of the pool of female sexual partners enhances African American men's standing within the existing system of hierarchical masculinities. Thus, within Black civil society, African American women in interracial love relationships face the stigma of being accused of being race traitors and whores, whereas African American men engaged in similar relationships can find their status as men raised.

Norms of racial solidarity that posit that African American men and women should support one another in every way aggravate this double standard. The rule of "marry within your race" is more easily enforced for Black women. But when Black men break the rule and seem to benefit from this transgression, community norms are brought to bear on them as well. Rejecting the idealized perspective of "love conquers all" advanced within *Guess Who's Coming to Dinner*, African American artists who adhere to the norm of racial solidarity routinely question and often reject outright interracial love and marriage relationships as being bad for Black people. For example, many of Spike Lee's films censure such relationships, reflecting a Black nationalist–inspired agenda in which to marry outside the "race" does disservice to the race. These themes are directly developed in *Jungle Fever*, Lee's 1991 feature-length film about a successful African American male architect who has an affair with Angela, his White Italian secretary. Leaving his beautiful and accomplished African American wife and daughter, Flipper seems bitten by "jungle fever," or a carnal (doglike) Black male attraction for White women. Flipper "flips" the script and brings the White woman home to meet his African American parents. As evidenced by the reaction of Flipper's parents (played by Ozzie Davis and Ruby Dee) when Flipper brought Angela home for dinner, Lee's message is clear. No *Guess Who's Coming to Dinner* liberal machinations occurred around the parental dinner table. Neither parent struggled to become "color-blind." Instead, Flipper's parents told Angela outright that her Whiteness was a problem and that she was not welcome. Despite Lee's efforts to pressure African American men to commit to Black women, one wonders why this need to pressure Black men to choose Black women as partners exists in the first place. If Black women were as worthwhile as White ones, why wouldn't Black men choose them?

African American women face a serious problem in this new desegregated America that cannot be resolved simply by branching out and pursuing White men as partners. Growing numbers of heterosexual African American women face bleak prospects for finding committed, loving relationships with men of any race. Within marketplace relationships of privilege and penalty, African American women's race and gender classification disadvantages them. As Maria Root observes, "Black women have been rendered less desirable by both race and gender and are thus partnered in intermarriages proportionately less than any other group. . . . Thus, when a Black woman suggests that 'white women are out to get any man they can' or 'are trying to take all the good Black men,' her statements reflect a demographic fact."[28] Unfortunately, rather than questioning the marketplace model and race and gender ideology that produces this "demographic fact," and Root conveniently ignores the growing problem of Black women alone and uncritically celebrates all interracial love relationships as "revolutionary." African American women seem to be the group most overlooked in a political economy that erases its own workings and appears to be much more concerned to protect the rights of individuals to "love who they want." Thus, the Black women who roll their eyes at interracial couples are not seen as sympathetic figures—they become recast as familiar stereotypical Black bitches who stand in the way of progress, in this case, the march toward a multiracial America.

This is a real conundrum—*Loving v. Virginia* granted *formal* rights to African American men and women to marry whomever they want. But the denial of realistic opportunities to do so coupled with a pernicious gender ideology that derogates Black womanhood has meant that the vast majority of heterosexual African American women lack *substantive* opportunities to exercise this freedom of choice. Moreover, those who do are labeled as less authentic Black women who become censured for somehow selling out the race. This double standard and the reality of so many African American women without partners is bound to lead to friction in how Black men and women interpret the interracial marriages that do exist. It also further exacerbates the strained relationships among heterosexual African American women and men.

Many Black men recognize how the power of Black community norms and lack of partners for African American women affects them. For example, Harlon Dalton tries to reconcile his commitment to African American political struggle and to African American women with his decision to marry a White woman: "Ultimately, I decided that if anything in life is personal, and therefore free from social obligation, it is our intimate relationships. And I took comfort in the fact that there are many, many ways to show love for my people. Nevertheless, I was, and remain, acutely aware that, in symbolic terms, marrying outside the race is easily seen as a rejection of Black people, and of Black women in particular. And symbols matter."[29] Recognizing that "symbols matter" and that, for many, his marriage breaks an important African American community norm, Dalton identifies intimate love relationships as one important site of individual, personal freedom. He defends his right to love whomever he wants as a right that all human beings should have. But despite Dalton's sensitivity in exploring painful issues, not all African American women accept his version of love. As Jill Nelson bitingly observes, "The more cautious among them insist that it's not that they consciously 'chose' a white woman, they 'just fell in love.' They conveniently cloak themselves in an adolescent notion of love as a state independent of history, politics, and cultural conditioning that we inadvertently and unintentionally 'fall' into, like a sinkhole."[30]

Because African American women are the ones left without partners and alone, apparently, African American women remain the group most bothered by this situation. Like the maid in *Guess Who's Coming to Dinner*, they remain stigmatized as "bitches" when they complain. For example, author Maria Root seems mesmerized by her own book's title. In *Love's Revolution*, she clearly sees interracial love and marriage as "revolutionary." At the same time, whereas she does describe the difficulties that African American women have in marrying interracially, she is far more concerned with protecting White women from "blame" for social relations that leave African American women without partners. Instead, she puts the responsibility not on the African American men and White women involved in such relationships but on the convenient target of White men: "White women are not to blame, however: the construction of whiteness and its control by white men are responsible. While white women are second-class citizens by gender, ironically they have more room to search for other partners."[31] In this universe, White women as "second-class citizens by gender" seemingly benefit from desegregation because they have "more room" to search for partners among those historically off-limits. Views such as these not only leave political and economic factors that frame the new racism unexamined, they conveniently let White women off the hook. They also reify long-standing images of White women either as passive creatures without agency or as moral women who, unlike their Black sisters, hold fast to the core American belief of "color blindness."[32]

Social and economic conditions certainly establish the parameters for interracial love relationships—after all, it is difficult to fall in love with someone of a different race whom you never meet because you attend racially segregated schools, live in racially segregated neighborhoods, and spend the bulk of your time with people of your own social class and citizenship status. Difference in the border zones of racial desegregation may increase the allure of the long forbidden "other"—Spike Lee's infamous "jungle fever" thesis. But the reasons why some African American men marry White women rather than African American women go beyond White women as forbidden fruit or White women's pursuit of Black men (the case of Black athletes, for example).

Harlon Dalton recognizes that many African American women question his decision to marry a White woman: "I realize that some of you are thinking, 'If you care about Black women so much, why didn't you marry one?' That is a perfectly fair question, especially in light of my suggestion that love and obligation are wellsprings of community. The answer begins with the simple yet profound fact that I fell in love with a woman who is White."[33] Dalton's comments are telling. His wife may be "White," but because White women are very diverse, the racial consciousness of White women is equally heterogeneous.

Some White women lack a consciousness of racism and only see their Black lovers through prevailing ideas of Black masculinity. To this day, I remain stunned by the memory of a small group of White women who approached me after a talk on a large, predominantly White, public university in a rural area in the Midwest. The girls announced that they were all dating Black men and that did not know any Black women who were willing to answer their questions. They wondered if I had any tips for them when they had their biracial babies. Unlike the many heterosexual African Americans who also routinely approach me after talks to share painful stories of how rejected they feel, especially by Black men, these White women had no doubt that they would marry Black men. They knew that they were part of "love's revolution." In contrast, other White women craft complex White identities through a prism of antiracist analysis. Dalton's wife Jill seems to fall into this category. Several months into their relationship, Jill asked him, "Why are you dating a White woman?" Dalton recalls, "that conversation had a profoundly liberating effect on me, for it let me know that Jill saw and understood herself as a person with a race and that she had no interest in trying to pretend that we could, or should, lead a colorblind or colorless existence."[34] For Jill, the task was not to erase Whiteness but to change its meaning in the context of the politics of color-blind America. By this decision, she became a race rebel.

In the 1990s, popular culture began to examine the issues within interracial love relationships. For example, recent feature films have begun to explore interracial relationships of African American women that grants them the type of individual freedom claimed by Black men and White women. The Black women depicted in these films are quite different from *Guess Who's Coming To Dinner*'s long-suffering mother or uppity maid, or of *Jungle Fever*'s Black professional women whose painful discussion of why Flipper and other Black male professionals show a predilection for White women remains legendary. For example, in *Waiting to Exhale*, when Bernadine (played by Angela Bassett) discovers that her spouse has been cheating on her with his *White* secretary, she throws him out of their luxurious house, puts his expensive suits in his car, and sets it on fire. "Would it be better if she were Black?" her husband asks. "No—it would be better if you were Black!" she replies. Long-suffering Black women are apparently out—dealing with the White Woman issue requires exhaling righteous anger.

Interracial love relationships are at the forefront of changing race relations in the United States, but the direction that they will go is far from settled. In this regard, the increasing visibility of biracial African Americans in scholarship and within popular culture and the partners they choose provides yet another angle of vision on the fate of the "same race, different gender" rule. Interestingly, the emerging archetype of the biracial Black child is typically female, light-skinned, and sporting a curly mop of hair that marks her as not-White but as also not-Black.[35] How will these Black biracial women respond to the "same race, different gender" rules? Apparently, middle-class women have far more freedom to love whomever they want than do working-class women. The 1998 film *Mixing Nia* takes up exactly this issue. Nia (played by Karyn Parsons), the highly educated, biracial daughter of a White Jewish father and a Black mother, quits her job at an ad agency over some racially offensive material. Recognizing that she knows little of the blackness that seems to be so important to her ad agency (they want her to market a questionable product to Black ghetto youth using icons from "authentic" Black culture), Nia tries to find a career as a writer. Through this quest, Nia encounters an updated version of the "tragic mulatto" whereby the old "tragic" flaw of mixed-race identity and rejection by Whites and Blacks alike becomes transformed into Nia's "tragic" flaw of feeling White, identifying with Whites, yet remaining saddled with the restrictions of being viewed as Black. Nia searches for her Black identity through an intimate love relationship with a Black Nationalist professor but eventually rejects him for the benefits of color blindness. Nia is free to date whomever she pleases, and she does. At the end of the film, however, she discovers her own story, a biracial one that grants her freedom to be an individual who can date, love, and be whomever she pleases. In an ideal world, all of those Black women alone would experience the same degree of freedom that seemingly is available to Nia.

The 1992 film *Zebrahead* provides one of the best analyses of crossing the color line presented within contemporary films. Here the forbidden relationship occurs among the young, the group that seemingly represents the future of America. But these are not affluent, suburban young people—the adolescents in *Zebrahead* are working-class, attend high school in Detroit, and are clearly of the hip-hop generation. In this context, Nikki a young brown-skinned African American girl from a single-parent home, meets Zeke, the White friend of her cousin. Zeke is no ordinary White boy. He loves Black culture, has Black friends, yet, unlike his White friends, he does not see Black culture and African Americans as primitive, promiscuous, and exotic. Zeke and Nikki fall in love and other African American young men resent their relationship. Nikki's cousin is accidentally killed, in part, because of his friendship with Zeke and for his acceptance of Nikki and Zeke's relationship. The sobering message of *Zebrahead* seems light years away from the upbeat humor of *Guess Who's Coming to Dinner*—love whom you like, but keep in mind that the "same race" rule is alive, your dinner guest may not be welcome, and crossing the color line can still get you killed.

BREAKING THE RULES: LOVING THE SAME IN YOU

In 1991, *P.O.V.* (*Point of View*), the public television series that features independently produced films, scheduled critically acclaimed director Marlon Riggs's video documentary *Tongues Untied*. The video explores the circumstances, politics, and culture of Black gay men using a mixture of styles ranging from social documentary to experimental montage, personal narrative, and lyric poetry. Relying on an array of Black and/or gay cultural forms, the video mixes the music of Billie Holiday and Nina Simone with the poetry of Essex Hemphill and Joseph Beam; it presents vogue dance and Snap! expression. *Tongues Untied* clearly fits within the mission of *P.O.V.* Yet, unlike Riggs's prior work, which had been shown with little controversy, *Tongues Untied* raised a firestorm of controversy. Seventeen of fifty major public television stations refused to show it, claiming that "community standards" would find it offensive. Some stations pointed to specific elements that might offend their audiences such as the frequent use of the word "fuck," a drawing of a penis, and a scene showing two men kissing. The video documentary also came under greater scrutiny due to its funding. Along with private donations, Riggs' had financed the video with a $5,000 grant from the National Endowment for the Arts (NEA), a federal agency supporting literary, visual, and performing artists. Moreover, because the *P.O.V.* series itself also received funding from the NEA, critics of *Tongues Untied* questioned whether government funding should support art that many found to be obscene. Responding to the controversy, Riggs vehemently opposed the charge of "obscenity." He expressed frustration at what he saw as mainstream Black America's "collusion" by its silence with this "nakedly homophobic and covertly racial assault." Riggs pointed out another purpose behind the "obscenity" rhetoric: the charge of being too "graphic" or "grossly offensive" provided the perfect pretext for "silencing a disenfranchised minority's attempt to end its subjugation and challenge the cultural terms of the majority's social control. Having deemed the language of black gay men unsuitable for public broadcast, tongues untied were peremptorily re-tied."[36]

Six years later, Cheryl Dunye's 1997 film *Watermelon Woman* also broke new ground, but this time for Black lesbians. With Dunye playing the lead role in a mock documentary, the plot of the film focuses on a young Philadelphia video store employee whose burning ambition to become a filmmaker fosters her determination to make a documentary. In the film, Cheryl becomes increasingly fascinated with an obscure Black actress who appeared in a number of Hollywood films in the 1930s, known only as the Watermelon Woman. Taking a cue from Black feminist historiography that has been devoted to documenting, recovering, and analyzing lost histories of African American women, the mock documentary traces Cheryl's efforts to reclaim the Watermelon Woman's past, a search that symbolizes efforts of Black lesbians to reclaim a closeted history. Using her camera rather than fiction as her primary tool of discovery, Dunye's *Watermelon Woman* explored a variety of themes of Black lesbian identity and sexuality. For one, it examined how norms of racial solidarity within African American communities affect LGBT Black people. Cheryl's best friend and coworker (also a lesbian) became uptight when Cheryl began a romance with a White customer. For another, *Watermelon Woman* depicts lesbian sexuality, a rarity in films that reach larger audiences. Moreover, lesbian sexuality occurs not between two African American women but across the lines of race. Whereas one reviewer described the film's love scenes as "the epitome of discreet eroticism," its depiction of lesbian sexuality sparked another NEA funding debate. "It is inconceivable that had the actors been of the same race but not the same sex, such a sequence could have caused such a furor.[37]

The controversies that greeted *Tongues Untied* and *Watermelon Woman* illustrate the difficulties that Black LGBT people face in toppling the "marry the opposite gender" rule. When they come out and are visible, whether partnered or not, all lesbian, gay, bisexual, and transgendered individuals break the rule of choose a different gender. But as revealed in the literature of LGBT African Americans, the politics of "coming out" have different consequences for Black Americans than for Whites. The visibility of Black LGBT individuals is doubly jarring in the context of a racialized history that constructs homosexuality as white. In this context, visible "out" Black gays and lesbians (let alone those who use the word "fuck," kiss one another, and shamelessly film their exploits as did characters in films by Riggs and Dunye) challenge heterosexist and racial norms adhered to by Whites and Blacks alike. In essence, "out" LGBT African Americans are inherently rebellious, regardless of their choice of love interest, the sexual practices they prefer, and/or whether they are sexually active at all.

Unlike African American heterosexual relationships, or interracial heterosexual relationships, the committed love *relationships* of African American lesbian, gay, bisexual, and transgendered people remain understudied and virtually invisible. Black LGBT people and politics are certainly more visible than ever before, especially regarding the process of coming out.[38] But when compared to the volumes written about Black heterosexual love relationships, historical and social scientific studies of the intimate love relationships and sexual practices of LGBT Black people remain far less common.[39]

When it comes to Black gays and lesbians, answering even relatively simple questions can take on major proportions. How many LGBT couples are there? How do they meet? How long do they stay together? How do they manage responsibilities within their households? How does one measure commitment among homosexual couples? Social science literature has a series of indicators to answer these questions for straight people. Within social science, for example, marriage is widely used as a primary indicator of committed love relationships. Yet relying solely on this indicator distorts the experiences of people who live together in committed partnerships, but who either choose not to marry (shack up) or who, like Black gays and lesbians, are forbidden to marry.[40] Social science research is making progress but LGBT relationships remain understudied.[41] Given this context, the results of the *Black Pride Survey 2000*, a survey of 2,645 African American attendees of nine regional Black Gay Pride celebrations does provide an important preliminary snapshot of the love relationships of Black LGBT people. While not a representative sample of Black LGBT people in the United States, the survey does provide an important supplement to the more general findings of the 2000 census.[42] The survey identified noticeable differences among men and women in committed relationships—Black lesbians were more likely to be in committed relationships than Black gay men—and also found that Black lesbians were more likely than Black gay men to have children living with them. This issue of marriage and domestic partnership was so high on the list of Black lesbians that it was identified as one of the top three issues facing Black LGBT people.[43]

As was the case for social science research prior to the *Black Pride Survey*, until the appearance of works such as *Tongues Untied* and *Watermelon Woman* in the 1990s, Black gays and lesbians had largely been written out of Black film and television histories. Through fiction, poetry, and interpretive essays, Black lesbian and bisexual writers such as Barbara Smith, Pat Parker, Audre Lorde, and June Jordan had long written about their lives and their relationships.[44] Essays and fiction by gay Black men have also explored themes of homosexual desire.[45] Black LGBT eroticism has existed, but it has neither been widely depicted in visual media nor in Black popular culture. Black gay and lesbian themes that until recently have been largely explored via fiction, poetry, and interpretive essays now move into the more visible and influential media of video, film, and public and cable television.

With love relationships so ignored by scholarship and media alike, the representations that do appear within popular culture can take on added importance, because, unlike the large number of films on Black heterosexual relationships and the growing treatment of interracial heterosexual relationships, representations of LGBT relationships and Black gay sexuality occur in an interpretive vacuum. As a general rule of thumb, Black gay and lesbian characters are denied both love relationships and sexual expression on film. Mainstream films typically relegate Black lesbians and Black gay men to stereotypical roles in which they are identified as homosexual but are denied on-screen sexual relationships. Reminiscent of the tragic mulatto, Black lesbians seem to have acquired the mantle of the tragic lesbian saddled with unrequited love, often for a White woman. In the feature film *Boys on the Side*, Whoopee Goldberg portrays Jane, a Black lesbian who loves Robin, a dying White woman. Jane unselfishly cares for Robin during the last days of her life. In this film, friendship is acceptable, with the notion of unrequited romantic and sexual love used to highlight the expressive energy of the friendship. The message about love seems to be that love cannot supersede heterosexuality and that sexual love can be expressed only through a friendship. In contrast to the tragic lesbian, Cleo, Queen Latifah's character in the 1996 feature film *Set It Off*, depicts the stereotypical image of the butch Black lesbian. The lesbian couple in *Set It Off* does not have a sex scene. Rather, their relationship is only a footnote used to explain the main character's butch demeanor. More typically, Black lesbians are simply absent.

For lesbian and gay African Americans, on-screen romantic relationships are more often implied that depicted. White lesbian relationships in mainstream films are more likely to contain sexual scenes, for example, the sex scenes between two White women in *Boys Don't Cry* and *Chasing Amy*. Films with Black lesbians are more discreet. For example, *The Color Purple, Daughters of the Dust*, and *The Women of Brewster Place* all present African American lesbian couples. However, in contrast to heterosexual sexuality, in all of the films, sexuality is suggested but rarely seen. In *Women of Brewster Place*, the lesbian couple clearly lives together in a romantic partnership, encounter the censure and ridicule of neighborhood residents who are aware of their lesbian relationship, yet the audience never sees the sexual nature of that relationship, even when the women are home alone together. Julie Dash's critically acclaimed independent film *Daughters of the Dust* (1992) also has lesbian characters, but here too, no space exists for explicit sexuality. The sexuality associated with Celie and Shug's lesbian relationship in Alice Walker's novel *The Color Purple* never makes it into the film version. With the exception of pornography, where explicit sexuality between two women of color is common practice, finding examples of two African American women engaged in a sexual act in a movie remains difficult.

Films such as *Tongues Untied* and the *Watermelon Woman* could happen only in a greatly changed intellectual and political climate in which love relationships that break the "same gender" rule have become more open. Through an increased visibility of Black LGBT people, and their being more vocal in claiming lesbian, gay, bisexual, and transgendered identities, Black LGBT people have identified several issues that shape Black gay love and sexuality. For one, the increasing visibility of gays and lesbians in wider society has enabled LGBT African Americans to question prevailing Black sexual politics. With the exception of large urban areas, historically, LGBT Black people have often remained closeted, tolerated within segregated African American communities just as long as they remained silent concerning their sexuality.[46] In contrast, in the post–civil rights era of desegregation, many LBGT African Americans are not ashamed of their sexual orientation, do not consider it to be a problem or a sin, and refuse to devalue it. Consider, for example, Donna Allegra's testimony of how she feels about her love of women:

> The upshot of my lesbian identity is that I fall in love with female people—and want to. I don't see this as a "lifestyle"—such a temporary-sounding term. It brings to mind this season's fall fashions or a layout of home decoration. . . . My lesbianism is more the ground zero of an emotional compass, ever searching out women. This orientation of my heart is not going to change because I don't want it to. I've never been tormented by my lesbianness. In fact, it's a favorite part of me, as Goddess given as being Black. What I have been tormented by is people's homophobia—their deliberate ignorance concerning my affectional orientation, their active offenses against me because of my sexuality. I am not the problem here.[47]

Allegra is not "tormented" by being a lesbian. Rather, she sees homophobia as the problem, not her own sexuality. This is the orientation she takes with her into her love relationships.

Allegra's comments speak to another important issue raised by Black gays and lesbians as having an important effect on their lives, namely, coping with heterosexual African Americans' often-negative reaction to homosexuality, especially Black same-sex desire and/or love relationships. Far too often, LGBT African Americans feel that they cannot remain within African American communities and have open, committed same-sex relationships. According to womanist theologian Kelly Douglas, the homophobia that many heterosexual Black people express toward LGBT people overall is one consequence of "sexual humiliation" that has left Black men and women vulnerable to adopting dysfunctional perceptions of masculinity and femininity. Moreover, this Black gender ideology also obliges them to "negate the humanity and worth of gay and lesbian persons whose ways of being challenge their distorted views of sexuality."[48] In this situation, the politics of respectability that suppress discussions of Black sexuality in general operate to police Black LGBT sexualities that are seen as being a threat to the integrity of the entire African American community. In this context, Black LGBT people may remain closeted within their African American families and Black civil society; yet, they also may live open "out" lives once they leave African American residential enclaves. Love relationships become negotiated in the context of shifting patterns of sexual identification marked by varying degrees of familiarity. Ironically, for LGBT African Americans, coming out of the sexual closet may require leaving the seeming safety of Black communities.

This theme of safety emerges as an important component of relationships of gay and bisexual Black men who are living on the Down Low (DL). While living ostensibly heterosexual lives, often with wives and girlfriends, Black men on the DL have sex with men. For many men on the Down Low, the label is both "an announcement of masculinity and a separation from white gay culture. To them, it is the safest identity available—they don't risk losing their ties to family, friends, and black culture."[49] In recent years, DL culture has grown out of the shadows and has developed its own contemporary institutions, for those who know where to look: websites, Internet chat rooms, private parties, and special nights at clubs. This subculture enables Black men on the DL to avoid the ridicule, rejection, and danger often encountered by gays who are out. Explaining why these men do not go to gay bars, "in a black world that puts a premium on hypermasculinty, men who have sex with other men are particularly sensitive to not appearing soft in any way."[50]

Leaving racially separate communities broadens the pool of potential love interests, but it also increases the possibilities that new partners may be non-Black. This tension fosters another important theme affecting Black LBGT love relationships, namely, the "same race" rule also affects African American lesbians, gays, bisexuals, and transgendered people. In this regard, LBGT African American love relationships share at least one issue with their heterosexual counterparts—interracial dating remains controversial. Moreover, as was the case with Black heterosexual love relationships, regardless of actual numbers, the visibility of Black LBGT people who have White partners and lovers compounds the issue. As Boykin observes, "gay interracial couples often face the scorn of Whites and Blacks alike. Derogatory terms like 'snow queen' (a Black person who primarily dates Whites) and 'dinge queen' (a White person who primarily dates Blacks) identify these modern day 'race traitors.'"[51]

Whites often view interracial LBGT sexuality and relationships as especially rebellious. Having a same-sex lover is shocking, but having one who is also Black is even more scandalous. This world of interracial LGBT

sexuality as inherently rebellious may resonate with White gays and lesbians whose sexual paradigms have had difficulty accommodating race and
whose politics often exclude African American people.[52] Not everyone
agrees that interracial LGBT sexuality is inherently rebellious. In his essay
"Dinge," Robert Reid-Pharr challenges the notion that interracial gay sexuality is a site of liberation, and thus muddies the waters for those who
would claim that interracial gay and lesbian love relationships are inherently progressive and that the sex act itself transcends everyday power relations. Using a psychoanalytic framework to challenge the assumptions of
queer theory that gay and lesbian sex is inherently rebellious and need not
be analyzed, Reid-Pharr argues that race operates within this form of sexual expression. His question "What do we think when we fuck?" suggests
that all forms of sexuality (including intraracial and interracial heterosexuality) are sites of acceptance and rebellion. As Reid-Pharr points out,
"what is more difficult to accept is the idea that the sexual act, at least as it
is performed between queers . . . is not necessarily a good, expansive, and
liberatory thing, a place in which individuals exist for a moment outside
themselves such that new possibilities are at once imagined and actualized."[53] Instead, he argues: "We do not escape race and racism when we
fuck. On the contrary, this fantasy of escape is precisely that which marks
the sexual act as deeply implicated in the ideological processes by which
difference is constructed and maintained."[54]

FOSTERING REBELLION

For African Americans coping with the multiple prisons and closets that
symbolize intersecting oppressions, it is important to develop more sophisticated understandings of freedom. In her 1999 memoir *The Prisoner's
Wife*, Asha Bandele describes how she came to fall in love with Rashid, a
prisoner who had been convicted of murder. Rashid's actual prison and
Asha's psychological one were contemporary manifestations of a historical
process of oppression. Her narrative explores how *love within a prison*
served as a form of rebellion. Their love for one another set both partners
on a path toward a freedom that recognized the constraints of prison yet
transcended its boundaries. The actual prison walls that separated her
from Rashid were real, not socially constructed. Just as Rashid could not
"break out" of prison, the structural constraints that circle Black people's

love relationships often limit choice. Asha also had her own internalized prisons, namely, the emotional scars that she carried due to sexual violence associated with racism, sexism, and heterosexism. Asha could rebel against the harm done to her by changing her consciousness, but this strategy had its limits. As individuals, neither Rashid nor Asha had the power to destroy the prisons of ghettoization and incarceration that circumscribed both of their lives.

Asha Bandele's memoirs may speak from the specificity of African American experience, in this case, a heterosexual love relationship with an incarcerated partner, but the themes she explores apply to all people who wish to love within situations that forbid them to do so:

> The prison itself played a significant role in solidifying how we were with each other, how close we would become. The prison, with all of its efforts to keep us unsteady, uncomfortable, and unable to love, became my adversary. Its stance against love automatically made me take a stance for love; I became a warrior. When I went to war, then, initially I thought I was battling against the bars and steel, the chains and cells, the brutal separation. . . . After enough time had passed that I was allowed some perspective, I came to see the battles quite differently, however. When all of my tactics and strategies had played out . . . in the end, the only one left in ruins was me. When the shock of seeing myself destroyed wore off, I realized it was not so terrible. The me in me who had been killed was the me who had gone through life with shifty eyes, the ones that always greeted love sideways, looking at it askance, always as a potential enemy. I tell Rashid this, about how I had once looked at love, and he said he understood. He said that it was how he felt once, before me, before us. This was how we came to see ourselves as rebels. We vowed a lifetime of battles against anything and anyone who tried to block our love from coming.[55]

Rashid's incarceration demanded that both partners define themselves differently and perceive one another differently than had they met in another time and place. Bandele recognized that the prison "played a significant role in solidifying how we were with each other, how close we would become" and decided to take a stance against it. Bandele came to see how her humanity had never been allowed to develop fully because she too had been in her own prison. Trying to beat prison by its own terms simply could not take her to the next step. "In the end, the only one left in ruins was me," she surmises.

The physical prison that incarcerated Rashid certainly curtailed both of their movements. But the larger prison that created it, namely, the history of racial oppression refracted through the lens of class, gender, and sexuality, presents a particular kind of prison that circumscribes all African American love relationships. The effects of past-in-present racism seen in contemporary demographics of schooling, housing, health, and jobs, and the deeply entrenched ideologies that justify these outcomes through a never-ending array of mass media images of Black masculinity and Black femininity speak to the necessity of Black dehumanization for the new racism. Ironically, the new prisons created by racial segregation and the erasure of Black pain through a blind commitment to color blindness now turns everything upside down. For African Americans, the mark of humanity (and, by implication, for everyone else) may be the ability to love fully, to see other people for who they are as fully human beings, to love within the context of oppression, and to bend or break the rules described here.

Asha and Rashid's courtship and marriage is not just another love story. For these two individuals, resistance came in rejecting the categories that confined them, seeing the actual and the larger societal prison for what it actually was, and engaging in the rebellious act of loving one another. When Asha saw what kind of woman she had become, one who "had gone through life with shifty eyes, the ones that always greeted love sideways, looking at it askance, always as a potential enemy," she realized how damaged she had been by trying to play by prison rules. Bandele and Rashid saw that oppression operates by distorting this basic ability to see and love one another as fully human beings. They decided to become rebels and claim their humanity, even within the strictures of a physical prison.

Asha and Rashid's love story is significant in that it points the way toward a different kind of love for individuals. Their story is certainly inspiring and can be read as a story of hope. However, whether these two individuals "make it or not" is not the issue. They are not "role models" whose actions should be emulated. The lesson here for Black women is not one of "go to prison and get yourself your own Rashid." Rather, their relationship of love within the context of prison points the way toward new self-definitions and new actions that recognize the humanity of those around us in the context of oppression. Such love need not be sexual, nor must it be within the same age group or across genders or within one race. Rather, this interior space of "love" described by Asha can serve as a space of freedom if only we are willing to imagine new possibilities.

NINE

WHY WE CAN'T WAIT
Black Sexual Politics and the Challenge of HIV/AIDS

On May 3, 2002, a group of South African citizens, international reporters, dignitaries, and common folk assembled in South Africa for a memorial service. Normally, such a ceremony would have attracted little attention. But this event was different because it marked the return of the remains of Sarah Bartmann, the so-called Hottentot Venus, to South Africa. Bartmann's homecoming had not been easy. After years of repeated requests by Nelson Mandela, South Africa's first postapartheid president, France finally agreed to release her remains. Greeting Bartmann as a forgotten ancestor 192 years after she left Capetown, the Khoi people placed her remains in a wooden coffin, the first ever to hold them. Commenting on the meaning of the memorial service, one sixty-three-year-old Khoisan woman remarked, "It is important for her to come back. She is one of ours."[1]

It was a bittersweet return, filled with the contradictions that confront people throughout the African Diaspora. Sarah Bartmann returned to a South Africa that bore little resemblance to the one that she left almost 200 years earlier. This South Africa was filled with immense promise and momentous problems. On the one hand, her remains arrived in a nation whose former policies of racial apartheid had come to symbolize the last vestige of a 500-year-old system of racial oppression. A democratically elected government now ran postapartheid South Africa, with Black Africans at the helm. Aspiring for a more just society, South Africa's freedom struggles had inspired worldwide respect and galvanized global antiracist initiatives. As a new multiracial democracy that seemingly escaped the widespread corruption plaguing other African nation-states, South Africa's citizens had approved one of the most progressive constitutions in the world. South Africa's many ethnic groups, women, children, and its lesbian, gay, bisexual, and transgendered citizens all found constitutional protection from discrimination and guarantees of human rights. The people of South Africa also recognized that, in order to progress, they needed to heal the wounds caused by their apartheid past. Recognizing the power of past-in-present racism, the members of South Africa's Truth and Reconciliation Commission sat through painful sessions in which people shared the tragic stories of how their children, parents, spouses, and loved ones had suffered under apartheid. The return of Sarah Bartmann's remains to this new progressive South Africa was part of this healing process of acknowledging the past in order to move into a promising future.

On the other hand, Bartmann's remains arrived in a South Africa confronting the enormous social problems of poverty, inadequate housing, poor health care, illiteracy, and unemployment. As the new government struggled to address these issues, it found itself confronting a major social problem that disproportionately affects its Black citizens and in ways that threaten their very survival. South Africa has one of the highest rates of HIV infection in the world and confronts a crisis of immense proportions. In South Africa, as elsewhere where HIV/AIDS is growing, the very future of Black communities is at stake.[2] Recognizing the magnitude of this crisis, citizens of South Africa (often in defiance of government officials) have joined together with those from other nations of continental Africa, the Caribbean, and other areas where HIV/AIDS constitute a major health crisis. All acknowledge that the global HIV crisis affects all people, yet it has especially devastating effects on Black people. Recognizing that the promise of a new South Africa could not be realized without tackling the problem of HIV/AIDS, many South African citizens took up the fight against HIV/AIDS.

When compared to their South African counterparts, Black American leaders and organizations have been far less vocal. Certainly the problems of HIV/AIDS among African Americans resemble those in South Africa and throughout the African Diaspora.[3] The political, economic, and social factors that frame the global HIV/AIDS pandemic also affect African Americans. Joblessness and high rates of poverty mean that poor and working-class African American men and women often lack access to housing, education, and health care, factors that would help keep them healthy. New forms of social control, for example, the growth of a prison system that incarcerates large numbers of Black men and disciplines them by condoning institutionalized rape, simultaneously raise rates of infection and suppresses protest. A powerful mass media masks these structural barriers by using controlling images of Black masculinity and Black femininity that stigmatize straights with a promiscuous Black hyper-heterosexuality and pathologize the sexual practices of LGBT Black people. Collectively, these social practices and the ideas that defend them underpin a powerful Black gender ideology that blames Black people for their own problems, in this case, the promiscuity that catalyzes disease and encourages African Americans to remain silent about their suffering.[4]

In this context, the spread of HIV/AIDS among African American men and women challenges African American politics' treatment of gender and sexuality. Because sexual contact constitutes one major trajectory of HIV contraction, the HIV/AIDS crisis reveals how the failure to criticize prevailing Black sexual politics places all African Americans at risk. Many African Americans fail to question dominant Black gender ideology and thus help replicate America's sexually repressive culture that takes special form within African American communities. For example, Black men who confuse masculinity with dominance and take these beliefs into their romantic relationships place their partners at risk. Whether straight, gay, or bisexual, Black men who make "booty calls" without condoms foster the spread of HIV. Black women who confuse femininity with submission and weakness fare no better. When partnered with these same men, heterosexual African American women who try to be the "strong" Black woman can end up being sexually exploited, economically used, and abandoned when they can no longer compete sexually in the marketplace. Labeling homosexuality as "white" suppresses recognition of the range of sexual identities among African Americans, further masking the spread of HIV within African American communities and retarding coalitions for AIDS activism.[5]

In a context in which HIV/AIDS is killing Black people, standing by and refusing to speak out about gender and sexuality within African

American communities contributes to the problem. It is impossible to craft an antiracist African American political agenda when the very people such an agenda claims to represent are so profoundly threatened with survival. Combating HIV/AIDS among African Americans certainly requires efforts to change existing social policies concerning education, health care, housing, and jobs. But it also requires developing a more progressive Black sexual politics among African Americans that aims to transform interpersonal relations and internal Black community politics. Such a politics might emphasize three core themes: first, a body politics grounded in the concept of the "honest body" that would enable individuals to reclaim agency lost to oppression; second, an ethic of honesty and personal accountability within all relationships that involve sexual contact; and third, increased importance placed on questions of gender and sexuality within African American politics. Changing interpersonal relations among African Americans and demanding more informed, responsible Black leadership concerning issues of gender and sexuality might catalyze a revitalized, broader antiracist social justice project.

HONEST BODIES: SEXUAL AUTONOMY AND BLACK BODY POLITICS

> If your heart and your honest body can be controlled by the state, or controlled by community taboo, are you not then, and in that case, no more than a slave ruled by outside force.
>
> —June Jordan[6]

A Black gender ideology that encourages Black people to view themselves and others as bitches, hoes, thugs, pimps, sidekicks, sissies, and modern mammies signals a dishonest body politics. In this situation, top-down power relations of race, class, gender, and sexuality permeate individual consciousness and tell African Americans how they should think about their own bodies.[7] Moreover, such power relations invade the body because they also instruct Black people how they should *feel* within their own bodies. This ideology severs mind, soul, and body from one another and helps structure oppression.[8] Taking gender-specific forms, African American men and women who come to see their bodies through the frames of the dominant society and who develop a consciousness based on these ideas are always on display. Where is the authentic, honest body in this context of dehumanization?

Honest bodies strive to treat the mental, spiritual, and physical aspects of being as interactive and synergistic. No one element becomes privileged over the other. Because honest bodies as described by June Jordan rejoin the mind, soul, and body, they become in one sense free. Starting with the mind, by interrogating one's own individual consciousness, is essential. Individuals who reject dominant scripts of Black gender ideology by fully accepting their own bodies "as is" move toward achieving honest bodies. What difference does it make if a Black woman is dark-skinned, or has long hair, or inherited "bootylicious" buttocks? Why place so much emphasis on evaluating Black men who are 5'5" as too short to date, or those with body-builder physiques as "hunks"? Black people may be bombarded with gender-specific images that deem Black bodies as less desirable if not downright ugly. But nowhere is it written that any African American need believe them. Because no organization, television network, hip-hop artist, or love partner can ever fully control what each of us thinks, individual consciousness remains a sphere of freedom. As individuals, we each have the power to reject prevailing ideas about gender and sexuality and to think about our own bodies differently.[9]

Developing honest bodies and a politics grounded in that fact thus begins from the inside out.[10] Less emphasis would be placed on how Black bodies look and how we should interpret them (scripts of Black masculinity and Black femininity) and more on how honest Black bodies feel, hear, and move. These are all elements of how individuals actually experience their bodies. We cannot actually "see" ourselves. Thus, expanding body politics beyond its current focus on the visual allows other themes to emerge, namely, new understandings of sexuality that rejoin ideas of soul and embodiment.[11]

There is evidence that Black people, however unintentionally, already draw upon a constellation of ideas and social practices that foreshadow a new body politics. In this regard, the meaning of *soul* among African Americans begins to expand ideas about sexuality itself.[12] An honest body would be in touch with its life spirit, or soul. A 1998 forum among Black intellectuals titled "Ain't We Still Got Soul?" generated a lively discussion about the meaning of soul and its connections to Black people and

Blackness. Thulani Davis notes, "in the world I grew up in, which was the segregated upper South, soul was the world we lived in."[13] Davis identifies elements of the soul culture such as, "being able to offer prayer from the heart" and "taking a solo—having something to say within the context of the room where you find yourself."[14] Ishmael Reed claims "soul is an English word that African Americans have borrowed to explain something that defies empirical investigation."[15] Clearly a booster of soul, Reed continues: "When we say soul, I think that we mean style, and there is no doubt that African Americans have a style, a way of cooking, of dancing, that's so attractive that even those who are pathologically hostile to Blacks adopt this style."[16]

The concept of soul fell out of favor in the 1980s and 1990s. Greg Tate identifies himself as a child who came of age in the late 1970s and that "by the time my generation reached its teens soul was something to be revered and parodied."[17] Tate describes his reactions to conference papers by Baraka, Reed, and Angela Davis who reconnected the term *soul* with its Yoruba, hoodoo, and Black nationalist roots: "I mulled how my own thirty-something generation and the hip hop generation's definitions of soul were more a function of reference than essence. In other words, soul wasn't nothing but a word to us—a way of describing how folk felt about the condition their condition was in back in the day."[18] Also describing a generational disconnect, Mark Anthony Neal uses the term the "post-soul aesthetic" to describe Black popular culture in the post–civil rights era. Neal claims that the post–civil rights era fostered Black identities that rendered many traditional ideas about Blackness meaningless.

Tate and Neal may be so focused on claiming a unique generational identity that they fail to see how the two periods of the post–civil rights era, namely, the legislative and social gains of the 1960s and 1970s, and the contemporary racial backlash that began in the 1980s and catalyzed punitive policies targeted toward Black youth, fostered the continuity of soul in different forms. As Portia Maultsby points out, "Soul is a concept that defines a distinctly Black worldview and a way of being. Because Black culture is not monolithic nor stagnant, each generation employs this concept in ways that reflect its unique set of circumstances, which are informed by cultural, social, and political environments."[20] Rhythm and blues (old school) and hip-hop may be differently soulful. The question lies less in choosing one form over the other than in examining how ideas about Black bodies, feelings, love, and sexuality have been configured within Black culture in the civil rights and post–civil rights eras. How did Black people feel about their bodies in response to the assaults of nineteenth- and twentieth-century scientific racism? How do Black people feel about their bodies now in the context of the new racism?

Black culture and its characteristic *soul* may be life affirming, but it is important to avoid the temptation to celebrate uncritically Black expressiveness (soul) as if it *already* constitutes a sphere of freedom. Black women who reject feminism, claiming a womanist politics for themselves where they are already liberated redefine Alice Walker's inclusive womanist vision for freedom in ways that minimize the workings of oppression.[21] Despite singing and dancing in church or partying in hip-hop venues, visiting Internet chat rooms or enjoying poetry slams, African Americans still experience the limitations of oppression. Here we can take lessons from the blues. As Angela Davis points out, "The blues idiom requires absolute honesty in the portrayal of black life. It is an idiom that does not recognize taboos: whatever figures into the larger picture of working-class African-American realities . . . is an appropriate subject of blues discourse."[22] For example, the blues contains numerous songs about prostitution, told from both the male and the female perspective. Typically, the blues do not criticize the institution, but rather treat it as real.

Across these different views of soul, one thing seems common. Soul is an inherently *embodied* concept and movement through time and space constitutes an important dimension of the expressive component of soul. Black dance provides an important template for developing honest bodies and a body politics grounded in them. As expressive (soulful) movement, Black dance links the soul with the body, the expressive, spiritual, and dynamism of life. Ishmael Reed provides a glimpse of the significance of Black dance to African Americans from all walks of life. In his essay "Introduction: Black Pleasure—An Oxymoron," Reed describes how pain and pleasure are omnipresent in Black experience, and how anything that helps Black people negotiate them is important: "one form of Black pleasure is that which makes life easier, no matter how difficult the circumstances under which this pleasure is experienced. Take dance. African American dance is used not only as a form of pleasure, but in African American religion throughout the hemisphere. Indeed, some of those religious dances have invaded American dance clubs, rendering Yoruba a pervasive, persistent cultural influence throughout most of the Western Hemisphere."[23] The meaning of dance to Black people may serve as a template for a nascent Black body politics grounded in the idea of the honest body. For example, Josephine Baker's answer to a reporter's query about her future suggests a way of being in her body that rejoins body and soul: "I shall dance all my life, I was born to dance, just for that. To live is to dance, I would like to die, breathless, spent, at the end of a dance."[24]

Baker's notion that "to live is to dance" illustrates the connection between soul (expressiveness as an individual life force) and embodiment (how people feel, move, and think within their bodies). It also points to a more expansive definition of sexuality as an embodied function. Because sexuality lies at the intersection of soul (individual expressiveness) and body (dance and movement), an expansive and redefined sexuality can serve as a critical site of struggle for an honest body. In this regard, sexual autonomy, namely, the ability to select one's own sexual orientation, sexual practices, and/or sexual partners, becomes ground zero in claiming an honest body.[25]

Rethinking sexual autonomy for Black people is essential for a body politics that rejoins mind, soul, and body. In this endeavor, Audre Lorde's work on the power of the erotic has been invaluable.[26] With its focus on the erotic, passion, and desire, Lorde's writing suggests that Black lesbian sexualities can be read as one expression of the reclamation of a despised Black female body. By claiming agency for Black lesbians, individuals whose race, gender, sexuality, and, in many cases, class, and age places them at the bottom of the social hierarchy, Lorde's work rescues Black female bodies that are most devalued and grants them respect.[27] Since Lorde's work over thirty years ago, Black female desire for women (or men) and agency concerning their own sexuality can now be more openly expressed. Certainly this theme of expanding Black female desire and pleasure permeates the work of Alice Walker, Gayl Jones, Gloria Naylor, Toni Morrison, and other major African American women writers.[28] Yet examining the various dimensions of sexual autonomy for Black women remains in its infancy. In *Longing to Tell: Black Women Talk about Sexuality and Intimacy*, Tricia Rose reports the sexual testimonies of Black women from all walks of life.[29] Realizing that American society is fixated on issues of race and sexuality, Rose saw that "we are bombarded by stories about sex and romance, but we almost never hear what black women have to say. The sexual stories that black women long to tell are being told in beauty parlors, kitchens, health clubs, restaurants, malls, and laundry rooms, but a larger, more accessible conversation for all women to share and from which to learn has not yet begun."[30] Black men too suffer from a silencing concerning the emotional, expressive, and erotic dimensions of their lives.[31]

Developing the sexual autonomy of honest bodies also invokes the power of the erotic, a force that is very different than the commodified sexuality pushed within mass media. This distinction between the erotic and sex (fucking), however, is far from clear, especially within contemporary Black popular culture. For example, Joan Morgan clearly confuses the type of erotic power proposed by Audre Lorde with the commodified sexuality that permeates hip-hop culture. In discussing the "ultimate truth about erotic power," Morgan argues: "without financial independence, education, ambition, intelligence, spirituality, and love, punanny alone isn't all that powerful. The reality is that it's easily replaceable, inexhaustible in supply, and quite frankly, common as shit. Women who value their erotic power over everything else stand to do some serious damage to their self-esteem."[32]

Rebelling against the rules and reclaiming the erotic means that Black straight and gay people alike can support one another in claiming honest bodies that are characterized by sexual autonomy. Using one's honest body engages all forms of sexual expression that bring pleasure and joy.[33] Overall, soul, expressiveness, spirituality, sensuality, sexuality, and an expanded notion of the erotic as a life force that may include all of these ideas seem to be tightly bundled together within this notion of an honest body that is not alienated from itself and where each individual has the freedom to pursue his or her sense of the erotic.

Two major challenges arise in advancing a philosophy of honest bodies that might catalyze a progressive Black body politics. For one, not all pleasure is political, and not all forms of sexual expression signal the presence of honest bodies. Seeking pleasure can simply be self-centered, self-serving, and selfish, the classic booty call in which one partner is unaware of the rules. In a context in which popular culture markets pleasure, especially sexual pleasure, as the antidote to alienation, and does so by using Black bodies and race as proxy for danger, excitement, forbidden practices, and sex, African Americans must be careful in embracing any strategy that claims pleasure as *inherently* transgressive.[34] Sexuality among African Americans must be understood in the context of structures of power (whether class, race, gender, or sexuality). Embracing "pleasure" without a broader understanding of how sexuality articulates with power relations of race, class, and gender, especially if the simple act of claiming pleasure is deemed inherently progressive, runs the risk of resurrecting stereotypes of Black people whereby ideas about Blackness remain culturally coded as sexual.

Another challenge for crafting a progressive body politics concerns countering the high level of sexual violence that permeates American society. Love, sexuality, and violence can be deeply intertwined and, for many Black people, separating them is not easy. Violence is often eroticized within American culture to the point where sexuality becomes understood through a prism of violence. For example, the threat of danger may heighten sexual attraction. Women who pass up good guys for thugs may find the attraction of rule breaking itself arousing. Taken further, some consumers of film and mass media find the high levels of victimization of Blacks, women, gays and lesbians, children, and poor people sexually stimulating. Certainly the movie industry and certain themes within hip-hop culture contribute to linking violence and sexuality. Violence may not be a sexual act per se, but its outcome may provide an arousal resembling that produced by sexual orgasm. Individuals who participate, however vicariously, in violence against an opponent may achieve heightened levels of excitement. For example, lynchings were public events at which Black men were often castrated, indicating that much more was at stake concerning White masculinity than punishing an individual wrongdoer.[35] Violence can also accompany deep feelings and passions that often are associated with love. Men who beat their wives would never consider hitting women about whom they cared little—strong feelings and "love" seem intertwined with the feelings that foster such behavior. Similarly, the degree of violence among Black men cannot all be attributed to the frustrations of dealing with racism. Instead, some violence among men may reflect the fear of a latent homoerotic love.[36]

Achieving honest bodies and the sexual autonomy that they promise will not be easy because, as James Baldwin points out: "people find it very difficult to act on what they know. To act is to be committed, and to be committed is to be in danger."[37] The struggle may be well worth the effort, especially in times of living with HIV/AIDS. Individuals living in honest bodies should do what they want with their bodies, and reject what they don't want. Yet how does one have pleasure and remain safe during an era when HIV constitutes such a danger? The old binary thinking that juxtaposed a politics of respectability to one of ill-repute (the derogated Black sexuality) promises safety through sexual abstinence ("just say no"). Yet the cost of safety is to deny bodily pleasure. When it comes to HIV/AIDS, a new path to an honest body defined by sexual autonomy mandates a commitment to thoughts, feelings, and actions that might place one in danger. Such a commitment involves living life differently such that, according to Baldwin: "to be sensual, I think, is to respect and rejoice in the force of life, of life itself, and to be *present* in all that ones does, from the effort of loving to the breaking of bread."[38] Thus, being in one's honest body becomes an essential part of the "force of life."

"READYING UP FOR SOME HONESTY:"
REBELLIOUS GENDER IDEOLOGY

Men have got to develop some heart and some sound analysis to realize that when sisters get passionate about themselves and their direction, it does not mean they're readying up to kick men's ass. They're readying up for honesty. And women have got to develop some heart and sound analysis so they can resist the temptation of buying peace with their man with self-sacrifice and posturing.
—Toni Cade Bambara[39]

Sexual contact constitutes one main source of HIV infection. Because sexual intimacy reflects an individual's relationship with his or her own body as well as how others see and value that body, individual sex acts are highly politicized. The danger posed by HIV/AIDS forces individual men and women to weigh the nature of each sexual contact, as well as all interpersonal relationships in which sexual expression might take physical form. For all African American men and women, straight and LGBT alike, "ready up for some honesty" concerning gender and sexuality is essential. However, "readying up for some honesty" is unlikely to happen in the absence of both a Black female and a male sexual autonomy, as well as a progressive Black gender ideology that helps Black men and women see other alternatives to those that currently exist.

Understanding how ideas about Black masculinity and Black femininity affect interpersonal relationships is intrinsically important, and it is necessary for addressing HIV/AIDS. Individual choice lies at the heart of any long-range solutions to HIV/AIDS. On the one hand, individual African American women and men can construct their own sexuality and that of their partners as sites of control and domination. When heterosexual men, for example, demand sexual intercourse without a condom, they become part of the HIV problem, whether or not they are infected with the HIV virus. When heterosexual women trade sexual favors for material gain without practicing safe sex, they too are part of the problem. On the other hand, when individual African American women and men strive to develop honest bodies and to reclaim the erotic as a site of freedom, and love as a source of affirmation for self and others, they challenge the spread of HIV/AIDS. Ironically, the much-maligned 1997 film *Booty Call* made these ideas explicit for heterosexuals by calling into question condom use in both committed relationships and mutual booty calls. The film explored one Black man's struggles to "ready up for some honesty" with his girlfriend by rejecting definitions of Black masculinity that rendered him an irresponsible boy. But the film did not stop with this endorsement of traditional heterosexual relationships. The film also sent another important message—sexual autonomy and sexual pleasure can be organized around the pleasure of a mutual booty call in which both parties agree to protect one another by practicing safe sex.

When it comes to HIV/AIDS, African American women and men, straight and LBGT, are all harmed by the refusal to "ready up for some honesty." One reason for the continued spread of HIV is that about half of people who carry the HIV virus have not been diagnosed as HIV positive, treated, or both. Many unknowingly transmit the virus to their sex partners. Take, for example, how the politics of gender and sexuality have affected the rapid growth of HIV/AIDS among poor Black women in the Mississippi Delta and across the rural South. Between 1990 and 2000, Southern states with large African American populations experienced a dramatic increase in HIV infections among African American women.[40] Most of the women lived in poverty, contracted HIV through heterosexual contact, and most found out that they were HIV positive when they became pregnant. Some women started having sex at very young ages, almost always with older men, and they found that they had little ability to persuade their partners to use condoms.[41] An informal sex-for-money situation existed, where nothing was negotiated up front, but where unstated assumptions existed in which women who engaged in casual sex with men would be rewarded with a little financial help, perhaps in paying the rent or in buying groceries. From the outside, these behaviors seem to support accusations of Black women's promiscuity, but the impoverished Black women who engaged in sex-for-money relationships desperately needed the money, especially if they had elderly parents or dependent children. They knew about HIV/AIDS but felt virtually powerless to take the steps needed to protect themselves from infection. Because they had so little control over other aspects of their lives, they felt that if God wanted them to get AIDS, then they resigned themselves to getting it.

The level of denial among these African American women who felt that testing positive for HIV could not happen to them resembles the stunning growth of a similar culture of denial among young Black gay men. Gay men account for the largest proportion of new HIV infections (43%), followed by people infected by heterosexual sex (27%), and intravenous drug users (23%).[42] Largely as a result of aggressive organizing and advocacy by gay White men, the disease leveled off in this population. Yet a study of approximately 5,700 gay men in six major U.S. cities reports that the rates of unawareness among Black gay men ages fifteen to twenty-nine are "staggeringly high." Among those found to have HIV, 90 percent of Blacks said that they did not know they were infected.[43] Given the history of AIDS activism among gay men, this lack of knowledge among Black gay men is disconcerting.

The emergence of a Black gay male subculture in which gay and bisexual Black men live on the Down Low (DL) aggravates this situation. The secretive nature of the DL subculture speaks to the linking of danger, dishonesty, and excitement. Popularized in the 1990s by singers TLC and R. Kelly, the term Down Low means "secret." It has a sexy ring to it, a hint that the person is doing something that is wrong but that "feels right." DL culture places a premium on pleasure and there is a certain degree of freedom in not having to fit within rigid sexual self-definitions. Men on the DL convey a strong sense of independence. At the same time, the Black masculine identities constructed within this subculture place Black gay and bisexual men at risk. Many DL guys search for the roughest, most masculine thugs, men who often do not use condoms. William, a participant in the Atlanta DL subculture, describes this phenomenon to journalist Benoit Denizet-Lewis: "Part of the attraction to thugs is that they're careless and carefree. Putting on a condom doesn't fit in with that. A lot of DL guys aren't going to put on a condom, because that ruins the fantasy." Denizet-Lewis draws out the implications of the lack of condom use: "It also shatters the denial—stopping to put on a condom forces guys on the DL to acknowledge, on some level, that they're having sex with men."[44]

As these examples suggest, the denial of honest bodies as well as the absence of honesty within heterosexual and homosexual relationships alike place everyone at risk. Despite the importance of HIV/AIDS, sexual practices associated with safe sex such as promoting condom use are still seen by far too many African American men as interfering with their pleasure and challenging a view of Black masculinity that glorifies sexual virility. Consider, for example, how the belief in having multiple sexual partners as an indicator of Black masculinity works to spread HIV, especially through unprotected sexual contact. When mass media figure Wilt Chamberlain bragged that he had engaged in sexual contact with over 10,000 women, he helped reinforce this notion that "real" Black men have multiple sexual partners. The level of denial of Black men living on the DL places their Black wives and girlfriends in harm's way. Public health officials are alarmed about men on the DL who spread HIV to unsuspecting wives and girlfriends—in 2001, almost two-thirds of women in the United States who found out they had AIDS were Black.[45] For some men and women, even testing positive for HIV does not serve as a deterrent to engaging in unprotected sex with unsuspecting partners. Behaviors such as these signal a fundamental reluctance to question Black gender ideology, especially the nexus of sexuality and violence that upholds hegemonic masculinity in the United States.

Overall, African Americans certainly need to "ready up for some honesty" in intimate love relationships. Doing so would enable individuals to tell the difference between the commodified sexuality and romantic love that are so heavily marketed within mass media and more complex notions of sexual autonomy and eroticism. As systems of oppression, racism, sexism, class exploitation, and heterosexism all gain power by denying sexual autonomy and annexing the power of the erotic for their own ends. In this context, reclaiming love and sexuality constitutes a necessary first step. At the same time, love and sexuality are insufficient for confronting the economic exploitation, political powerlessness, and sexual violence of the new racism. "Love" is often what is manipulated within relationships of domination. Can "love" conquer violence in an abusive relationship? Would "loving" their masters really have toppled the system of slavery?

Identifying the micro-politics of intimate love relationships as a sphere of freedom is alluring, but as the HIV/AIDS epidemic reminds us, sexuality is not necessarily a place of freedom. Instead, manipulating sexuality, annexing the power of the erotic, and using both to deny the very humanity of love constitute important mechanisms of social control. This annexation perverts African Americans' understandings of their own bodies and frames how everyone else perceives and treats Black people. For philosopher Michel Foucault, whose pioneering work has profoundly affected understandings of sexuality and power, "Sexuality is not opposed to and subversive of power. On the contrary, sexuality is a 'dense transfer point' of power."[46] When tied to his work on the disciplinary power of bureaucracies (the case of prisons for African Americans under the new racism), sexuality becomes an important terrain of control under hegemonic social relations that squeeze out all dissent.

Critical race theorist Paul Gilroy certainly supports this view. Gilroy paints a gloomy picture of the possibilities for finding freedom within sexual relationships. Noting that the word *freedom* is disappearing from the vocabulary of Blacks in the West, Gilroy argues that the yearning for freedom is being transported into a different, private mode, one that he calls "racialized biopolitics."[47] Within Gilroy's schema, because literal freedom has been won, Blacks search for substantive freedom by escaping into personal relationships and striving for freedom via the release provided by sexual orgasms. Just as drug addicts become addicted to the pleasure and/or avoidance of pain provided by their drug of choice, sexuality can provide a similar release. But what happens, queries Gilroy, when the internal space of pleasure becomes emblematic of Black politics? During prior periods of freedom struggle, "wild, intense sexual activity between consenting heterosexual adults in private" signaled African American success in claiming spaces of privacy.[48] Now, however, because marketplace relations of Black popular culture have found a way to annex these "dense transfer points" of contemporary oppression, private sites of Black sexual expression are no longer rebellious. As evidence for this gloomy view of love relationships, Gilroy argues: "the sharpest break between the older traditional patterns and the newer biopolitics is evident where what were once love stories have mutated into sex stories."[49] Stated differently, the people dancing to Missy Elliott's "Get Yr Freak On" may feel free, but the economic and political mandates of the new racism want them to buy CDs, clothing, gym shoes, liquor, cell phones, and use these material possessions as substitutes for the abscence of deep love in their lives.

Robert Reid-Pharr also expresses skepticism about the ability of the erotic to hold its own in the context of new social relations. On the one hand, Reid-Pharr believes that the homoeroticism of gay sexuality constitutes a potential sphere of freedom. For example, despite the regressive racial and gender politics that framed the 1995 Million Man March on Washington, he describes moments of transcendence that felt like freedom: "If freedom were truly the ultimate goal of the march, then it was freedom of a discrete, limited kind: freedom from the crushing burden of images—the criminal, the addict, the vengeful lover, the victim, the invalid. Instead, we were presented with an ocean of men, orderly, directed, clean-cut, and remarkably eloquent."[50] For Reid-Pharr, the source of freedom at the march lay in Black men's ability to create a Black male space that kept the damaging effects of Black gender ideology at bay. Despite his claims that love, sexuality, and freedom are intertwined, Reid-Pharr also cautions that eroticism cannot be installed as a new "model" for sexual liberation: "What is more difficult to accept is the idea that the sexual act, at least as it is performed between queers . . . is not necessarily a good, expansive, and progressive thing, a place in which individuals exist for a moment outside themselves such that new possibilities are at once imagined and actualized."[51]

What a complex world Foucault, Gilroy, and Reid-Pharr present, one in which even the interior space of Black consciousness may have lost the power to love, or to even try. In their worlds, domination, which operates both by structuring power from the top down through disciplinary means such as prisons and by annexing the power of the erotic available to each individual human being, has won. Certainly those Black men and women who engage in unsafe sex, and who physically, emotionally, and/or sexually abuse one another, fit this profile. In the sobering world produced by HIV/AIDS, these works provide an important corrective against overly optimistic views of human nature that counsel us that "love" is the answer. At the same time, this interior space of sexuality, sensuality, the erotic, and love does not always serve as a dense transfer point of power that disempowers African American men and women. When it comes to individual consciousness, new knowledge of progressive Black sexual politics can generate important behavioral changes that make intimate love relationships key sites of rebellion.

In readying up for some honesty, African American men and women might refashion the relationship between love and freedom in ways that expand our understanding of the connections among soul, spirituality, embodiment, sensuality, expressiveness, eroticism, and sexuality. Take, for example, James Baldwin's discussion of love as a spiritual journey and as a means of moving toward "liberation" or freedom: "To be with God is really to be involved with some enormous, overwhelming desire, and joy, and power which you cannot control, which controls you. I conceive of my own life as a journey toward something I do not understand, which in the going toward, makes me better. I conceive of God, in fact, as a means of liberation and not as a means to control others. Love does not begin and end the way we seem to think it does. Love is a battle, love is a way; love is a growing up."[52] Baldwin places his discussion of love in a spiritual context, but such love need not be associated with an organized religion nor recognize God as the head of a church. This mature notion of love at its fullest imvolves bringing an honest body to a fully human relationship. How many African Americans are ready for that kind of honesty?

BUILDING COMMUNITY:
LOVE AND BLACK EMPOWERMENT

It's clear to me that I spent too much time in the past believing it
was necessary to mobilize entire armies against the devastating
effects of racism, and not enough time considering how one person
can help another person to heal from those effects. A chain, after
all, is only as strong as its individual links, and it seems to me now
that the way to help strengthen my community as a whole is to
improve the quality of my relationships—romantic and otherwise—with individual Black folks I meet every day. To do this

requires tearing down all the walls I've built around myself and
taking a long, hard look inside; what I've already discovered, much
to my surprise, is that the view isn't really all that bad.

—Quinn Eli[53]

The issues raised by the HIV/AIDS epidemic suggest that the need for a
progressive Black sexual politics is far from an abstract, academic concern.
Advocates from around the globe lobby for effective treatment and prevention initiatives, for example, making HIV medications available to all
who need them and a good public health effort to educate people about the
disease and how they can protect themselves. But what does prevention
really mean? As the African American women in Mississippi and the
African American gay men in major U.S. cities suggest, prevention
requires going much further than information about disease transmission
and free access to condoms. Definitions of Black masculinity and Black
femininity, the recognition of an array of sexual identities (straight, gay,
lesbian, bisexual, and transgendered), questions concerning sexual practices and when "safe sex" is truly "safe," ideas about whether and when to
get tested for the HIV virus and how to reveal the outcome to one's sexual
partners, all are questioned by the presence of HIV/AIDS. These issues
require new understandings of Black body politics, new interpersonal relationships that "ready up for some honesty," and new conceptualizations of
the idea of *Black community* and the politics it might engender.

One way that African Americans might move toward a progressive
Black sexual politics lies in developing inclusionary definitions of Black
community. Despite its disfavor within contemporary academic circles, the
phrase *Black community* is one that many ordinary African Americans recognize and use, if only to mourn its seeming loss. The language of community encompasses two main ideas. The first views community as being
synonymous with family and/or people. In this case, the term *Black community* is used interchangeably with the phrase *Black people*. Both concepts
view all Blacks as connected and reference the physical, emotional, and psy-
chic spaces in which Black people "belong."[54] This use connotes moral, ethical associations whereby African American families, neighborhoods,
churches, fraternal organizations, and civic organizations serve as places of
acceptance and safety that affirm African American individuals. Providing
respite from racial oppression, ideally, Black "communities" become spaces

in which Black people can be honest with one another and find recognition and acceptance. This view of Black community also invokes views of Black leadership whereby African Americans with more talent, skills, and resources devote them to building up the community. Because Black people are seen as organically connected, these "race" men and women work on behalf of the "race's" progress.[55] Black humanity is affirmed without question within such communities. This idealized view of Black community involves claiming a Black identity that is grounded in a moral, ethical framework of acceptance of each African American individual.

The HIV/AIDS crisis reveals that the majority of African Americans experience neither their communities nor their relations with other Black people in this fashion. Instead, a narrow Black identity politics that demands an unquestioned loyalty to one version of Blackness consistently privileges some versions of Blackness and disadvantages others.[56] Such politics routinely derogate and exclude African Americans who are the wrong sexual orientation; who love significant others that are the wrong color; who do not wear expensive clothes and gym shoes; who are deemed to be too young or too old to express a worthwhile opinion; or whose gender merits that they take a back seat in families, churches, and other Black organizations. African Americans as a group are politically harmed by this perversion of Black identity politics that installs rigid social hierarchies within the boundaries of race and then requires unquestioned loyalty to the "race." This version of Black identity politics also undercuts the very definition of community that it seemingly represents. Without developing moral, ethical communities that fully accept and support each African American individual, how can African Americans meet the challenge of HIV/AIDS? Why should non–Black American citizens care about African Americans if Black people do not value and care for one another?

The language of community also connotes a second main idea, namely, a political solidarity whereby people see themselves as part of a larger political entity that shares a common agenda. In the context of the new racism, Black people as a cultural community would also constitute a political community charged with developing an antiracist politics. Black antiracist politics would strive to empower African Americans as a collectivity in order to solve problems that disproportionately affect the broader Black community, in this case, the HIV/AIDS epidemic. This understanding of community comes with its own set of problems. For one, being

Black is insufficient for building a political agenda because the needs and perceptions of African Americans vary greatly. For another, political communities typically have some sort of ideology or philosophy that bind them together by explaining their current predicaments and suggesting strategies for change. But no ideology *by itself* can explain HIV/AIDS let alone craft a political agenda that will help people deal with it.[57] Finally, because HIV/AIDS (as is the case for virtually every social issue) does not affect just Black people, solutions require coalitions with other groups who share a similar agenda. Addressing the challenges of HIV/AIDS certainly requires a broad-based, coalition politics. But one might ask, given the deeply entrenched nature of racism in the United States, how long-lasting these coalitions would be when the immediacy of the issue in question fades? When it comes to HIV/AIDS, for example, what arguments would be so compelling that they would convince affluent gay White men in the West to throw in their lot with poor South African adolescent girls and vice versa? What ideologies would sustain such a coalition?[58]

Responding to HIV/AIDS requires building Black communities that encompass both meanings of community, namely, a revitalized Black identity politics that recognizes the significance of gender and sexuality and political communities that work for Black empowerment, primarily as part of broader coalitions with other groups. For both connotations of community, the relationships that Black individuals have with one another become ground zero for a revitalized Black community politics. Love relationships are essential because they are the glue that holds Black community together.

On its most basic level, love relationships between two people constitute a community of two members. For example, the love relationship between Asha and Rashid described in Bandele's memoir *The Prisoner's Wife* (as discussed at the end of chapter 8) points to the significance of an ethic of care in building a more politicized understanding of oppression and how it might be resisted. By recognizing patterns of sameness and difference that joined them, they constructed a community of two. Asha and Rashid's story suggests that if these two individuals can recognize one another's humanity, love one another despite their faults, and commit to one another in the harsh environment that destroys love and therefore self (the actual prison and the metaphorical prisons of racism, sexism, etc.) then love and commitment constitute important qualities for a progressive

Black sexual politics. This politicized love is grounded in a type of commitment to self and others that comes from seeing Black humanity in the context of oppression, and recognizing that choosing to love in that context is a political act.

The message is simple—take a stand against oppression, love a Black woman; take a stand against oppression, love a Black man. Such love is extremely difficult to co-opt. There have always been Ashas and Rashids in Black America, people who refused to follow the rules. However, we either fail to recognize them and/or just do not know what to make of them. More important, we have not been encouraged to *be* them in the contexts of our everyday lives.

Love certainly holds a prominent place in African American intellectual traditions. Perhaps the best known is Martin Luther King, Jr.'s concept of "beloved community." King spoke of the need to cultivate a three-dimensional love for God, Self, and Others that in turn might serve as a framework for community. King may have popularized the concept of beloved community, but contemporary scholars now use it to rethink the workings of gender and sexuality. Take, for example, theologian Kelly Douglas's discussion of how agape, spirituality, and sexuality are linked and have a place within Christian theology. Spurred on by the inaction of Black churches in confronting HIV/AIDS, Douglas searched for theology that would provide an alternative interpretive framework designed to change the church's approach to sexuality:

> The love of God made manifest in Jesus is what has come to be understood as agape. Agape is God's love. It is an active love, the giving of oneself for the sake of justice and the building of an authentically human community. . . . A positive embrace of human sexuality is critical to agape, and it is crucial for those who would radiate what it means to be created in the image of God. Human sexuality is what provides men and women with the capacity to enter into relationships with others. Sexuality is that dimension of humanity that urges relationship. Sexuality is a gift from God that, if properly appreciated, helps women and men to become more fully human by entering into loving relationships.[59]

Kelly suggests that embracing this notion of agape fosters a politics whereby the beloved community should protect its most vulnerable members. In this context, HIV/AIDS would not be seen as a crosscutting issue that only affects some members of the community, but rather a consensus issue whereby the community recognized how its very being was threatened by what was happening to its most vulnerable members. Versions of the beloved community in general and of a notion of a Black beloved community that finds space for all of its members and is complete with their heterogeneity are not a luxury. In confronting the challenge of HIV/AIDS, such a notion of community is essential.

How does one actually build such a beloved community that would be affirming of all Black people yet simultaneously would be accepting of a broader social justice agenda? Within African American history, striving for a beloved community has not been an abstraction; it has guided political activism. One significant feature of the civil rights movement was that, because agape addressed freedom struggles of *actual* and not imagined Black communities, one finds models of women and men who tried to build beloved communities in reality. For example, Ella Baker's notion of group-centered leadership suggests a very different form of community organization and, by implication, conception of freedom. From Baker's perspective, the very idea of leading people to freedom was a contradiction in terms. Freedom required that people stop relying on leaders and develop the capacity to analyze their own social position and understand their collective ability to change the circumstances of their lives. In one interview she stated, "Strong people don't need strong leaders. My basic sense of it has always been to get people to understand that in the long run they themselves are the only protection they have against violence or injustice. . . . People have to be made to understand that they cannot look for salvation anywhere but to themselves."[60]

The civil rights movement provides important insights concerning how African Americans tried to build a beloved community that would be affirming of African Americans yet simultaneously focused on a broader social justice agenda. Yet because its challenge lay in confronting deeply entrenched patterns of legal racial segregation, it faced markedly different challenges than those associated with joblessness, inner-city decay, the commodification of Black popular culture, and other manifestations of the new racism. It is one thing to say that Black people should love one another and that this should serve as the basis for community and for an impassioned politics. It is entirely another to conceptualize how a beloved community can be accomplished within contemporary America. Divisions among African Americans make notions such as beloved community seem like an unattainable abstraction. Black youth in particular remain alienated from these ideas, associating them with either the "near obsessive national attention given to praising the long gone civil rights movement" or dismissed by caricaturing the Black Power movement.[61] Such praise and/or dismissal ignores the fact that Black youth who have come of age during the four decades following the civil rights movement not only have *not* seen its promise of a beloved community come to fruition, they have been deemed the problem of America (not its hope for the future).

What will it take for Black people to love one another? The power on this one seems to be entirely in our own hands. What will it take for more African Americans to arrive at a place at which we can say: "Yes, my spirit is liberated, even here behind a wall, a razor-wire fence, and four electronically locked doors. Here with Rashid, I have never felt so open, so free, or for that matter, and by extension, never so close to God."[62] We currently have no language for the "love" needed for this endeavor, only terms that get us close. In a context in which "fucking" serves as a poor substitute for a sense of the erotic that might nourish body and soul, and in which courts protect child pornography on the Internet as bona fide expressions of free speech, popular notions of "romantic love" create more problems than they solve. So we have to start small, by thinking through what is needed for a new gender ideology for everyone and for new types of relationships for African American women and men based on these fresh ways of seeing others and ourselves. Forging our own original paths might enable us to develop a progressive Black sexual politics that one day will meet the challenge of HIV/AIDS.

THE POWER OF A
FREE MIND

Any real change implies the breakup of the world as one
has always known it, the loss of all that gave one an
identity, the end of safety. And at such a moment,
unable to see and not daring to imagine what the future
will now bring forth, one clings to what one knew; to
what one possessed or dreamed that one possessed. Yet,
it is only when a man is able, without bitterness or self-
pity, to surrender a dream he has long cherished or a
privilege he has long possessed that he is set free—he
has set himself free—for higher dreams, for greater
privileges.

—James Baldwin[1]

James Baldwin tells us much about the process of negotiating
the paradoxes of Black gender ideology within the confines of
contemporary Black sexual politics. When it comes to romantic
love relationships, for example, far too many heterosexual
African American women cling to what they "know" and try to
apply existing gender scripts even when such scripts have little
hope of success. "Maybe if I had longer hair, lighter skin, and
smaller lips; maybe if I talked more quietly and let him think
that he is right when I know that he's not; maybe if I share him
with other women, I'll be able to keep a man," many speculate.
"I have to be strong to compensate for his weaknesses," they
reason. The loss of what one "dreamed that one possessed" can

be even more insidious. Most men see gender equality with women as a defeat and this perception affects their relationships both with women and with one another. Young, working-class African American men, for example, can engage in violence toward one another and toward women for no apparent reason, in part because they do not feel powerful and fear the loss of an expected male entitlement. "He tried to steal my gym shoes; she 'dissed' me; he was looking at my woman; he was looking at my ass; all that skeezer wanted was my money; s/he deserved what s/he got," they rationalize. Violence comes in defense of an illusionary respect that all desire but few really possess. "I may spend the rest of my life in prison for murdering that 'bitch'/ 'nigger'/ 'faggot,'" some reason, "but now I know that I'm a man." So much fear accompanies being African American—fear of being unloved, alone, disrespected, ignored, ridiculed, too visible, invisible, silenced, or forgotten.

In this situation of fear in which every modicum of privilege may be staunchly defended, defying existing Black sexual politics can signal "the loss of all that gave one an identity" and "the end of safety." With so much at stake, no wonder so few African American women and men dispute, let alone openly and in public, prevailing Black sexual politics. Many complain about their love lives (or lack thereof), but few challenge the social structures that bring about their unhappiness. But without challenging a U.S. sexual politics that installs a hegemonic White masculinity in the center of all assessments of human worth as the gold standard against which we are all measured (and that includes White men); that masks the gender-specific forms of political economy that keep far too many African American women dependent on welfare and African American men locked up in prison; that defends these state practices by reconfiguring institutionalized lynching and rape as forms of sexualized violence suitable for controlling African American populations; and that justifies the new racism with a media that is saturated with updated, class-specific images of bucks and jezebels, how can African Americans develop a more progressive Black sexual politics?

Given the potential loss of perceived privileges let alone the very real threat of loss of safety, why do it at all? Why rock the boat and defy prevailing Black sexual politics? Certainly one reason concerns efforts to avoid the abuse that routinely accompanies playing by the rules. Slaves ran away because they knew that they were being exploited and victimized. Their prisons were clear to them. Women who leave abusive relationships see safety not in staying with their batterers but in leaving them. Gays, lesbians, bisexuals, and transgendered individuals choose to leave the closet because the emotional abuse of remaining closeted may be more damaging than the physical danger of being identifiably "out." Given the mistreatment that so many African American men and women experience due to the body politics that accompany ideas about Black sexuality as well as the gender politics expressed via views of Black masculinity and Black femininity, rejecting prevailing Black sexual politics may provide a respite from abuse.

But there's more. Baldwin also holds out the heady possibilities of the *benefits* that might ensue should individuals try to change both the systems that confine them and their reactions to those systems. For African American women, straight and gay alike, relinquishing the cherished dream of finding a sexual partner of the appropriate race, gender, social class, age, skin color, and religion may be the precise action needed to be "set free" to find a more complex love. For African American men, straight and gay alike, surrendering the seeming privileges of being their mothers' "baby boys," or the extra attention afforded Black men who are deemed to be an "endangered species," or the ability of heterosexual Black male college students to exploit the sex-ratio imbalance to get as many women as they want, or the perpetual excuses many African American men offer for decidedly bad behavior ("racism made me do it—can't a brother catch a break?") may be the price of being "set free." For African American women, men, and transgendered people, the dreams catalyzed within a context of oppression remain limited—oppression crowds out the possibilities of new, more liberatory dreams.

Confronting existing gender ideology, prevailing notions of Black sexuality, and the social relations that they justify raises an important question of how to move toward freedom in the context of oppression. With prison as the metaphor for Black life, freedom becomes its antithesis. Prison can be literal—actual laws and customs that foster forms of subordination of race, class, gender, and sexuality. Prison can also be figurative—ideas about heterosexism and about masculinity and femininity can keep some African Americans as securely locked up in small worlds as the most powerful laws. As Gaines points out, "a jail is a jail, but the greatest imprisonment of all and, therefore, the greatest freedom, too, is in your mind."[2] Within the confines of race, African Americans police one another, using the cross-cutting weapons of sexuality, gender, and class. Is it possible to craft a new gender ideology, new understandings of Black sexuality, and new social class relations that are not predicated upon dominance? For African Americans as a group, collective freedom struggles require a progressive sexual politics. For individuals, claiming new identities of race, gender, and sexuality, and seeing one another in honest and loving ways, reverses the process of dehumanization associated with oppression. In essence, struggling to both redefine Black masculinity and Black femininity in ways that are life affirming and live one's life by those new self-definitions may be what is needed to move toward "higher dreams," "greater privileges," and, ultimately, a degree of personal freedom that can never occur when one lives by someone else's rules.

How do we do this? How might we translate the desire to change into action strategies that might produce honest bodies, honest loving relationships, and African American community politics predicated upon a love ethic? Toni Cade Bambara points to the enormity of the task of developing the power of a free mind that will catalyze the type of progressive Black sexual politics suggested here: "Perhaps we need to face the terrifying and overwhelming possibility that there are no models, and that we shall have to create from scratch."[3] Starting from scratch is difficult. But the importance of this task cannot be underestimated because, as the challenges of HIV/AIDS reveal, African American survival may depend on it. Acceptance and escape constitute important, timeworn, and often effective strategies. They do grant individuals a place within existing power relations. Yet neither strategy challenges the historical Black gender ideology that resurrects ideas about "weak men, strong women" and places them in service to the new racism. Neither acceptance nor escape can support a progressive Black sexual politics because neither constructs alternatives to current arrangements.

African Americans need to rebel against the ideas and practices that disempower us. African Americans need different conceptions of femininity and masculinity that do not simply mimic those of White men and women, but that reflect the needs of actual lived Black experience and that contribute toward building a true democracy in the United States. In this context, Black people must rebel against existing Black sexual politics throughout the entire system; from the micro-politics that frame the one-on-one interactions of everyday life; through trying to change the ethos of the Black Church and other Black community organizations; through the macro-politics of building new social movements with other groups who are engaged in similar social justice initiatives. Rebellion without direction, however, can be fruitless. Sanyika Shakur came to this realization after spending years in prison: "little did I know that I had been resisting all my life. By not being a good black American I was resisting. But my resistance was retarded because it had no political objective. . . . Repression is funny. It can breed resistance, though it doesn't mean that the resistance will be political, positive, or revolutionary."[4]

Rebellions are usually the purview of youth because they have the most to gain and the least to lose. African American youth in partnership with White youth were at the forefront of the civil rights struggles; Black youth formed the core of the Black power movement; and Black South African youth gave up years of their education to resist the policies of apartheid. Rebellious youth who are armed with a vision and the knowledge and skills needed to build a movement can work wonders. When it comes to issues of gender and sexuality, Black youth must lead the way in the next phase of antiracist struggle because failing to do so virtually guarantees them an impoverished future. Surrendering old dreams should enable Black people to dream new ones. In this sense, as James Baldwin suggests, Black people may set ourselves free, "for higher dreams, for greater privileges."

NOTES

INTRODUCTION

1. Collins 2000a.
2. Collins 1998.
3. Sexuality and sexual orientation are social constructs that are connected to gender scripts, the constellation of behaviors a culture deems appropriate or even ideal for men and women. These roles include not only behavior but also attitudes and emotions that are seen as being a normal man or woman. Because gender scripts are frequently used to define the parameters of sexuality, all forms of sexuality must be understood as reflecting a specific culture (Greene 2000, 240).
4. Collins 2000a.
5. See, e.g., Staples 1979.
6. Thomas 1996.
7. I write extensively about the concept of critical social theory in *Fighting Words*. Critical social theory constitutes theorizing about the social in defense of economic and social justice. What makes critical social theory "critical" is its commitment to justice, for one's own group and/or for that of other groups. Where social group differences exist such that some groups are privileged while others are oppressed, achieving social justice requires resisting oppression. Thus, while individuals matter, I emphasize justice as a group-based phenomenon. Questions of justice and fairness typically fall outside the scope of traditional definitions of social theory, yet they emerge as central to critical social theory. See *Fighting Words* for a comprehensive analysis of critical social theory (Collins 1998).
8. This project relies upon a broad corpus of empirical and conceptual studies that have been done by others. The edited volumes *Words of Fire* and *Traps* provide solid introductions to questions of masculinity and femininity within African American communities (Guy-Sheftall 1995; Byrd and Guy-Sheftall 2001). Donna Franklin's *Enduring Inequality* provides an historical summary of Black family life and love relationships (Franklin 1997). For readers who are unfamiliar with the internal dynamics of African American communities, *Gender Talk*, coauthored by Johnnetta Cole and Beverly Guy-Sheftall contains a comprehensive overview of the struggle for women's equality within Black communities (Cole and Guy-Sheftall 2003). *Black Sexual Politics* places these and similar works in a broader theoretical and political context.
9. Cole and Guy-Sheftall 2003, xxxi, xxxiv.

10. Both the incidence and mortality rates of prostate cancer for Black men show marked racial patterns. Between 1988 and 1992, the incidence and mortality rates for prostate cancer were 34 percent and 123 percent higher, respectively, for Black men than for White men (Stanford et al. 1999, 48). Breast cancer, the most common form of cancer among women in the United States, shows similar patterns. Incidence rates are higher as are mortality rates, primarily because, relative to White women, a larger percentage of Black women's cancers are diagnosed at a later, less treatable stage.

11. Definitions of sexuality are notoriously difficult to pin down. For example, the *Oxford Paperback Dictionary and Thesaurus* describes *sexuality* as the "fact of belonging to one of two sexes" and has having "sexual characteristics, impulses, etc." What does this mean? The dictionary's definition of the term *sex* is more specific: As a noun, the dictionary defines *sex* as a "group of males or females collectively," the "fact of belonging to either group," or as "sexual instincts, desires, activity, etc." In its colloquial use, sex refers to "sexual intercourse." The dictionary also lists a definition that connotes the sex act: "carnal knowledge, coitus, consummation of marriage, copulation, coupling, fornication, intercourse, intimacy, lovemaking, mating, sexual intercourse, sexual relations, union." These definitions are much more narrow than my use of sexuality here. For more information, consult the website at http://www.askoxford.com/dictionary/sexuality.

12. For an extended discussion of these three approaches, see Collins 2000a, 128–148. Also, queer theory's conceptual move to distinguish between gender and sexuality has been vital to the development of new vocabularies of all sorts, including those used here.

13. Ironically, often under the guise of intersectionality, the black/white race relations paradigm becomes expanded to what essentially becomes a white and all others race relations paradigm.

14. McKinnon 2001, 1.

15. Brazil (182 million) has the largest population of people of African descent in the New World. However, because Brazil also has a unique history of racial classification, it is difficult to specify its racial makeup. All population statistics were taken from http://emuseum.mnsu.edu/information/population.

16. In this context, capitalizing the terms *Whites* and *White American* serves the same purpose. In any place where one might substitute Italian, Puerto Rican, French, or British as population groups with identifiable histories, I capitalize *Black*. I also capitalize the terms *Black* and *White* when they are used as adjectives that clearly refer to specific population groups, for example, Black neighborhoods or White-run corporations. I also capitalize the terms Black and White even though they reference ideologies or concepts, whether self-defined or imposed, for example, Black feminism, ideologies of Black sexuality developed in conjunction with ideologies of White supremacy, constructs of hegemonic White masculinity and hegemonic Black femininity. The phrase *Black sexual politics* illustrates these crosscutting meanings. It refers alternately to a set of ideas, practices, and people that are already in place as well as to a constellation of ideas and behaviors that this volume hopes to foster. I had hoped to distinguish among these varying uses, but capitalizing *Black* in some places and not in others was ultimately confusing and unwieldy. I recognize that these distinctions are not always clear-cut, but for now, they will have to suffice.

CHAPTER ONE

1. Asante 1993.
2. The details of this version come from (Fausto-Sterling 1995). Depending on the intent of the author, Sarah Bartmann's story takes on different meanings. For example, Anne Fausto-Sterling's account focuses on the nineteenth-century scientists who relentlessly probed her body and used Bartmann as a vehicle for redefining Western concepts of race, gender, and sexuality. Fausto-Sterling's version points out how we learn much more about European scientists themselves via their treatment of Sarah Bartmann than we gain any accurate information about her. In contrast, in his groundbreaking essay "The Hottentot and the Prostitute: Toward an Iconography of Female Sexuality," Sander Gilman's account traces how ideas about the Hottentot Venus as an icon of Black sexuality were crucial to nineteenth-century European perceptions of women's sexuality (Gilman 1985, 76–108). Advancing a materialist analysis, Zine Magubane takes issue with Gilman's claim that, by the eighteenth century, the sexuality of African men and women became the icon for deviant sexuality in general. Rather, Magubane contends that the Bartmann exhibition encapsulated the debates that were occurring concerning colonial labor needs (Magubane 2001). Grounded in a cultural studies framework, Susie Prestney explores how the image of the Hottentot Venus was central to conceptions of difference, especially those of freak shows and similar spectacles (Prestney 1997). Taking a different approach, Yvette Abrahams challenges the flawed historiography on the Khoi people and indigenous people in general that places Bartmann outside history (Abrahams 1998). Finally, my own rendering of this narrative in *Black Feminist Thought* (Collins 2000a, 136–137, 141–145), and in this volume aim to place Sarah Bartmann in an intersectional analysis of how race, class, gender, and sexuality affect women of African descent.
3. Bederman 1995, 1–5.
4. I use the terms *representations*, *stereotypes*, and *controlling images* to refer to the depiction of people of African descent within Western scholarship and popular culture. Each term has a different history. Representations need not be stereotypical and stereotypes need not function as controlling images. Of the three, controlling images are most closely tied to power relations of race, class, gender, and sexuality. For a discussion of controlling images, see Collins 2000a, 69–96.
5. As used here, the term *invented* resembles Benedict Anderson's notion of an *imagined* community (Anderson 1983). In his important study of nationalism, Anderson contends that members of nations can never know one another. They "imagine" or "invent" a community. Racial categories such as White, Black, and native are all, in this sense, invented. Also, the term *discourse* has a particular meaning of a set of ideas and practices that, when taken together, organize both the way a society defines certain truths about itself and the way it deploys social power. An invented discourse is in some sense an oxymoron in that all discourses are social constructions that simultaneously shape and reflect actual social relations. For a good use of the term *invented* as the frame of an argument, see Oyèrónké Oyèwùmí's book *The Invention of Women: Making an African Sense of Western Gender Discourses* (Oyewumi 1997). All invented discourses typically contain contradictions and are often hotly contested, certainly the case with invented discourses on Black sexuality. For historical treatments of the invention of discourses of Black sexuality, see Jordan 1968, 136–178, especially 150–151; and D'Emilio and Freedman 1997, 34–37.

6. Collins 2000a, 69–96.
7. Abrahams 1998; Maseko 1998.
8. Morton 1991; Jewell 1993; Davis 1994; Asante 1994; Turner 1994.
9. The theme of primitivism of non-Western peoples was used to justify colonialism and slavery. For an analysis of how this idea was constructed and used, see
   Young 1995; Torgovnick 1990; McClintock 1995.
10. The term *Latina* addresses some of the multifaceted debates within contempo-
    rary racial theory that demonstrate the fluidity of racial classification. Research
    on how the different histories of people of African descent within Latin American
    countries coupled with a philosophy of "racial democracy" shows how Latin
    American populations approach race and ethnicity differently (Winant 2001,
    219–248). In this context, Lopez's history as a Puerto Rican is significant, espe-
    cially regarding the changing meaning of race in the United States as evidenced
    in the 2000 census (Rodriguez 2000). The category *Latina* refers to a wide range
    of national histories and migration streams into a new American ethnicity of
    Hispanic. Historically, Puerto Ricans have been viewed as reflecting a mulatto
    mixture resulting from European and African backgrounds as compared to a mes-
    tizo mixture of European and Indian of Chicana or Mexican-American popula-
    tions. But the very categories of mulatto and mestizo may mask more than they
    reveal about the fluidity of racial and ethnic classification throughout the
    Americas. Both Puerto Rico and Mexico have varying combinations of racial
    mixtures, a situation that generates different approaches to skin color, hair tex-
    ture, and the racial order itself. These ideas become layered upon North American
    ideas concerning race.
11. D'Emilio and Freedman 1997, 102–103.
12. Ironically, the theme of racial mixture of African, Indians, and Whites falters
    when Spain and Portugal are in the mix. Latinas have Spanish blood, but the
    Whiteness of this lineage can be questioned. Moors brought dark skin and Islam
    to Spain and intermingled with its peoples. Ferdinand and Isabella were cele-
    brated for unifying Spain, "civilizing" it, and insisting on Catholicism as the way
    to prove membership and belonging in the emerging Spanish nation. Thus,
    Moors with their heathen Muslim beliefs and their dark skin became coded as sav-
    ages.
13. The relationship among colonialism, European nationalism, and women has been
    explored by a variety of authors. For a representative work, see Yuval-Davis 1997.
14. People of African descent were not the only ones whose sexuality was patholo-
    gized in this process. Whereas the black/white binary is the anchor that frames all
    others, different race/gender groups found their sexuality differentially stereo-
    typed and pathologized in this process. Enslaving people of African descent not
    only required enforcing the master/slave relationship, it also required erasing the
    presence of indigenous peoples (who faced genocidal policies) as well as claiming
    land that had been historically governed by Mexico (Takaki 1993). Racial ideolo-
    gies constructed the sexualities of multiple groups in relation to one another
    (D'Emilio and Freedman 1997). Justifying slavery also required establishing a
    social class hierarchy among Whites while hiding the effects of this hierarchy
    under the assumed privileges attached to Whiteness.
15. For an early discussion of Black male sexuality, see Jordan 1968, 151–152. For
    more recent works that build on historical work, see Ferber 1998; Riggs 1999;
    Jones 1993.

16. For an analysis of how this process operated in the late nineteenth and early twentieth centuries, see Somerville 2000; Bederman 1995.

17. For a classic work on this process, see Hoch 1979.

18. The changes generated by postcoloniality, global capitalism, and new technologies have sparked a lively debate about the contours and meaning of the new racism in the United States. Some scrutinize the transformation of contemporary U.S. society as a racialized social system composed of structural and ideological dimensions (Bonilla-Silva 1996). When it comes to African Americans, structurally, American society has not made the gains in desegregating its housing, schools, and employment promised by the civil rights movement (Massey and Denton 1993). One study of Atlanta, Georgia, revealed that neighborhood-level racial resegregation is emerging as a new spatial pattern within major American cities, even those with a politically enfranchised and highly visible Black middle class (Orfield and Ashkinaze 1991). Other research points to the growth of a prison-industrial complex as an important new site for institutionalized racism confronting working-class and poor African Americans and Latinos (Miller 1996). Ideologically, a belief in upholding "color blindness" masks the continued inequalities of contemporary racism. By proclaiming that equal treatment of *individuals* under the law is sufficient for addressing racism, this ideology redefines *group*-based, antiracist remedies such as affirmative action as being "racist" (Crenshaw 1997). For a critique of color blindness and an analysis of how this racial ideology merits rethinking in the United States, see Guinier and Torres 2002.

19. For a thorough analysis of how globalization shapes contemporary racial formations, see Winant's analysis of the United States, South Africa, Brazil, and Europe in the post–World War II era (Winant 2001). Feminist analysis has also produced a broad literature on globalization and women's economic status, some of it focused on racism, sexism, and issues of globalization. For representative theoretical work in this tradition, see Alexander 1997; Mohanty 1997. African American scholars have also focused more attention on the global political economy. For representative works in this tradition, see Wilson 1996; Brewer 1994; Squires 1994.

20. Bauman 1998, 9.

21. Lusane 1997, 114.

22. M. Jacqui Alexander's discussion of the tourist industry in the Bahamas provides an especially insightful analysis of the effects of globalization on nation-state autonomy and on social problems within the Bahamas (Alexander 1997).

23. Cultural studies and studies of mass media underwent massive growth after 1980. For general work on the media, see Gitlin 2001. For race and media, see Entman 2000. The field of Black cultural studies has generated a range of literature. For representative works, consult Bobo 1995; Kelley 1994; Kelley 1997; Rose 1994; Wallace 1990; Gilroy 2000; Ransby and Matthews 1993; Gates 1992; Neal 2002; Watkins 1998; Cashmore 1997; Caponi 1999; Dent 1992b; Hall 1992; and Dyson 1996.

24. Kitwana 2002.

25. Clarke 1983, 199.

26. D'Emilio and Freedman suggest that the suppression of a range of sexual practices was part of colonization. Comparing the sexual practices of Native Americans, which varied widely, with European colonialist perceptions of such practices, in every region where Europeans and indigenous peoples came into

contact, Europeans judged the sexual life of natives as "savage" and their own practices as "civilized." For example, most indigenous peoples did not associate either nudity or sexuality with sin. They accepted premarital intercourse, polygamy, or institutionalized homosexuality, all practices that were condemned by European church and state (D'Emilio and Freedman 1997, 6–7). They point out, "perhaps the most striking contrast between English and Indian sexual systems was the relative absence of sexual conflict among native Americans, due in part to their different cultural attitudes toward both property and sexuality. . . . In cultures in which one could not 'own' another person's sexuality, prostitution—the sale of sex—did not exist prior to the arrival to European settlers. Rape—the theft of sex—only rarely occurred, and it was one of the few sexual acts forbidden by Indian cultures" (D'Emilio and Freedman 1997, 8).

27. D'Emilio and Freedman 1997, 16.

28. A 1995 report published by the Social Science Research Council charts the political difficulties that have plagued scientific studies of sexuality within American social science (di Mauro 1995).

29. Hegemony is also a mode of social organization wherein the dissent of oppressed groups is absorbed and thereby rendered politically useless. Moreover, in hegemonic situations, power is diffused throughout a social system such that multiple groups police one another and suppress each other's dissent. For example, if African Americans come to believe the dominant ideology and accept ideas about Black masculinities and Black femininities constructed within the dominant framework, then Black political dissent about gender and about all things tied to gender becomes weakened. Because they are used to justify existing social hierarchies, hegemonic ideologies may seem invincible. But ideologies of all sorts are never static. Instead, they are always internally inconsistent and are always subject to contestation (Magubane 2001).

30. Remez 2000.

31. This history of suppression of sex education and the limits on discussions that do exist have an especially negative impact on African American adolescents. HIV/AIDS has had a significant impact on African American youth. For statistics, see http://www.cdc.gov/hiv/pubs/Facts/afam.pdf.

32. For an analysis of talk shows, especially the production of "trashy" talk shows, see Grindstaff 2002. Grindstaff does not emphasize race, but her study of how talk shows replicate and reproduce ideas about social class and gender provides insight into the general process of ideology construction and contestation. She notes that talk shows are typically geared to women, feature working-class guests, and aim to display ordinary people engaged in extraordinary behavior.

33. Mark Anthony Neal and Hortense Spillers offer two different interpretations of the emergence of the term "baby daddy" to describe unmarried fatherhood among African American men. Neal's chapter "Baby Mama (Drama) and Baby Daddy (Trauma): Post-Soul Gender Politics" uses Black popular culture (Neal 2002, 57–97). In contrast, Spillers's essay "Mama's Baby, Papa's Maybe: An American Grammar Book," also examines unmarried fatherhood in the context of American race relations and the exploitation of Black bodies under slavery (Spillers 2000).

34. Grindstaff borrows the phrase the "money shot" from pornography to describe the efforts of producers to get ordinary people to deliver strong emotions such as joy, sorrow, rage, or remorse that can be seen in visible, bodily terms. Crying, shaking, running, and other evidence of emotion besides just talk are solicited. As

Grindstaff points out, "Like pornography, daytime talk is a narrative of explicit revelation in which people 'get down and dirty' and 'bare it all' for the pleasure, fascination, or repulsion of viewers. Like the orgasmic cum shot of pornographic films, the money shot of talk shows makes visible the precise moment of letting go, of losing control, of surrendering to the body and its 'animal' emotions" (Grindstaff 2002, 19). This is why Mr. Povich followed the woman backstage—he was in search of an authentic money shot.

35. Sociologist Abby Ferber describes how White supremacist literature remains obsessed with this theme of interracial sexuality generally and of protecting the body of the White woman (and thus the White race) from Black penetration. White women who willingly partner with Black men become redefined as "darkened," trashy women (Ferber 1998).

36. West 1993, 83.

37. The works of Black women writers repeatedly identify how they are encouraged to keep silent about gender problems within African American communities. For example, African American scholars Johnnetta Cole and Beverly Guy-Sheftall recount how their volume on the struggle for women's equality within African American communities goes against racial discourse that counsels Black women not to "air dirty laundry" about gender and sexuality (Cole and Guy-Sheftall 2003, xxiii–xxxviii). They name their book *Gender Talk* in an effort to reverse these silences.

38. Sex role theory has generated considerable critique. Michael Messner summarizes five common problems with sex role theory: (1) it focuses on individualistic, voluntary levels of analysis that minimize institutional power relations; (2) it implies a false symmetry between men and women that masks gender oppression; (3) it uses the male sex role to create a falsely universalized (middle-class, White, heterosexual) norm and measures deviance using this standard; (4) it relies on binary ideas about gender that reify biological notions of male and female sex categories; and (5) it is inadequate for examining changes in gender ideology, especially resistance (Messner 1998, 258). Messner points out that sociologists do not use the terms "race roles" or "class roles" when describing other social inequalities: "we may speak of race or class *identities*, but we do so within the context of an understanding of the historical dynamics of race and class *relations*" (Messner 1998, 258). R. W. Connell offers a comparable critique: "the conceptualization of gender through role theory . . . reifies expectations and self-descriptions, exaggerates consensus, marginalizes questions of power, and cannot analyze historical change" (Connell 1992, 735). By the 1980s, a more historicized and politicized language of gender relations virtually supplanted the language of sex role theory within sociology, although not within psychology, education, social work, and other disciplines.

39. In his classic work on stigma, Erving Goffman examines the strategies used by people who are stigmatized to manage a "spoiled identity" (Goffman 1963). While scholars often use Goffman's work to explore the management of stigma by individuals, here I use the concept to explore how Blacks as a group respond to the stigma of Blackness that is evidenced by a seemingly deviant Black sexuality.

40. African American organizational response to HIV illustrates this stance of avoidance (Cohen 1999, 250–292). Political theorist Cathy Cohen contends that the NAACP, the Urban League, and the Southern Christian Leadership Conference exemplify national Black organizations that have been "uneven at their best moments and neglectful in their worst" (Cohen 1999, 258). The sexual miscon-

duct of prominent Black male political leaders never raised the types of debates within African American communities concerning the gender politics involved. For example, the NAACP chose to cover up the sexual harassment case against then head Ben Chavis. The paternity suit filed against politician Jesse Jackson was ridiculed but not analyzed.

41. For an overview of gender and Black churches, see Cole and Guy-Sheftall 2003, 102–127. Recalling their own upbringings in Southern Christian churches, Cole and Guy-Sheftall summarize the principal lessons about gender: "That God is a male and that Jesus is both white and male; that the relationship between women and men in everyday life is to be like that between God and His church, for God is the head of the church, and all members are to follow Him; and that God and all of His people will look down on a 'bad woman' (for example, one who gets pregnant out of wedlock) and praise 'a virtuous woman' (for example, one who is a loyal helpmate to her husband and a good mother to her children)" (Cole and Guy-Sheftall 2003, 104).

42. I focus on established Black political organizations in this section, but it is important to note that these organizations appeal to older African Americans. These traditional players in African American politics have been joined by the hip-hop generation, a segment of Black youth who express contradictory positions on gender and sexuality. They do not vote, but their importance within popular culture gives their ideas a greater visibility among Black youth than the programs of established African American organizations (Kitwana 2002, 175–194).

43. Forms of biological racism that reached their peak during the eugenics movement and historical ideas about race that emerged from this view of the world have been disproved. However, recent developments within genetics, for example, the mapping of human DNA in the Human Genome Project, the increasing use of DNA identification in criminal justice, and controversies that now surround the use of genetic information in medical and insurance records all suggest that biology and race are still closely linked. For a discussion of issues of racism and science, see the essays in Harding 1993.

44. Wieviorka 1997, 139.

45. Wieviorka 1997.

46. For an insightful social science study of White racial attitudes, see Bonilla-Silva 2001. For an analysis of strategies of everyday racism that operate without a clear color line, see Essed 1991. In my own work, I identify four domains of power that collectively provide a framework for conceptualizing race and similar systems of oppression. The four domains are structural, disciplinary, hegemonic, and interpersonal. Under color-blind racism, for example, the hegemonic domain has increased in importance such that it generates ideologies that mask how race frames public policy in social institutions (structural), the differential application of rules to Blacks and Whites within schools, jobs, and other organizational settings (disciplinary) and how individuals treat one another in everyday life (interpersonal). For an extended discussion of the domains as sites for Black women's resistance, see Collins 2000a, 273–290.

47. In 1999, 55 percent of Blacks but only 22 percent of non-Hispanic Whites lived in the central cities of metropolitan areas (McKinnon and Humes 2000, 2).

48. Dawson 1994.

49. Wilson generated controversy by suggesting that class was increasing in importance within African American communities and pointed out that social class may

be well on its way toward becoming a crosscutting issue for African Americans (Wilson 1978).

50. Cohen 1999, 14–15.
51. Scott 1990.
52. Kelley 1994, 8.
53. Gilroy 2000.
54. Lorde 1984, 53–59.

CHAPTER TWO

1. For a comprehensive analysis of this same theme as it applies to African American women, see my discussion of the new politics of containment in chapter 2 of *Fighting Words* (Collins 1998, 11–43).
2. Kitwana 2002, 23.
3. For discussions of various aspects of globalization, race, and inequality, see Bales 1999; Lusane 1997; Bauman 1998; Mohanty 1997.
4. For a general overview of how race operates in a transnational framework, see Winant 2001. The framework of transnationalism is less often applied to African American experiences than those of Latinos.
5. For representative works on new racist ideologies, see Crenshaw 1997; Guinier and Torres 2002; Bonilla-Silva 2001; and Goldberg 1993. For race and media, see Entman 2000. For representative works in the field of Black cultural studies, consult Kelley 1994; Kelley 1997; Gates 1992; Neal 2002; Dent 1992b; Hall 1992; Dyson 1996.
6. For example, much attention has been given to the important issue of the poor school performance of African American youth (Fordham 1996), and Black males in particular (Arnett Ferguson 2000). Afro-Caribbean immigrants to the United Kingdom express similar concerns with their children's performance. This theme of Black youth being denied access to education and/or receiving differential treatment by schools run by dominant groups reappears across societies. Despite similar disadvantages among Black youth worldwide, a transnational discourse addressing issues peculiar to Black youth has not yet surfaced.
7. For a comprehensive treatment of racial formation theory, see Omi and Winant 1994.
8. The literature on slavery is vast and I make no effort to review it here. This section relies on material from Jordan 1968, 24–32, 216–265 and Torgovnick 1990, 3–11. Despite Orlando Patterson's troublesome analyses of the gendered aspects of slavery (see, Patterson 1998), his classic cross-cultural analysis of slavery analyzes chattel slavery as one of several forms within a global context (Patterson 1982). Material in this section is also drawn from general African American historiography, in particular, Takaki 1993, 51–76 and 106–138; Berry 1994; Franklin 1992; Gutman 1976; and also from feminist scholarship on slavery, in particular, Giddings 1984; Jones 1985; White 1985a.
9. Omolade 1994, 7.
10. Collins 2000a, 72–84.
11. A variety of authors analyze contemporary representations of Black masculinity in relation to this foundational controlling image of the buck. For work in this tradition, see Hoch's discussion of White men as heroes and Black men as "beasts" (Hoch 1979). See also, Dines 1998; Turner 1994; Harrison 2001.

12. Berry 1994, 14–26.
13. For an overview of contemporary work that analyzes masculinity in terms of patriarchy, see Messner 1998, 1990; Connell 1995.
14. For general works that examine Black masculinity within the interpretive framework put forth here, see Carbado 1999b, 1999c; Riggs 1992, 1999; Thomas 1996.
15. Angela Davis presented one of the earliest and most comprehensive analyses of institutionalized rape as a tool of domination (Davis 1978). Davis reports that legal institutions not only do not punish institutionalized rape, they actually encourage and support it as an extension of public policy. For example, rapes by soldiers and rapes of imprisoned peoples are not punished. I take up this theme more thoroughly in chapter 7.
16. Kapsalis 1997; White 1985a.
17. Spillers 2000, 73.
18. Berry 1994.
19. Frazier 1948; Moynihan 1965.
20. For a discussion of gender arrangements and marriage, see Gutman 1976. For discussions of the idea of gender equality, see White 1985a; Davis 1981.
21. See, for example, Thompson 1983; Sudarkasa 1981.
22. Patterson 1998, 3.
23. Patterson 1998, 25.
24. Oliver and Shapiro 1995, 13–15.
25. Berry 1994.
26. Dash 1996, 79.
27. For analyses of the climate for African Americans, see Giddings 1984. For a discussion of the content of images, see Morton 1991; Jewell 1993; Turner 1994. For discussions of race and sexuality in late-nineteenth- and early-twentieth-century America, see Somerville 2000; Bederman 1995.
28. For discussions of the myth of the Black male rapist and its connection to lynching during this period, see Bederman 1995, 45–76, and Wiegman 1993. For a literary analysis of this theme, see Harris 1984.
29. Giddings 1992, 443.
30. Franklin 1995, 74.
31. Ida B. Wells-Barnett was the first African American critic to link the myth of the Black rapist to state-sanctioned lynching. Wells-Barnett argued that social and economic factors catalyzed lynching, not the behavior of African American men. See Wells-Barnett's reprinted pamphlets in Wells-Barnett 2002.
32. D'Emilio and Freedman 1997, 107.
33. Collins 2002, 14.
34. Hill 1997, 25.
35. Hill 1997, 29.
36. Hill 1997, 36–37.
37. Marks 1989.
38. A research tradition of urban ethnographies that is too vast to cite here describes how these trends were organized in different American cities. The material in this section is taken from Marks 1989, 137–151.
39. Carby 1992, 754.
40. Carby 1992, 739.
41. Carby 1992, 746.
42. Higginbotham 1993, 185–229.

43. I'm thinking here of the alliance between C. Delores Tucker, president of the National Political Congress of Black Women, and former Reagan administration official William Bennett in response to the profanity, violence, and misogyny in gangsta rap. For a summary, see George 1998, 188–192.

44. Carby 1992, 745.

45. Higginbotham 1993, 193.

46. Davis 1998, 44. Material in this section is taken from Davis.

47. Davis 1998, 44.

48. During this period, gender reassignments were not an option as they are for contemporary transgendered individuals. For this reason, I omit the category of transgendered from this discussion. There was, however, a prominent gay, lesbian, and bisexual presence in Harlem. Contemporary queer readings of some of the major works of the Harlem Renaissance provide a window into literary figures (see, e.g., Somerville 2000; Julien 1992). More contemporary works such as anthropologist William Hawkeswood's study of Black gay men in Harlem (Hawkeswood 1996), and Audre Lorde's memoirs about 1950s New York (Lorde 1982) suggest a community with a long history that precedes the dominance of the closet from the 1950s to the 1980s. Sociologist Steve Seidman reminds us that the closet is a historically specific entity (Seidman 2002, 29).

49. During this same period, heterosexism as a system of power grew in tandem with the color line, and it relied upon a similar logic of segregation that was differently organized and deployed. For an extended discussion of this period, see Somerville 2000, 1–14.

50. See, for example, Kennedy and Davis 1994; Lorde 1982.

51. Black middle-class women also found it difficult to contest prevailing norms of femininity. Because they were often held up as symbols of the race, a common practice within nationalist-inspired group politics (see, e.g., Davis 1998, 44), middle-class Black women were further restricted by the politics of respectability. Their lifestyles were on display as visible signs that Black women were not inherently sexually wanton.

52. Nelson 1997, 63.

53. Carbado 1999a, 177.

54. Robinson 2000, 237–238.

55. Root 2001.

56. Wilson 1978.

57. McKinnon and Humes 2000, 2.

58. Five measures of racial residential segregation are typically used. Evenness measures the differential distribution of the population. Exposure measures potential contact among racial groups. Concentration refers to the relative amount of physical space occupied by a racial group. Centralization indicates the degree to which a racial group is located near the center of an urban area. Clustering measures the degree to which racial groups live disproportionately in contiguous areas (Iceland, Weinberg, and Steinmetz 2002, 7–10). The literature reports declines in residential racial segregation for African Americans across all five measures. However, the largest metropolitan areas (1 million or more population) had higher residential segregation than the middle-sized ones (500,000 to 999,999), which in turn had higher rates than smaller ones. The size of the metropolitan area and the size of the Black population within it seem to matter. Three of the five indexes showed a pattern of higher segregation in places with a higher percentage of

Blacks in 2000, while two showed the reverse. In particular, as the percentage of the population that is Black increased, Blacks were (1) less likely to be evenly spread across the metropolitan area; (2) less likely to share common neighborhoods with Whites (isolation index); and (3) more likely to live near other Blacks (spatial proximity index) (Iceland, Weinberg, and Steinmetz 2002, 63).

59. For an analysis of racial segregation, see Massey and Denton 1993. Also, see Oliver and Shapiro 1995, 15–23. In 2000, the five most segregated metropolitan areas for Black people were Milwaukee, Detroit, Cleveland, St. Louis, and Newark. Cincinnati, Buffalo, and New York were roughly tied for sixth place, and the top ten was rounded out by Chicago and Philadelphia (although Philadelphia was roughly tied with Kansas City, New Orleans, and Indianapolis) (Iceland, Weinberg, and Steinmetz 2002, 68). By 2000, African Americans constituted a sizeable percentage of the populations of large American cities. Of the ten largest areas in the United States, Detroit had the largest proportion of Black people (83 percent), followed by Philadelphia (44 percent), and Chicago (38 percent). Two places—New York and Chicago—together accounted for nine percent of the total Black population. The ten largest places for Blacks accounted for 20 percent of the total Black population (McKinnon 2001, 7).

60. McKinnon 2001.

61. The criteria used to define social class, for example, educational attainment, occupational level, and income, affect estimates of the size of the Black middle class. Here I emphasize occupational characteristics because these demonstrate race/gender patterns that are central to the arguments in this book.

62. Race and gender differences characterize this movement of African Americans into professional and managerial jobs. In 1999, the proportion of employed non-Hispanic White men (32 percent) in managerial and professional occupations was almost twice that of Black men (17 percent). Non-Hispanic White women (35 percent) were more likely than Black women (24 percent) to be in these positions. In this regard, White men and women were far closer in occupational status (32 and 35 percent) than Black men and women (17 and 24 percent) (McKinnon and Humes 2000).

63. This heterogeneity within the Black middle class should not obscure the major differences between middle-class Blacks and Whites. For an analysis of these differences in income and wealth, see Oliver and Shapiro 1995, 91–125.

64. Graham 2000.

65. Iceland, Weinberg, and Steinmetz 2002, 3–4.

66. Patillo-McCoy 1999.

67. Patillo-McCoy 1999, 123.

68. Race and gender also influenced the continued concentration of Black men and women in less desirable jobs. For example, Black men (17 percent) are more than twice as likely as White men (8 percent) to work in service occupations and almost twice as likely (31 percent compared to 17 percent) to be operators, fabricators, and laborers. Black women (27 percent) were more likely than non-Hispanic White women (15 percent) to be employed in service occupations (McKinnon and Humes 2000, 4). In essence, gender-segmented jobs of laborers and service work continued to characterize the occupational experiences of poor and working-class African Americans.

69. Much has been written about the PRWOR Act. For a discussion of how this act fits into a frame of "welfare racism," see Neubeck and Cazenave 2001, 115–144.

70. Kitwana 2002, 48.
71. Squires 1994.
72. McKinnon and Humes 2000, 5.
73. McKinnon and Humes 2000, 6.
74. Franklin 1997b, 153–214.
75. Miller 1996, 1–9.
76. Kitwana 2002, 71–76.
77. Kitwana 2002, 76.
78. McKinnon and Humes 2000, 2.
79. Definitions of poverty seem to matter greatly in who gets counted as poor. In 1998, the official poverty threshold for a family of four was $16,600, leaving a sizeable gap between the $25,000 income threshold reported here and official poverty. Whatever the family composition, Black families are poorer than White ones, with families headed by Black women with no spouse present poorer than all. In 1998, poverty was highest in families maintained by women with no spouse present: 41 percent for Blacks compared to 21 percent for non-Hispanic Whites (McKinnon and Humes 2000, 6).
80. Varying explanations have been given for these patterns. William Julius Wilson's research links patterns of family organization to the changing contours of economic opportunities in Black urban neighborhoods (Wilson 1996; Wilson 1987). Wilson's research highlights how growing joblessness among African American men in the 1960s and 1970s correlates with (but does not necessarily cause) increasing rates of African American mother-child families. His work documents how the emergence of mother-child families among working-class African Americans can be attributed, in part, to a changing political economy that disadvantaged U.S. Blacks. Others criticize capitalist development itself (Squires 1994).
81. Anderson 1999.
82. The crisis within contemporary gender politics sparked Cole and Guy-Sheftall to write their book: "Now is a particularly critical time for *Gender Talk* because of what we perceive to be an embattled Black, mostly male leadership, a deepening crisis in Black male-female relationships, an embrace of patriarchal family values, and a backlash against feminism and Black feminists" (Cole and Guy-Sheftall 2003, xxxii).
83. Cole and Guy-Sheftall 2003, 186.
84. Dickerson 2000.
85. Chambers 1996, 44.
86. Chambers 1996, 46.
87. Golden 1995, 68.
88. Bales 1999, 6.
89. Robinson 2000, 74.

CHAPTER THREE

1. The field of postcolonial studies contains many works that examine how ideas generally, and sexual discourse in particular, was essential to colonialism and to nationalism. In this field, the works of French philosopher Michel Foucault have been pivotal in challenging prior frameworks heavily grounded in Marxism and in Freudian psychoanalysis. Here I rely on two main ideas from the corpus of Foucault's work. The first, expressed in his classic work *Discipline and Punish*, concerns the strategies that institutions use to discipline populations and get them

to submit under conditions of oppression (Foucault 1979). The second idea concerns the normalization of such power through the use of hegemonic ideologies. Volume I of Foucault's *The History of Sexuality* uses sexuality to illustrate this normalization of power (Foucault 1980). Despite the enormous impact that Foucault has had on studies of power, few works analyze his treatment of race. Ann Stoler's *Race and the Education of Desire* is exemplary in this regard (Stoler 1995). Stoler examines how Foucault's analyses of sexuality in European societies can be read also as an analysis of race. In this chapter, I rely on many of Stoler's insights. For a comprehensive overview of works on Foucault and sexuality that do not deal with race, see Stoler 1995, 19, n. 1. For a description of the specific manipulation of sexual discourse within colonialism, see McClintock 1995; Gilman 1985; and Young 1995, 90–117.

2. Jordan 1968, 3–43.

3. Jordan 1968, 136–178.

4. See, for example, White 1985a.

5. Despite the marginality of all LGBT Black people, subpopulations did not place issues of sexuality on the public agenda at the same time or in the same way. Black lesbians raised issues of heterosexism and homophobia in the 1980s, fairly early in modern Black feminism. For classic work in this tradition, see Combahee River Collective 1982; Lorde 1982; Smith 1983; and Clarke 1983. For a representative sample of more recent works, see Clarke 1995; Gomez and Smith 1994; Moore 1997; Gomez 1999; Greene 2000; Smith 1998. In contrast, works by gay Black men achieved greater prominence later. See, for example, Hemphill 1991; Riggs 1992. *Tongues Untied*, the documentary by the late Marlon Riggs, represents an important path breaking work in Black gay men's studies in the United States (*Tongues Untied* 1989). More recently, work on Black masculinity that analyzes homosexuality has gained greater visibility. See Hutchinson 1999; Riggs 1999; Thomas 1996; Carbado 1999c; Hawkeswood 1996; Simmons 1991.

6. Cohen and Jones 1999, 88.

7. Mandela 1994, 341. Foucault suggests that the prison serves as an exemplar of modern Western society (Foucault 1979). The techniques used to discipline and punish deviant populations constitute a punishment industry. Prisons operate by controlling populations via disciplining the body. Foucault's work on sexuality also emphasizes regularization and discipline, only this time via creating discourses of sexuality that also aim to control the body (Foucault 1980). For an analysis of Foucault's treatment of race, sexuality, and gender, see Stoler 1995.

8. Wideman 1984, 52.

9. For works that detail the effects of welfare state policies on African Americans, see Quadagno 1994; Brewer 1994; Neubeck and Cazenave 2001. For general works on state policy and African American economic well-being, see Squires 1994; Massey and Denton 1993; Oliver and Shapiro 1995. For analyses of jobs and urban economies, see Wilson 1996; 1987.

10. West 1993.

11. In the 1980s, homicide became one of the leading causes of death of young Black men (Oliver 1994). For work on the vulnerability of Black youth in inner cities, see Anderson 1978; 1990; 1999; Canada 1995; Kaplan 1997; Kitwana 2002.

12. Anderson 1999.

13. Anderson 1999.

14. Anderson 1978; 1990; 1999.

15. As quoted in Cole and Guy-Sheftall 2003, 139.
16. Mandela 1994, 367–368.
17. Mandela 1994, 341.
18. Rose 1994, 21–61; George 1998, 1–21.
19. Sociologist Steve Seidman traces the emergence and decline of the closet as a metaphor describing contemporary LGBT politics (Seidman 2002). Seidman dates the closet as reaching its heyday in the 1950s and early 1960s during the early years of the cold war. In his research, he was surprised to find that many contemporary gay Americans live outside the social framework of the closet. Seidman suggests that the two main ways that gay life has been understood since 1969, namely, the coming-out narrative or the migration to gay ghettoes, may no longer be accurate: "as the lives of at least some gays look more like those of straights, as gays no longer feel compelled to migrate to urban enclaves to feel secure and respected, gay identity is often approached in ways similar to heterosexual identity—as a thread" (Seidman 2002, 11). Unfortunately, Seidman's methodology did not allow him to explore the ways in which Black LGBT people have similar and different experiences.
20. Both science and religion advanced different justifications for stigmatizing homosexuals. Until recently, Western medicine and science viewed sexuality as being biologically hardwired into the human species and obeying natural laws. Heterosexual sexual practices and reproduction were perceived as the "natural" state of sexuality, and all other forms of sexual expression were classified as deviant. Religion offered similar justifications. Promiscuity and homosexuality emerged as important categories of "unnatural" sexual activity that normalized monogamous heterosexuality within the context of marriage and for purposes of reproduction.
21. This is Foucault's argument about biopower, the normalization of practices that enable society to discipline individual bodies, in this case, sexual bodies, and groups, in this case, straights and gays, as population groups that become comprehensible only in the context of discourses of sexuality. This view prevailed until shifts within the study of sexuality in the 1980s and 1990s.
22. Seidman 1996, 6.
23. The term *queer* often serves as an umbrella term for lesbian, gay, bisexual, transgendered, and anyone else whose sexuality transgresses the status quo. Not everyone claims the term as an identity or statement of social location. Some argue that the term erases social and economic differences among lesbians and gay men, and others consider it to be derogatory. Still others use the term to acknowledge the limitless possibilities of an individual's sexuality. They see terms such as *gay*, *lesbian*, and *bisexual* as misleading in that they suggest stable sexual identities. Beyond these ideological differences, I do not use the term *queer* here because LGBT African American people do not prefer this term. When participants in the *National Black Pride Survey 2000* were asked which label from a very extensive list came closest to describing their sexual orientation, 42 percent self-identified as gay, 24 percent chose lesbian, 11 percent chose bisexual, and 1 percent marked transgendered. In contrast to high levels of agreement on gay and lesbian, "queer" was one of the least popular options (1 percent). As the survey reports, "Black GLBT people do not readily, or even remotely, identity as 'queer'" (Battle et al. 2002, 19).
24. LGBT politics and the "queering" of sexuality has been one important dimension of the post–civil rights era and Seidman contends that the postcloseted world

of the post–civil rights era has shown greater acceptance of LGBT people. Yet, suggests Seidman, acceptance may come with a price. Today, LGBT people are under intense pressure to fit the mold of the "good gay citizen" to be monogamous and to look and act normal. This image may be safe, but it continues to justify discrimination against those who do not achieve this ideal (Seidman 2002).

25. Here I use the framework of "domains of power" to examine the convergence of racism and heterosexism. Briefly, race, sexuality, gender, class, and other systems of oppression are all organized through four main domains of power. The structural domain of power (institutional policies), the disciplinary of power (the rules and regulations that regulate social interaction), the hegemonic domain of power (the belief systems that defend existing power arrangements), and the interpersonal domain of power (patterns of everyday social interaction) are organized differently for different systems of oppression. Here I use this model as a heuristic device to build an argument about the interconnections of racism and heterosexism. For a discussion of the framework and its applicability in Black feminist politics, see chapter 12 of *Black Feminist Thought* (Collins 2000a, 273–290).

26. For a discussion of the *Loving* decision and its effects on interracial marriage, see Root 2001. For the full definition of the Defense of Marriage Act, see U.S. Census Bureau 2000.

27. Racism and heterosexism share this basic cognitive frame, and it is one shared by other systems of power.

28. Clarke 1983.

29. Both sets of ideas also serve as markers for constructing both heterosexuality and homosexuality within the wider society. Prior to the social movements of the civil rights era that called increased attention to both racism and heterosexism, racial protest was contained within the prisons of racially segregated neighborhoods and LGBT protest within the invisibility of individual closets.

30. Mudimbe 1988; Appiah 1992.

31. Young 1995, 90–117; McClintock 1995.

32. Jordan 1968, 7.

33. Jordan 1968, 5. Jordan suggests that the reactions of the English differed from those of the Spanish and the Portuguese who for centuries had been in close contact with North Africa and who had been invaded by peoples both darker and more civilized than themselves. The impact of color on the English may have been more powerful because England's principal contact with Africans came in West Africa and the Congo, areas with very dark-skinned Africans. Thus, "one of the fairest-skinned nations suddenly came face to face with one of the darkest peoples on earth" (Jordan 1968, 6).

34. Torgovnick 1990, 18–20.

35. Historically, scientific racism has made important contributions to creating and sustaining myths of Black promiscuity as well as constructing a normalized heterosexuality juxtaposed to the alleged deviancy of White homosexuality. The scientific racism of medicine, biology, psychology, anthropology, and other social sciences constructed both Black promiscuity as well as homosexuality and then spent inordinate time assisting state and religious institutions that aimed to regulate these practices. For general discussions of race and science, see Gould 1981; Harding 1993; Zuberi 2001.

36. Fausto-Sterling 1995.

37. Foucault 1979.

38. Haraway 1989, 262. In this context, studying animals that were clearly not human but close to it might reveal what granted Europeans their humanity and Africans their putative bestiality. Here the interest in animal behavior as a form of human behavior uninterrupted by culture appears. Within primatology, monkeys and apes have a privileged relation to nature and culture, in that "simians occupy the border zones" (Haraway 1989, 1). "In Africa, the primate literature was produced by white colonists and western foreign scientists under no pressure until well after independence to develop scientific, collegial relations with black Africans. African primates, including the people imagined as wildlife, modeled the 'origin of man' for European-derived culture. . . . Africa became a place of darkness, one lacking the enlightenment of the West. India has been used to model not the 'origin of man,' but the 'origin of civilization.' Both are forms of 'othering' for western symbolic operations, but their differences matter" (Haraway 1989, 262).

39. Collins 2000a, 69–96.

40. Wiegman 1993, 239.

41. Quoted in Kapsalis 1997, 37. Understandings of Black women's promiscuity also build upon a deep historical theme within Western societies that links deviant sexuality with disease. The hypervisible, pathologized portion of Black women's sexuality centered on the icon of the whore, the woman who demands money for sexual favors. This image is pathologized in that prostitutes were associated with ideas about disease and pollution that bore stark resemblance to ideas about the threat of racial pollution so central to conceptions of whiteness grounded in purity (Giddings 1992, 419).

42. Baker 1993, 43.

43. Baker 1993, 33–60.

44. Dwyer 2002. This case also resembles the well-known case of the Scottsboro boys in which a group of Black men were convicted of allegedly raping White women. They too were eventually exonerated.

45. White 1985a.

46. Gould 1981; Zucchino 1997; Amott 1990; Brewer 1994; Neubeck and Cazenave 2001.

47. Roberts 1997, 4.

48. In a context in which the United States has the highest teen pregnancy rate in the Western world, the even higher rates of teen pregnancy among African American adolescents is a cause for alarm. Many factors influence high rates of pregnancy among young Black women. For example, adult men, some of whom may have coerced girls to have sex with them, father most of the babies born to teen mothers. Studies show that as many as one in four girls are victims of sexual abuse (Roberts 1997, 117).

49. See Gould 1981; Lubiano 1992; Zucchino 1997; Neubeck and Cazenave 2001.

50. Roberts 1997, 152.

51. As quoted in Cole and Guy-Sheftall 2003, 165.

52. For a discussion of the type of racial reasoning that generates ideas of racial authenticity, see Cornel West's "The Pitfalls of Racial Reasoning" (West 1993, 21–32).

53. These same pressures fostered views of homosexuals as invisible, closeted, and assumed to be White. Normalized White heterosexuality became possible and hegemonic only within the logic of both racism and heterosexism.

54. The general use of the term "the Black Church" refers to Black Christian churches

in the United States. This includes any Black Christian who worships and is a member of a Black congregation. The formal use of the term refers to independent, historic, and Black-controlled denominations that were founded after the Free African Society in 1787. For a listing, see Monroe 1998, 297, n. 1. For a general history of the Black Church, see Lincoln 1999. For analyses of Black women's participation in the Black Church, see Douglas 1999; Gilkes 2001; Higginbotham 1993.

55. See, Patillo-McCoy 1999, especially Patillo-McCoy 1998.
56. Lincoln 1999, xxiv.
57. Douglas 1999.
58. Cole and Guy-Sheftall 2003, 116.
59. Cole and Guy-Sheftall 2003, 120.
60. Cohen 1999, 276–288.
61. Simmons 1991.
62. For a discussion of the family networks of Black gay men in Harlem, see Hawkeswood 1996. Also, see Battle et al. 2002, 13–17.
63. Higginbotham 1993, 185–229.
64. Somerville 2000.
65. Julien 1992, 274.
66. Davis 1998.
67. Davis 1998, 3.
68. Kennedy and Davis 1994.
69. Lorde 1982.
70. Monroe 1998, 281.
71. Comstock 1999, 156.
72. Comstock 1999, 156.
73. Boykin 1996, 90.
74. Boykin 1996, 19.
75. Moore 1997; McCready 2001.
76. Smith 1990, 66.
77. Boykin 1996, 81.
78. "Skeleton in Newark's Closet: Laquetta Nelson Is Forcing Homophobia Out into the Open" 2003.

CHAPTER FOUR

1. The Funny Pages: List of Penises 15.
2. Jordan 1968, 3–43.
3. For an analysis that argues that body politics are a Western phenomenon and that African societies place far less emphasis on the body, see Oyěwùmí 1997.
4. Fausto-Sterling 1995; Giddings 1992.
5. Kennedy 2002, 48. The effectiveness of this strategy is debatable.
6. Kelley 1997; Mercer 1994; Rose 1994; Wallace 1990; Giddings 1992; Riggs 1992; Dyson 1993; Neal 2002; Dent 1992b; Hall 1992.
7. I use the terms *representations*, *stereotypes*, and *controlling images* to refer to the depiction of people of African descent within Western scholarship and popular culture. Each term has a different history. Representations need not be stereotypical and stereotypes need not function as controlling images. Of the three, controlling images are most closely tied to power relations of race, class, gender, and sexuality. For a discussion of controlling images, see Collins 2000a, 69–96.

8. Kennedy 2002, 63.

9. Bogle 1989, 252.

10. One commentator fails to see the complexities of the race and gender politics in some of Grier's movies and places her with a framework of an undifferentiated "superbitch:" "In *Foxy Brown* alone, Grier thrashes a call girl in a bar, slashes the throat of another woman, cremates two men to death, and castrates a third and delivers his genitals in a pickle jar to his womanfriend as a warning. . . . It didn't matter what Grier's slated role was, her character type remained the same—whorish superbitch who bedded with anyone including her professed enemies" Freydberg 1995, 234–235. Grier certainly did all of these things, but she was not a whore and her actions were politically motivated.

11. Nelson 1997, 102.

12. Nelson 1997, 102.

13. Souljah 1999, 4.

14. Souljah 1999, 4.

15. Marriott, 126.

16. Marriott, 126.

17. Roberts 1995.

18. Roberts 1995, 79.

19. Jones 1994, 80.

20. Torgovnick 1990, 90.

21. See the discussion in chapter 6 of how images of White femininity, especially concerning physical beauty, operate as a hegemonic gender ideology for all women.

22. Cole and Guy-Sheftall 2003, 182–215.

23. Latifah 1999, 3.

24. For a discussion of the family ideal as it affects African American women, see Collins 2000a, 46.

25. Roberts 1997, 153.

26. Roberts 1997, 152. Even worse are those women who remain on drugs, sell their bodies, and decide to keep their children. Those Black women who engage in sex work in order to support their children are especially chastised. The hoochie mama popularized in Black popular culture constitutes a bad mother who sells sex and neglects her children. The derogated Black mother who is on drugs also fits within this nexus of representations of bad Black mothers.

27. Two groups of children cost the state little: (1) those children whose middle-class and affluent parents absorb the costs of their education, health care, recreational services either through supporting private institutions or through living in suburbs that limit public services to residents; and (2) children of undocumented immigrants whose citizenship status renders them ineligible for state services and/or fearful of claiming state services to which they are entitled. The first group is groomed to take over professional and managerial positions while the latter can be used to fill the increasing service sector jobs. The majority of African American children, half of whom live in poverty but who by virtue of citizenship remain entitled to public benefits, fall into neither of these two categories. The result—Black children become increasingly expendable.

28. Collins 1999; Roberts 1997.

29. For discussions of race, welfare, and population control, see Collins 1999; Neubeck and Cazenave 2001.

30. Roberts 1997, 122–142.

31. Roberts 1997, 143–148.
32. For general discussions of race and the American social welfare state, see Quadagno 1994; Brewer 1994; Neubeck and Cazenave 2001.
33. Davis 1998; Roberts 1995.
34. Roberts 1995, 324.
35. Emerson 2002, 116.
36. Emerson 2002, 126.
37. Emerson 2002, 127.
38. McPherson 2000, 189.
39. McPherson 2000, 189.
40. "Skeleton in Newark's Closet: Laquetta Nelson Is Forcing Homophobia Out into the Open" 2003.
41. For a discussion of *The Cosby Show* and race relations in the 1980s, see Jhally and Lewis 1992.
42. The professional success of the character of Claire Huxtable required erasing the actual high degree of discrimination that faces African American women in the legal profession. To get some sense of a sea change in media depictions of this theme, one need only compare the image of Claire Huxtable to that of Teri Joseph (played by actress Nicole Ari Parker) on Showtime's original series *Soul Food*. Joseph is a high-powered Chicago lawyer aiming to juggle a career and family obligations. Unlike Claire Huxtable, who managed to make partner in record time as a mother of five children, childless Teri has a degree from a prestigious law school, works extremely long hours, is devoted to her job, yet is passed over for promotion to partner.
43. The Anita Hill/Clarence Thomas media event sparked numerous articles and at least two edited volumes entirely devoted to the case; see Smitherman-Donaldson 1995; Morrison 1992. Yet work on Oprah Winfrey, a figure who has had a far greater impact on American popular culture, remains neglected.
44. Bogle 1989, 82.
45. Grindstaff 2002.
46. Aldaraca 1995.
47. Aldaraca 1995, 214.
48. Jhally and Lewis 1992.
49. Magubane 2001.

CHAPTER FIVE

1. This notion of booty as the spoils of war spurs a series of related meanings, namely, commonly acquired plunder that will be divided among the winners. Also, the phrase "to play booty" appears in the history of the term *booty*, in this case, to join with confederates in order to "spoil" or victimize another player. In other words, when two players act falsely in order to gain a desired object, they "play booty."
2. The term *booty* also has special significance for Black femininity, for example, the fascination with Black female buttocks discussed in chapter 4 as a sign of racial difference. However, booty does not have the same function in shaping Black femininity as that played in framing Black masculinity. The dual meaning of booty as property and as sexual conquest is central to definitions of masculinity and Black men's access to both has been blocked in American society. Because manhood is

an active endeavor that must be constantly defended and proved (through acts such as sexual conquest, having money, etc.) conceptions of Black masculinity are dependent on Black women's behavior, in this case, the booty. In contrast, Black femininity has no comparable dependence on male behavior. Black women can still be women without any need to call attention to their booties or to engage in booty calls. In this sense, men have much more at stake regarding their masculinity than women.

3. Anderson 1978; 1990; 1999.
4. Platt 2002, 18.
5. Platt 2002, 23.
6. One puzzle is how White audiences can admire Black men's athletic bodies yet fear actual African American men. By arguing that commodified bodies are actually "flesh" that is then sold on the open marketplace, Hortense Spillers investigates the complicated mechanisms that join Black male athletes with their adoring fans. Reducing Black men's bodies to "flesh" in order to objectify them for reasons of profit, yet marketing those same bodies as objects of desire, introduces unsolvable contradictions (Spillers 2000, 60).
7. George 1998, 53.
8. Awkward 1999.
9. Boyd 2000, 65.
10. Boyd and Shropshire 2000, 7.
11. Neal 2002, 144.
12. Platt 2002, 45–46.
13. Platt 2002, 124.
14. Platt 2002, 125.
15. Platt 2002, 128–129.
16. Platt 2002, 128.
17. Platt 2002, 128.
18. Platt 2002, 125–126.
19. Platt 2002, 24.
20. Boyd 2000, 66.
21. Human Rights Watch 2001, 27. For additional material on incarceration, see Davis 1997; Tonry 1995; Hutchinson 2001.
22. In contrast, young White youth who mimic the styles of thug life may do so as a fashion statement because they are guaranteed access to education and jobs regardless of their youthful rebellion. For discussions of the phenomenon of White appropriation of Black culture, see the articles in Tate 2003.
23. Wilson 1996; Canada 1995; Anderson 1999; Kitwana 2002.
24. Dyson argues that Tupac pursued themes that covered rap's subgenres: conscious rap, political hip-hop, party music, hedonism rap, thug rap, and ghettocentric rap. He notes that Tupac was also skilled at several modes of address within hip-hop such as the dis rap, the hip-hop eulogy, the maternal letter, and the pastoral letter to keep hope alive (Dyson 2001, 64).
25. Dyson 2001, 49.
26. Dyson 2001, 64.
27. Dyson 2001, 64.
28. George 1998, 139.
29. Ogbar 1999, 172.
30. Ogbar 1999, 173.

31. Kennedy 2002, 38–55.
32. Kennedy 2002, 48.
33. Dines 1998, 294.
34. For a provocative analysis of Black male sexuality and the importance of the body, see Kobena Mercer's essay on racial fetishism in the work of photographer Robert Mapplethorpe, Mercer 1994, 171–219.
35. Fair and Astroff 1991.
36. Fair and Astroff 1991, 65.
37. Fair and Astroff 1991, 73.
38. *Los Angeles Times*, April 30, 1990.
39. *New York Times*, September 17, 1990.
40. Fair and Astroff 1991, 68.
41. Fair and Astroff 1991, 69.
42. Smith 1983, 142.
43. Angela Davis identifies the power that the idea of the Black male criminal or thug has for many White Americans that made the Horton incident work: "The fear of crime has attained a status that bears a sinister similarity to the fear of communism as it came to restructure social perceptions during the fifties and sixties. The figure of the 'criminal'—the racialized figure of the criminal—has come to represent the most menacing enemy of American society" Davis 1997, 270.
44. Kellner 2001.
45. Guerrero 1993, 239.
46. This process has long worked with mass media, especially sports. Babe Ruth was an icon of American sports because the White working-class origins of a large segment of the American population saw baseball and his place in it as speaking for them. Similarly, for many working-class African Americans, Muhammad Ali represented a new politics of racial defiance that refused to bow down to the buddy image. In this context, "Jordan's overall image, while popular, is one devoid of the character substance and specific cultural identity so integral to both Ruth and Ali" (Boyd and Shropshire 2000, 6).
47. Jones 1993, 252. Black male heterosexuality is a repressed discourse characterized by powerlessness and reaction (Jones 1993, 252). This subordination is especially evident in Black buddy films in that Black buddies are rarely depicted engaged in loving sex acts. Rather, as Jones suggests, "The sexuality of the Black male is realized through individualized, physical dominance rather than sex itself, when realized at all" (Jones 1993, 251). Physical dominance typically occurs through violence and, as a result, the sexuality of Black characters is constructed through the violent action of the film. The result—a Black male heterosexuality emerges that is grounded in sexuality without a sex act.
48. Carby 1998, 190.
49. Seidman 2002, 128–129.
50. Riggs 1999, 307.
51. In summer 2003, the ailing Bravo network picked up this theme of the gay buddy with its smash series *Queer Eye for a Straight Guy*. Using five gay men (four of whom were White), the show builds upon the theme of the gay buddy by providing help to a straight guy who needs assistance with some sort of major event, for example, proposing to his girlfriend or asking his girlfriend to move in with him.
52. Denizet-Lewis 2003, 30.
53. Arnett Ferguson 2000.

54. The appeal of machismo that has been associated with Black Nationalist philosophy may stem in part, from this perception that Black intellectuals have "sold out," and that Black male intellectuals in particular are "punks." Black Nationalism is patriarchal, but its adherents have few qualms about challenging White male authority.

55. Boyd 2000, 67.

56. Interestingly, because this rhetoric of color blindness seems to challenge ideas of White supremacy, it makes it doubly difficult to contest. Ferber argues that the White supremacist discourse that she studied required a difference/equality distinction that was violated by interracial sexuality. Within this framework, race and gender differences are constructed as hierarchical and necessary. Thus, efforts to erase hierarchy are reinterpreted as efforts to do away with racial and/or gender differences. As Ferber points out, "an equality that recognizes differences is impossible within this framework" (Ferber 1998b, 70). At the same time, the framework of equality provides no space as well for bona fide "differences" that can be used to remedy past and present inequalities. The result is an impotent antiracist and feminist discourse that is trapped between tenets of White supremacy and a head in the sand color blindness. Neither can address current inequalities in desegregated environments.

57. Dalton 1999a, 333.

CHAPTER SIX

1. Bambara 1970, 108. Traditional gender ideology holds that, ideally, men and women should complement one another because neither gender is complete without the other. Relying on assumptions of heterosexuality, each gender has appropriately masculine and feminine attributes that, when combined, fit together smoothly to make a couple whole. Moreover, this logic of gender complementary offers a view of gender equality based on male and female differences. Ideally, men and women have distinctive responsibilities that also complement one another. Men lead and women follow. Men care for women by protecting them from harm and ensuring their financial security. Women care for men by supporting them in any way they can. This traditional gender ideology is not inherently flawed because many men and women rely upon these standards to build affirming, lifelong partnerships and family lives. The problem occurs when this traditional gender ideology becomes the norm for evaluating everyone's experiences.

2. Bambara 1970, 101.

3. Black family research has often uncritically accepted the assumption of gender complementarity associated with sex role theory. For example, both William E. B. Du Bois and E. Franklin Frazier's work on African American families identified as problematic gender norms that differed from those characterizing White middle-class families. Frazier describes African American gender arrangements as a "Black matriarchy" and, as a result, is accused of endorsing the "weak men, strong women" thesis. Neither author saw a deficient gender ideology as the sole or even the primary cause of African American poverty and political powerlessness. Instead, they explore how social structures associated with capitalist development and with racism interfered with African Americans' ability to fulfill traditional gender roles. This basic framework that social structures retarded African American ability to fulfill traditional gender roles was transformed yet again and

moved into public policy forums in 1965 with the publication of the Moynihan report, *The Negro Family: The Case for National Action*. This volume marked the beginnings of the modern debate on Black gender ideology (Moynihan 1965). For a discussion of these issues, see Franklin 1997a.

4. Family researchers first raised the issue of how gender ideology worked to privilege the nuclear family over other configurations (Andersen 1991). Black feminist analyses identify similar issues. See, for example, Jordan 1992; Lorde 1984; Gilkes 2001.

5. The general use of the term "the Black Church" refers to Black Christian churches in the United States. For a general history of the Black Church, see Lincoln 1999.

6. See Patillo-McCoy 1999, especially Patillo-McCoy 1998.

7. Douglas 1999.

8. Collins 1989.

9. Spillers 2000, 74.

10. Torgovnick 1990, 42.

11. Torgovnick 1990, 55.

12. Hegemony is a mode of social organization that relies on ideology to make oppressive power relations seem natural and normal. One goal of hegemonic ideologies is to absorb the dissent of oppressed groups, thereby dissipating its political effects. For example, if African Americans come to believe the dominant Black gender ideology circulated within the mass media, then Black political dissent about gender and sexuality becomes weakened. Hegemonic ideologies may seem invincible. But ideologies of all sorts are never static but instead are always internally inconsistent and are resisted (Magubane 2001).

13. Emerging in conjunction with a men's movement, and influenced by Western feminism (although this debt is not typically acknowledged) as well as the constructionist turn in the American academy in the 1990s, gender scholarship rejected the apolitical and nonhistorical framework of traditional sex role theory. New analyses of masculinity approached it as a system of gender power. "To understand a system of inequality, we must examine its dominant group—the study of men is as vital for gender analysis as the study of ruling classes and elites is for class analysis," argued R.W. Connell (Connell 1992, 736). Within this framework, the term "hegemonic masculinity" came to refer to the dominant form of masculinity in any given society and created the space to view representations of White masculinity and Black masculinity not as descriptions of nature but as social constructions rooted in American power relations.

Rejecting the term "patriarchy" as overly simplistic, at any given moment a range of masculinities exists in any social order, including masculinities that are hegemonic, marginalized, and subordinated. Some key features characterize hegemonic masculinity. First, hegemonic masculinity is defined in relation to the subordination of women *and* in relation to other subordinated and marginalized masculinities (Messner 1990, 205). Second, hegemonic masculinity does not refer to a personality type or an actual male character. Rather, it describes a set of prescriptive social norms, symbolically represented, that operate as a crucial part of daily, routine activities (Wetherell and Edley 1999, 336). Third, the constellation of ideas and social practices that constitute hegemonic masculinity are accepted, rejected, and performed by men from diverse social class groupings, racial/ethnic groups, ages, and religions. Whereas men are not equal in their ability to control the very definitions of masculinity itself, the vast majority of men are, in some fashion, complicit in upholding hegemonic masculinity (Connell 1995). Finally, the power relations that construct these relational masculinities enable the erasure of whiteness, class privilege, and assumptions of heterosexuality, in short, the workings of hegemonic masculinity itself. As a result, hegemonic discourses of American masculinity operate as unquestioned truths. Ironically, despite the ubiquity of gender, race, class, and sexuality in constructing American masculinity, masculinity can be discussed without referencing these systems at all.

Over time, this literature on masculinities devoted increasing attention to the socially constructed nature of hegemonic masculinities in relation to a variety of other constructed masculinities across differences of class, race, ethnicity, and sexuality. Masculinity itself was seen as highly heterogeneous and relational, with masculinities constructed in relation to one another emerging as an important area of study (Connell 1992, 1995). One important idea now possible with the emergence of this literature is that, from the perspectives of subordinated groups, all masculinities are in some sense hegemonic—a situation in which, for example, White men encounter a hegemonic White masculinity of what a White man should be and do, and Black men encounter equally hegemonic ideas about what Black men should be and do. In a sense, there are levels of hegemonic masculinity, all designed to control.

14. Kimmel 2001.
15. Freydberg 1995, 2257.
16. Freydberg 1995, 2257.
17. "Skeleton in Newark's Closet: Laquetta Nelson Is Forcing Homophobia Out into the Open" 2003.
18. This fear of feminization may help explain why many Black men reject feminism: "it is the idea of feminism connected to a perverse notion of the feminine that in the historical memory of Black men conjures up images of feminization, castration, and ultimately death" (Lemons 1997, 45). In everyday life, such men are viewed as being emasculated or, in Black vernacular, "pussy whipped."
19. Initially, sports operated as a White, middle- and upper-class male-created homosocial cultural space that provided elite men a psychological separation from the perceived "feminization" of society while providing symbolic proof of male superiority. As Messner observes, "it is not simply the bonding among men and the separation from women, but the physicality of the activity which gives sports its saliency in gender relations" (Messner 1990, 204). Over time, as this space became dominated by working-class White men, by Black men, and most recently by women, sport delivers less of this "symbolic proof of White male superiority."
20. Anderson 1999, 9–10.
21. The concept of a "family wage" also leads to pay discrimination against women. It argues that men should be paid more than women because men have the responsibility of financially supporting their wives and children. In contrast, women are more likely to have babies and leave the labor market to care for them.
22. Connell 1992, 748.
23. Connell 1992, 736.
24. Dalton 1999a, 333.
25. This theme of body politics has a prominent place in feminist theory. For discussions of women's biology and human nature, see Bordo 1993. For an alternative analysis of the meaning of the body within Western societies, see Oyěwùmí 1997.
26. Banks 2000, 28.

27. Patterson 1982, 61.
28. Patterson 1982, 61.
29. Banks 2000, 29.
30. Girls constitute a related benchmark used to construct hegemonic femininity. Girls are allegedly pure, innocent, and sexual virgins. They should be unspoiled. Interestingly, representations of young women/girls within contemporary popular culture contain the contradictions currently plaguing views of young White womanhood. On the one hand, women are expected to aspire to a body type that approximates that of adolescent girls. The inordinate pressure placed on thinness within U.S. society advances a social norm that values youth. At the same time, these same inordinately thin adolescent girls are dressed as highly sexualized women within high fashion. Black women as sexualized, full-figured women become juxtaposed to the thin, young, fragile and increasingly ornamental and sexualized young White girls.
31. Torgovnick 1990, 53. This theme of White female submissiveness also appears in other major icons of Western popular culture. For example, the various remakes of *King Kong* take this need to rescue White womanhood from sexual predators to an entirely new level. With King Kong theorized to be symbolic of Black men as animals or "apes" run amuck, just as Jane needed saving from the predators in the jungle, the White woman in Manhattan needed saving from a lustful Kong now transplanted to an urban jungle (Dines 1998).
32. Naylor 1988, 28.
33. Gomez 1999, 174. Gomez observes that Black lesbians are rarely represented on film or in print and that, if they are, the fully developed characters presented by Audre Lorde or Alice Walker are missing. Instead, Black lesbians are typically presented as tragic (television adaptation of *The Women of Brewster Place*), as peripheral to the main story, or as caricature (Cleo played by Queen Latifah). Given this history, the character of Kima on the HBO series *The Wire* constitutes a breakthrough character.
34. Collins 2000b.
35. For general discussions of Black women, family, and work, see Giddings 1984; Jones 1985.
36. This recognition does not mean that race and gender discrimination were given equal weight within African American politics. Black feminist analyses of Black women's subordination have long been present, but, until the post–civil rights era, they have functioned as a minor strand within Black community politics (Collins 2000a).
37. Calmore 2001.
38. Petterson 1997.
39. Petterson 1997, 605.
40. Neal 2002, 68.
41. Black women's unwillingness to confront the SBW image can foster Black women's vulnerability to domestic violence (Richie 1996) as well as their experiences with incest and sexual abuse (Wilson 1994; White 1985b).
42. Baldwin 1993, 217.
43. Mercer 1994, 171–220.
44. Mercer 1994, 174.
45. See the photograph on p. 186 in Mercer 1994, 174.
46. Denizet-Lewis 2003, 30.

47. This was a major plank in the platform of turn-of-the-twentieth-century Black Club Women (Giddings 1984).
48. For discussions of hypersegregation, see Massey and Denton 1993. For discussions of the erosion of Black institutions, see Gregory 1994.
49. Jones 1994, 92.
50. McClary and Walser 1994.
51. Racial integration may be one marker of the post–civil rights era, but it is clear that it has been accompanied by dramatic increases in the incarceration rates of African American men. In the last half of the twentieth century, especially during the post–civil rights era, the incarceration rates of African Americans in relation to Whites went up dramatically. In 1933, Blacks were incarcerated at a rate approximately three times that for Whites. By 1950, the rate was 4 to 1; in 1960, it was 5 to 1; in 1970 it was 6 to 1, and by the 1980s, it was 7 to 1 (Miller 1996, 88). Various expressions of racial bias in all phases of the criminal justice system have, by now, been well documented as producing this outcome (Miller 1996, 48–88).
52. This growing interconnectedness of prison, street, and youth culture, with the importance given to hierarchies of masculinity, became repackaged and sold within the commodified relations of global mass media. These ideas now permeate not only African American culture but also have become markers of a new form of authentic Blackness.

CHAPTER SEVEN

1. Hill 1997, 13.
2. African Americans may have lost far more than Anita Hill as a result of Thomas's appointment. Routinely aligning himself with its most conservative wing, Thomas's record on the Supreme Court concerning racism has been disappointing to labor organizations, women's constituencies, and civil rights groups. Anita Hill also suffered personal loss. In the ten years following the hearings, Hill experienced hate mail, unwanted phone calls, and death threats. In contrast, Thomas has remained on the Supreme Court, enjoying its privileges. Hill was virtually run out of her job as a law professor at the University of Oklahoma and underwent persistent harassment by students, colleagues, and strangers on the street (Hill 1997).
3. Crenshaw 1992, 405.
4. Wells-Barnett 2002; Davis 1978.
5. For a discussion of consensus and cross-cutting issues within Black politics, see Cohen 1999.
6. Lynching has not always been so central to Black antiracist politics. See historian Paula Giddings' analysis of Black leadership, which initially took little action concerning lynching before Ida B. Wells-Barnett's solitary crusade (Giddings 2001).
7. Beck and Tolnay 1992, 22.
8. Harris 1984, 19.
9. Beck and Tolnay 1992, 7–8.
10. Gender analyses shed light on why castration reappears in accounts of Black male lynchings. Robyn Wiegman provides a psychoanalytic analysis of lynching that examines its power in terms of national identity—the end of slavery constituted a rebirth of the nation that needed to develop new race relations. African American bodies were no longer commodities, and making this transition from slavery to the

reenslavement of Jim Crow de jure segregation required a complicated process of reworking Black male sexuality and African American masculinity. Wiegman suggests that lynching served as a "threat of ritualized death" that provided one means for hegemonic White masculinity to be rearticulated within the uncertainties of postemancipation. As Wiegman points outs, "not only does lynching enact a grotesquely symbolic—if not literal—sexual encounter between the white mob and its victim, but the increasing utilization of castration as a preferred form of mutilation for African American men demonstrates lynching's connection to the sociosymbolic realm of sexual difference. In the disciplinary fusion of castration with lynching, the mob severs the black male from the masculine, interrupting the privilege of the phallus, and thereby reclaiming, through the perversity of dismemberment, his (masculine) potentiality for citizenship" (Wiegman 1993, 224).

11. Collins 2000a, 53–55.
12. Dash 1996, 225.
13. Dash 1996, 226.
14. Dash 1996, 226.
15. In 1892, Ida B. Wells-Barnett learned firsthand the lengths to which some White citizens of Memphis were willing to go to maintain African American political and economic subordination. In March, Memphis Whites lynched three successful African American managers of a grocery business. Wells knew all three men, and also understood that they were resented because their store successfully competed with a White store. This painful personal experience of her friends' lynching was a turning point in Wells-Barnett's commitment to social justice activism. Wells-Barnett wrote an editorial that, for 1892, advanced the shocking hypothesis that not only were African American men often falsely accused of rape but also that because some White women were attracted to Black men, some sexual relations that did occur between African American men and White women were consensual. Fortunately, when the editorial appeared, Wells-Barnett was out of town or she too might have been lynched. Memphis citizens burned down the *Free Speech* and threatened Wells-Barnett's life if she ever returned to Memphis. This shocking catalyst marked the beginning of Ida Wells-Barnett's impressive over-twenty-year crusade against lynching that took the form of going on speaking tours, publishing editorials, preparing pamphlets, organizing community services, participating in women's and civil rights groups, and publishing *Southern Horrors, A Red Record, and Mob Rule in New Orleans*, three of Wells-Barnett's important pamphlets on lynching (Wells-Barnett 2002).
16. Wells-Barnett 2002, 6.
17. James 1996; Giddings 2001.
18. These ideas come from Ann Stoler's excellent analysis of Michel Foucault's ideas about race. Stoler states: "as 'private wars' were cancelled and war was made the prerogative of states, as war proper moves to the margins of the social body, as society is 'cleansed of war-like relations' that this 'strange,' 'new' discovery emerged, one in which society itself was conceived as an entity saturated with the relations of war" (Stoler 1995, 64–65).
19. Bandele 1999, 86.
20. See Wilson 1994 and Pierce-Baker 1998, 117–139. African American adolescent mothers also report that the fathers of their babies are much older men (Kaplan 1997).
21. Painter 1992, 213.

22. Pierce-Baker 1998, 64.
23. Cleage 1993.
24. Pierce-Baker 1998, 91.
25. West 1999, 59.
26. Because so many African American women live in large, racially segregated urban areas, Black women more likely to be victims of rape than White women—reported rapes are 1.4 to 1.7 times higher. Yet such women are less likely to have their rape cases come to trial than White women, and they are less likely to get convictions for those cases that do come to trial. Moreover, African American women who are sexually assaulted are less likely to use rape-counseling services. It is important to stress that patterns of Black male violence against Black women occur within a broader social context in which the routinization of violence works to desensitize everyone to its effects. Viewing one's first violent movie may be shocking—viewing the fiftieth film has far less impact. The genre of stalker films that make raping and killing women a spectator sport contributes to this broader climate of violence against women. Black men whose violent behavior is targeted toward Black women are certainly not immune from these societal pressures.
27. Bell 1999, 240.
28. Childhood sexual assault (Maya Angelou's *I Know Why the Caged Bird Sings* and Toni Morrison's *The Bluest Eye*); family violence (see Alice Walker's fiction, especially *The Color Purple* and *The Third Life of George Copeland*), and the effects of rape on African American women (Gayl Jones's *Eva's Man*) have all been explored in African American women's fiction. Black women's essays examine similar themes. Statements about the pain of rape (Austin 1993), rape as a tool of political control (Davis 1981), and the pervasiveness of violence in African American civil society (Cleage 1993) all have received considerable treatment in African American women's writings. Increasingly, womanist theologians are providing a new interpretive context that encourages Black women to speak out about abuse. See Douglas 1999 and West 1999.
29. Awkward 1999, 137.
30. Wyatt 1992, 87.
31. Pierce-Baker 1998, 136.
32. Supplementing survey data with interviews with 126 African American and 122 White women in the Los Angeles area conducted by a same race interviewer, Wyatt investigated women's perceptions of rape. Wyatt's interviewers also asked the question, "Why do you think you were victimized?" African American women were significantly more likely than White women to offer explanations about their victimization that involved the riskiness of their living circumstances (Wyatt 1992, 84).
33. Wyatt 1992, 85.
34. Pierce-Baker 1998, 124.
35. Pierce-Baker 1998, 161.
36. West 1999, 58.
37. Omolade 1994, 89.
38. Powell 2000, 74.
39. Miller 1996, 1–9.
40. Human Rights Watch 2001, 3.
41. Human Rights Watch 2001, 5.
42. Human Rights Watch 2001, 7.

43. Human Rights Watch 2001, 8.
44. Miller 2000, 300.
45. Material in this section is taken from Miller 2000, 300.
46. Miller 2000, 302.
47. Miller 2000, 303.
48. Miller 2000, 303.
49. Human Rights Watch 2001.
50. Sociologist R. W. Connell offers an explanation for the fluidity of gender categories: "In our culture, men who have sex with men are generally oppressed, but they are not definitively excluded from masculinity. Rather, they face structurally-induced conflicts about masculinity—conflicts between their sexuality and their social presence as men, about the meaning of their choice of sexual object, and in their construction of relationships with women and with heterosexual men" (Connell 1992, 737).
51. Human Rights Watch 2001, 70.
52. Violence targeted against gay Black men can be especially vicious, in part, because gay Black men become suitable targets for the violence. Some guards view homosexuality as an open invitation to sexuality. As one prisoner, who was heterosexual, recalled: "I had an officer tell me that 'faggots like to suck dick, so why was I complaining'" (Human Rights Watch 2001, 114).
53. Pinar 2001, 1031–1046. Given the myth of the Black rapist, placing Black men in prison situations in which they are encouraged to rape other men produces the very stereotype created in the postemancipation era. Black men become dangerous, a reason to keep them locked up.
54. Human Rights Watch 2001, 169.
55. Human Rights Watch 2001, 216.
56. Pinar 2001, 1119.
57. Pinar 2001, 1053–1057.
58. Human Rights Watch 2001, 109–122.
59. Human Rights Watch 2001, 171.
60. Human Rights Watch 2001, 168.
61. African American men constituted 42 percent of those admitted to prison in 1981 and, by 1993, had become an unsettling 55 percent of those admitted (Miller 1996, 55).
62. (Miller 1996, 97). Sociologist Elijah Anderson describes the code of the street in which demanding respect and exhibiting toughness function as important dimensions of Black masculinity within inner-city neighborhoods (Anderson 1999). In his lengthy study of lynching and prison rape, William Pinar identifies another connection between prison culture and masculine identity: "Prisons are not alien womanless worlds in which men resort to unimaginable acts. Prisons disclose the profoundly womanless worlds most men in fact inhabit, in which women are fundamentally fictive, units of currency in a homosocial economy . . . perhaps most men 'live' in an all-male world intrapsychically from which women are aggressively banished. It is a sign of manhood" (Pinar 2001, 1119).
63. Oliver 1994.
64. Canada 1995.
65. McCall 1994; Shakur 1993.
66. Anecdotal, unpublished material.
67. Morgan 1999, 73.

CHAPTER EIGHT

1. Root 2001, 1. This rule may seem natural, but it actually requires constant reiteration. Most people encounter widespread societal pressure to get married. Should there be any confusion about the definition of marriage, the 1996 Federal Defense of Marriage Act felt compelled to clarify it: "In determining the meaning of any Act of Congress, or of any ruling, regulation or interpretation of the various administrative bureaus and agencies of the United States, the word 'marriage' means only a legal union between one man and one woman as husband and wife, and the word 'spouse' refers only to a person of the different sex who is a husband or wife" (U.S. Census Bureau 2000). One wonders just who is attacking marriage if Congress feels that it must pass laws to "defend" it.

2. Social movements for Black and Latino civil rights, for women's rights, and for the rights of lesbian, gay, bisexual, and transgendered (LGBT) people, among others, profoundly changed historical relations of segregation. Whether racial segregation in schools, housing, and public life; of gender segregation of women and men into separate spheres of life; of heterosexuals from gays and lesbians through the forced closeting of sexual minorities; and of national policies that excluded immigration from Latin America, Asia, Africa, and the Caribbean, rigid forms of segregation are all giving way to an imperfect desegregation. Despite higher rates of residential racial segregation for African Americans than Whites, especially those living in large cities, rates of residential racial segregation dropped between 1980 and 2000 (Iceland, Weinberg, and Steinmetz 2002, 59–76). On average, all women still earn less than men, but White women in particular are closing the occupational gap—in 1999, 35 percent of non-Hispanic White women were in professional and managerial jobs compared to 32 percent of non-Hispanic White men (McKinnon and Humes 2000, 4). Assumptions about marriage and about LGBT partnerships are changing. In the 2000 census, 5.5 million couples reported living together without being married, up from 3.2 million in 1990. The majority of unmarried-partner households had partners of the different sex (4.9 million), but about 1 in 9 had partners of the same sex (Simmons and O'Connell 2003, 1). Assumptions concerning American citizenship are also changing. The Census Bureau estimated that by 2002 the foreign-born population numbered 32.5 million people, accounting for 11.5 percent of the total U.S. population (U.S. Census Bureau 2003).

3. In 1998, 60 percent of all White men over the age of fifteen were married. In contrast, 41 percent of Black men fell in this category. Marital rates for White and Black women were even more disparate. For White women, 57 percent were married whereas 36 percent of Black women were married. A sizeable proportion of African Americans remain unmarried (which does not necessarily mean living without a partner)—46 percent of Black men and 41 percent of Black women were never married (U.S. Census Bureau 1999). Marital rates among African Americans may be in decline, but it is important to note that, despite the lower rates, Black men (41 percent) are more likely to be married than Black women (36 percent).

4. Marital rates are not adequate evidence of commitment. The marital rates mask the prevalence of unmarried partnerships among African Americans. Black men and women (never married, widowed, and divorced) may be identified as unmarried yet live with opposite-sex partners in unmarried-partner households. In 2000, approximately 15.5 percent of all households maintained by African

American couples contained unmarried opposite-sex partners. In other words, the marital rate may be a less accurate measure of committed heterosexual relationships among African Americans than among Whites (7.3 percent) or Asians (4.0 percent) where opposite-sex, unmarried-partner households are lower (Simmons and O'Connell 2003, 6).

5. The decline in marriage accelerated in the 1970s. In 1970, 57 percent of Black men and 54 percent of Black women were married. By 1980, 49 percent of Black men and 44 percent of Black women were married (U.S. Census Bureau 1999). A variety of factors have been identified as contributing to these patterns of decline. Black marriages fail at higher rates than in previous years and many African Americans no longer choose to marry at all (Franklin 1997b). Many dating relationships and marriages remain characterized by emotional and/or physical violence (Richie 1996; Wilson 1994; White 1985b; Cleage 1993).

6. Collins 2000a, 151–160.

7. Recent research suggests that Black middle-class experiences differ from those of their White counterparts. For one, middle-class Black people are more likely to live in closer proximity to poor and working-class Black people (Patillo-McCoy 1999).

8. Moreover, not all poor and working-class Black people live in racially segregated neighborhoods. The guests on the popular talk shows discussed in chapter 1 who underwent paternity tests were typically from different races.

9. Omolade 1994, 80.

10. Carbado 1999b, 420.

11. Cose 2003.

12. McCall 1997, 37.

13. Kitwana 2002, 104.

14. Bell 1999, 243–244.

15. Morgan 1999, 130–131.

16. Dalton 1999a, 124.

17. Morgan 1999, 121–122.

18. Sterk-Elifson 1994, 114.

19. Gilroy 2000, 204.

20. Morgan 1999, 74–75.

21. Smith 1999, 117.

22. Washington 1996, 1121.

23. Bandele 1999, 114.

24. In the two decades following this momentous decision, Whites intermarried with non-Whites and interracial marriage grew at least 500 percent (Root 2001, 6). Despite this statistical increase, the overall rate of interracial marriage remained small—only 1.3 percent of married couples over age fourteen were in interracial marriages in the 1970s. However, when it came to African Americans, this "500 percent increase" masked significant racial patterns. Because African Americans and White Americans constitute *numerically* large population groups, Black-White intermarriages represent the greatest *number* of relationships. Statistically, however, African Americans remained the *least* likely group to marry interracially with Whites.

25. The 1960 census counted 51,000 Black-White couples, fairly evenly divided between Black husbands with White wives (25,000) and Black wives with White husbands (26,000). During the 1960s, however, the number of African American men married to White women increased to 41,000, whereas the numbers of

African American women married to White men remained virtually the same. Thus, during the 1960s, Black-White intermarriages increased only because of an increase in the number of African American men marrying White women. By 1980, approximately 80 percent of all Black-White intermarriages involved a Black man and a White woman—an estimated 9.5 percent of African American men who got married at all married White women. By the 1990 census, gender differences in patterns of Black-White intermarriage were even more pronounced. Numerically, the number of Black-White marriages in the 1980s nearly doubled, jumping from 121,000 couples in 1980 to 213,000 couples in 1990. The increase of Black men marrying White women continued its upward path—the 94,000 couples reported in 1980 had mushroomed to 159,000 such couples by 1990. Statistically, however, because African American women also began to enter into interracial marriages, by 1990 approximately 75 percent of Black-White marriages were between a Black man and a White woman. The rate of intermarriage for Black women with White men, which had stayed fairly constant from 1960 to 1980, doubled during the 1980s, jumping from 27,000 in 1980 to 54,000 in 1990. This would have been a remarkable increase had it not been for the continued increase in marriages between Black men and White women. These figures are taken from Root (Root 2001, 179–188). See Root's appendix for a comprehensive discussion of all patterns of intermarriage, not just Black/White couples.

26. Root 2001, 169.
27. Ironically, an African American woman and a White man brought forward the *Loving v. Virginia* case that overturned laws against interracial marriage.
28. Root 2001, 11.
29. Dalton 1999b, 125.
30. Nelson 1997, 108.
31. Root 2001, 11.
32. Despite efforts to construct White women as either "blameless innocents" or as heroic champions of a democratic, color-blind America, it is important to remember that much is at stake for individual White women who love and/or marry African American men. Even within the changed legal and social climate of desegregation, their families and friends may see heterosexual White women who enter into interracial partnerships with African American men as violating some historical taboos. Contemporary White supremacist literature, in particular, has been obsessed both with interracial sexuality and with explaining White women's seemingly free participation in it. Within this literature, a White woman who thinks for herself and chooses a Black male sexual partner becomes an unthinkable abomination. The only satisfactory explanation is that these women have been "brain raped," stripped of free will and thereby not responsible for their actions (Ferber 1998a).
33. Dalton 1999b, 124.
34. Dalton 1999b, 125.
35. Two things here—these biracial Black women are replacing more "authentic" looking Black women in movies, televisions ads, music videos, and other arenas of popular culture that call for Black women. Moreover, biracial Black women are the ones depicted with struggles over their racial identity. In the fictional world of media, biracial Black men are depicted as being far less bothered by the color line.
36. Riggs 2002. Black British film and visual media has been far more open in exploring issues of gay sexuality. For example, British filmmaker Isaac Julien's film *Looking for Langston* also raised considerable controversy with its then shocking

thesis concerning Langston Hughes and homosexuality. Julian's 1991 film *Young Soul Rebels* also examines the love relationship of Black gay men.

37. Thomas 1997. As uncommon as images of interracial lesbian love relationships are, it is even more unusual to see one that involves a woman who is neither Black nor White. The love relationship of Evy, a Latina, and Kia, an African American woman, in the 1994 film *Go Fish* constitutes one exception. Even here, their relationship was not the focus of the film. The character of Kima on the HBO show *The Wire*, played by an actress of African American and Korean American heritage, also breaks new ground in this regard.

38. Boykin 1996; Hawkeswood 1996; Moore 1997; Smith 1999.

39. For exceptions to this situation, see Boykin 1996; Wekker 2000; Johnson 2000; Battle et al. 2002.

40. Because LGBT people are not allowed to marry, relying on traditional data sources to gauge commitments to LGBT relationships remains difficult. The treatment of LGBT households in the 1990 and 2000 censuses illustrates the difficulties of gathering basic demographic data on the extent of LGBT committed relationships, let alone dynamics within those relations. In 1990, the response "unmarried partner" was added as an option to the census question on household relationship, and in both the 1990 and 2000 censuses the terms "spouse" and "unmarried partner" were defined and asked the same way. In both censuses, if a person was identified as the "spouse" of the householder and was the same sex as the householder, the "spouse" response was flagged for further review and allocation, that is, assignment of a value other than originally reported by the person. Yet the analysis of this data differed in the two censuses. In 1990, the edit and allocation process did not allow the same-sex "spouse" combination to occur. In contrast, in 2000, when the combination occurred, the term "unmarried partner" was substituted for the term "spouse," thus allowing the category of same-sex unmarried partner to appear for the first time (U.S. Census Bureau 2000). Certainly same-sex, unmarried partnerships existed before the Census Bureau recognized them in 2000, but the very process of collecting and analyzing data has been a major factor in the closeting and subsequent visibility of LGBT committed relationships and families.

41. For example, the findings in *Married and Unmarried-Partner Household: 2000*, the first report ever issued by the Census Bureau on unmarried partners, contains information on people who reported living in different-sex and same-sex partnerships. For African Americans in racially homogeneous partnerships, the report notes that 16.9 percent of Black households are maintained by different-sex unmarried couples, and 1.4 percent are maintained by same-sex unmarried partners (Simmons and O'Connell 2003 , 6). Because the material from the 2000 census will be released over time, and because the 2010 census may provide the first ten-year overview of trends in same-sex unmarried partner households, it will take time for reputable government sources such as the census to document trends in same-sex partnerships.

42. Regarding gender, men comprised 58 percent of the sample, women 40 percent, and transgendered people 2 percent. Regarding sexual identity, the study reports that 63 percent of the men in the sample self-identified as gay and 13 percent as bisexual. For women, 61 percent self-identified as lesbian, 12 percent selected gay, and 10 percent chose bisexual. Less than 1 percent of men, women, or transgendered individuals self-identified as "queer" (Battle et al. 2002, 19).

43. Battle et al. 2002, 26.

44. Jordan 1992; Smith 1998; Lorde 1982.
45. Hemphill 1991; Smith 1999.
46. For example, Gloria Hull's retrieval and collection of the papers of Alice Dunbar suggests that Dunbar was a deeply closeted lesbian. Urbanization created new opportunities for Black gays and lesbians to find one another and, in many cases, build communities that reached across racial lines. Thus, the visibility of Black gay and lesbian love relationships became more possible and prominent within new city spaces. For example, through oral histories, the award-winning book *Boots of Leather, Slippers of Gold* re-creates the social norms of lesbian communities in Buffalo, New York, in the 1940s and 1950s. African American lesbians are presented as being simultaneously a marginal part of the larger community of White lesbians, yet having a social structure of their own that operated largely within the confined, segregated world of Black Buffalo (Kennedy and Davis 1994). In a similar fashion, Audre Lorde's autobiographical *Zami* is an important work that describes from an insider perspective, lesbian communities in New York City during this same period. From Lorde's autobiography, one can learn about the types of love relationships that were available to Black lesbians (Lorde 1982). More recently, the 2000 census identifies how unmarried partner households of all types are concentrated in central cities as compared to the concentration of married partner households in suburbs or rural areas (Simmons and O'Connell 2003, 2–3).
47. Moore 1997, 149.
48. Douglas 1999, 128.
49. Denizet-Lewis 2003, 31.
50. Denizet-Lewis 2003, 32.
51. Boykin 1996, 107.
52. For analyses of issues that affect the politics of Blacks and gays, see Cohen and Jones 1999.
53. Reid-Pharr 2001, 97.
54. Reid-Pharr 2001, 98. In her analysis of interracial lesbian relationships in film, Pellegrini proposes a similar psychoanalytic argument by exploring the ways in which Blackness works in films that were directed by White men and in some cases, White women (Pellegrini 1997). Arguing that all love relationships constitute some combination of sameness and difference, the problem confronted by lesbian films when both of the women are White lies in maintaining the distinction between female homosocial bonding and female homosexuality. Watching two White women engaged in a lesbian relationship raises too many questions about close female friendships for White audiences. In this context, Blackness bears the burden of helping the audience displace these uncomfortable questions onto the historically forbidden, interracial sexual relationship. By articulating lesbian difference through racial difference, the films can avoid, or potentially avoid, homophobic equations of same-sex love with narcissistic love of the same.
55. Bandele 1999, 72–73.

CHAPTER NINE

1. Swarns 2002.
2. The magnitude of the problem in continental Africa is staggering. For example, a 2002 report issued jointly by the United Nations Program on AIDS, UNICEF, and the U.S. Agency for International Development reported that HIV/AIDS had left

11 million African children orphans, defined as children under age fifteen who lose one or both parents. This number is expected to rise to 20 million in Africa by 2010. Most of the AIDS orphans do not lose their parents as infants, but years later when they are of school age (Altman 2002b). More than half of South Africa's fifteen-year-olds will die of AIDS-related diseases, government officials predict (Swarns 2001).

3. African Americans are more at risk for contacting AIDS than other racial/ethnic groups. In 1998, African Americans represented 37 percent of all AIDS cases ever reported to the Center for Disease Control. In 2000, Black Americans accounted for 43 percent of AIDS cases (Altman 2002a, 1). Almost half (45%) of new AIDS cases reported in the United States in 1998 were African American. Moreover, not only are HIV/AIDS rates in the United States increasing faster among African Americans than among other groups, much of the increase is occurring in African American women. Among those who acquired HIV through heterosexual sex, from 1994 through 2000, Black women accounted for nearly half and Black male heterosexuals accounted for an additional 25 percent (Altman 2002a, 1). Age also matters—Black youth in the United States have been hard hit by HIV/AIDS. In 1998, young African Americans represented more than half (57%) of new AIDS cases reported among those thirteen to nineteen years old (Kaiser Family Foundation 2000, 5).

4. Ideas about disease associated with modern/Western medicine emerged in a scientific context that was preoccupied with issues of biology, race, and gender. The concepts of health juxtaposed to those of sickness and disease constituted an important binary woven throughout those discussed in earlier chapters. These beliefs served as the basis for long-standing taboos on intermarriage and on interracial sexuality. Western science was deeply implicated in creating these relationships (Gould 1981; Fausto-Sterling 1992). Exploring the connections between sexuality and disease was of special interest. Europeans defined Blacks as another species, a diseased, degenerate "race," and saw sexual contact between Whites and Blacks as polluting and causing disease among the allegedly superior White race. Similar beliefs framed European understandings of social class, this time encapsulated with European perceptions of prostitutes as a lower social class and as a group who also carried disease and pollution. In this way, sexuality, disease, race, gender, and class mutually constructed one another. Within this logic, sexuality and disease became intricately connected and gained meaning from one another. On the one hand, one way to maintain allegedly normal sexuality is to portray alternative sexualities as deviant. People who engaged in taboo sexual practices or in sexual practices with taboo people became stigmatized as being "sick" or were liable to become "polluted" or "diseased" if they continued the forbidden contact. Groups stigmatized in this fashion included homosexuals and prostitutes. Victorian prostitutes—working-class White women—were accused of spreading syphilis and were stigmatized as "bad women." As historian Paula Giddings points out, this association of Black sexuality with disease has striking predecessors in the nineteenth century: "In the medical metaphors of the day, the sexual organs of sexual women were not only hotbeds of moral pathology, but of disease. In the nineteenth century the great fear was of a sexually transmitted disease that was spreading among the population, was incurable, and after invading the body, disfigured and decomposed it in stages. The name of the disease was syphilis, and it was the era's metaphor for the retribution of sexual sin" (Giddings 1995, 419).

5. For a discussion of coalitions between African Americans and LGBT people, see Brandt 1999.

6. Jordan 1992.

7. In the 1990s, ideas about the body became widespread in literary criticism and in cultural studies. For work that examines this trope of the body to explore issues that affect Black women, see especially Holloway 1995; Roberts 1997; Carby 1992; Bennett and Dickerson 2001. For work on Black men's bodies, see Cunningham 1996.

8. This splitting speaks to the theme of double consciousness first proposed by African American intellectual William E. B. DuBois one hundred years ago whereby the mind was split from the body and Black people were dominated because they learned to think about themselves through the lens of racial ideology. This argument preceded contemporary views of internalized oppression whereby controlling images of Black masculinity and Black femininity are believed and shape self-perception. DuBois does not speak of how that double consciousness also disrupts how people feel in their bodies, the theme that I raise here.

9. I write extensively about this concept in chapter 5 of *Black Feminist Thought*. See "The Power of Self-Definition" (Collins 2000a, 97–122).

10. This approach diverges from current work in body politics that views the body as "skin" and equates it with a canvas on which scripts of domination are written. The focus of this outside/in approach becomes the social scripts themselves. I am indebted to this approach and have certainly relied upon it in this volume. But to me, this version of body politics underemphasizes individual agency, will, and spirit. Actual people disappear to be replaced by abstract social actors and social scripts. Phrases such as "the black body" and "my Black body" catalyze different politics. For an overview of this outside/in body literature and an example of its use, see Mohanram 1999.

11. One feature of the Western emphasis on the mind concerns the reliance on visual metaphors and seeing as a cultural frame for analyzing society. When people get an idea, they say, "I see what you mean." Reading this book is an exercise in thinking that depends on the visual. But how might an honest body politics operate if visual metaphors were no longer privileged in this way? How might an honest body politics operate if other ways of knowing were also incorporated into models of body politics?

12. As a term that emerged in the context of the Black arts movement of the 1960s, soul remains a slippery concept to identify. Black scholars point out how difficult it is to define soul: "Although we may not know specifically what soul 'is,' we still may be able to recognize it" (Guillory and Green 1998, 3). Soul may be gaining new favor: "In some ways, the concept of soul may serve us far better than race ever will. While statisticians and clinicians . . . discern Blackness through a variety of biological and social attributes, soul remains an abstract and evocative site for identity formation" (Guillory and Green 1998, 2). Portia Maultsby provides one of the most comprehensive definitions of soul: "Soul, as a concept, originated in African-American communities during the late 1960s. It evolved from the ideology of Black Power, which promoted Black nationalism. Therefore, soul has both sociopolitical and cultural functions and meanings. From a sociopolitical perspective, it advocated self-awareness, Black empowerment, and a Black identity. From a cultural perspective, it identified expressions symbolic of a Black style or a Black way of doing things, as well as a range of traditions unique to African Americans" (Tate et al. 1998, 270).

13. Tate et al. 1998, 275.

14. Tate et al. 1998, 276.
15. Tate et al. 1998, 281.
16. Tate et al. 1998, 281.
17. Tate et al. 1998, 269.
18. Tate et al. 1998, 269–270.
19. Neal 2002, 3. In his work on Black popular culture, Mark Anthony Neal takes an ethereal view of soul, claiming that it emerged in conjunction with African American modernity and was premised on the production of "positive" representations of Blackness that could be used to counter the negative ones long associated with racism. Within this definition, claiming soul was a way for African Americans to identify a racial essence that distinguished them from their oppressors. Two distinctive political moments of Black activism, namely, the 1920s and the 1960s, both produced Black arts movements that investigated Black culture and identified its significance for Black political struggle. Culture and identity, especially the construction of positive Black identities, were central to both political moments.
20. Tate et al. 1998, 282.
21. Collins 1998, 61–65.
22. Davis 1998, 107.
23. Reed 1998, 169.
24. Asante 1994, 78.
25. Spirituality (expressiveness) and sexuality may also be directly linked. Many African cultures have long demonstrated an intrinsic connection between spirituality and sexuality (Douglas 1999, 84). Kelly Douglass describes these connections: "Spirituality concerns a person's connection to God and, thus, inevitably involves her or his sexuality. . . . [S]exuality is that fundamental dimension of human beings that governs intimate, sensual, affective, emotional, and sexual relationships. Human sexuality and spirituality are inextricably linked because both involve a person's relationship to God" (Douglas 1999, 84). Like soul, the concept of spirituality also has the potential to expand sexual meanings and move men and women toward sexual autonomy.
26. Lorde 1984, 53–59.
27. Hammonds 1997, 181.
28. One outcome of their work is that forms of women's sexual desire and expression that have been labeled nasty, dirty, or forbidden (the hallmark of the Western invention of Black sexuality) may no longer be so. As Gina Dent observes, oral sex serves as a "code for black women's pleasure, gay sexuality, and other illicit practices, including drug use in black communities" (Dent 1992a, 14).
29. Rose 2003.
30. Rose 2003, 4.
31. Building on Lorde's work, Black men have only recently begun to explore similar questions of Black male desire, agency, and eroticism across diverse sexualities (Carbado 1999c). Robert Reid-Pharr suggests that much that has been written about sexuality, a basic bodily activity, but that this literature says little about the physicality of sexuality itself. Reid-Pharr takes queer theory to task, arguing that new theories of sexuality must find ways to influence how people act, and not just how they think. "The task that awaits all of us, then, is to speak desire plainly, to pay attention to what we think when we fuck. It is the particular task of white men to give up the comforts of naiveté, of banal gestures to racial inclusion. The work before us is precisely to put our own bodies on the line. We much refuse to allow

the production of a queer theory so reified that it does nothing to challenge the way we interact, the way we think, and the way we fuck. We must insist on a queer theory that take the queer body and what we do with it as a primary focus" (Reid-Pharr 2001, 98).

32. Morgan 1999, 224.

33. This concept of honest bodies may also have links to spirituality and a relationship with God. Working within traditions of Christian theology, Douglas argues for a Black sexual politics that protects the historical realness of God's revelation in Jesus, one that requires a theological understanding of the body. Bodies are not worshipped within this tradition, but rather are appreciated both as "temples of God" and as the medium of God's love. God was distinctly revealed in human history only by becoming embodied. Moreover, human beings can come to know and be in relationship with one another only by reaching out to one another with their bodies, and accepting one another as being embodied (Douglas 1999, 118).

34. The growing impoverishment of the phrase the personal is political illustrates these problems. As British cultural critic Kobena Mercer observes, "sexual politics is narrowed down first to sexuality, then to the self. It strikes me that this 'self-centeredness' is a characteristic of white sexual politics, or rather it is an interpretation of 'the personal is political' which is made in a highly individualistic manner that tends to exclude questions of race because it is so preoccupied with 'self' at the expense of the 'social'" (Mercer 1994, 148).

35. Harris 1984; Hall 1983; Wiegman 1993; Pinar 2001.

36. Within literature, E. Lynn Harris explores this theme through the character of Basil Henderson, a Black bisexual football player who has difficulty coming to terms with his sexuality. Henderson pursues gay men as sexual partners yet lashes out, often violently, at gay men who pursue him.

37. Baldwin 1963, 9.

38. Baldwin 1963, 43.

39. Bambara 1970, 109.

40. For example, in Mississippi, 28.5 percent of those reporting new HIV infections in 2000 were Black women, up from 13 percent in 1990. In Alabama, the number rose to 31 percent from 13 percent whereas in North Carolina, it rose to 27 percent from 18 percent (Sack 2001).

41. Data in this paragraph are from Sack 2001.

42. Data in this paragraph are from Altman 2002a, 1.

43. Altman 2002a, 1.

44. Denizet-Lewis 2003, 32.

45. Denizet-Lewis 2003.

46. Stoler 1995, 3. Also see, Foucault 1980, 1979.

47. Gilroy 2000, 185.

48. Gilroy 2000, 184. Angela Davis makes a similar argument in her claim that Black women's blues was a public text that wrestled love relationships away from either White or Black male control (Davis 1998).

49. Gilroy 2000, 195.

50. Reid-Pharr 2001, 174–175.

51. Reid-Pharr 2001, 97.

52. Baldwin 1993, 136.

53. Eli 1995, 143.

54. This use of community is derogated because it is seen to reflect nineteenth-century

racist beliefs used to construct understandings of race itself. Benedict Anderson's important work *Imagined Communities* describes this process of constructing modern nation states from the imagined communities of people who never meet (Anderson 1983). Anderson's argument has been extended to the social construction of races, which in the climate of the new racism, sees races as equally imagined. The origins of ideas of race as family may lie in nineteenth-century politics and science, but the historical experiences that have accompanied these ideas now have a life of their own. Despite the fiction of "race" for Black people, the reality of race persists through shared experiences that are not directly attributable to racism. For a discussion of this use of "race" among Black people, see Higginbotham 1992.

55. For discussions of these concepts, see selected works by Gilkes 2001; Carby 1998; Higginbotham 1993.

56. This criticism of Black identity politics has been raised from many directions. For a classic representative work, see West 1993, 21–32.

57. Ideological commitment can only go so far because ideologies gain credence and fall out of favor based on their ability to explain current social phenomena. Liberalism, Marxism, multiculturalism, Black nationalism, feminism, queer theory, and other political ideologies all claim the rightness of their cause and aim to organize groups around their core principles. Yet these ideologies often work at cross purposes and can divide African American populations more than they unite them. Ideological groups always exclude those who somehow violate the party line, no matter how right it can appear to be to its supporters. The HIV/AIDS crisis reveals the limitations of current Black political agendas (typically the false choice of racial integration versus Black separatism) that fail to make issues of gender and sexuality central to their platforms.

58. Racism in the United States provides a pristine example of the shifting nature of racial coalitions. Differences of class, age, gender, sexuality, and race do not disappear simply because a social movement has managed to transcend them for one moment in time. For example, the absence of protest by White women during the challenges to affirmative action in the early 2000s suggests that White women abandoned this coalition when they perceived it as no longer serving their interests. Increasingly cast as a program for racial/ethnic minorities who needed "help," affirmative action came under attack. Similarly, the racial coalitions that culminated in the 1963 March on Washington seem a distant past in the context of segregated suburbs. Whites have left the coalition and voted with their feet.

59. Douglas 1999, 115.

60. Payne 1989, 893.

61. Kitwana 2002, xx.

62. Bandele 1999, 138.

AFTERWORD

1. Baldwin 1993, 117.

2. Gaines 1994, 191.

3. Bambara 1970, 109.

4. Shakur 1993, 330.

GLOSSARY

binary thinking: a system of thought that divides concepts into two oppositional categories, for example, white/black, man/woman, heterosexual/homosexual, saint/sinner, reason/emotion, and normal/deviant.

Black community: a set of institutions, communication networks, and practices that help African Americans respond to social, economic, and political challenges confronting them. Also known as Black civil society.

Black sexuality: a set of ideas invented about the sexual practices of people of African descent that have been used to justify Black subordination. Ideas about Black sexuality underlie dominant societal beliefs about Black masculinity and Black femininity.

Black sexual politics: a set of ideas and social practices shaped by gender, race, and sexuality that frame Black men and women's treatment of one another as well as how African Americans are perceived and treated by others.

capitalism: an economic system based on the private ownership of the means of production. Capitalism is typically characterized by extreme distributions of wealth and large differences between the rich and the poor.

color blindness: a racial ideology that gained prominence during the post–civil rights era that argues that using racial language perpetuates racism.

commodification: in capitalist political economies, land, products, services, and ideas are assigned economic values and are bought and sold in marketplaces as commodities.

controlling images: the gender-specific depiction of people of African descent within Western scholarship and popular culture. The terms *representations* and *stereotypes* also describe this phenomenon. Representations need not be stereotypical and stereotypes need not function as controlling images. Of the three, controlling images are most closely tied to power relations of race, class, gender, and sexuality.

critical social theory: bodies of knowledge and sets of institutional practices that actively grapple with the central questions facing groups of people differently placed in specific political, social, and historical contexts characterized by injustice. What makes critical social theory "critical" is its commitment to justice, for one's own group and/or for that of other groups.

disciplinary practices: a way of ruling that relies on bureaucratic hierarchies and techniques of surveillance. Institutionalized rape and lynching are disciplinary practices that have been used to uphold oppression.

discourse: a set of ideas and practices that, when taken together, organize both the way a society defines certain truths about itself and the way it puts together social power.

globalization: the increasing concentration of capital in the hands of a relatively small number of transnational corporations. Two effects of globalization are greater influence on the world economy than that of nation-states, and a global distribution of wealth and poverty that privileges Western European, North American, and other advanced industrial nations.

hegemony: a form of social organization that uses ideology to create taken-for-granted ideas that are used to justify oppression. Hegemonic conditions absorb and depoliticize oppressed groups' dissent and encourage individuals and groups to police one another and suppress each other's dissent.

heterosexism: an ideology and system of power that defines what constitutes normal and deviant sexuality and distributes social rewards and penalties based on this definition. Heterosexism and its accompanying assumptions of heterosexuality operate as a hegemonic or taken-for-granted ideology. For example, the term *sexuality* itself is used so synonymously with *hetero-sexuality* that schools, churches, and other social institutions treat hetero-sexuality as natural, normal, and inevitable.

homophobia: holding or expressing negative beliefs and actions toward gay, lesbian, bisexual, and/or transgendered people.

hyper-heterosexuality: a thesis developed within Western societies that views people of African descent as being sexually promiscuous and engaging in sexual practices that resemble those of animals.

identity politics: a way of knowing that sees lived experiences as important to creating knowledge and crafting group-based political strategies.

ideology: a body of ideas reflecting the interests of a particular social group. Racism, sexism, and heterosexism all have ideologies that support social inequality. Ideologies are never static and always have internal contradictions.

intersectionality: analysis claiming that systems of race, economic class, gender, sexuality, ethnicity, nation, and age form mutually constructing features of social organization, which shape African American experiences and, in turn, are shaped by African Americans.

oppression: an unjust situation in which, systematically and over a long period of time, one group denies another group access to the resources of society. Race, gender, class, sexuality, nation, age, and ethnicity constitute major forms of oppression.

paradigm: an interpretive framework used to explain social phenomena.

political economy: the way of organizing power relations and the economic system of a society. Capitalism has a distinctive political economy characterized by large differences in wealth between social classes and major differences in power where wealthy people have more power than poor people.

racial solidarity: the belief that members of a racial group have common interests and should support one another above the interests of members of other racial groups.

racism: a system of unequal power and privilege in which humans are divided into groups or "races" with social rewards unevenly distributed to groups based on their racial classification. In the United States, racial segregation constitutes a fundamental principle of how racism is organized.

scientific racism: a specific body of knowledge about Blacks, Asians, Native Americans, Whites, and Latinos produced within biology, anthropology, psychology, sociology, and other academic disciplines of Western science. Scientific racism was designed to prove the inferiority of people of color.

segregation: a constellation of policies that separate groups based on the belief that proximity to the group deemed to be inferior will harm the allegedly superior group. Though currently forbidden by law in the United States, racially segregated neighborhoods, schools, occupational categories, and access to public facilities persist.

social class: in its most general sense, social groups differentiated from one another by economic status, cultural forms, practices, or ways of life. Social class refers to a group of people who share a common placement in a political economy.

social justice project: an organized, long-term effort to eliminate oppression and empower individuals and groups within a just society.

transnationalism: a view of the world that sees certain interests as going beyond the borders of individual countries. Whereas internationalism emphasizes the relationship between nation-states, transnationalism emphasizes processes that transcend nations, for example, migration, capital flight, and the creation of new Diasporic populations.

BIBLIOGRAPHY

"The Funny Pages: List of Penises." Web page [accessed July 2, 2003]. Available at http:funnies.paco.to/PenisList.html.

Tongues Untied. 1989. Marlon T. Riggs. 1 videocassette (55 min.): San Francisco, CA: Frameline.

"Skeleton in Newark's Closet: Laquetta Nelson Is Forcing Homophobia Out into the Open." Web page [accessed July 30, 2003]. Available at http://www.theg-ully.com/essays/gaymundo/030619_race_gays_newark.html.

Abrahams, Yvette. 1998. "Images of Sara Bartman: Sexuality, Race, and Gender in Early-Nineteenth-Century Britain." *Nation, Empire, Colony: Historicizing Gender and Race*. Ed. Ruth Roach Pierson and Nupur Chadhuri, 220–236. Bloomington: Indiana University Press.

Aldaraca, Bridget A. 1995. "On the Use of Medical Diagnosis as Name-Calling: Anita F. Hill and the Rediscovery of 'Erotomania.'" *Black Women in America*. Ed. Kim Marie Vaz, 206–221. Thousand Oaks, Calif.: Sage.

Alexander, M. Jacqui. 1997. "Erotic Autonomy as a Politics of Decolonization: An Anatomy of Feminist and State Practice in the Bahamas Tourist Industry." *Feminist Genealogies, Colonial Legacies, Democratic Futures*. Ed. M. Jacqui Alexander and Chandra Talpade Mohanty, 63–100. New York: Routledge.

Altman, Lawrence K. 2002a. "Many Gay Men in U.S. Unaware They Have HIV, Study Finds." Web page [accessed July 13, 2002]. Available at http://www.nytimes.com/2002/07/08/health/08AIDS.html.

———. 2002b. "AIDS Leaving Grim Legacy of Orphans, Report Says." Web page [accessed July 10, 2002]. Available at http://www.nytimes.com/2002/07/1.../10.

Andersen, Margaret L. 1991. "Feminism and the American Family Ideal." *Journal of Comparative Family Studies* 22, no. 2: 235–246.

Anderson, Benedict. 1983. *Imagined Communities: Reflections on the Origin and Spread of Nationalism*. London: Verso.

Anderson, Elijah. 1978. *A Place on the Corner*. Chicago: University of Chicago Press.

———. 1990. *Streetwise: Race, Class, and Change in an Urban Community*. Chicago: University of Chicago Press.

———. 1999. *Code of the Street: Decency, Violence and the Moral Life of the Inner City*. New York: W. W. Norton.

Appiah, Kwame Anthony. 1992. *In My Father's House: Africa in the Philosophy of Culture*. New York: Oxford University Press.

Arnett Ferguson, Ann. 2000. *Bad Boys: Public Schools in the Making of Black Masculinity*. Ann Arbor: University of Michigan Press.

Asante, Kariamu Welsh. 1993. "Josephine Baker." *Black Women in America: An Historical Encyclopedia*. Ed. Darlene Clark Hine, 75–78. Vol. 1. New York: Carlson Publishing.

————. 1994. "Images of Women in African Dance: Sexuality and Sensuality as Dual Unity." *Sage* 8, no. 2 (fall): 16–19.

Austin, Dorisjean. 1993. "The Act Behind the Word." *Wild Women Don't Wear No Blues: Black Women Writers on Love, Men and Sex*. Ed. Marita Golden, 147–60. New York: Anchor.

Awkward, Michael. 1999. "'You're Turning Me On': The Boxer, the Beauty Queen, and the Rituals of Gender." *Black Men on Race, Gender, and Sexuality*. Ed. Devon W. Carbado, 128–46. New York: New York University Press.

Baker, Houston A. 1993. *Black Studies, Rap, and the Academy*. Chicago: University of Chicago Press.

Baldwin, James. 1963. *The Fire Next Time*. New York: Vintage.

————. 1993. *Nobody Knows My Name*. New York: Vintage.

Bales, Kevin. 1999. *Disposable Slavery: New Slavery in the Global Economy*. Berkeley: University of California Press.

Bambara, Toni Cade. 1970. "On the Issue of Roles." *The Black Woman: An Anthology*. Ed. Toni Cade Bambara, 101–110. New York: Signet.

Bandele, Asha. 1999. *The Prisoner's Wife: A Memoir*. New York: Scribner.

Banks, Ingrid. 2000. *Hair Matters: Beauty, Power, and Black Women's Consciousness*. New York: New York University Press.

Battle, Juan, Cathy J. Cohen, Dorian Warren, Gerard Fergerson, and Suzette Audam. 2002. *Say It Loud, I'm Black and I'm Proud: Black Pride Survey 2000*. New York: The Policy Institute of the National Gay and Lesbian Task Force.

Bauman, Zygmunt. 1998. *Globalization: The Human Consequences*. New York: Columbia University Press.

Beck, E. M., and Stewart E. Tolnay. 1992. "A Season for Violence: The Lynching of Blacks and Labor Demand in the Agricultural Production Cycle in the American South." *International Review of Social History* 37: 1–24.

Bederman, Gail. 1995. *Manliness and Civilization: A Cultural History of Gender and Race in the United States, 1890–1917*. Chicago: University of Chicago Press.

Bell, Derrick. 1999. "The Sexual Diversion: The Black Man/Black Woman Debate in Context." *Black Men on Race, Gender, and Sexuality: A Critical Reader*. Ed. Devon W. Carbado, 237–247. New York: New York University Press.

Bennett, Michael, and Vanessa D. Dickerson, eds. 2001. *Recovering the Black Female Body: Self-Representations by African American Women*. New Brunswick, N.J.: Rutgers University Press.

Berry, Mary Frances. 1994. *Black Resistance, White Law: A History of Constitutional Racism in America*. New York: Penguin Press.

Bobo, Jacqueline. 1995. *Black Women as Cultural Readers*. New York: Columbia University Press.

Bogle, Donald. 1989. *Toms, Coons, Mulattoes, Mammies, & Bucks: An Interpretive History of Blacks in American Films*. New York: Continuum.

Bonilla-Silva, Eduardo. 1996. "Rethinking Racism: Toward a Structural Interpretation." *American Sociological Review* 62 (June): 465–480.

————. 2001. *White Supremacy and Racism in the Post–Civil Rights Era*. Boulder, Colo.: Lynne Rienner Publishers.

Bordo, Susan. 1993. *Unbearable Weight*. Berkeley: University of California Press.

Boyd, Todd. 2000. "Mo' Money, Mo' Problems: Keepin' It Real in the Post-Jordan Era." *Basketball Jones: America Above the Rim*. Ed. Todd Boyd and Kenneth L. Shropshire, 59–67. New York: New York University Press.

Boyd, Todd, and Kenneth L. Shropshire. 2000. "Basketball Jones: A New World Order?" *Basketball Jones: America Above the Rim*. Ed. Todd Boyd and Kenneth L. Shropshire, 1–11. New York: New York University Press.

Boykin, Keith. 1996. *One More River to Cross: Black and Gay in America*. New York: Anchor Books.

Brandt, Eric, ed. 1999. *Dangerous Liaisons: Blacks, Gays, and the Struggle for Equality*. New York: The New Press.

Brewer, Rose. 1994. "Race, Class, Gender and U.S. State Welfare Policy: The Nexus of Inequality for African American Families." *Color, Class and Country: Experiences of Gender*. Ed. Gay Young and Bette J. Dickerson, 115–127. London: Zed.

Byrd, Rudolph P., and Beverly Guy-Sheftall, eds. 2001. *Traps: African American Men on Gender and Sexuality*. Bloomington: Indiana University Press.

Calmore, John O. 2001. "Race-Conscious Voting Rights and the New Demography in a Multiracing America." *North Carolina Law Review* 79, no. 5: 1254–81.

Canada, Geoffrey. 1995. *Fist, Stick, Knife, Gun: A Personal History of Violence in America*. Boston: Beacon Press.

Caponi, Gena Dagel, ed. 1999. *Signifyin(g), Sanctifyin', & Slam Dunking: A Reader in African American Expressive Culture*. Amherst: University of Massachusetts Press.

Carbado, Devon W. 1999a. "The Construction of O.J. Simpson as a Racial Victim." *Black Men on Race, Gender, and Sexuality*. Ed Devon W. Carbado, 159–193. New York: New York University Press.

———. 1999b. "Epilogue Straight Out of the Closet: Men, Feminism, and Male Heterosexual Privilege." *Black Men on Race, Gender, and Sexuality*. Ed Devon W. Carbado, 417–447. New York: New York University Press.

———. 1999c. "Introduction: Where and When Black Men Enter." *Black Men on Race, Gender, and Sexuality*. Ed Devon W. Carbado, 1–17. New York: New York University Press.

Carby, Hazel V. 1992. "Policing the Black Woman's Body in an Urban Context." *Critical Inquiry* 18: 738–755.

———. 1998. *Race Men*. Cambridge, Mass.: Harvard University Press.

Cashmore, Ellis. 1997. *The Black Culture Industry*. New York: Routledge.

Chambers, Veronica. 1996. *Mama's Girl*. New York: Riverhead Books.

Clarke, Cheryl. 1983. "The Failure to Transform: Homophobia in the Black Community." *Home Girls: A Black Feminist Anthology*. Ed. Barbara Smith, 197–208. New York: Kitchen Table Press.

———. 1995. "Lesbianism: An Act of Resistance." *Words of Fire: An Anthology of African-American Feminist Thought*. Ed. Beverly Guy-Sheftall, 241–251. New York: The New Press.

Cleage, Pearl. 1993. *Deals with the Devil: And Other Reasons to Riot*. New York: Ballantine.

Cohen, Cathy J. 1999. *The Boundaries of Blackness: AIDS and the Breakdown of Black Politics*. Chicago: University of Chicago Press.

Cohen, Cathy J., and Tamara Jones. 1999. "Fighting Homophobia versus Challenging Heterosexism: 'The Failure to Transform' Revisited." *Dangerous Liaisons: Blacks, Gays, and the Struggle for Equality*. Ed. Eric Brandt, 80–101. New York: The New Press.

Cole, Johnnetta Betsch, and Beverly Guy-Sheftall. 2003. *Gender Talk: The Struggle for Women's Equality in African American Communities*. New York: Ballantine.

Collins, Patricia Hill. 1989. "A Comparison of Two Works on Black Family Life." *Signs* 14, no. 4: 875–84.

———. 1998. *Fighting Words: Black Women and the Search for Justice*. Minneapolis: University of Minnesota Press.

———. 1999. "Producing the Mothers of the Nation: Race, Class and Contemporary U.S. Population Policies." *Women, Citizenship and Difference*. Ed. Nira Yuval-Davis, 118–129. London: Zed Books.

———. 2000a. *Black Feminist Thought: Knowledge, Consciousness, and the Politics of Empowerment*. New York: Routledge.

————. 2000b. "Gender, Black Feminism, and Black Political Economy." *Annals of the American Academy of Political & Social Science* 568 (March): 41–53.

————. 2002. "Introduction to *On Lynchings*." *On Lynchings*. Ed. Ida B. Wells-Barnett, 9–24. Amherst, N.Y.: Humanity Books.

Combahee River Collective. 1982. "A Black Feminist Statement." *But Some of Us Are Brave*. Ed. Gloria T. Hull, Patricia Bell Scott, and Barbara Smith, 13–22. Old Westbury, N.Y.: Feminist Press.

Comstock, Gary David. 1999. "'Whosoever' Is Welcome Here: An Interview with Reverend Edwin C. Sanders II." *Dangerous Liaisons: Blacks, Gays, and the Struggle for Equality*. Ed. Eric Brandt, 142–157. New York: The New Press.

Connell, R. W. 1992. "A Very Straight Gay: Masculinity, Homosexual Experience, and the Dynamics of Gender." *American Sociological Review* 57 (December): 735–751.

————. 1995. *Masculinities*. Cambridge: Polity Press.

Cose, Ellis. 2003. "The Black Gender Gap." *Newsweek* March 3: 46–51.

Crenshaw, Kimberlé Williams. 1992. "Whose Story Is It Anyway? Feminist and Antiracist Appropriations of Anita Hill." *Race-ing Justice, En-Gendering Power*. Ed. Toni Morrison, 402–440. New York: Pantheon Books.

————. 1997. "Color Blindness, History, and the Law." *The House That Race Built*. Ed. Wahneema Lubiano, 280–288. New York: Pantheon.

Cunningham, George P. 1996. "Body Politics: Race, Gender, and the Captive Body." *Representing Black Men*. Ed. Marcellus Blount and George P. Cunningham, 131–154. New York: Routledge.

Dalton, Harlon L. 1999a. "AIDS in Blackface." *Black Men on Race, Gender, and Sexuality*. Ed. Devon W. Carbado, 324–337. New York: New York University Press.

————. 1999b. "Pull Together As Community." *Black Men on Race, Gender, and Sexuality: A Critical Reader*. Ed Devon W. Carbado, 120–127. New York: New York University Press.

Dash, Leon. 1996. *Rosa Lee: A Mother and Her Family in Urban America*. New York: Basic Books.

Davis, Angela Y. 1978. "Rape, Racism and the Capitalist Setting." *Black Scholar* 9, no. 7: 24–30.

————. 1981. *Women, Race, and Class*. New York: Random House.

————. 1994. "Afro Images: Politics, Fashion, and Nostalgia." *Critical Inquiry* 21, no. 2: 37–45.

————. 1997. "Race and Criminalization: Black Americans and the Punishment Industry." *The House That Race Built*. Ed. Wahneema Lubiano, 264–279. New York: Pantheon.

————. 1998. *Blues Legacies and Black Feminism: Gertrude "Ma" Rainey, Bessie Smith and Billie Holiday*. New York: Vintage.

Dawson, Michael C. 1994. *Behind the Mule: Race and Class in African-American Politics*. Princeton, N.J.: Princeton University Press.

D'Emilio, John, and Estelle B. Freedman. 1997. *Intimate Matters: A History of Sexuality in America*. Chicago: University of Chicago Press.

Denizet-Lewis, Benoit. 2003. "Double Lives on the Down Low." *New York Times Magazine*, August 3, 28–33+.

Dent, Gina. 1992a. "Black Pleasure, Black Joy: An Introduction." *Black Popular Culture*. Ed. Gina Dent, 1–19. Seattle: Bay Press.

————, ed. 1992b. *Black Popular Culture*. Seattle: Bay Press.

Dickerson, Debra J. 2000. *An American Story*. New York: Anchor.

di Mauro, Diane. 1995. *Sexuality Research in the United States: An Assessment of the Social and Behavioral Sciences*. New York: Social Science Research Council, Sexuality Research Assessment Project.

Dines, Gail. 1998. "King Kong and the White Woman: *Hustler* Magazine and the Demonization of Black Masculinity." *Violence against Women* 4, no. 3 (June): 291–307.

Douglas, Kelly Brown. 1999. *Sexuality and the Black Church: A Womanist Perspective*. Maryknoll, N.Y.: Orbis.

Dwyer, Jim. 2002. "Reinvestigation of Park Jogger Case Leaves Some Officials with Doubts" *New York Times*, A15. September 28.

Dyson, Michael Eric. 1993. *Reflecting Black: African-American Cultural Criticism*. Minneapolis: University of Minnesota Press.

———. 1996. *Between God and Gangsta Rap: Bearing Witness to Black Culture*. New York: Oxford University Press.

———. 2001. *Holler If You Hear Me: Searching for Tupac Shakur*. New York: Basic Books.

Eli, Quinn. 1995. "A Liar in Love." *Speak My Name: Black Men on Masculinity and the American Dream*. Ed. Don Belton, 137–143. Boston: Beacon Press.

Emerson, Rana A. 2002. "'Where My Girls At?' Negotiating Black Womanhood in Music Videos." *Gender & Society* 16, no. 1: 115–135.

Entman, Robert M., and Rojecki Andrew. 2000. *The Black Image in the White Mind: Media and Race in America*. Chicago: University of Chicago Press.

Essed, Philomena. 1991. *Understanding Everyday Racism: An Interdisciplinary Theory*. Newbury Park, Calif.: Sage.

Fair, Jo Ellen, and Roberta J. Astroff. 1991. "Constructing Race and Violence: U.S. News Coverage and the Signifying Practices of Apartheid." *Journal of Communication* 41, no. 4: 58–74.

Fausto-Sterling, Anne. 1992. *Myths of Gender: Biological Theories about Women and Men*. New York: Basic Books.

———. 1995. "Gender, Race, and Nation: The Comparative Anatomy of 'Hottentot' Women in Europe, 1815–1817." *Deviant Bodies: Critical Perspectives on Difference in Science and Popular Culture*. Ed. Jennifer Terry and Jacqueline Urla, 19–48. Bloomington: Indiana University Press.

Ferber, Abby L. 1998. *White Man Falling: Race, Gender, and White Supremacy*. Lanham, Md.: Rowman & Littlefield.

Fordham, Signithia. 1996. *Blacked Out: Dilemmas of Race, Identity, and Success at Capital High*. Chicago: University of Chicago Press.

Foucault, Michel. 1979. *Discipline and Punish: The Birth of the Prison*. New York: Schocken.

———. 1980. *The History of Sexuality Vol. I: An Introduction*. New York: Vintage Books.

Franklin, Donna L. 1997. *Ensuring Inequality: The Structural Transformation of the African-American Family*. New York: Oxford University Press.

Franklin, Vincent P. 1992. *Black Self-Determination: A Cultural History of African-American Resistance*. Brooklyn, N.Y.: Lawrence Hill Books.

———. 1995. *Living Our Stories, Telling Our Truths: Autobiography and the Making of the African-American Intellectual Tradition*. New York: Scribner.

Frazier, E. Franklin. 1948. *The Negro Family in the United States*. New York: Dryden.

Freydberg, Elizabeth Hadley. 1995. "Sapphires, Spitfires, Sluts, and Superbitches: Aframericans and Latinas in Contemporary American Film." *Black Women in America*. Ed. Kim Vaz, 222–243. Thousand Oaks, Calif.: Sage.

Gates, Henry Louis. 1992. *Loose Canons: Notes on the Culture Wars*. New York: Oxford University Press.

George, Nelson. 1998. *Hip Hop America*. New York: Penguin.

Giddings, Paula. 1984. *When and Where I Enter: The Impact of Black Women on Race and Sex in America*. New York: William Morrow.

———. 1992. "The Last Taboo." *Race-ing Justice, En-Gendering Power*. Ed. Toni Morrison, 441–465. New York: Pantheon.

————. 2001. "Missing in Action: Ida B. Wells, the NAACP, and the Historical Record." *Meridians: Feminism, Race, Transnationalism* 1, no. 2: 1–17.

Gilkes, Cheryl Townsend. 2001. *If It Wasn't for the Women: Black Women's Experience and Womanist Culture in Church and Community*. Maryknoll, N.Y.: Orbis.

Gilman, Sander L. 1985. *Difference and Pathology: Stereotypes of Sexuality, Race, and Madness*. Ithaca, N.Y.: Cornell University Press.

Gilroy, Paul. 2000. *Against Race: Imagining Political Culture Beyond the Color Line*. Cambridge, Mass: Belknap Press of Harvard University Press.

Gitlin, Todd. 2001. *Media Unlimited: How the Torrent of Images and Sounds Overwhelms Our Lives*. New York: Henry Holt.

Goffman, Erving. 1963. *Stigma: Notes on the Management of Spoiled Identity*. Englewood Cliffs, N.J.: Prentice Hall.

Goldberg, David Theo. 1993. *Racist Culture: Philosophy and the Politics of Meaning* Cambridge, Mass.: Blackwell.

Golden, Marita. 1995. *Saving Our Sons: Raising Black Children in a Turbulent World*. New York: Doubleday.

Gomez, Jewell, and Barbara Smith. 1994. "Taking the Home Out of Homophobia: Black Lesbian Health." *The Black Women's Health Book: Speaking for Ourselves*. Ed. Evelyn C. White, 198–213. Seattle: Seal Press.

Gomez, Jewelle. 1999. "Black Lesbians: Passing, Stereotypes and Transformation." *Dangerous Liaisons: Blacks, Gays, and the Struggle for Equality*. Ed. Eric Brandt, 161–177. New York: The New Press.

Gould, Stephen Jay. 1981. *The Mismeasure of Man*. New York: Norton.

Graham, Lawrence Otis. 2000. *Our Kind of People: Inside America's Black Upper Class*. New York: HarperPerennial.

Greene, Beverly. 2000. "African American Lesbian and Bisexual Women." *Journal of Social Issues* 56, no. 2: 239–249.

Gregory, Steven. 1994. "Race, Identity and Political Activism: The Shifting Contours of the African American Public Sphere." *Public Culture* 7, no. 1: 147–164.

Grindstaff, Laura. 2002. *The Money Shot: Trash, Class, and the Making of TV Talk Shows*. Chicago: University of Chicago Press.

Guerrero, Ed. 1993. "The Black Image in Protective Custody: Hollywood's Biracial Buddy Films of the Eighties." *Black American Cinema*. Ed. Manthia Diawara, 237–246. New York: Routledge.

Guillory, Monique, and Richard C. Green, eds. 1998. *Soul: Black Power, Politics, and Pleasure*. New York: New York University Press.

Guinier, Lani, and Gerald Torres. 2002. *The Miner's Canary: Enlisting Race, Resisting Power, Transforming Democracy*. Cambridge, Mass.: Harvard University Press.

Gutman, Herbert. 1976. *The Black Family in Slavery and Freedom, 1750–1925*. New York: Random House.

Guy-Sheftall, Beverly, ed. 1995. *Words of Fire: An Anthology of African-American Feminist Thought*. New York: New Press.

Hall, Jacqueline Dowd. 1983. "The Mind That Burns in Each Body: Women, Rape, and Racial Violence." *Powers of Desire: The Politics of Sexuality*. Ed. Ann Snitow, Christine Stansell, and Sharon Thompson, 329–349. New York: Monthly Review Press.

Hall, Stuart. 1992. "What Is This 'Black' in Black Popular Culture?" *Black Popular Culture*. Ed. Gina Dent, 21–33. Seattle: Bay Press.

Hammonds, Evelynn M. 1997. "Toward a Genealogy of Black Female Sexuality: The Problematic of Silence." *Feminist Genealogies, Colonial Legacies, Democratic Futures*. Ed. M. Jacqui Alexander and Chandra Talpade Mohanty, 170–181. New York: Routledge.

Haraway, Donna. 1989. *Primate Visions: Gender, Race, and Nature in the World of Modern Science.* New York: Routledge, Chapman & Hall.

Harding, Sandra, ed. 1993. *The "Racial" Economy of Science: Toward a Democratic Future.* Bloomington: Indiana University Press.

Harris, Trudier. 1984. *Exorcising Blackness: Historical and Literary Lynching and Burning Rituals.* Bloomington: Indiana University Press.

Harrison, C. Keith. 2001. "From Paul Robeson to Althea Gibson to Michael Jordan: Images of Race Relations and Sport." *Michael Jordan, Inc. Corporate Sport, Media Culture, and Late Modern America.* Ed. David L. Andrews, vii–xii. Albany: State University of New York Press.

Hawkeswood, William G. 1996. *One of the Children: Gay Black Men in Harlem.* Berkeley: University of California Press.

Hemphill, Essex, ed. 1991. *Brother to Brother: New Writings by Black Gay Men.* Boston: Alyson Publications.

Higginbotham, Evelyn Brooks. 1992. "African-American Women's History and the Metalanguage of Race." *Signs* 17 (winter): 251–274.

———. 1993. *Righteous Discontent: The Women's Movement in the Black Baptist Church 1880–1920.* Cambridge, Mass.: Harvard University Press.

Hill, Anita. 1997. *Speaking Truth to Power.* New York: Doubleday.

Hoch, Paul. 1979. *White Hero, Black Beast: Racism, Sexism, and the Mask of Masculinity.* London: Pluto Press.

Human Rights Watch. 2001. *No Escape: Male Rape in U.S. Prisons.* New York: Human Rights Watch.

Hutchinson, Darren Lenard. 1999. "'Claiming' and 'Speaking' Who We Are: Black Gays and Lesbians, Racial Politics, and the Million Man March." *Black Men on Race, Gender, and Sexuality.* Ed. Devon W. Carbado, 28–45. New York: New York University Press.

Hutchinson, Earl Ofari. 2001. "Hardest Hit by the Prison Craze." Web page [accessed March 24, 2002]. Available at http://www.salon.com/news/feature/2001/01/12/black_women/print/html.

Iceland, John, Daniel H. Weinberg, and Erika Steinmetz. 2002. *Racial and Ethnic Residential Segregation in the United States: 1980–2000,* U.S. Census Bureau, Series CENSR-3. Washington, D.C.: U.S. Government Printing Office.

James, Joy. 1996. "The Profeminist Politics of W. E. B. DuBois with Respects to Anna Julia Cooper and Ida B. Wells Barnett." *W. E. B. DuBois on Race and Culture.* Ed. Bernard W. Bell, Emily R. Grosholz, and James B. Stewart, 141–160. New York: Routledge.

Jewell, K. Sue. 1993. *From Mammy to Miss America and Beyond: Cultural Images and the Shaping of U.S. Social Policy.* New York: Routledge.

Jhally, Sut, and Justin Lewis. 1992. *Enlightened Racism.* Boulder, Colo.: Westview Press.

Johnson, Cary Alan. 2000. "Hearing Voices: Unearthing Evidence of Homosexuality in Precolonial Africa." *The Greatest Taboo: Homosexuality in Black Communities.* Ed. Delroy Constantine-Simms, 132–148. New York: Alyson Books.

Jones, Jacqueline. 1985. *Labor of Love, Labor of Sorrow: Black Women, Work, and the Family from Slavery to the Present.* New York: Basic Books.

Jones, Jacquie. 1993. "The Construction of Black Sexuality: Towards Normalizing the Black Cinematic Experience." *Black American Cinema.* Ed. Manthia Diawara, 247–256. New York: Routledge.

Jones, Lisa. 1994. *Bulletproof Diva: Tales of Race, Sex, and Hair.* New York: Doubleday.

Jordan, June. 1992. *Technical Difficulties: African-American Notes on the State of the Union.* New York: Pantheon Books.

Jordan, Winthrop D. 1968. *White Over Black: American Attitudes toward the Negro, 1550–1812.* New York: W. W. Norton.

Julien, Isaac. 1992. "Black Is, Black Ain't: Notes on De-essentializing Black Identities." *Black Popular Culture*. Ed. Gina Dent, 255–275. Seattle: Bay Press.

Kaiser Family Foundation. 2000. "The State of the HIV/AIDS Epidemic in America." *Kaiser Family Foundation*, April.

Kaplan, Elaine Bell. 1997. *Not Our Kind of Girl: Unraveling the Myths of Black Teenage Motherhood*. Berkeley: University of California Press.

Kapsalis, Terri. 1997. *Public Privates: Performing Gynecology from Both Ends of the Speculum*. Durham, N.C.: Duke University Press.

Kelley, Robin D. G. 1994. *Race Rebels: Culture, Politics, and the Black Working Class*. New York: Free Press.

———. 1997. *Yo' Mama's DisFUNKtional!: Fighting the Culture Wars in Urban America*. Boston: Beacon Press.

Kellner, Douglas. 2001. "The Sports Spectacle, Michael Jordan, and Nike: Unholy Alliance?" *Michael Jordan, Inc. Corporate Sport, Media Culture, and Late Modern America*. Ed. David L. Andrews, 37–63. Albany: State University of New York Press.

Kennedy, Elizabeth Lapovsky, and Madeline D. Davis. 1994. *Boots of Leather, Slippers of Gold: The History of a Lesbian Community*. New York: Penguin Books.

Kennedy, Randall. 2002. *Nigger: The Strange Career of a Troublesome Word*. New York: Pantheon.

Kimmel, Michael S. 2001. "Masculinity as Homophobia: Fear, Shame, and Silence in the Construction of Gender Identity." *Men and Masculinity: A Text Reader*. Ed. Theodore F. Cohen, 29–41. Belmont, Calif.: Wadsworth Press.

Kitwana, Bakari. 2002. *The Hip Hop Generation: Young Blacks and the Crisis in African-American Culture*. New York: Basic Books.

Latifah, Queen. 1999. *Ladies First: Revelations of a Strong Woman*. New York: Quill.

Lemons, Gary L. 1997. "To Be Black, Male, and 'Feminist' —Making Womanist Space for Black Men." *International Journal of Sociology and Social Policy* 1, no. 2: 35–61.

Lincoln, C. Eric. 1999. *Race, Religion, and the Continuing American Dilemma*. New York: Hill & Wang.

Lorde, Audre. 1982. *Zami, A New Spelling of My Name*. Freedom, Calif.: Crossing Press.

———. 1984. *Sister Outsider: Essays and Speeches*. Freedom, Calif.: Crossing Press.

Lubiano, Wahneema. 1992. "Black Ladies, Welfare Queens, and State Minstrels: Ideological War by Narrative Means." *Race-ing Justice, En-Gendering Power*. Ed. Toni Morrison, 323–63. New York: Pantheon Books.

Lusane, Clarence. 1997. *Race in the Global Era: African Americans at the Millennium*. Boston: South End Press.

Magubane, Zine. 2001. "Which Bodies Matter? Feminism, Poststructuralism, Race, and the Curious Theoretical Odyssey of the 'Hottentot Venus.'" *Gender and Society* 15, no. 6: 816–834.

Mandela, Nelson. 1994. *Long Walk to Freedom: The Autobiography of Nelson Mandela*. Boston: Little, Brown.

Marks, Carole. 1989. *Farewell, We're Good and Gone: The Great Black Migration*. Bloomington: Indiana University Press.

Marriott, Robert. 2000. "'Blowin' Up." *Vibe*: 126–132.

Maseko, Zola. 1998. *The Life and Times of Sara Baartman: "The Hottentot Venus."* New York: First Run/Icarus Films.

Massey, Douglas S., and Nancy A. Denton. 1993. *American Apartheid: Segregation and the Making of the Underclass*. Cambridge, Mass.: Harvard University Press.

McCall, Nathan. 1994. *Makes Me Wanna Holler: A Young Black Man in America*. New York: Random House.

———. 1997. *What's Going On: Personal Essays*. New York: Random House.

McClary, Susan, and Robert Walser. 1994. "Theorizing the Body in African-American Music." *Black Music Research Journal* 14: 75–84.

McClintock, Anne. 1995. *Imperial Leather: Race, Gender, and Sexuality in the Colonial Contest.* New York: Routledge.

McCready, Lance. 2001. "When Fitting In Isn't an Option, or, Why Black Queer Males at a California High School Stay Away from Project 10." *Troubling Intersections of Race and Sexuality: Queer Students of Color and Anti-oppressive Education.* Ed. Kevin K. Kumashiro, 37–54. New York: Rowman & Littlefield.

McKinnon, Jesse. 2001. *The Black Population: 2000.* Vol. C2KBR/01–5. U.S. Census Bureau. Washington, D.C.: U.S. Government Printing Office.

McKinnon, Jesse, and Karen Humes. 2000. *The Black Population in the United States: March 1999.* Current Population Reports, Series P20–530. U.S. Census Bureau. Washington, D.C.: U.S. Government Printing Office.

McPherson, Tara. 2000. "Who's Got Next? Gender, Race, and the Mediation of the WNBA." *Basketball Jones: America Above the Rim.* Ed. Todd Boyd and Kenneth L. Shropshire, 184–197. New York: New York University Press.

Mercer, Kobena. 1994. *Welcome to the Jungle: New Positions in Black Cultural Studies.* New York: Routledge.

Messner, Michael A. 1990. "When Bodies Are Weapons: Masculinity and Violence in Sport." *International Review of the Sociology of Sport* 25: 203–217.

———. 1998. "The Limits of 'The Male Sex Role': An Analysis of the Men's Liberation and Men's Rights Movements' Discourse." *Gender & Society* 12, no. 3: 255–276.

Miller, Jerome G. 1996. *Search and Destroy: African-American Males in the Criminal Justice System.* New York: Cambridge University Press.

Miller, Teresa A. 2000. "Sex and Surveillance: Gender, Privacy and the Sexualization of Power in Prison." *George Mason University Civil Rights Law Journal* 10, no. 2: 291–356.

Mohanram, Radhika. 1999. *Black Body: Women, Colonialism, and Space.* Minneapolis: University of Minnesota Press.

Mohanty, Chandra Talpade. 1997. "Women Workers and Capitalist Scripts: Ideologies of Domination, Common Interests, and the Politics of Solidarity." *Feminist Genealogies, Colonial Legacies, Democratic Futures.* Ed. M. Jacqui Mohanty Chandra and Talpade Alexander, 3–29. New York: Routledge.

Monroe, Irene. 1998. "Louis Farrakhan's Ministry of Misogyny and Homophobia." *The Farrakhan Factor: African-American Writers on Leadership, Nationhood, and the Minister Louis Farrakhan.* Ed Amy Alexander, 275–298. New York: Grove Press.

Moore, Lisa C., ed. 1997. *Does Your Mama Know? An Anthology of Black Lesbian Coming Out Stories.* Austin, Texas: Redbone Press.

Morgan, Joan. 1999. *When Chickenheads Come Home to Roost: My Life as a Hip-Hop Feminist.* New York: Simon & Schuster.

Morrison, Toni, ed. 1992. *Race-ing Justice, En-Gendering Power: Essays on Anita Hill, Clarence Thomas, and the Construction of Social Reality.* New York: Pantheon Books.

Morton, Patricia. 1991. *Disfigured Images: The Historical Assault on Afro-American Women.* New York: Greenwood Press.

Moynihan, Daniel Patrick. 1965. *The Negro Family: The Case for National Action.* Washington, D.C.: U.S. Government Printing Office.

Mudimbe, V. Y. 1988. *The Invention of Africa: Gnosis, Philosophy, and the Order of Knowledge.* Bloomington: Indiana University Press.

Naylor, Gloria. 1988. "Love and Sex in the Afro-American Novel." *The Yale Review* 78, no. 1: 19–31.

Neal, Mark Anthony. 2002. *Soul Babies: Black Popular Culture and the Post-Soul Aesthetic.* New York: Routledge.

Nelson, Jill. 1997. *Straight, No Chaser: How I Became a Grown-up Black Woman.* New York: G. P. Putnam's Sons.

Neubeck, Kenneth J., and Noel A. Cazenave. 2001. *Welfare Racism: Playing the Race Card against America's Poor*. New York: Routledge.

Ogbar, Jeffrey O. G. 1999. "Slouching toward Bork: The Culture Wars and Self-Criticism in Hip-Hop Music." *Journal of Black Studies* 30, no. 2: 164–183.

Oliver, Melvin L., and Thomas M. Shapiro. 1995. *Black Wealth/White Wealth: A New Perspective on Racial Inequality*. New York: Routledge.

Oliver, William. 1994. *The Violent Social World of Black Men*. New York: Lexington Books.

Omi, Michael, and Howard Winant. 1994. *Racial Formation in the United States: From the 1960s to the 1990s*. New York: Routledge.

Omolade, Barbara. 1994. *The Rising Song of African American Women*. New York: Routledge.

Orfield, Gary, and Carole Ashkinaze. 1991. *The Closing Door: Conservative Policy and Black Opportunity*. Chicago: University of Chicago Press.

Oyěwùmí, Oyèrónké. 1997. *The Invention of Women: Making an African Sense of Western Gender Discourses*. Minneapolis: University of Minnesota Press.

Painter, Nell. 1992. "Hill, Thomas, and the Use of Racial Stereotype." *Race-ing Justice, En-Gendering Power*. Ed. Toni Morrison, 200–214. New York: Pantheon Books.

Patillo-McCoy, Mary. 1998. "Church Culture as a Strategy of Action in the Black Community." *American Sociological Review* 63 (December): 767–784.

———. 1999. *Black Picket Fences: Privilege and Peril among the Black Middle Class*. Chicago: University of Chicago Press.

Patterson, Orlando. 1982. *Slavery and Social Death: A Comparative Study*. Cambridge, Mass.: Harvard University Press.

———. 1998. *Rituals of Blood: Consequences of Slavery in Two American Centuries*. Washington, D.C.: Civitas Counterpoint.

Payne, Charles. 1989. "Ella Baker and Models of Social Change." *Signs* 14, no. 1: 885–899.

Pellegrini, Ann. 1997. "Women on Top, Boys on the Side, but Some of Us Are Brave: Blackness, Lesbianism, and the Visible." *College Literature* 24, no. 1: 83–98.

Petterson, Stephen M. 1997. "Are Young Black Men Really Less Willing to Work?" *American Sociological Review* 62: 605–613.

Pierce-Baker, Charlotte. 1998. *Surviving the Silence: Black Women's Stories of Rape*. New York: W. W. Norton.

Pinar, William F. 2001. *The Gender of Racial Politics and Violence in America: Lynching, Prison Rape, and the Crisis of Masculinity*. New York: Peter Lang.

Platt, Larry. 2002. *New Jack Jocks: Rebels, Race, and the American Athlete*. Philadelphia: Temple University Press.

Powell, Kevin. 2000. "Confessions." *MS,* April/May, 73–77.

Prestney, Susie. 1997. "Inscribing the Hottentot Venus: Generating Data for Difference." *At the Edge of International Relations: Postcolonialism, Gender & Dependency*. Ed. Phillip Darby, 86–105. New York: Pinter.

Quadagno, Jill. 1994. *The Color of Welfare: How Racism Undermined the War on Poverty*. New York: Oxford University Press.

Ransby, Barbara, and Tracye Matthews. 1993. "Black Popular Culture and the Transcendence of Patriarchal Illusions." *Race and Class* 35, no. 1: 57–68.

Reed, Ishmael. 1998. "Introduction: Black Pleasure—An Oxymoron." *Soul: Black Power, Politics, and Pleasure*. Ed. Monique Guillory and Richard C. Green, 169–171. New York: New York University Press.

Reid-Pharr, Robert F. 2001. *Black Gay Man*. New York: New York University Press.

Remez, Lisa. 2000. "Oral Sex among Adolescents: Is It Sex or Abstinence?" *Family Planning Perspectives* 32, no. 6: 298–304.

Richie, Beth E. 1996. *Compelled to Crime: The Gender Entrapment of Battered Black Women*. New York: Routledge.

Riggs, Marlon T. "Current Online: Marlon Riggs on the 'Tongues' Episode." Web page [accessed September 8, 2002]. Available at http://www.current.org/prog/prog114g.html.

Riggs, Marlon T. 1992. "Unleash the Queen." *Black Popular Culture*. Ed. Gina Dent, 99–105. Seattle: Bay Press.

———. 1999. "Black Macho Revisited: Reflections of a SNAP! Queen." *Black Men on Race, Gender, and Sexuality*. Ed. Devon W. Carbado, 306–311. New York: New York University Press.

Roberts, Dorothy E. 1997. *Killing the Black Body: Race, Reproduction, and the Meaning of Liberty*. New York: Pantheon Books.

Roberts, Robin. 1995. "Sisters in the Name of Rap: Rapping for Women's Lives." *Black Women in America*. Ed. Kim Marie Vaz, 323–333. Thousand Oaks, Calif.: Sage.

Robinson, Randall. 2000. *The Debt: What America Owes to Blacks*. New York: Plume.

Rodriguez, Clara E. 2000. *Changing Race: Latinos, the Census, and the History of Ethnicity in the United States*. New York: New York University Press.

Root, Maria P. P. 2001. *Love's Revolution: Interracial Marriage*. Philadelphia: Temple University Press.

Rose, Tricia. 1994. *Black Noise: Rap Music and Black Culture in Contemporary America*. Hanover, N.H.: Wesleyan University Press.

———. 2003. *Longing to Tell: Black Women Talk about Sexuality and Intimacy*. New York: Farrar, Straus and Giroux.

Sack, Kevin. 2001. "AIDS Epidemic Takes Toll on Black Women." Web page [accessed December 2, 2001]. Available at http://www.nytimes.com/2001/07/03/health/03AIDS.

Scott, James C. 1990. *Domination and the Arts of Resistance: The Hidden Transcripts*. New Haven, Conn.: Yale University Press.

Seidman, Steven. 1996. "Introduction." *Queer Theory/Sociology*. Ed. Steven Seidman, 1–29. Malden, Mass.: Blackwell.

———. 2002. *Beyond the Closet: The Transformation of Gay and Lesbian Life*. New York: Routledge.

Shakur, Sanyika. 1993. *Monster: The Autobiography of an L.A. Gang Member*. New York: Atlantic Monthly Press.

Simmons, Ron. 1991. "Some Thoughts on the Challenge Facing Gay Intellectuals." *Brother to Brother: New Writings by Black Gay Men*. Ed. Essex Hemphill, 211–228. Boston: Alyson Publications.

Simmons, Tavia and Martin O'Connell. *Married-Couple and Unmarried-Partner Households: 2000*, CENSR-5. 2003. U.S. Census Bureau. Washington, D.C.: U.S. Government Printing Office.

Smith, Barbara, ed. 1983. *Home Girls: A Black Feminist Anthology*. New York: Kitchen Table Press.

———. 1990. "The NEA Is the Least of It." 65–67.

———. 1998. *The Truth That Never Hurts: Writings on Race, Gender, and Freedom*. New Brunswick, N.J.: Rutgers University Press.

Smith, Charles Michael, ed. 1999. *Fighting Words: Personal Essays by Black Gay Men*. New York: Avon.

Smitherman-Donaldson, Geneva. 1995. *African American Women Speak Out on Anita Hill–Clarence Thomas*. Detroit: Wayne State University Press.

Somerville, Siobhan B. 2000. *Queering the Color Line: Race and the Invention of Homosexuality in American Culture*. Durham, N.C.: Duke University Press.

Souljah, Sister. 1999. *The Coldest Winter Ever*. New York: Pocket Books.

Spillers, Hortense J. 2000. "Mama's Baby, Papa's Maybe: An American Grammar Book." *The Black Feminist Reader*. Ed. Joy James and T. Denean Sharpley-Whiting, 57–87. Malden, Mass.: Blackwell.

Squires, Gregory D. 1994. *Capital and Communities in Black and White: The Intersections of Race, Class, and Uneven Development*. Albany: State University of New York Press.

Stanford, J. L., R. A. Stephenson, L. M. Coyle, R. Correa, J. W. Eley, F. Gilliland, B. Hankey, L. N. Kilonel, C. Kosary, R. Ross, R. Severson, and D. West. 1999. *Prostate Cancer Trends 1973–1995*. NIH Pub. No. 99–4543. SEER Program, National Cancer Institute, Bethesda, Maryland.

Staples, Robert. 1979. "The Myth of Black Macho: A Response to Angry Black Feminists." *Black Scholar* 10, no. 6: 24–33.

Sterk-Elifson, Claire. 1994. "Sexuality among African-American Women." *Sexuality Across the Life Course*. Ed. Alice S. Rossi, 99–126. Chicago: University of Chicago Press.

Stoler, Ann Laura. 1995. *Race and the Education of Desire: Foucault's History of Sexuality and the Colonial Order of Things*. Durham, N.C.: Duke University Press.

Sudarkasa, Niara. 1981. "Interpreting the African Heritage in Afro-American Family Organization." *Black Families*. Ed. Harriette Pipes McAdoo, 37–53. Beverly Hills, Calif.: Sage.

Swarns, Rachel L. 2001. "South Africa's AIDS Vortex Engulfs a Rural Community." Web page [accessed December 2, 2001]. Available at http://www.nytimes.com/2001/11/25/health/25AIDS.html.

———. 4 May 2002. "Mocked in Europe of Old, African Is Embraced at Home at Last." *New York Times*, sec. A, p. 3.

Takaki, Ronald T. 1993. *A Different Mirror: A History of Multicultural America*. Boston: Little, Brown.

Tate, Greg, ed. 2003. *Everything but the Burden: What White People Are Taking from Black Culture*. New York: Broadway Books.

Tate, Greg, Portia Maultsby, Thulani Davis, Clyde Taylor, and Ishmael Reed. 1998. "Ain't We Still Got Soul?" Roundtable Discussion. *Soul: Black Power, Politics, and Pleasure*. Eds. Monique Guillory and Richard C. Green, 269–283. New York: New York University Press.

Thomas, Kendall. 1996. "'Ain't Nothin' Like the Real Thing': Black Masculinity, Gay Sexuality, and the Jargon of Authenticity." *Representing Black Men*. Ed. Marcellus Blount and George P. Cunningham, 55–69. New York: Routledge.

Thomas, Kevin. March 28, 1997. "The Watermelon Woman: Wry 'Woman' Explores Race, Sexuality." *Los Angeles Times*.

Thompson, Robert Farris. 1983. *Flash of the Spirit: African and Afro-American Art and Philosophy*. New York: Vintage.

Tonry, Michael. 1995. *Malign Neglect: Race, Crime, and Punishment in America*. New York: Oxford University Press.

Torgovnick, Marianna. 1990. *Gone Primitive: Savage Intellects, Modern Lives*. Chicago: University of Chicago Press.

Turner, Patricia A. 1994. *Ceramic Uncles and Celluloid Mammies: Black Images and Their Influence on Culture*. New York: Anchor.

U.S. Census Bureau. 1999. "Marital Status of the Population 15 Years Old and Over, by Sex and Race: 1950 to Present." Web page [accessed March 17, 2003]. Available at http://www.census.gov/population/socdemo/ms-la/tabms-1.txt.

U.S. Census Bureau. 2000. "Technical Note on Same-Sex Unmarried Partner Data from the 1990 and 2000 Censuses." Web page [accessed March 16, 2003]. Available at http://www.census.gov/population/www/cen2000/samesex.html.

U.S. Census Bureau. 2003. "Foreign-Born Population Surpasses 32 Million Census Bureau Estimates." Web page, [accessed March 16, 2003]. Available at http://www.census.gov/Press-Release/www/2003/cb03-42.html.

Wallace, Michele. 1990. *Invisibility Blues: From Pop to Theory*. New York: Verso.

Washington, Elsie B. 1996. *Uncivil War: The Struggle between Black Men and Women*. Chicago: The Noble Press.

Watkins, S. Craig. 1998. *Representing: Hip Hop Culture and the Production of Black Cinema*. Chicago: University of Chicago Press.

Wekker, Gloria. 2000. "Mati-ism and Black Lesbianism: Two Ideal Typical Expressions of Female Homosexuality in Black Communities of the Diaspora." *The Greatest Taboo: Homosexuality in Black Communities*. Ed. Delroy Constantine-Simms, 149–162. New York: Alyson Books.

Wells-Barnett, Ida B. 2002. *On Lynchings*. Amherst, N.Y.: Humanity Books.

West, Cornel. 1993. *Race Matters*. Boston: Beacon Press.

West, Traci C. 1999. *Wounds of the Spirit: Black Women, Violence, and Resistance Ethics*. New York: New York University Press.

Wetherell, Margaret, and Nigel Edley. 1999. "Negotiating Hegemonic Masculinity: Imaginary Positions and Psycho-Discursive Practices." *Feminism & Psychology* 9, no. 3: 335–356.

White, Deborah Gray. 1985a. *Ar'n't I a Woman? Female Slaves in the Plantation South*. New York: W.W. Norton.

White, Evelyn C. 1985b. *Chain, Chain, Change: For Black Women Dealing with Physical and Emotional Abuse*. Seattle: Seal Press.

Wideman, John Edgar. 1984. *Brothers and Keepers*. New York: Penguin.

Wiegman, Robyn. 1993. "The Anatomy of Lynching." *American Sexual Politics*. Ed. John C. Fout, and Maura Tantillo, 223–245.

Wieviorka, Michel. 1997. "Is It So Difficult to Be an Anti-Racist?" *Debating Cultural Hybridity: Multi-cultural Identities and the Politics of Anti-racism*. Ed. Pnina Werbner and Tariq Modood, 139–53. London: Zed.

Williams, Sherley A. 1986. *Dessa Rose*. New York: William Morrow.

Wilson, Melba. 1994. *Crossing the Boundary: Black Women Survive Incest*. Seattle: Seal Press.

Wilson, William Julius. 1978. *The Declining Significance of Race*. Chicago: University of Chicago Press.

———. 1987. *The Truly Disadvantaged: The Inner City, the Underclass, and Public Policy*. Chicago: University of Chicago Press.

———. 1996. *When Work Disappears: The World of the New Urban Poor*. New York: Knopf.

Winant, Howard. 2001. *The World Is a Ghetto: Race and Democracy since World War II*. New York: Basic Books.

Wyatt, Gail Elizabeth. 1992. "The Sociocultural Context of African American and White American Women's Rape." *Journal of Social Issues* 48, no. 1: 77–91.

Young, Robert J. C. 1995. *Colonial Desire: Hybridity in Theory, Culture and Race*. New York: Routledge.

Yuval-Davis, Nira. 1997. *Gender and Nation*. Thousand Oaks, Calif.: Sage.

Zuberi, Tukufu. 2001. *Thicker than Blood: How Racial Statistics Lie*. Minneapolis: University of Minnesota Press.

Zucchino, David. 1997. *The Myth of the Welfare Queen*. New York: Scribner.

INDEX